25.00

HERBERT F. QUINN, now partly retired, was formerly Professor of Political Science at Concordia University.

The increasing momentum of the separatist movement in Quebec under René Lévesque and the Parti Québécois has focused renewed attention on the history of French-Canadian nationalism. Professor Quinn begins this work on the period following the first world war, and in his revised and expanded edition, carries it up to the rise of the Parti Québécois and the victory of a more radical over a more conservative nationalism.

The nationalism of the 1920s led to the formation and rise to power of the Union Nationale party of Maurice Duplessis in the 1930s. A study of the Union Nationale, its origins, its policies, its victories, and its defeats provides the background essential to an understanding of Quebec politics today.

Two new chapters follow the history of the party from 1960 to 1973, the year in which the Union Nationale disappeared from the legislature. These chapters cover three political developments: the inauguration of the Quiet Revolution by Jean Lesage's Liberal party; the unexpected return to power of the Union Nationale in 1966, which was followed shortly by its decline and demise in 1973; and the rise of the new nationalist party, the Parti Québécois, which replaced the Union Nationale as the main opposition to the Liberals.

'Quinn's book is a valuable primer of Quebec politics that should aid in the understanding of the province's traditions and modern problems.'
Globe Magazine

Herbert F. Quinn

THE UNION NATIONALE

Quebec Nationalism
from Duplessis to Lévesque

SECOND ENLARGED EDITION

UNIVERSITY OF TORONTO PRESS

Toronto Buffalo London

© University of Toronto Press 1963
Toronto Buffalo London
Reprinted 1967, 1970, 1974
Second enlarged edition 1979

Printed in Canada

Canadian Cataloguing in Publication Data

Quinn, Herbert F., 1910–
   The Union nationale

   Bibliography: p.
   Includes index.

   ISBN 0-8020-2318-5 bd.   ISBN 0-8020-6347-0 pa.

   1. Union nationale (Canada) 2. Quebec (Province)—Politics and
government—1936–1960.° 3. Quebec (Province)—Politics and government—
1960–1976.° 4. Nationalism—Quebec (Province) I. Title.

JL259.A58Q86 1979   329.9'714   c79-094542-8

Contents

Preface

THE GROWTH OF A SEPARATIST MOVEMENT in Quebec in recent years, and the spectacular gains made by Réal Caouette and his Social Credit party in the federal election of 1962, have focused considerable attention on the politics of that province on the part of English Canada. It is not always recognized, however, that these developments are but two expressions of a French-Canadian nationalism whose origins can be traced back to the period following the First World War. The nationalism of the 1920's resulted in the formation and rise to power of the Union Nationale party of Maurice Duplessis in the 1930's. A study of the Union Nationale, its origins, its policies, its victories and its defeats, is therefore an essential condition for an understanding of the currents of discontent sweeping Quebec today, and the questioning which is taking place among French Canadians concerning the validity of the constitutional arrangements embodied in the Confederation pact of 1867.

This book arises from an interest in Quebec politics which goes back twenty-five years as my first article on this subject was published in the *Dalhousie Review* in 1938. It is based, therefore, not only on the usual formal sources for a historical study—articles, newspapers, pamphlets, government documents, and so on—but also on impressions gained over this long period from innumerable discussions and correspondence with party leaders, organizers, and candidates, and on information picked up from attendance at countless political meetings, conventions, and other party gatherings.

Although I have been mainly concerned with the Union Nationale party, the book can, in many respects, be looked upon as a political history of Quebec from the end of the First World War to 1960, for I have devoted considerable attention to the Liberal party and the minor political movements. Political developments have been described against the background of the industrial revolution which has been changing the face of Quebec ever since the First World War. Moreover, an attempt has been made to show the relationship between the various political parties and the trade unions, the farmers' organizations, the nationalist and patriotic associations, and the many Catholic Action groups.

In the preparation of this study I received help and assistance from many individuals, only a few of whom can be mentioned here. I wish to express my thanks and appreciation for the constructive criticism and encouragement of Professor Thomas P. Peardon of Columbia University, under whose direction the study was originally prepared as a doctoral dissertation. Professor Wynne Francis of the Department of English, Sir George Williams University, gave me invaluable aid in editing the text for publication. I am indebted to my former colleague, Dr. G. O. Rothney of Memorial University, a keen student of Quebec politics during the many years he taught at Sir George Williams, for turning over to me his sizable collection of newspapers, clippings, pamphlets, and periodicals, dealing with Quebec politics during the period between 1930 and 1950. I would like to thank Miss F. G. Halpenny and the editorial staff of the University of Toronto Press for their suggestions and many forms of assistance in putting the manuscript through its various stages. Finally, my wife, who read successive versions of the study, helped in innumerable ways and prevented me from making many errors both of fact and of judgment.

HERBERT F. QUINN

Sir George Williams University
May, 1963

Preface to
Second Enlarged Edition

THE FIRST EDITION OF THIS BOOK, published in 1963, brought the story of the Union Nationale up to its defeat at the hands of the Liberal party in 1960. In the eighteen years which have elapsed since that date, a number of important changes have taken place on the Quebec political scene. These changes may be summed up in three key developments: the Quiet Revolution introduced by Jean Lesage's Liberal party in the 1960s; the unexpected return to power of the Union Nationale in 1966, which was quickly followed by its rapid decline and demise in the election of 1973; the rise of a new nationalist party in the late 1960s, the Parti Québécois, which soon replaced the Union Nationale as the spokesman for Quebec nationalism and the chief opposition to the Liberal party.

The main purpose of the two additional chapters in this second edition is to fill the gap in Quebec's political history between 1960 and 1973. The first of these chapters describes how the Union Nationale successfully met the challenge of the Quiet Revolution and returned to power in 1966, while the second one describes how the party failed to meet the second challenge of the new nationalism of the sixties and went into a steady decline. These two chapters deal, therefore, not only with the history and policies of the Union Nationale, but also with those of the Liberals and the Parti Québécois.

Although this second edition ends the story with the election of 1973, it has been found necessary to make some comments on what appeared to be the rebirth of the Union Nationale under a new leader, Rodrigue Biron, in the election of 1976. My comments appear in a brief postscript in which it is argued that, in spite of certain similarities between the party which died in 1973 and the one which was resurrected in 1976, Biron's party cannot be looked upon as the traditional Union Nationale of Duplessis and Johnson. From my viewpoint the story of the Union Nationale, which has been the subject of my deep interest for around forty-five years, has come to an end.

Only a few changes have been made in the text of the first edition: pages 186 to 191 of Chapter IX have been eliminated as superfluous with the addition of the new chapters; the tables in the Appendix originally numbered IV and V are now VII and VIII and have been updated; the Index has been revised to cover the new chapters and two additional sections have been added to the Bibliography; the new chapters are X and XI, while the last chapter of the first edition, "Conclusions," now becomes Chapter XII.

Although the historical and cultural background of Quebec politics, as described in Chapter I, has changed in some important respects since this chapter was written, it is still valid as a description of the main characteristics of Quebec society during most of the Duplessis era. Important changes since that time, particularly in regard to the role of the Church, are described in those parts of the new chapters dealing with the Quiet Revolution and the New Nationalism. It might also be pointed out that even though the theoretical conclusions in Chapter XII refer only to the period up to 1960, they are still relevant for any society with the characteristics of Quebec before the Quiet Revolution.

It would be worthwhile here to note a few differences in political terminology between Quebec and the rest of Canada. Some of the Quebec terms are of long standing, while others became common usage in the sixties: electoral districts are not referred to as ridings, but as "comtés"; the head of the government is not called Premier, but Premier Ministre; the name of the legislature was changed in 1968 from Assemblée Legislative to Assemblée Nationale; a member is referred to as a "député," rather than a M.L.A., or M.P.P. Since the sixties the term usually used for Quebec, with obvious nationalist overtones, is "Etat du Québec," rather than Province of Quebec.

I wish to express appreciation to my son, Kevin, who gave me invaluable assistance in drawing up the statistical tables and in proofreading the various drafts of the study; and to Mrs. Josie Christensen of the Political Science Department, Concordia University, for her time-consuming and conscientious work in typing the manuscript. I would also like to thank R. I. K. Davidson and the editorial staff of the University of Toronto Press for their suggestions and assistance in putting the manuscript through its various stages.

HERBERT F. QUINN

Sir George Williams Campus
Concordia University
February, 1979

Introduction

THE PROVINCE OF QUEBEC is unique on the North American continent in
that it is the only political unit made up of a people who are predominantly French and at the same time predominantly Roman Catholic.[1] The people of Quebec, descendants of settlers who came over
from France three centuries ago, have, during the intervening years,
succeeded in retaining, almost unchanged, their language, their religion, their legal and educational systems, and even many of their
customs. As a consequence, they constitute a small, homogeneous
ethnic group, with a culture, way of life, and set of values quite different in most respects from those prevailing throughout the rest of the
continent.

In noting that the people of Quebec are the guardians of French
culture in North America another important point must be borne in
mind. The cultural values and institutions which the French Canadians have maintained and fostered during the greater part of their
history have not been those of Revolutionary France, but those of the
Ancien Régime. It was not the France of Voltaire, Rousseau, and the
ideals of 1789, but the France of Corneille and Racine, Bossuet and
Louis XIV, which was the most important influence in the early development of this society. The Revolution had comparatively little impact
on French Canada because the Catholic Church, whose influence was
dominant at the time, was successful in insulating the people of
Quebec from such revolutionary doctrines as liberalism, democracy,

[1]In 1951, 82 per cent of the province's total population was of French origin,
and 87.9 per cent were Roman Catholics. See Quebec, Department of Trade and
Commerce, *Statistical Year Book*, 1953, 81 and 87.

and secularism. While it is true that at different times during the nineteenth century radical and anti-clerical ideas from France were adopted by some of Quebec's political leaders, the hierarchy was able to prevent these ideas from spreading to the mass of the people. When cultural contacts between France and Quebec became more extensive after World War I the ideas which were most influential among the French-Canadian *élite* were those of the modern representatives of the Catholic tradition in France, such as Péguy, Mauriac, Mounier, and Maritain. It is only since the Second World War that those writers who are in the secular and anti-clerical tradition, such as Gide, Malraux, Camus, and Sartre, have found a receptive audience in some intellectual circles.[2]

There is one other respect in which the province of Quebec differs from many other regions in North America. Within the past fifty years or so it has passed through an industrial revolution which has transformed it from a backward rural and agrarian society into an advanced urban and industrial one. This transformation has been brought about primarily through the activities of British and American capital seeking profitable fields for investment; French-Canadian capital has played a negligible role in the process. Like all such revolutionary changes, industrialization altered considerably the social and economic structure of Quebec society, and presented a serious challenge to the traditional way of life and values of the French Canadian. It also had an important impact on the pattern of politics in that province. It is this latter aspect of industrialization which we are concerned with here.

This book is a study of the political party which dominated Quebec politics during the most intensive phase of industrialization. The origin of the party in question, the Union Nationale, can be traced back to a nationalist movement which began to develop shortly after the First World War. One of the most significant characteristics of this nationalist movement was its opposition to the widespread changes which industrialism was making in the French Canadian's way of life and to the fact that the economy of the province was dominated by foreign capital. The Union Nationale succeeded in driving the Liberal party from power in 1936, and remained in office until 1939. Although the

[2]The nature of existing cultural contacts between France and Quebec is discussed in D'Iberville Fortier, "Les relations culturelles franco-canadiennes," *Esprit*, nos. 193–4 (août-sept. 1952), 247–58. In regard to the influence of Mounier and Maritain on French-Canadian thought in the 1930's, see Michael K. Oliver, "The Social and Political Ideas of French-Canadian Nationalists, 1920–1945," unpublished doctoral dissertation, McGill University (1956), chap. v.

party was defeated by the Liberals in the election of the latter year, it was to return to power in 1944 and remain in office until defeated a second time by the Liberal party in 1960.

The first two chapters of the book provide some background material on the factors conditioning the French Canadian's approach to politics and the early political history of Quebec. There is then a description of the growth of opposition in the 1920's to the Liberal party's policy of industrialization, and an explanation of how this opposition led to the formation of the Union Nationale and its rise to power under the leadership of Maurice Duplessis in 1936. This account is followed by an analysis of the economic and social policies pursued by the first and second Union Nationale administrations—from 1936 to 1939, and from 1944 to 1960. The main purpose of this analysis is to show how Duplessis transformed the Union Nationale from a party of radical nationalism to a party of conservative nationalism by pursuing policies which constituted a complete reversal of the programme of reform on which it had been elected to office in 1936. The next few chapters explain why the Union Nationale, in spite of this repudiation of its original programme, was able to return to power in 1944 after its serious defeat of 1939, and remain in office until 1960. The concern here is to demonstrate the important role which Duplessis' opposition to certain policies of the federal government played in his electoral victories, and to describe some of the administrative and electoral practices which also helped to keep the Union Nationale in power. Finally, there is the story of how the policies of the party eventually aroused the antagonism of a number of influential groups and organizations in the province, and how the Liberal party under Jean Lesage managed to capture the support of these dissatisfied elements and to bring about the defeat of the Union Nationale just one year after the death of Duplessis in 1959.

To the political scientist the history of a political movement like the Union Nationale is a case study of the pattern of parties and politics under a particular set of conditions and in a particular type of economic and social environment. As such it should provide some insights into the functioning of the party system in other societies where the background and conditions are similar and contribute to the growing body of theory dealing with political behaviour. There is therefore a brief concluding chapter in which a few comments are made concerning certain aspects of the political process which this study of Quebec politics has brought to light.

THE UNION NATIONALE

Quebec Nationalism from Duplessis to Lévesque

CHAPTER I

The Historical and Cultural Background
of Quebec Politics

IN UNDERTAKING A STUDY of the political system of any society it is essential first of all to understand the nature of those historical and cultural elements in a people's background which have conditioned their thinking and affected their attitude towards the party struggle. Three main factors have always been dominant in the French Canadian's approach to politics: his preoccupation with the maintenance of his cultural values and the safeguarding of his interests against the English-speaking majority in Canada; his strong adherence to the doctrines and social philosophy of Roman Catholicism as interpreted by his clergy; and his lack of democratic convictions and of an adequate understanding of parliamentary government, in spite of his association with democratic institutions.

THE STRUGGLE FOR CULTURAL SURVIVAL

The success of the people of Quebec in maintaining a French and Catholic culture for over three hundred years on a continent where the vast majority are English-speaking and Protestant has often been referred to as "the French-Canadian miracle." This "miracle" has only been possible, however, because the people of that province, as well as their leaders, have always shown a determination to survive, a "will to live" as a cultural group. The French Canadians have had a sense of mission, of a duty to preserve French Catholic culture in America against all forces which would destroy it. This sense of mission has given them a direction, a goal which has aided them greatly in maintaining their identity. In a speech delivered to the Société Saint Jean-Baptiste in 1939, Abbé Lionel Groulx, a leading Quebec historian, analysed their feeling of identity in this way:

Nous sommes des Français, mais des Français d'une certaine variété. Depuis trois cents ans nous vivons séparés politiquement du vieux pays d'origine. Des impératifs historiques et géographiques rigoureux nous ont contraints à nous forger des institutions politiques, juridiques, économiques, des coutumes et des mœurs qui nous sont propres . . . Sous des aspects divers, nous sommes l'Américain le moins européen, et le plus européen des Américains. Le moins européen, parce que, plus que les autres et depuis plus longtemps que les autres, déracinés de l'Europe et rivés à l'Amérique. Le plus européen, parce que plus tendus, par nos antennes culturelles, vers le vieux continent.[1]

As a result of his determination to retain his cultural distinctiveness, the French Canadian, ever since 1763, has been engaged in an intermittent, and at times bitter, struggle against assimilation by the dominant English group.

During the greater part of the period from the conquest to Confederation the French Canadians were under the rather arbitrary rule of a colonial governor, sent out from England, who in most respects was answerable only to the Colonial Office at home. It is true that in 1791 Lower Canada, as Quebec was called at the time, was granted a legislative assembly, but it had little effective control over the executive, and not until 1848 was a truly responsible or democratic system of government established. Although it cannot be said that the period of colonial government was characterized by cruel or harsh treatment of the French population, it was a difficult time for the people of Quebec.[2] They were, after all, a conquered people under a government of English Protestants who had always looked upon the French as traditional enemies and who hated and despised the religion they practised. In spite of the fact that the Quebec Act, 1774, guaranteed them certain rights, such as the use of their own civil law and the practice of their religion, they still had to wage a continual struggle to maintain these rights. They might be free to practise their religion, but it was the Anglican Church which received preferential treatment from the government, though only a small minority in the colony were adherents of that faith. There was more than one attempt on the part of the English minority in the Legislative Assembly to make English the only official language. The English colonists also monopolized

[1]*Le Devoir*, 24 juin 1939.
[2]For a sympathetic description of the French-Canadian struggle in this early period, see A. R. M. Lower, *Colony to Nation* (1st edition, Toronto, 1946), chaps. XIII and XVII.

most of the better-paid positions in the administration. On occasion the more radical French-Canadian critics of the government found their journals censored or suppressed. In fact, until the 1840's, there were always prominent individuals in the colonial administration who looked forward to the time when the French Canadians would abandon their language, and possibly their religion, and become assimilated into the English group. This was certainly the hope of Lord Durham as a result of his study of the problems of government in the North American colonies.

A new period in the history of French Canada began with the enactment of the British North America Act in 1867, which brought Britain's scattered colonies in North America together in a new self-governing dominion. Confederation did not by any means end the French Canadian's struggle for cultural survival, nor did it eliminate the necessity for waging a continuous fight to protect his interests as a group. It did, however, change the nature of that struggle in some respects.

It is true that in the new federal state the French were a majority in one province, Quebec, and were thus in a position to enact a great deal of legislation which would conform to their particular values and way of life. In the division of legislative powers under the British North America Act the provinces were given control over such important areas of legislation as municipal institutions, education, the solemnization of marriage, hospitals and asylums, property and civil rights. The wide interpretation which was later to be given to the property and civil rights clause by the Judicial Committee of the Privy Council extended provincial jurisdiction over the whole field of labour and social legislation. But while the French Canadians were secure in their control over the province of Quebec, they had little hope of ever becoming the dominant group in any other province, although in time there were to be sizable French minorities in such provinces as New Brunswick and Ontario.[3] Most important of all, there was little likelihood of their ever winning a majority of the seats in the federal legislature, as it soon became apparent that the French Canadians were to be a permanent minority in a country which was overwhelmingly English-speaking.

As a result of the new situation in which he found himself after the establishment of the Dominion of Canada, the French Canadian's

[3]By 1951 there were 197,631 people of French origin in the province of New Brunswick out of a total population of 515,697. The figures for Ontario were 477,677 out of 4,597,542. Quebec, Department of Trade and Commerce, *Statistical Year Book*, 1953, p. 81.

approach to politics since 1867 has been dominated by three major objectives: ¹ to maintain, and even extend, the rights of French-Canadian minorities in other provinces; ² to retain intact the legislative powers of the province under the British North America Act against all attempts by the federal government to extend its authority; ³ and to expand the autonomy of Canada within the Commonwealth and eliminate any possibility of Canada becoming involved in Great Britain's foreign policy or Great Britain's wars. The strong stand adopted by the French Canadian on these different issues has from time to time resulted in serious clashes with the dominant English group and imposed heavy strains on both the unity of the country and the federal structure of government.

The concern of the people of Quebec about the position of the French minorities in other provinces arises from the fact that, when the British North America Act was enacted, it did not give to these minorities the same guarantees and rights as it accorded to the English Protestant minority in Quebec in regard to such things as the use of the English language in the legislature and in public documents, and state support for Protestant schools.⁴ The general attitude of the people of Quebec on this issue has been that, at least in the spirit of the confederation act which they tend to look upon as a compact between two nationalities, French Canadians in other provinces should be treated in the same way as English Protestants in Quebec. The refusal of the other provinces to accept this point of view has caused serious tensions between the two language groups at different times. In 1896, for instance, Quebec was aroused over the action of the government of Manitoba in eliminating financial assistance for the French Catholic schools in that province. Again, during the First World War, considerable resentment developed in Quebec when the province of Ontario decided to make English the principal language of instruction in all schools in the province, including those in areas where practically all of the pupils were French-speaking.

In regard to the maintenance of provincial autonomy against encroachment by the federal power, it would not be correct to say that this has been an attitude peculiar to the province of Quebec. Like the states in the United States, all the provinces in Canada have, at one time or another, been concerned about the maintenance of their constitutional rights. It has been the province of Quebec, however,

----

⁴The province of Ontario is an exception in the matter of education. The British North America Act guaranteed to the Roman Catholic separate schools in that province the maintenance of the rights which they enjoyed before Confederation.

which has always been the most reluctant to relinquish any part of the legislative power of the province as set forth in the British North America Act.

This emphasis in Quebec on the necessity of maintaining intact the rights of the province is not difficult to understand. The fact that the French Canadians constitute a majority in that province alone means that it is the only one where they are in a position to deal with economic, social, and cultural problems in their own way. Only in Quebec can they be sure that any laws which are passed will accord with their particular value system and their particular interests, as they see them. They insist, quite correctly, that any provincial powers ceded to the federal government are powers handed over to an authority which will always be controlled by an English-speaking majority in the House of Commons and in the cabinet. This majority has a different culture and a different set of values and, however well intentioned it may be, can hardly be expected either to understand fully or to appreciate the point of view of the French Canadian. Probably one of the best illustrations of the nature of this problem is to be found in the field of education. While English Canada has shown an increasing trend in favour of secular, non-religious education, most of the people of Quebec are still convinced that education should be religiously oriented. For all these reasons they have looked upon the maintenance of provincial rights as a matter of life and death in their struggle for cultural survival.[5]

When we come to the question of the autonomy of Canada within the Commonwealth, and a policy of non-participation in Great Britain's wars, we are dealing with the issue most crucial of all to the French Canadian. It is also the one which has been the cause of the most serious cleavages between the two language groups. The French Canadian's attitude in this matter is basically a reaction to that of the dominant English group.

In turn, the attitude of the English Canadian towards relations with Great Britain can be understood only if we realize that his reaction reflects the fact that he is often a comparatively recent arrival in Canada. Most English Canadians are the descendants of immigrants who arrived in Canada from the British Isles within the last seventy-five or hundred years. As a consequence, right up to the Second World War their sentimental attachment to Great Britain as the "mother country" has been very strong. To many of them, even as late as the

[5]The clearest statement of the Quebec argument for provincial autonomy is to be found in: Quebec, *Report of the Royal Commission of Inquiry on Constitutional Problems* (Québec, 1956), vol. II, pt. 3.

1930's, the United Kingdom, rather than Canada, was the homeland. As a result of these close bonds the average English Canadian has always been strongly opposed to any policies which would in any way weaken Canada's relations with Britain. Until comparatively recently, he has usually been an imperialist or centralizer, rather than an autonomist, in his conception of Canada's role in the Commonwealth.[6] His close attachment to Britain has meant that he has tended to equate at all times the interests of Canada with those of the former country. Most important of all, he has insisted that when Britain is threatened by war, Canada must be at her side, for the mother country must be defended in time of need. This does not mean, of course, that the defence of Britain has been the only factor in the English Canadian's readiness to participate in the last two World Wars, and particularly in the 1939–45 conflict. His historical background, in which the struggle for individual liberties and parliamentary institutions has played such an important part, has made him receptive to the idea of fighting in defence of liberty and democracy.[7]

The attitude of the French Canadian towards the question of relations with Britain has also been conditioned by his historical background, and as a result it is diametrically opposite to that of the other language group. The fact that the French Canadian has been on the North American continent for over three hundred years, and that he rejected the France of the Revolution, has meant that his ties with that country were broken long ago. It is Canada, not France, and certainly not Britain, which he looks upon as his mother country. Canada is the only country to which he has any real attachment or to which he owes allegiance. He is convinced that just as Britain (or France) at all times pursues its national interest, so Canada should do the same. With this different set of attitudes it is not surprising that ever since 1867 the people of Quebec have been strongly opposed to close ties with Britain and have fought for the independence and autonomy of Canada within the Commonwealth, the latter being looked upon as a loose federation of sovereign states.

This historical background also explains why the French Canadian is opposed to Canada's automatic participation in any war in which Britain might become involved. He cannot, of course, be expected to

[6]In a recent study, G. V. Ferguson of the *Montreal Star* expresses the opinion that it was between the two World Wars that English Canada "swung out of its former semi-colonial ways of thinking and into a broad and genuine nationalism." See "The English-Canadian Outlook," in Mason Wade, ed., *Canadian Dualism* (Toronto, 1960), p. 14.

[7]See R. A. Mackay and E. B. Rogers, *Canada Looks Abroad* (Toronto, 1938), pp. 285–7.

respond to any appeal to defend the mother country. Moreover, his absorption in his own affairs, and in his struggle for survival, has made him feel far removed from the quarrels of Europe. His concept of the defence of Canada has always been limited to a defence of Canada's shores. Also, his lack of strong democratic convictions, discussed later in this chapter, leaves him unmoved by any appeal to participate in a war "to make the world safe for democracy." All of this has resulted in a strong isolationism which has seen both World Wars as part of a struggle for power between rival imperialisms, a struggle in which the smaller nations would be well advised not to become involved.[8] With such a viewpoint, it is not surprising that the First and Second World Wars created serious crises in the relationship between Quebec and the rest of Canada.

THE ROMAN CATHOLIC WAY OF LIFE

The second factor to be borne in mind in any study of Quebec politics is that we are dealing with a society which is predominantly Roman Catholic. Moreover, the type of Catholicism found in Quebec is quite different from that prevalent in many parts of France and Italy where a considerable number of the people are only nominal Catholics who seldom attend religious services, pay no attention to the moral directives of the clergy, and do not adhere to the social philosophy of the Church. The French Canadian's whole pattern of thinking, his system of values and way of life, have to a very large extent been moulded by the doctrines and social philosophy of Roman Catholicism. This philosophy has up to now been the major determinant of his attitude towards such questions as the nature and purpose of man, the relationship between the individual and the state, the role of the family in society, the questions of divorce and birth control, the right of private property, and the relative merits of socialism and capitalism.[9]

[8]For a clear exposition of the French-Canadian point of view on participation in European wars see François-Albert Angers, "Pourquoi nous n'accepterons jamais la conscription pour service outre mer," L'Action Nationale, XIX, 2 (fév.-mars 1942).

[9]According to a classification worked out by a French sociologist, the people of Quebec would fall into the category of "dévots," as contrasted with the "conformisme saisonnier" characteristic of large numbers of people in France and Italy. The latter term refers to those whose religious activities are limited to marriage in the Church, receiving its last rites, and possibly attending mass at Christmas and Easter. Gabriel le Bras, Introduction à l'histoire de la pratique religieuse en France (Paris, 1942), I, chap. i. As recently as 1955 a Gallup Poll showed that 93 per cent of the people of Quebec attended church at least once a week as contrasted to 44 per cent for the neighbouring province of Ontario (Montreal Star, June 29, 1955).

Although there has been no official union of Church and State in Quebec since 1763, the Roman Catholic Church has been the most important influence in the shaping of the French Canadian's basic institutions and in the safeguarding of his traditions.[10] Its activities have not been confined to strictly religious matters, but have also extended to intellectual, professional, economic and social life. The Church has organized or sponsored youth movements, professional associations, co-operatives, trade unions, and farmers' organizations. It has built hospitals, orphanages, and homes for the aged, and in fact has provided many of the social welfare facilities which in the other provinces have been the responsibility of the state.[11] The influence of the Church has been particularly important in the field of education. It has always effectively controlled the educational system under an arrangement whereby the school commissions elected by the property owners pay for the construction and maintenance of buildings, as well as the salaries of the teachers, while the Church has jurisdiction over the training of the teachers and sets down the basic principles to be followed in the organization of the curriculum.[12]

One reason for the wide area of influence and control which the Church has always exercised over Quebec society is to be found in the early history of that province. During the French régime the settlers in North America were accustomed to following the directives and leadership of two different authorities, one civil, one religious. The first was represented in the person of the Governor of the colony, and the second in the Bishop of Quebec. With the English conquest one of the sources of direction and leadership disappeared, for the French settlers could hardly be expected to look upon the English colonial administration as a legitimate civil authority. There was still the Church, however, as only a comparatively small number of the clergy had returned to France, and it was natural enough that the people should turn to it as the only organization capable of providing them with effective guidance and leadership. By force of circumstances the clergy thus became the source of authority for the French Canadian, not only on strictly religious and moral questions, but also on economic, social, educational, and political matters. Its dominant position in the colony was strengthened by the fact that the British Colonial

[10]See Jean-C. Falardeau, "The Changing Social Structures," in Falardeau, éd., *Essais sur le Québec contemporain* (Québec, 1953), pp. 112–16.

[11]The extent to which the Church has been responsible for public welfare and education in Quebec has been pointed out in: Canada, *Report of the Royal Commission on Dominion-Provincial Relations* (Ottawa, 1940), Book I, p. 227.

[12]See Charles Bilodeau, "Education in Quebec," *University of Toronto Quarterly*, XXVII, 3 (April, 1958), 402–4.

Office, after some hesitation, decided to permit the Roman Catholic Church to retain many of the rights it had enjoyed under the French régime. Although the leading role of the clergy in political affairs was to be challenged by the slow growth of a new lay leadership after 1800, the Church has been able to retain its pre-eminent position in most of the other fields up to the present time.

Another reason for the strength of the Church in Quebec is that, in contrast to some Catholic countries, the clergy has never been set off from the mass of the people by being recruited from any one particular class. It has also been remarkably free from corruption and scandal and has seldom had to face the accusation of luxurious living. Unlike France, where the higher clergy, even after the Revolution of 1789, came largely from the aristocracy and the upper middle class, the clergy in Quebec has always come from all walks of life. If it is an *élite*, it is one which anyone may enter whatever his birth, wealth, or social status. The late Cardinal Archbishop of Quebec, for instance, was the son of a shoemaker. The present Cardinal Archbishop of Montreal is the son of a small shopkeeper.[13] All of this has meant that, in spite of the important role that the clergy has played in Quebec, the average French Canadian has not looked upon it as a tyranny imposed from without nor as an oppressive force exercising a moral dictatorship.

Perhaps the most important factor of all in the ability of the Church to retain the loyalty of the people of Quebec is its close association with the struggle for cultural survival. In its determination to foster and maintain Roman Catholicism as the religious faith of the people of Quebec, the clergy has been the champion of one of the characteristics of French-Canadian culture which sets it apart from that of the rest of the continent. This distinctiveness has strengthened the French Canadian in his resistance to assimilation. Moreover, the clergy has not only been concerned with protecting the French Canadian from the influence of Protestant or secular beliefs; it has also been a staunch defender of those other basic characteristics of his way of life. For instance, the clergy has usually been in the front line of the fight to maintain the language rights of French minorities in other provinces. Thus it can be seen that, like the Roman Catholic Church in Ireland and Poland, one of the reasons for the popular support enjoyed by the Church in Quebec has been the important contribution it has made to the cause of national survival. A French-Canadian labour leader writes,

13The wide social base from which the clergy is recruited has been pointed out by J.-C. Falardeau in "Rôle et importance de l'Eglise au Canada Français," *Esprit*, nos. 193–4 (août-sept. 1952), p. 227.

"Si le clergé régnait, c'est qu'il savait représenter les aspirations populaires, c'est qu'il s'appuyait sur la confiance sans réserve que mettait en lui l'immense majorité des citoyens."[14]

To understand the role that the Roman Catholic Church has played in Quebec society, it is essential that we grasp the main principles underlying the particular way of life which the leaders of that Church have been so determined to maintain. For the moment we will be concerned only with the basic features of the ideal Christian society advocated by members of the clergy during the period prior to industrialization, that is, roughly until the First World War. Further developments in the thinking of the Church after that time, particularly in regard to economic and social matters, will be dealt with later.[15]

The most important principle of the philosophy of life which the Church in Quebec always held up as an ideal was the primacy of spiritual over material values.[16] (This is not to suggest, of course, that the religious ideals of the Church in Quebec, as described here, are essentially different from those held by the Roman Catholic Church in other areas and countries.) Man's activities in this world were to be subordinated to the goal of everlasting happiness in the next. The possession of divine grace and the Christian virtues was more important than success in worldly affairs and the higher incomes which went with it. The Church also rejected the view that religion was purely a matter of inner experience and one's own private affair. It insisted that a man's religious beliefs could not be divorced from other aspects of his daily life. The spirit of Christianity had to embrace and penetrate not only the individual life of man but also his life in society. His economic activities, for instance, must at all times be guided by the Christian principles of truth and justice.

The three basic institutions in the Church's conception of the ideal Christian society were the family, the parish, and the school.[17] The function of the family was first of all the biological one of reproduction, and the desirability of large families was always stressed. The family was also looked upon as an economic and social unit and was expected to provide for many of the needs of its members in these areas. Its organization was on a hierarchical basis, with the father as

[14]Gérard Pelletier, "D'un prolétariat spirituel," *Esprit*, nos. 193–4 (août-sept. 1952), p. 198.

[15]See *infra*, pp. 54–7.

[16]A good short description of the Church's ideal of the Christian society is to be found in Maurice Tremblay, "Orientations de la pensée sociale," in Falardeau, éd., *Essais sur le Québec contemporain*.

[17]See André Montpetit, "Les institutions sociales," in Esdras Minville, éd., *Notre Milieu* (Montréal, 1946), chap. XIV.

ruler and head and his wife in a subordinate position. Anything which tended to destroy the growth and solidarity of the family, such as birth control and divorce, was to be absolutely rejected.

The parish, the second key institution of this ideal society, was the larger unit made up of all the families in a given area. Although its functions were primarily religious, the Church felt that any social life, other than that on a familial basis, should be centred in the parish. The parish was to be not merely a religious unit but an all-inclusive community which provided its members with their whole field of activity. The parish priest was the leader of this community just as the father was the head of the family. The authority and guidance of the priest, therefore, extended to a large range of matters other than those of a purely religious nature.

The school, the other basic institution of this society, was to supplement and extend the work of the family and the parish in the formation and development of the Christian personality. To this end all levels of education had to be permeated by the value system of Catholicism, for the Church insisted that no system of instruction could really be called education unless it was based on religious principles. It had to be oriented towards the supernatural, and put its greatest emphasis not on the pursuit of material aims but on the saving of one's soul through the practice of the Christian virtues. A Quebec educationist writes: "Education must be based upon man's spiritual nature and eternal destiny. It is not confined to man's mere physical, ethical and intellectual development. It should fit him for eternity as well as for time. . . . If it does not bring him nearer to God it is a failure."[18]

It should also be pointed out that the Church always held that higher education was for the *élite* rather than the masses and that it had to be built around the hard core of classical studies. Thus, it was an educational system better suited to turning out priests, doctors, lawyers, and other professional people, rather than the accountants, engineers, and technicians required by an industrial society.

Another important aspect of the social thought of the Church in Quebec was the strong conviction that, if these basic institutions of a Christian society were to be safeguarded and developed, it was essential that the French Canadian retain his rural way of life. In the view of the Church, a rural society not only provided an environment in conformity with man's basic nature but was also the form of existence most likely to lead to a virtuous life. Any mass movement from the

[18]Father Henri Saint-Denis, "French-Canadian Ideals in Education," in *French-Canadian Backgrounds: A Symposium* (Toronto, 1940), pp. 24–5.

rural areas to the towns was considered an unjustifiable desertion of the countryside which would endanger the faith and religious values of the French Canadian. The Church was to cling to this ideal of a rural society of land-owning proprietors until the end of World War II. Nor was it alone in this respect. Many French-Canadian intellectuals were also convinced that if the people of Quebec were to survive as a distinct French and Catholic society in North America they must remain faithful to their peasant vocation.[19]

A few qualifications must now be added to this description of the extremely important part played by the Roman Catholic Church in the evolution of Quebec society. The fact that the Church has been the most important single influence in the formation of the French-Canadian outlook does not mean that it has been the only influence. Nor does it mean that the leaders of the Church have always been successful in overcoming every challenge to their ideals and goals; for instance, the opposition of the hierarchy to industrialization did not prevent Quebec from developing into a modern industrial society, although it is probably true that this opposition slowed up the process to some extent, particularly in its early stages.[20] To take another example, since the latter part of the nineteenth century the French Canadian has tended more and more to resent the interference of the clergy in questions he considers to be of a purely political nature. This has been particularly true of those occasions, admittedly rather rare, when the French Canadian has felt that the policies and objectives of the Church run counter to his interests as a minority ethnic group. In the next chapter we shall see how Laurier's Liberal party was successful in winning a majority of Quebec seats in the elections of 1891 and 1896 in spite of strong opposition from the hierarchy. From that time onward the leaders of the Church have usually been careful to adopt a position of official neutrality as between different parties, although on occasion they have criticized a particular politician or a particular policy.

THE LACK OF A DEMOCRATIC PHILOSOPHY

In addition to his struggle for cultural survival and his adherence to the Roman Catholic way of life, a third factor in the background of the French Canadian must be considered, if we are to understand his

[19]See Tremblay, "Orientations de la pensée sociale," p. 199.
[20]Between 1867 and 1940 large quantities of money, manpower, and natural resources were expended on church-sponsored back-to-the-land and colonization projects. See Esdras Minville, "La Colonisation," in Minville, éd., L'Agriculture (Montréal, 1944), p. 306.

approach to politics. This is his attitude towards democratic institutions and parliamentary government.

The system of parliamentary democracy to be found in the province of Quebec appears, on the surface, similar in every respect to that which exists in the other provinces and at the federal level. There is a lower house called the Legislative Assembly, elected by universal suffrage for a maximum period of five years, and an upper house called the Legislative Council, whose members are appointed by the provincial executive and whose functions are similar to those of the Canadian Senate. The leader of the largest party in the Assembly is appointed Prime Minister by the Lieutenant Governor. The Prime Minister then proceeds to select a cabinet, which is responsible to the lower house of the legislature and must therefore resign if it loses the confidence of that house. The rules of procedure in the legislature are modelled on those of the federal legislature, which in turn are modelled on those of the British Parliament. Whenever an election is called any person who is eligible to vote may present himself as a candidate, and any political party is free to organize, to propagate its ideas, and to support or oppose the government which happens to be in office.

In spite of the similarity in form of the system of government in Quebec to that of the other Canadian provinces, there is one basic difference which makes it impossible to call that province a truly democratic society. Although the French Canadian may have a democratic system of government, he has never really understood or accepted the theoretical principles and assumptions on which parliamentary democracy is based. Concepts such as "the sovereignty of the people," "the responsibility of government to the governed," or "civil rights" play little or no part in his political thinking. In other words we are presented with the paradox of a people with democratic institutions but without strong democratic convictions. This raises two obvious questions: how did this unusual situation develop; and how has the lack of a democratic ideology affected the way in which parliamentary government has functioned in Quebec?

One of the reasons for the lack of a democratic ideology on the part of the people of Quebec is historical. Under the French régime all powers of government were concentrated in a governor, whose responsibility lay mainly in the field of military affairs, and an intendant, who dealt with economic, financial, and judicial matters.[21] Although on rare occasions assemblies of prominent citizens might be called, in

21See Guy Frégault, Le Civilisation de la Nouvelle France, 1713–1744 (Montréal, 1944), chap. III.

general the vast majority of the people of New France had no opportunity to participate either in decision-making at the political level, or in exercising control over the government. Unlike the New England colonies to the south, there was not even that limited, but important form of political participation which is to be found wherever local and municipal institutions have been established.[22] In short, the governmental system under which the people of New France lived was a form of despotism similar in most respects to that of the *Ancien Régime* at home.

As a result, when the British assumed control over Canada in 1763 they found a people who, unlike themselves, had no tradition of a bitter struggle against an absolute monarchy in order to set up representative institutions and establish the principle of the rights of the individual against the state. Nor did that vast ideological unheaval some years later, the French Revolution, have any impact on French-Canadian thinking. Owing to the predominant influence of the Church at the time, the French Canadians heard very little about the radical ideas of such revolutionary manifestos as the *Declaration of the Rights of Man and Citizen*.[23] Thus, when democratic institutions gradually made their appearance in Quebec, during the period from 1791 to 1848, they were an innovation introduced by the conquerors. Although there were a number of reasons why the British Colonial Office decided to take this step, probably the most important one was the considerable pressure exerted by the newly arrived United Empire Loyalists from the south, who were opposed to arbitrary government and demanded the same type of popular institutions as they had enjoyed in the former British colonies from which they had fled.

The French Canadians were willing enough to accept these democratic institutions, although they did not really understand them or appreciate the values on which they were based. As one authority on Canada's constitutional development has expressed it:

The vast majority of the electors had no conception of the political machine which they were called on to create. . . . An apathetic, conservative, docile and non-political people were entrusted with a constitution implying knowledge and insight. No attempt had been made to instruct them in its ordinary workings, much less in those delicate, intangible conventions and indeterminate traditions which gave it force and vitality.[24]

---

[22]See K. G. Crawford, *Canadian Municipal Government* (Toronto, 1954), pp. 20–2.

[23]The reaction of the Church in Quebec to these revolutionary ideas is described in Arthur Maheux, "French Canadians and Democracy," *University of Toronto Quarterly*, XXVII, 3 (April, 1958), 345.

[24]W. P. M. Kennedy, *The Constitution of Canada, 1534–1937* (2nd edition; London, 1938), pp. 88–9.

From the point of view of democratic theory, parliamentary government was accepted by the people of Quebec for the wrong reasons. It was welcomed in that province, not because of any conviction that all government should be responsible to the governed, but because French-Canadian leaders were quick to grasp the value of representative institutions as a means of defending the interests and cultural values of the group against the autocratic rule of the colonial governor. Later on, after Confederation, these same institutions were an effective means of defending the interests of the province of Quebec, and of the French Canadians in other provinces, against the domination of the English-speaking majority in Canada. In other words, although with the passage of time the French Canadian was to acquire some knowledge of the values underlying democratic government, his main interest in parliamentary institutions was that they were a weapon, not against autocratic government as such, but against any government, autocratic or otherwise, which happened to be dominated by the English. This attitude of the French Canadian towards democracy is described by one writer: "Pour lui, la démocratie s'est tout de suite identifiée à la lutte pour ses droits religieux et linguistiques. Il s'est servi de la démocratie plutôt qu'il n'y a adhéré comme à une doctrine."[25]

Still another reason for the lack of a democratic ideology among the people of Quebec arises out of the important role that the Church has played in this society. First of all, it must be borne in mind that in its internal structure the Roman Catholic Church is an authoritarian institution; decisions are made from the top down rather than the reverse. Directives in regard to doctrine and policy flow down from the Pope to the bishops, to the lower clergy, to the layman.[26] The fact that the French-Canadian Catholic, in contrast to the English Protestant, has been accustomed to look to authority for decisions in such an important area as religious doctrine and practice, has tended to make him look to authority in other matters as well, including politics. Although the authority to which he looks in the latter case is lay, rather than clerical, this kind of attitude is hardly conducive to the development of a vigorous democratic society.

[25]F. R. Scott, "Canada et Canada-Français," *Esprit*, nos. 193–4, (août-sept. 1952), 185. See also Pierre-Elliott Trudeau, "Some Obstacles to Democracy in Quebec," *Canadian Journal of Economics and Political Science*, XXIV, 3 (Aug., 1958), 297–311.

[26]This does not mean that the policies of the Church are completely unaffected by pressures from below. It is fairly well known that when Pope Leo XIII issued his encyclical *Rerum Novarum* on the labour problem in 1891, he was to a very considerable extent merely giving official papal sanction to social theories which had originated with Catholic thinkers, both clerical and lay, in France and Germany.

An even more important aspect of the Church's influence on the French Canadian's attitude towards democracy can be traced back to the political theory of Roman Catholicism in the nineteenth century. During the greater part of that century, the Church in France and other European countries was to a very large extent opposed to the growth of liberalism and democracy. The French Revolution of 1789, and the revolutions which swept Europe in 1848, convinced the Church that the new ideologies were necessarily linked with anti-clericalism, secularism, atheism, and the absence of law and order.[27] There was also the fact that the Church's attitude towards government was based on the concept of a Natural Law which laid down the proper norms governing the actions of individuals and states, and it could not accept, therefore, Rousseau's doctrine of the sovereign people as the ultimate source of all law and authority. In reaction to the democratic movement the Church in Europe during the last century was usually allied with the landed aristocracy, and tended to favour monarchical government of a more or less absolutistic kind. A change in this attitude only began very slowly after the 1890's when Pope Leo XIII advised French Catholics to rally to the Republic.

Although the political theory of the Church in Quebec, as in Europe, emphasized tradition, order, and obedience to authority, and showed a lack of enthusiasm for democratic ideals,[28] it is true that the Roman Catholic hierarchy in that province, like other French Canadians, readily accepted British parliamentary institutions once they were established. Like the lay leaders they quickly grasped the advantages which these institutions offered in the struggle of the French Canadian to maintain his cultural values, including those of a religious nature. Moreover, their experience with the particular type of liberal democracy introduced by the English taught them that this form of government was not necessarily linked to atheistic, anti-clerical, and secular doctrines.

The lack of a democratic ideology on the part of the people of Quebec has affected seriously the proper functioning of parliamentary government in that province. For one thing it has meant that the majority of French Canadians tend to look upon government, not as an agency whose power and authority stems from the people, not in

[27]An excellent description of the impact which the European revolutions of 1848 had on the thinking of Pope Pius IX is to be found in E. E. Y. Hales, *Pio Nono* (London, 1954).

[28]The opposition of the Church in Quebec to radical and liberal ideas imported from France after the Revolution of 1848 is described in M. Ayearst, "The *Parti Rouge* and the Clergy," *Canadian Historical Review*, XV, 4 (Dec., 1934), 390–405.

the sense of "our government," but as a force external to, and above the people, which makes laws they must obey and levies taxes they must pay.[29] This attitude has had a rather curious result: government expenditures made in the ordinary course of administration for such things as public works or social services have usually been looked upon, not as a right of the citizen, but as a special favour or privilege granted by the government. The party in power has a particular advantage as its expenditure of government money, particularly at election time, enables it to pose as a benefactor whose generosity should be rewarded by voting it back into office. There is little real grasp of the obvious fact, particularly among the voters in the rural areas, that the source of the money which governments spend is the people themselves and that, as a consequence, government expenditures are not simply favours granted by the party which happens to be in power.

There are other ways in which the lack of understanding of democratic values has affected the functioning of parliamentary institutions in Quebec. The average Quebec voter is left unmoved by flagrant breaches of the spirit of fair play on the part of the majority party towards the opposition in the legislature. He is not likely to be aroused by such abuses as partisanship on the part of the Speaker, the refusal of the government to grant the opposition sufficient time to discuss bills, or the use of a large majority in the Assembly to stifle investigation of government departments and manipulate the electoral machinery to its own advantage.[30] Because the French Canadian has had no tradition of a struggle to establish the principle of legislative control over the public purse, he is unconcerned whenever proper budgetary procedures are not followed by the government.

In pointing out the shortcomings of parliamentary government as it functions in Quebec it is not meant to imply that these weaknesses are to be found only in that province. The operation of democratic government in some of the other provinces has often left much to be desired. In Quebec, however, the development of healthy democratic institutions has been a much slower process because of the peculiarities in the historical background of the French Canadian which have been described in this chapter.

[29]See editorials, *Le Devoir*, 20 juillet, 27 déc. 1956.

[30]For the entirely different reactions of English and French Canadian to certain abuses in procedure in the House of Commons in 1956, see André Laurendeau, "Nous et les Anglo-Saxons," *Le Devoir*, 12 juin 1956.

CHAPTER II

The Pattern of Quebec Politics, 1867-1919

BEFORE DESCRIBING THE DIFFERENT DEVELOPMENTS which were to lead to the formation of the Union Nationale, it is necessary to provide a brief outline of the pattern of Quebec politics between 1867 and 1919, that is, from Confederation until the end of the First World War. This political history may be divided into two periods: the first from 1867 to 1896, and the second one from 1896 to 1919.

During most of the period from 1867 to 1896 the people of Quebec supported the Conservative party in both federal and provincial politics. The party captured a majority of Quebec seats in every federal election except those of 1874 and 1891;[1] in provincial politics the Conservatives won every election except those of 1878, 1886, and 1890.[2] The strength of the party in Quebec during these post-Confederation years was to a considerable extent due to the political skill and perception of John A. Macdonald, the Conservative leader. Macdonald recognized and accepted the fact that the different historical and cultural background of the French Canadian made it inevitable that on many matters of national concern he would have a point of view different from that prevailing in the rest of Canada. As a consequence, the Conservative leader never failed to take into consideration the particular interests and attitudes of the people of Quebec when he was formulating policy. On one occasion he stated, "No man in his senses can suppose that the country can for a century to come be governed by a totally unfrenchified government. If a British-Canadian desires to conquer, he must 'stoop to conquer.' He must make friends of the French

[1]See E. P. Dean, "How Canada has Voted: 1867 to 1945," *Canadian Historical Review*, XXX, 3 (Sept., 1949), 233.
[2]See Appendix A, Table VII.

without sacrificing the status of his race or his religion. He must respect their nationality."[3] Macdonald was astute enough to form a working alliance with influential French-Canadian politicians of conservative tendency, such as Georges Etienne Cartier, and always made sure that the province of Quebec had good representation in his cabinets.[4]

Another important factor in the strength of the Conservatives in Quebec was that the party had the solid support of the Roman Catholic hierarchy during the latter half of the nineteenth century. The Liberals, the other major party, at that time had a radical, anti-clerical wing in Quebec called the *Rouges*, who had come under the influence of the revolutionary ideas which were widespread in France and other European countries around 1848. Among other things, the *Rouges* opposed any kind of co-operation between Church and State, and many of them were advocates of secular rather than religious education.[5] As a result, the Liberals had to contend with the uncompromising hostility of the leaders of the Church who actively campaigned against them in every election.[6] Although there was growing resentment on the part of many French Canadians against clerical interference in politics, for the first two decades after Confederation the opposition of the Church made it extremely difficult for the Liberals to make much headway in Quebec.

In spite of the political skill of Macdonald and the support of the clergy, the dominant position of the Conservative party in Quebec was to come to an end shortly before the turn of the century. The particular issue which brought about the downfall of Macdonald's party was a controversy which arose in the 1880's between French and English Canada over the status of the Métis, half-breeds of French-Indian descent living in the Canadian northwest. Shortly after Confederation a considerable amount of unrest had developed among this small group living on the edge of civilization because of their growing conviction that the ownership of their lands, and their traditional hunting and fishing rights, were being threatened by the arrival of English settlers from Ontario, who proposed to exploit this area. After a number of

[3]A. D. Lockhart, "The Contribution of Macdonald Conservatism to National Unity, 1854–78," *Canadian Historical Association, Report*, 1939, p. 125.

[4]The skill of Macdonald in bringing together divergent groups and interests to form the Conservative party is described in F. H. Underhill, "The Development of National Parties in Canada," *Canadian Historical Review*, XVI, 4 (Dec., 1935), 368–75.

[5]M. Ayearst, "The *Parti Rouge* and the Clergy," *Canadian Historical Review*, XV, 4 (Dec., 1934), 391.

[6]The campaign of the Church against the Liberal party is described in J. S. Willison, *Sir Wilfrid Laurier and the Liberal Party* (Toronto, 1903), I, chaps. x–xii.

protests and petitions to the Conservative government at Ottawa proved of no avail, the Métis in what is today Saskatchewan revolted in 1885 and set up a provisional government at Batoche under Louis Riel. Riel had been in exile in the United States as he had been involved in a somewhat similar uprising on the Red River in Manitoba in 1870. As a military operation the Northwest Rebellion of 1885 amounted to very little, and it was put down quite easily by a handful of federal troops. Riel was taken prisoner and a short while later put on trial for the murder of an English settler, Thomas Scott, who had been shot on the orders of Riel during the earlier Red River uprising. An English-speaking jury brought in a verdict of guilty, but with a recommendation of mercy.[7]

If the Northwest Rebellion was unimportant militarily, it was an altogether different story from the political point of view. From the beginning of the controversy the French Canadians in Quebec were in sympathy with the grievances of the Métis whom they looked upon as their "blood brothers." However, it was not until Riel was put on trial that they really became aroused, and then the whole affair became for Canada the major political issue of the day. While English Canada looked upon Riel as a common murderer who should be executed, French Canada looked upon him as a national hero, the symbol of French-Canadian resistance to assimilation and domination by the majority group. Within a comparatively short time all the latent antagonism and distrust between the two language groups had come to the fore. Macdonald's Conservative government was immediately placed in a difficult position between the two fires. The Conservative leader temporized by twice postponing the execution of Riel. Finally, however, he capitulated to the pressure from the Ontario wing of his party, led by the strongly anti-French and anti-Catholic Orange Lodges, and the execution was carried out.

The effect of the Riel affair on Quebec politics was far reaching. The Quebec wing of Macdonald's party was split in two, for most Conservatives in that province, as well as practically all of the Liberals, had opposed the execution of Riel. Just previous to the execution sixteen Conservative members of Parliament from Quebec had sent a telegram to Macdonald protesting that such action on the part of the government would be an act of cruelty. The most important result of this

[7]For a French-Canadian account of the Riel rebellion, and its impact on politics, see Robert Rumilly, *Histoire de la Province de Québec*, V, *Riel*, (2ème édition; Montreal, 1942). A different point of view is to be found in George F. G. Stanley, *The Birth of Western Canada* (Toronto, 1936, 1961).

whole controversy was the rapid growth of nationalist sentiments among the people of Quebec and the formation of a new provincial party called the Parti National, which pledged itself to fight the federal government by all constitutional means. The new party was led by Honoré Mercier, who up to that time had been the leader of the provincial Liberal party. Although composed mainly of former Liberals, the Parti National also included a number of former Conservatives.

In the provincial election of 1886 the resentment of the French Canadians against "the hangmen of Ottawa," as the Macdonald government was called, enabled the Parti National to defeat the Quebec wing of Macdonald's party. The Conservatives had been in control of the provincial administration during practically all of the period from 1867 onwards.[8] Mercier could not rest content, however, until he had brought about the defeat of Macdonald himself. He therefore proceeded to throw his powerful party organization behind the Liberal party in the federal elections of 1887 and 1891.[9] The result was that in the election of the latter year the Liberal party, now under the leadership of a French Canadian, Wilfrid Laurier, won more Quebec seats in the federal legislature than the Conservatives for the first time since 1874. Thirty-five Liberals were elected as compared to thirty Conservatives.

Although Mercier's administration at Quebec City became involved in some serious financial scandals in the early 1890's, and his party broke up shortly afterwards, there is little doubt that the nationalist movement which he led was the decisive factor in destroying the dominant position of the Conservative party in Quebec. It is true that the latter party made something of a comeback by winning the provincial election of 1892, but its triumph was short-lived, for it was again defeated in the election of 1897. During the next sixty years the Conservative party was seldom successful in obtaining any significant support from the people of Quebec in either federal or provincial elections.

The political history of Quebec after 1896 was to be one of Liberal domination. In the provincial sphere, after defeating the Conservatives in the election of 1897, the party was to remain in office for the next thirty-nine years, that is, until it was defeated by the Union Nationale in the election of 1936. In the field of federal politics the Liberals were

[8]A list of Quebec administrations from 1867 to 1960 is to be found in Appendix A, Table VIII.

[9]In regard to Mercier's role in the federal election of 1887, see Rumilly, *Riel*, pp. 226–33. For the election of 1891 see R. Rumilly, *Histoire de la Province de Québec*, VI, Les "*Nationaux*," pp. 200–11.

to win a majority of Quebec seats in every election from 1891 right up to 1957.[10] There was only one occasion during this long period when the federal wing of the party had to contend with any kind of strong opposition from Quebec. This occurred in the early 1900's when a certain amount of dissatisfaction with Laurier's policy of token participation in the Boer War, and his decision to build a Canadian navy, led to the formation of a new nationalist movement headed by Henri Bourassa, a Montreal journalist and former Liberal member of Parliament.[11] Although Bourassa's nationalists were not successful in breaking the Liberal control over the province, they did help to bring about the downfall of the Laurier government by winning twenty-seven out of Quebec's sixty-five seats in the federal election of 1911. This loss by the Liberals in Quebec, coupled with substantial losses to the Conservatives in the other provinces, forced Laurier to resign and brought the federal Conservative party back into office. Bourassa's movement disintegrated around the beginning of the First World War.

There were several reasons for the success of the Liberals in retaining the support of the Quebec voter after 1896. One was that by the turn of the century the party had lost whatever anti-clerical or secular tendencies it ever had, and was no longer considered suspect by most of the clergy. This transformation was due largely to the efforts of Laurier, the Liberal leader, who devoted himself to the task of bringing about a *rapprochement* between his party and the Church. Laurier insisted continually that the principles for which he and his party stood drew their inspiration from the moderate reformist type of liberalism found among such English leaders as Gladstone rather than from the doctrinaire anti-clerical liberalism found on the Continent.[12]

The strength of the Liberals was based also on the stand taken by the party on the question of provincial autonomy, an issue which, as we have seen, had always been of particular concern to the people of Quebec. In this regard, although both the major parties had usually been guided by the principle that the rights of the provinces under the British North America Act must be respected, it was the Liberals who,

[10]See Dean, "How Canada has Voted," for election figures up to 1945. For the elections of 1949, 1953, 1957, 1958, 1962 see *Canadian Parliamentary Guide,* 1950, 1954, 1958, 1959, 1963.

[11]Bourassa's movement is described in Jean-C. Bonenfant and Jean-C. Falardeau, "Cultural and Political Implications of French-Canadian Nationalism," Canadian Historical Association, *Report,* 1946, pp. 66–71.

[12]Laurier's commitment to the principles of English liberalism was affirmed in a famous speech he made in Quebec City in 1877 on "Political Liberalism." See Willison, *Laurier and the Liberal Party,* I, chap. xii.

from 1867 until the beginning of World War II, "were the more solicitous for the maintenance of all provincial prerogatives."[13] While this statement applied to the party at both the federal and the provincial levels, naturally enough it was the provincial wing in Quebec which was the most uncompromising in its opposition to any centralization of powers in the hands of the federal authority. This was particularly true of the administration of L. A. Taschereau, Liberal Prime Minister of the province from 1920 to 1936. Taschereau resolutely opposed the slightest encroachment on the rights of the province by the central government, even when the latter was under the control of the federal wing of his own party.[14] The Quebec leader went so far as to insist that no changes could be made in the British North America Act without the consent of all the provinces.[15]

However, the most important factor in the consistent loyalty of the French Canadian to the Liberal party was that the latter not only stood for the autonomy of the provinces within the federal system, but was also the greatest proponent of the autonomy of Canada within the Commonwealth. It was the Conservatives rather than the Liberals who always took the most pride in the British connection and who usually opposed any policies likely to weaken Canada's ties with Great Britain. For example, the Conservatives fought Laurier's proposal in 1910 to establish a separate Canadian navy on the grounds that such a step would adversely affect the interests of the Empire and threaten its unity. For the same reason the party opposed the plans of the Liberals to negotiate a reciprocal trade agreement with the United States. The slogan under which the Conservatives fought the election of 1911 was "no truck nor trade with the Yankees."[16]

The most convincing proof for the French Canadian that the Conservative party would have Canada make greater sacrifices in support of imperial policies than the Liberals was provided by the divergent attitude of the two parties towards the nature and extent of Canada's

13R. M. Dawson, *The Government of Canada* (1st edition; Toronto, 1947), p. 505.

14Taschereau's determination to defend the autonomy of the province was expressed quite forcibly in the Speech from the Throne in the 1928 session of the Assembly. See *Canadian Annual Review*, 1927–8, p. 412. See also: Quebec, *Report of the Royal Commission of Inquiry on Constitutional Problems* (Quebec, 1956), I, 100.

15*Canadian Annual Review*, 1926–7, 343.

16A. R. M. Lower, *Colony to Nation* (2nd edition; Toronto, 1949), p. 430. The traditional policy of the Conservatives of close ties with Great Britain is also pointed out in J. R. Williams, *The Conservative Party of Canada, 1920–1949* (Durham, N.C., 1956), pp. 222–7.

participation in the First World War. When that war broke out in 1914 the federal administration was under the control of the Conservative party led by Prime Minister Robert Borden. Borden assured the British government that it could depend on the full support of the Canadian people, and made preparations to send a military contingent overseas. This policy received the strong endorsement of Laurier's Liberal party. Although Canada's entry into the war at Britain's side did not arouse the same wild enthusiasm in Quebec as in the rest of the country, the average French Canadian was not opposed to such a move so long as recruiting was on a voluntary basis. He would then not be compelled to enlist unless he wanted to do so, and, in fact, the number of volunteers from Quebec was proportionately much smaller than that of the other provinces.[17] By 1917, however, the voluntary system had broken down and could no longer provide sufficient manpower for Canada's commitments overseas. Borden thereupon decided to call upon Laurier and his Liberal party to join the Conservatives in a coalition government which would introduce conscription. After some deliberation Laurier turned down Borden's offer to join his cabinet, and instead opposed vigorously the proposal to adopt a compulsory system of recruitment. In this stand Laurier had the solid support of the Quebec Liberals: most of his followers in the other provinces, however, swung their support behind Borden. The cabinet which finally put the conscription bill through Parliament, therefore, was predominantly Conservative, although it also contained a number of English-speaking Liberals.

A wave of resentment swept across Quebec following the introduction of conscription, and the bitterness and antagonism between the two language groups in Canada reached their greatest intensity since the Riel affair. An important result of this controversy was the destruction of what little support the Conservatives still retained in Quebec, making it impossible for the party to capture any sizable number of seats for a long time to come. The Liberal party, on the other hand, was greatly strengthened because of the stand taken by Laurier and the Quebec Liberals, in spite of the fact that most of the English Liberals had sided with Borden. To the average Quebec voter the Liberal party had become the strongest bulwark against Canadian involvement in "imperialist ventures." This was dramatically illustrated in the provincial election of 1919 when the Liberal party won

[17]It is estimated that during the whole period of the war some 200,000 volunteers came from Ontario, but only 50,000 from Quebec, and of the latter large numbers were English-speaking. See Lower, *Colony to Nation*, p. 466.

forty-three out of the eighty-one seats in the legislature by acclamation; the Conservative party did not consider it worthwhile to even put up a candidate in these electoral districts.[18] Here was the unusual situation of a party winning an election a week before the voting started. The Liberals' control over the Quebec administration was not to be seriously challenged until the 1930's.

From this brief outline of the political history of Quebec from 1867 to the end of the First World War one significant conclusion at least is obvious. The willingness of the people of Quebec to support any particular party in the years from 1867 to 1919 was determined largely by the extent of that party's sympathy for the attitudes and interests of the French Canadians as a minority cultural group. During the greater part of the time the vast majority of Quebec voters supported one of the two major Canadian parties, the Conservatives or the Liberals, depending upon which one was most favourable to the French-Canadian point of view at the moment. There were occasions, however, when the people of Quebec, or a sizable proportion of them, became convinced that the Quebec wings of the old parties were not adequately defending their interests on some controversial issue. This usually resulted in the growth of nationalist movements whose leaders pledged themselves to make an aggressive stand against any threat to the French Canadian's traditional way of life. The basic difference between the nationalists and the Quebec members of the old parties was that the former were more intransigent in their defence of French-Canadian interests and less willing to compromise with the English-Canadian point of view when a serious controversy developed between the two language groups.

It is important to point out that the type of nationalism we are discussing here is of the defensive rather than the expansionist kind. It is concerned with the maintenance of existing rights and interests rather than the extension of the influence and attitudes of the group to other peoples and other areas.[19] It may be looked upon as the natural reaction of a minority ethnic group when confronted with a serious threat to its cultural survival. It expresses the determination of a people to

[18]See Jean Hamelin, Jacques Letarte, and Marcel Hamelin, "Les élections provinciales dans le Québec," *Cahiers de Géographie de Québec,* 7 (Oct. 1959–Mar. 1960), 38.

[19]There have been a number of individual nationalists, however, who have put forward the idea that French Canada has a "divine mission" to spread the "superior values" of French and Catholic culture in North America. See Bonenfant and Falardeau, "Cultural and Political Implications of French-Canadian Nationalism," pp. 65–6.

remain themselves. A Quebec historian of the nationalist school writes:

> Qu'est-ce que le nationalisme? C'est tout simplement la manifestation de la solidarité naturelle qui existe entre les membres d'un groupe humain ayant une tradition historique et culturelle qui lui donne un caractère propre. . . .
>
> Le nationalisme n'est pas un sentiment ou un mouvement artificiel. Il est la conséquence de la nécessité qui oblige l'homme à vivre en société. Forcés de s'unir pour réaliser des tâches communes, les membres d'un même groupe humain, placé sur un territoire limité dans l'espace, s'habituent à agir et à penser collectivement. Encadrés par des dirigeants qui ont la responsabilité de maintenir leur cohésion, héritiers d'une culture qui se différencie des autres, liés entre eux par un réseau d'intérêts matériels puissants, inspirés par des idéaux qui leur sont propres, ils s'affirment comme collectivité en s'opposant aux sociétés qui les environnent.[20]

A nationalist movement similar in many respects to those of Mercier and Bourassa was to make an appearance on the Quebec political scene shortly after the end of the First World War. It was to differ from the earlier movements, however, in that one of its main concerns was with an entirely new threat to the traditional interests and way of life of the French Canadian. This new school of nationalist thought was aroused over the policy pursued by successive Liberal régimes of promoting the industrialization of Quebec by encouraging foreign capital to invest in the province—an industrialization process which not only resulted in a system of absentee ownership of Quebec industry, but also destroyed the old rural society whose maintenance most French-Canadian leaders had always considered essential for cultural survival.

[20]Michel Brunet, *La Présence anglaise et les Canadiens* (Montreal, 1958), p. 235.

CHAPTER III

The Challenge of Industrialism and the
Growth of Nationalism

INASMUCH AS ONE of the most important characteristics of the nationalist movement which led to the formation of the Union Nationale was its opposition to the economic policies pursued by the Liberal party, we must first study the nature of those policies and their impact on the old rural Quebec society.

When the Liberal party came into office just before the turn of the century, the province of Quebec conformed fairly closely to the ideal of the rural and agrarian society favoured by the Church. Agriculture and other extractive industries were the basis of the province's economy, although there was also a certain amount of manufacturing.[1] With the exception of a few large industries in the Montreal and Quebec areas, however, such manufacturing as existed was integrally related to the farm economy and consisted of sawmills, brickyards, tanneries, blacksmith shops, small foundries, and manufacturers of simple farm machinery. Most of it was carried on in small establishments with little capital and every few workers.[2]

[1]It is estimated that out of a total production of $150,000,000 at the end of the nineteenth century, agriculture contributed 65 per cent, forestry 25 per cent, manufacturing 4 per cent, fishing and mining around 2 per cent each. Albert Faucher and Maurice Lamontagne, "History of Industrial Development," in Jean-C. Falardeau, éd., Essais sur le Québec contemporain (Québec, 1953), p. 28.

[2]The description of the old rural society in this chapter is based largely on Everett C. Hughes, French Canada in Transition (Chicago, 1943), chaps. II–IV. Hughes's interpretation of the evolution of French Canada has been criticized by Philippe Garigue in Etudes sur le Canada Français (Montréal, 1958). It has been defended, however, by Hubert Guindon in "The Social Evolution of Quebec

During this early period the majority of the people of the province lived in rural areas, for there were almost no large urban centres other than Montreal and Quebec City.[3] Families were large; there were sometimes as many as ten or twelve children. The parish was the centre of community life, and the parish priest played a dominant role. Aside from the clergy, the *élite* of this rural society were the doctors, lawyers, and other professional people who had attended one of the many classical colleges.

This agrarian economy was characterized by mixed farming rather than specialized crops, and, although some of it was exported, most of the produce was sold in local markets. The standard of living of the average farmer was not very high and his cash income was quite small, but he was by no means poverty-stricken. In the first place, the main system of land tenure was that of the family farm, owned by those who worked it; tenant farming was practically unknown. Moreover, the farmer was not completely dependent on the sale of his farm produce for his livelihood. If necessary, he could be highly self-sufficient. His farm could meet the needs of his family for meat and vegetables; fuel in the form of firewood was readily available; members of the family could make most of their clothes; and the large size of the average family made a cash layout for hired labour unnecessary. Owing to this high degree of self-sufficiency, the farmer's standard of living, modest though it might be, was not affected by fluctuations in the demand for his products to the same extent as it would have been in a more advanced and specialized agrarian society.

The important role that the Liberal party was to play in the trans-formation of this rural and agrarian society into a modern capitalist economy arose out of two basic convictions held by all successive Liberal administrations from 1897 to 1936. In contrast to the idealiza-tion of the rural life found among the leaders of the Church and some of the intelligentsia, the Liberals believed that the well-being and prosperity of the people of Quebec were dependent on the exploitation of the province's rich resources of timber, minerals, and hydro-electric power, and the rapid development of manufacturing industries. Sec-ondly, they were convinced that this necessary exploitation and devel-opment was the task of private rather than public enterprise. The preference for private enterprise on the part of the Quebec Liberals

Reconsidered," *Canadian Journal of Economics and Political Science*, XXVI, 4 (Nov., 1960), 533–51.

[3]According to the census of 1901, 60 per cent of the population lived in rural areas. Quebec, Department of Trade and Commerce, *Statistical Year Book, 1947*, p. 83.

was not too surprising. The party had discarded the anti-clerical aspects of nineteenth-century liberalism but retained the economic principles of that particular philosophy. The most important of these principles was a belief that government ownership of industry or any kind of intervention in "the smooth functioning of the economic order" was harmful and could be disastrous.

However, in its effort to further the development of the province's natural resources under a system of private enterprise, the Liberal party was faced by the problem that in a predominantly rural society of farmers, artisans, and shopkeepers, there was little domestic capital available for investment. When, therefore, around the turn of the century, British, American, and English-Canadian entrepreneurs began to show some interest in the province as a field for profitable invest- ment, they received every inducement and encouragement from the Liberal administration. Prior to the First World War, British and American pulp and paper companies were given grants in perpetuity of enormous tracts of public domain. Foreign and English-Canadian capitalists were given the right to exploit the vast water power resources of the province, a policy in sharp contrast to that of the neighbouring province of Ontario, which was then setting up a publicly owned electric power system. In order to induce British and American manufacturing concerns to establish branch plants in Quebec, the province offered exemption from certain types of taxation. Legislation was enacted giving private enterprise monopoly control of public utili- ties in Montreal and other cities.[4]

These policies of the Liberal party resulted in a certain amount of industrial development in the period before the First World War, but the industrialization of Quebec did not really get under way until the Taschereau administration of 1920–36. Like his predecessors L. A. Taschereau was an economic liberal, with an attitude not too different from the "rugged individualism" of Herbert Hoover in the early thir- ties. He was also as firmly convinced as previous Liberal leaders that the prosperity and well-being of the people of Quebec were dependent on the rapid industrial development of the province under a system of private enterprise. A Quebec historian thus describes Taschereau's economic philosophy:

. . . il ne croit pas à la colonisation mais à l'industrie, il ne croit pas à l'étatisme mais à l'initiative privée, il ne croit pas à la chance mais au

[4]This legislation was passed in spite of the fact that there was considerable public sentiment in the early twentieth century for municipal ownership of such utilities. See Robert Rumilly, *Histoire de la Province de Québec*, XII, *Les Ecoles du nord-ouest* (Montréal, 1944), pp. 112–15.

labeur. Il veut l'aisance des ouvriers, mais dans le respect des droits patronaux. Il tient la prospérité des grandes firmes pour la source majeure du bien-être général.[5]

Taschereau extended and intensified the traditional Liberal policy of grants of land, tax exemptions, and other concessions to foreign capital interested in exploiting the province's water power, mineral, and timber resources or in opening manufacturing plants. Foreign capital was also encouraged by the government's policy of a minimum of restriction and control over such matters as public utility rates, corporation financing, and the sale of securities. The important hydro-electric industry, for instance, was allowed to develop in its early days "in an environment of unfettered private enterprise that public utilities seldom enjoy."[6] Taschereau firmly believed that taxes must be kept at the lowest possible level so as not to "paralyze progress and stop initiative."[7] The various forms of social legislation must be avoided as much as possible, not only because they increased the financial burden of the taxpayer, but also because they were a form of "state paternalism" which destroyed the initiative and sense of responsibility of the individual.[8]

Perhaps one of the most attractive aspects of Taschereau's policies to the foreign investor was the attitude of the administration towards labour legislation. While it would not be true to say that the Liberal leader was opposed to all such legislation, his laissez-faire economic philosophy made him reluctant to introduce those measures which would guarantee the worker adequate wages and proper working conditions and give full legality to his attempts to organize and bargain collectively. Although certain legislation was enacted in 1925 giving some legal status and recognition to trade unions and the bargaining process, it was not strong enough to strengthen appreciably the position of the workers or to give much impetus to the growth of the trade union movement.[9] Nor did it prevent the formation of company-dominated unions where management was determined to head off the

[5]Ibid., XXV, Alexandre Taschereau (Montreal, 1952), p. 20.
[6]J. H. Dales, Hydroelectricity and Industrial Development: Quebec, 1898–1940 (Cambridge, Mass., 1957), p. 30.
[7]Canadian Annual Review, 1925–6, p. 377.
[8]This was Taschereau's main argument in rejecting the proposals put forward by various groups that Quebec establish a system of old age pensions. Ibid., 1928–9, p. 386.
[9]One authority on Quebec's labour legislation contends that it was not until a court decision was handed down in 1942 that the complete legality of trade unions in that province was definitely established. Jacques Perrault, "L'Evolution juridique," in Falardeau, éd., Essais sur le Québec contemporain, p. 135.

organization of independent and relatively militant international (American) unions.[10] Even where such international unions did exist they were often refused recognition by employers. The net result of Liberal labour policy was that the formation of trade unions was a slow and difficult process and the vast majority of Quebec workers still remained unorganized by the early 1930's.[11] The employer was thus provided with a plentiful supply of cheap and docile labour, and labour costs were a good deal lower than in the neighbouring province of Ontario.[12]

As a consequence of the economic policies of Taschereau and his predecessors, the province of Quebec had been transformed by the early 1930's into a predominantly industrial society, although agriculture continued to play an important role in the economy.[13] The province was now a major producer of aluminium, ships, aircraft, asbestos, textiles, and boots and shoes. It was the largest producer of pulp and paper in Canada, and the development of its abundant sources of electric power resulted in the establishment of large chemical and electrometallurgical industries. Montreal, the main industrial area in Quebec, had become the centre for the processing of various raw materials such as sugar, oil, and tobacco; it was also an important centre for the production of electrical and transportation equipment and metal products. The province had begun to produce copper, gold, zinc, and other minerals in some quantity.[14]

The new industrial society was characterized by large-scale industries employing hundreds and sometimes thousands of workers in a single plant, using mass production methods, and possessing large quantities of intricate capital equipment. An even more important characteristic was the concentration of ownership and control. In many industries huge monopolies developed through the merging of existing

[10]A French-Canadian Jesuit who had played an active part in the Catholic trade union movement in the 1920's admits that at that time many of these organizations were little more than company unions. See the comments of Jacques Cousineau, S.J., in Maurice Tremblay, "Orientation de la pensée sociale," Falardeau, éd., Essais sur le Québec contemporain, p. 212.

[11]In 1931 only 10.66 per cent of wage earners were organized into trade unions. See Appendix A, Table IX.

[12]In 1924 the average yearly wage in manufacturing industries in Quebec was $883.00 compared to $1,039.00 in Ontario. Dominion Bureau of Statistics, Canada Year Book, 1926, p. 414.

[13]By 1931, about 27 per cent of the labour force was still engaged in agriculture, as compared to 37 per cent in industry, and 36 per cent in commerce and services. Hughes, French Canada in Transition, p. 24.

[14]For a brief description of the industrial development of Quebec up to the beginning of the Second World War see Faucher and Lamontagne, "History of Industrial Development," pp. 32–3.

firms or the forcing of smaller competitors out of business.[15] In some cases large-scale operations were required by technological factors; in many others the only reason was the desire for control of the market and higher profits. Quebec had now become not only an industrial society, but one in which a few large monopolies played leading roles.

The policy of industrialization pursued by the Liberal party from the turn of the century to the 1930's had, of course, certain advantages for the people of Quebec. The new industries provided employment for the surplus population of the rural areas. This surplus population was the direct result of the system of inheritance in the old rural society. The practice was for each farmer to pass on his farm intact to one of his sons and provide for the others by buying new farms. By the turn of the century, however, it was becoming more and more difficult to find suitable farm land for the non-inheriting sons. As a result they began to migrate to the towns and cities in search of employment.[16] Although the wages paid to these new urban workers might not be very high, they enjoyed more cash income than they had known on the farm. The new industrial towns also provided additional markets for those who still remained in agricultural pursuits. Other occupational groups, such as merchants and professional people, benefited from the increased purchasing power of rapidly growing urban communities.

Whatever the immediate economic benefits flowing from the new economy, it was nevertheless quite clear that industrialization had serious implications for the people of Quebec: first, it presented an entirely new and serious challenge to the maintenance of those basic institutions and values which were part of their traditional culture and way of life; secondly, it made a revolutionary change in the economic status of the average French Canadian.

The challenge which industrialization presented to the traditional way of life arose from the mass migration that it brought about from the rural areas to the cities. This migration tended to destroy the old static rural society whose maintenance most French-Canadian leaders had always considered essential for cultural survival. Whereas in 1900 roughly 60 per cent of the people of Quebec lived in rural areas, by 1931 the province was 63 per cent urban.[17] As the province became more urbanized, the nature and function of two of the basic institu-

[15]The steady trend towards centralization of control and growth of monopoly in Quebec industry from the turn of the century until 1938 is described by F. A. Angers, "Les institutions économiques," in E. Minville, éd., Notre milieu (Montréal, 1946), pp. 381–92.

[16]Some of the problems arising out of the Quebec system of inheritance are discussed in Hughes, French Canada in Transition, pp. 4–9 and 20.

[17]Quebec, Statistical Year Book, 1947, p. 83.

tions of the traditional society, the family and the parish, were radically transformed. Urban life made the solidarity of the family and the patriarchal authority of the father extremely difficult to maintain. The head of the family was now in the economically unstable position of a wage earner, and was very often only one of several wage earners in the family, one of whom might be his wife. The large families which, as a source of farm labour, had been an asset in the rural society, became a liability and increased financial burden in the urban setting. The parish, which had been not only a religious unit but also an all-embracing community, lost this social function in the city. The parish priest began to lose some of his traditional authority, if not in religious matters, at least in other fields. Nor did the close and intimate relationship which had always existed between the pastor and his parishioners survive in the towns and cities.[18]

Undoubtedly the most serious effect of industrialization from the point of view of the Church was that it presented a threat to the religiously oriented scale of values of the old peasant society. The industrialists brought with them, not only their language, but also the secular value system of the English-speaking world with its emphasis on material well-being as against the primacy of the spiritual. Inspired by the principles of economic liberalism, they also brought the idea of a self-regulating economic order divorced from all ethical considerations. In this stress on well-being in this world rather than in the hereafter the industrialists in their continual search for profits, and the trade unions in their continual search for higher wages, were both diametrically opposed to the traditional value system of this Roman Catholic society.

The other important aspect of industrialization was that in the new economy the French Canadian played an essentially subordinate role. As Quebec became a modern industrial society of large capitalistic enterprises owned and operated by English, American, and English-Canadian industrialists, the economic status of the majority of French Canadians changed from that of land-owning proprietors, or skilled artisans working in their own shops, to that of wage and salary earners working for an alien employer. Moreover they were employed in the lower paid jobs in industry, for most of the higher managerial and white-collar jobs were in the hands of English-speaking people.[19] One of the reasons for this was that the industrialists to a very large extent brought with them their own managers, technicians, and white-collar

[18]In regard to the impact of industrialism on the family and the parish, see Jean-C. Falardeau, "The Changing Social Structures," in Falardeau, éd., *Essais sur le Québec contemporain,* pp. 110–14.
[19]See Hughes, *French Canada in Transition,* Table 45, p. 205.

personnel, or recruited them among English Canadians. Another factor was that the Church-controlled system of higher education, with its emphasis on classical studies, was not equipped to provide the engineers, managers, and accountants needed in an industrial society.

Although the changed economic status of the French Canadian had brought him a somewhat higher standard of living than that to which he had been accustomed, the old sense of independence and security had been destroyed. The stability of the static rural society had now given way to the instabilities and uncertainties of a dynamic market economy subject to periodic breakdowns in the form of depressions, with consequent unemployment, falling incomes, and deprivation. Nor did this loss of a sense of security touch only those people who in one way or another had become dependent on the smooth functioning of the new industrial system for their livelihood; it also applied to the sizable minority still engaged in farming and other non-industrial pursuits. Agriculture had become more and more specialized, and the farmer now produced largely for Canadian, and to some extent for world markets. This meant a higher cash income and better standard of living as long as conditions were prosperous, but it also meant that the farmer had lost his self-sufficiency and that his livelihood depended now on fluctuations in demand on national and world markets over which he had no control. The small French-Canadian shopkeeper and businessman had to meet the stiff competition of the large English-owned establishments, and in the trend towards monopoly some of the companies which disappeared, or were absorbed, were old and well-established French-Canadian concerns. The professional class might enjoy a higher income but their old prestige and leading role in the community were now challenged by the new managerial group which industrialism had brought with it.

In view of the widespread nature of the changes brought about in the way of life of the people of Quebec and their subordinate role in the new economy, it was perhaps inevitable that the Liberal policy of industrialization would meet with a certain amount of opposition from various sections of the population. What could hardly have been anticipated, however, even as late as 1930, was that this opposition would result in the rise of a new and powerful nationalist movement which would eventually challenge the Liberal domination of Quebec politics.

NATIONALIST OPPOSITION TO INDUSTRIALIZATION

It was when the tempo of industrialization was accelerated under the Taschereau administration that organized and coherent opposition to the Liberal policy of industrialization began to develop. This opposition came mainly from two sources: one was a small group of nationalist intellectuals who called themselves La Ligue d'Action Française; the other, certain Catholic Action organizations sponsored by the Church.

L'Action Française was formed during the First World War by a few followers of Henri Bourassa, the veteran nationalist leader who had campaigned against the naval policies of Laurier's Liberal party in the federal election of 1911.[20] When it was formed, L'Action Française had the limited objective of promoting the use of the French language in commerce and industry and defending the language rights of French minorities in other provinces.[21] Shortly after the war, however, it expanded its scope and aims, emerging as a full-fledged nationalist movement determined to defend and promote all those traditional rights and interests of the French Canadian as a distinct cultural group.

L'Action Française was never to have a very large membership, but it quickly gained influence and prestige in intellectual circles in the early 1920's and succeeded in attracting prominent individuals playing an active role in all phases of French-Canadian life, the professions, business, the Church, politics, and education. The most outstanding figure was Abbé Lionel Groulx, a professor of history at the University of Montreal, whose nationalistic ideas were to have a tremendous influence on the youth of the province for the next three decades. In 1918 Groulx became the editor of a monthly review published by L'Action Française and called by the same name.

While L'Action Française never became directly affiliated with any political party, it was to be the most important single agency in the formulation and development of a nationalist ideology which was to have a revolutionary impact on political developments in the province. Like previous nationalist movements, L'Action Française was concerned with the defence of the rights of French Canadians in other provinces, and the maintenance of the autonomy of the province within the federal system; it was also opposed to close ties with Britain or involvement in Britain's wars. It differed considerably from the earlier forms of nationalism, however, in its awareness of the serious nature of the economic problem, that is, of the threat which industrialization presented to the maintenance of the traditional cultural

[20]The group was originally called La Ligue des Droits du Français, but changed its name to La Ligue d'Action Française in 1918. In this chapter the shorter name of L'Action Française will be used. Although the name of this organization, as well as some of its ideas, were borrowed from the French movement led by Maurras, there was no direct link with the latter.

[21]Mason Wade, *The French Canadians, 1760–1945* (Toronto, 1955), pp. 865–6.

system, and of the subordinate role which the French Canadian played in the new economy. This recognition by a nationalist group, for the first time, of the importance of the economic problem was influenced to a large extent by a sharp but brief postwar depression in 1921 which brought with it a considerable amount of economic hardship. The main theme of the articles published in *L'Action Française* that year (vols. V-VI) was "l'enquête sur le problème économique."

From the early 1920's onward L'Action Française carried on a relentless campaign against the industrial system in all its ramifications. This campaign had two aspects. The first one arose out of the opposition on the part of most nationalists to industrialism as such, because of the challenge which the steady migration to the towns presented to the old rural way of life of the people of Quebec.[22] This point of view was shared by the Roman Catholic hierarchy. Both the nationalists and the hierarchy attempted to stem the migration to the urban areas by eulogizing the superior values of the rural environment and by warning the people of Quebec of the dire consequences for the survival of their culture if the desertion of the countryside continued.[23] To a certain extent an attempt was made to turn back the clock by organizing a back-to-the-land and colonization movement.[24] But the nationalists and the Church could not avoid recognizing the impossibility of completely reversing the industrialization process, and their solution here was to suggest that its tempo be slowed down and some kind of balance be struck between an industrial and an agrarian society.[25]

The second aspect of the nationalists' campaign against the industrial system was their vigorous protest against the subordinate role of the French Canadian in the new economy and his reduction to a mere wage earner. They strongly resented the fact that the ownership and control of the province's wealth and natural resources were in the hands of foreign capitalists, while the French Canadians had become, to use an expression popular at the time, "hewers of wood and drawers of water." To the nationalists the greater participation of the people

[22]See Antonio Perrault, "La Défense de notre capital humain: utilisation de notre capital humain," *L'Action Française*, XVI, 4 (oct. 1926), 195.

[23]The hierarchy issued a pastoral letter along these lines in 1923. See *Canadian Annual Review*, 1923, p. 610. The Church was not to give up its ideal of a rural and agrarian society until well into the 1940's.

[24]See the proposals put forward by Alexandre Dugré, S.J., "La Défense de notre capital humain: par la colonisation," *L'Action Française*, XVI, 3 (sept. 1926), 130–53.

[25]This was the solution suggested by Henri Bourassa all through the 1920's. See "L'Election provinciale de 1927: les conservateurs de Québec battus par les conservateurs d'Ottawa," *Le Devoir*, 11 fév. 1950, p. 47.

of Quebec in the economic development of their province was a matter of simple social justice. The extent of this resentment against the role played by foreign capital in the economy is illustrated by the following statement made by one of the prominent members of L'Action Française:

Presque partout l'étranger nous domine, nous tient. . . . Nos gouvernants . . . ont laissé des gens d'autre langue, d'autre race, s'emparer à vil prix de presque tout notre patrimoine. Que nous reste-t-il encore, dans l'ordre visible, matérial? Nos champs. Et même aux environs des grandes villes, nous en avons déjà trop cédé aux spéculateurs étrangers. . . . Nous sommes prospères, dit-on. Le vrai, c'est que les autres le sont, chez nous, et que, chez nous, nous les servons.[26]

The one weak spot in this campaign of the nationalists against the industrial system was that, although they insisted that the people of Quebec must regain control over their natural resources and wealth, there was no general agreement as to the specific steps by which this economic emancipation was to be brought about. Some of the suggestions put forward by different members of L'Action Française were that legislation be enacted forbidding the exploitation of Quebec's natural resources by Americans; that there should be more stringent government regulation of timber-cutting by foreign-controlled lumber and pulp and paper companies; and that the exploitation of the province's water power should be rigidly controlled and reserved for Canadian companies. The most widely suggested remedy, and the one on which all nationalists were certainly in agreement, was that the growth and development of small-scale French-Canadian business establishments should be encouraged, and that they should be given preferential treatment by the provincial government.[27]

The most important point to be noted in all these suggestions is that these nationalists of the 1920's with the exception of Henri Bourassa, were opposed not so much to capitalism in general as to large-scale English and American capitalism specifically.[28] The most logical

[26]Georges Pelletier, "Les Obstacles économiques à l'indépendance du Canada Français," L'Action Française, VIII, 2 (août 1922), 66–7.

[27]The various solutions to the problem of industrialism proposed by various members of L'Action Française between 1921 and 1928 are outlined in Wade, The French Canadians, pp. 878–90.

[28]Bourassa's critique of capitalism may be summarized here. The nationalist leader had travelled in Europe and had been much impressed by the attempts of the Catholic social movement in Belgium to find a middle way between the extremes of laissez-faire capitalism and Marxian socialism. Bourassa made a distinction between capitalism and its "abuses." He was not opposed to private property but to its concentration in the hands of a few individuals. He criticized modern capitalism for its "cult of money" and "exploitation of the working man,"

solution for any group like L'Action Française, which was concerned about the control exercised by foreign capital over the economic life of the province, would have been a sweeping programme of socialization. This would have taken the wealth of the province out of the hands of the English and put it under the control of a provincial government which would always be French-dominated. This solution was generally rejected, however, for, leaving aside a few public utilities, government ownership played little part in the thinking of L'Action Française. Widespread socialization was contrary to the Catholic social philosophy to which this group adhered, and which indeed it tended to interpret in a rather conservative fashion.[29]

Aside from L'Action Française, the other major source of opposition to industrialization in the period following the First World War was several Catholic Action groups sponsored by the hierarchy. These groups were formed because of the hierarchy's growing realization that, although it might still look upon the rural society as the ideal, most French-Canadians now lived in urban areas, and that this changed environment presented problems for the maintenance of the faith which the Church had hitherto not been called upon to cope with. With the parish in the urban setting no longer the integrating unit of community life and the intimate bond which linked the faithful to the parish priest broken, the increasing danger of the spiritual alienation of the urban masses was only too apparent. It had become necessary to insulate the French Canadian from the ideas and value system of a secular world by ensuring that his various fields of activity were concentrated in organizations inspired by Catholic doctrines and principles.

The most important of these organizations sponsored by the Church was a Catholic trade union movement launched in 1921 when a few scattered unions in different parts of the province amalgamated under

---

and looked upon it as a threat to the family, to the livelihood of the farmer, and to small-scale business enterprise. He was particularly opposed to cartels, trusts, and to large enterprises like the chain stores and the public utility companies. He was a strong advocate of the right of workers to organize and bargain collectively, although he tended to prefer the Catholic rather than the international unions. Probably the best description of the social philosophy of this controversial figure is to be found in Michael K. Oliver, "The Social and Political Ideas of French-Canadian Nationalists, 1920–1945," unpublished doctoral dissertation, McGill University, 1956, chap. II. See also a famous speech made by Bourassa in Quebec City in 1931 entitled, "Capitalisme, Bolchevisme, Christianisme," reprinted in *Le Devoir*, 11 fév. 1950, p. 49.

[29]Unlike Bourassa, most of the nationalists seemed unaware that the Church, while attacking the socio-economic doctrines of socialism, also rejected economic liberalism. The social philosophy of the Church is discussed, *infra*, pp. 54–7.

the name of the Confédération des Travailleurs Catholiques du Canada (C.T.C.C.).[30] When the C.T.C.C. was first formed the main concern of the Catholic hierarchy was not so much to strengthen the bargaining position of the French-Canadian worker as to protect him from the secularizing influence of the international (American) unions, which were just beginning to get a foothold in the province. Not only were these unions foreign, but they were also neutral in religious matters, and for that reason were looked upon by the bishops as "anti-Christian and materialistic."[31]

Another Church-sponsored occupational grouping was a farmers' union called the Union Catholique des Cultivateurs (U.C.C.), which was organized in 1924. Its purpose was to protect and promote not only the spiritual but also the material welfare of the farmers, and thus stem the flight from the land. One of the most important activities of the U.C.C. was the sponsoring of colonization schemes to open up new farming areas in the more remote parts of the province.[32]

Other Catholic Action organizations were a farmers' co-operative movement, formed in 1922, and called Coopérative Fédérée de Québec; the Caisses Populaires, or credit unions; and a province-wide youth organization called Association Catholique de la Jeunesse Canadienne-Française (A.C.J.C.). The last two organizations were actually formed before the War, but now assumed increased importance in the eyes of the hierarchy. In the early thirties more specialized youth organizations were set up, such as the Jeunesse Ouvrière Catholique (J.O.C.) for young workers, the Jeunesse Agricole Catholique (J.A.C.) for young farmers, and the Jeunesse Etudiante Catholique (J.E.C.) for students.

In theory the activities of these various organizations were limited to advancing the religious and economic interests of their members, and they were supposed to be neutral in politics. In practice they were all strongly nationalistic and outspoken critics of the foreign industrialists. In fact, many of the leaders of these various groups were also members of L'Action Française. The C.T.C.C. was opposed to the industrialists, not so much because they were capitalists, but because they were American or British instead of French-Canadian. This organization was equally opposed to the international unions which

[30]For a good description of the origin, history, and philosophy of the C.T.C.C., see Alfred Charpentier, "Historique de la C.T.C.C.," Programme-souvenir, Congrès annuel, et vingt-cinquième anniversaire de la Confédération des Travailleurs Catholiques du Canada (Québec, 1946), pp. 13–36.

[31]H. A. Logan, Trade Unions in Canada (Toronto, 1948), p. 594.

[32]For the origin and history of the U.C.C., see Firmin Létourneau, L'U.C.C. (La Trappe, Québec, 1949).

industrialism had brought with it, and its yearly conventions were characterized by violent attacks on these unions.[33] The main grievance of the U.C.C. was that the large lumber, pulp and paper, and power companies had appropriated huge tracts of potential farm land, thus narrowing the agrarian sector of the economy and making it difficult for farmers to find new farm land for their sons. Its opposition was intensified in 1926 when a power development of a pulp and paper company in the Lake St. John district resulted in the flooding of the land of large numbers of farmers in that area.[34] As for the various youth organizations, they tended to be more nationalist than Catholic. This was particularly true of the A.C.J.C., which had played an active part in all nationalist movements since its formation in 1904, and had always been associated with the promotion of the concept of "le mystique national."[35]

In their campaign against the industrial system L'Action Française and the Catholic Action groups had the support of at least two of the important dailies in the province—L'Action Catholique, the semi-official organ of the Archbishop of Quebec City, and the Montreal nationalist daily Le Devoir, which was still under the direction of Henri Bourassa in the 1920's. Although Bourassa's main interest had shifted to federal politics, he still found time to make strong attacks on the industrial system. In fact, his opposition to the rapid pace of industrialization went back to 1910 when Le Devoir was founded.

In spite of the vigour of the campaign carried on by these various groups and publications all through the twenties, they were not particularly successful in stemming the flight from the land or in arousing any widespread opposition to the foreign industrialists among the people of Quebec. The average French Canadian, preoccupied with the struggle to protect his rights and interests at the political level, was slow to grasp the more subtle challenge presented by the growth of an industrial society through the intervention of foreign capital. He was not yet fully aware of the significance of the changes which industrialism had brought about in his traditional way of life; nor did he understand clearly the nature of his subordinate position in the new economy. As long as that economy was prosperous industrialization was welcomed because it provided greater opportunities for employment and a somewhat higher income for most people.

[33]See, for instance, the description of the 1922 convention in Robert Rumilly, Histoire de la Province de Québec, XXVI, Rayonnement de Québec (Montreal, 1953), p. 104.

[34]See Létourneau, L'U.C.C., p. 111.

[35]Jean-C. Bonenfant and Jean-C. Falardeau, "Cultural and Political Implications of French-Canadian Nationalism," Canadian Historical Association, Report, 1946, p. 67.

This lack of interest in the nationalistic ideas of L'Action Française on the part of the people of Quebec, and the rather complacent attitude towards the foreign industrialists, was to change suddenly in the early 1930's as a result of the world-wide breakdown of the economic system. The impact of the depression in Quebec was much the same as in other provinces and countries: mass unemployment, falling incomes, bread lines, and deprivations affecting all sections of the people. Industrial production fell off sharply, and large numbers of people, able and willing to work, could not find jobs. Many of those who managed to retain their positions had to take sizable cuts in wages and salaries. Farmers and other primary producers, unable to find markets for their produce, also found themselves in a precarious financial position. Many of them migrated to the cities, thus increasing the burden on relief rolls. Professional people, merchants, and other middle class groups all experienced drastic reductions in income.

With the depression of the 1930's the ideas of the nationalist intellectuals and their bitter antagonism towards all aspects of the industrial system spread rapidly among the masses of the people. This ready acceptance of the nationalist ideology was not too difficult for the average French Canadian once he awakened to the fact that the ownership and control of the economic system which was the cause of all his hardships were in the hands of foreign industrialists. Resentment against the capitalistic system as such quickly became coupled with antagonism towards the English-speaking people who dominated it.

Not only did nationalistic ideas begin to spread more rapidly under the impact of the depression, but they also took a more radical turn. Le Devoir and L'Action Française, which changed its name to L'Action Nationale in 1932, intensified their attacks against "les étrangers" exploiting the province's natural resources.[36] The nationalist press was particularly critical of "the electricity trust," which became the symbol of irresponsible economic power.[37] There were several reasons for singling out this particular industry. It was based on the exploitation of an important natural resource and provided the motive power for all other industries in the province. Through the device of interlocking directorates the power companies were intimately connected with many other large industries, particularly with such financial institutions as banks and insurance companies. The situation was similar to that prevailing in the United States about the same time, in that

[36]The increasingly radical trend found in the articles published in L'Action Nationale in the early thirties is described in Wade, The French Canadians, pp. 903–4.

[37]In regard to nationalist agitation against the power companies, see J. H. Dales, Hydroelectricity and Industrial Development: Quebec, 1898–1940, p. 224.

methods of financing could not always bear close scrutiny, profits were often fantastically high, and the rates paid by the consumer were excessive.[38]

As the depression deepened anti-English feeling grew rapidly and "Quebec for the French Canadians" became the slogan of the day. Nationalistic and anti-English feeling was widespread among the working classes dependent for their livelihood on an alien employer who in many cases maintained his profit margin by drastically cutting wages and salaries. For instance, one large American-controlled textile company, with net profits in 1933 of 24 per cent on invested capital, paid weekly wage rates averaging $13.43 for males and $9.73 for females. This was based on a 55-hour week. Ninety male and 130 female workers were paid wages of less than $8.00 per week.[39]

Nationalistic sentiments were also found among the small French-Canadian merchants and businessmen, who were less able than their large English competitors to withstand the impact of the sharp reduction in sales, and as a consequence were involved in a desperate struggle to stave off bankruptcy. In reaction to this situation they organized a movement called L'Achat Chez Nous to try and convince the people of the province that they should only buy goods manufactured by French-Canadian firms and make their purchases solely from French-Canadian merchants. For a short while during the thirties branches of L'Achat Chez Nous were to be found in all parts of the province.

Another section of the population strongly influenced by the ideas of the nationalists was the youth of the province. Fresh from schools and colleges, they were entering a world which had no place for them in its economic structure. In the early thirties all kinds of nationalist leagues and societies were organized among university students or recent graduates. Practically all of these organizations had the same basic characteristics: they were anti-English and anti-trust, they glorified the French-Canadian "race," and they were often tinged with anti-Semitism. Some of these groups went so far as to propose the separation of Quebec from the rest of Canada and the establishment of a French-Canadian state on the banks of the St. Lawrence. However, although these organizations were extremely vocal and attracted a good deal of public attention at the time, their influence was limited, their membership was small, and none of them lasted very long.

[38]For the abuses connected with the financing of the Montreal Light, Heat, and Power Company, see *ibid.*, pp. 115–23.
[39]See Canada, *Report of the Royal Commission on Price Spreads* (Ottawa, 1937), p. 118. Similar examples of such exploitation are to be found in chapter v of the Report.

The most important aspect of the spread of nationalistic ideas among the people of Quebec was its effect on the fortunes of the Liberal party. When L'Action Française and the Catholic Action groups had begun their campaign against the industrial system back in the early twenties it was inevitable that they would also be critical of the political party which had promoted and fostered it. The nationalists felt that the Liberals had betrayed the true interests of the province by their policy of concessions and grants to the industrialists. As long as the economy was prosperous, and the various nationalist groups represented only a small proportion of the electorate, the Liberals could safely ignore all such criticism. The strength of the party's position was indicated by the fact that in the election of 1927, the last one before the depression, it was successful in capturing seventy-five of the eighty-five seats in the legislature.[40] When, however, the breakdown of the economic system resulted in widespread economic unrest and the rapid growth of the nationalist ideology, the Liberals found themselves in a difficult position. They were now confronted by demands from all parts of the province that the government take energetic measures to alleviate the serious economic situation, curb the power of the foreign industrialists, and return control over the natural resources of his province to the French Canadian.

In the face of this growing discontent the Quebec government, like that of the other provinces, set up a system of direct relief grants to the unemployed in co-operation with municipal and federal authorities, and inaugurated a certain number of public works in order to provide additional jobs.[41] Paradoxically, however, for a party which had done so much to promote the industrialization of the province, the Liberals pinned their faith on a back-to-the-land movement as the best solution for unemployment and as a means of relieving pressure on relief rolls in the cities.[42] Needless to say, this was a point of view which was supported by both the nationalists and the Church. In co-operation with the clergy the government embarked on an ambitious colonization programme involving subsidies and other forms of financial assistance to all those individuals who could be induced to take up farming in the undeveloped frontier areas of the province. The government also spent large amounts of money in building roads, schools, and other public works in the colonization districts. Certain other reforms were also introduced. In response to pressure from the

[40]See Appendix A, Table VII.

[41]In regard to the economic policies pursued by the Liberals in an attempt to solve the problems resulting from the depression, see Canada, *Report of the Royal Commission on Dominion-Provincial Relations* (Ottawa, 1940), Book I, 193.

[42]See Speech from the Throne, 1931-2 Session, *Canadian Annual Review*, 1932, p. 170.

trade unions, and particularly the Catholic syndicates, a Ministry of Labour was established, and a statute was passed called the Collective Labour Agreements Extension Act, which strengthened to some extent the bargaining position of the workers. In answer to the nationalist criticisms of "the electricity trust," a provincial Royal Commission was appointed to investigate the financing and rate structure of the electric power companies.

In spite of these different measures, the government was not particularly successful in materially improving the economic situation or satisfying the demands of the nationalists. To a certain extent this was due to factors beyond its control. Obviously the problems confronting the government were not confined to the province of Quebec, but were the result of the world-wide breakdown of the economic system. The failure of the Liberal administration, however, was also due to the fact that its philosophy of laissez-faire made it reluctant to intervene in the economy and enact the drastic reforms which would have at least partially improved social conditions. Although the government spent sizable amounts on direct relief, it refused to launch any really comprehensive programme of social legislation on the grounds that public revenues were not inexhaustible and that private charity must also come to the aid of the unemployed. In spite of the large sums spent in promoting the back-to-the-land movement, these colonization projects had comparatively little effect in solving the problem of urban unemployment or in decreasing the pressure on relief rolls.[43] It was only too clear that the back-to-the-land solution was completely unrealistic in a society which was well on the road to industrialization and where 63 per cent of the population were already living in urban areas. The fact that this faith in colonization as a means of solving Quebec's problems was shared by the nationalists and the Church did not make it any less of an illusion.

Perhaps most important of all, the Liberal party's close ties with the industrialists made it unwilling to adopt the vigorous measures demanded by the nationalists to curtail the dominant role played by foreign capital in the economy of the province. The government did not take any effective steps to regulate the exploitation of the province's natural resources; it was reluctant to introduce legislation which would lower the rates charged by public utility companies and eliminate watered stock and other abuses in financing. Although such labour legislation as the government enacted was of some value to the trade union movement, it was still inadequate. As a result, the

[43]See *Royal Commission on Dominion-Provincial Relations*, Book I, 193.

large employers continued to be favoured by a labour market where the vast majority of the workers were unorganized.

The unwillingness, or inability, of the Liberal party to put into effect the economic and social reforms demanded by the nationalists, its failure to solve the problem of unemployment, and its close ties with the foreign industrialists led to increasing disillusionment among the people of Quebec with Taschereau's administration. The resentment against the economic system had now become directed against not only the English-speaking capitalists who owned and controlled it but also the political party which had promoted and fostered it. Nor was this opposition confined to the Liberal party's economic policies. The average voter was also beginning to become aroused by the accumulating evidence that the administration was characterized by nepotism, excessive use of patronage, and electoral corruption. As a climax to this widespread dissatisfaction with the Taschereau administration, all the various groups in the province opposed to the policies of the régime formed a coalition, just previous to the election of 1935, and launched a new political movement called the Union Nationale, whose avowed purpose was to drive the Liberal party from power.

CHAPTER IV

The Formation and Rise to Power
of the Union Nationale

THE UNION NATIONALE had its origin in a revolt which took place
within the ranks of the Liberal party in the early 1930's. This revolt
began when a group of young left-wing Liberals, who called themselves L'Action Libérale Nationale (A.L.N.), became dissatisfied with
the party's conservative economic policies and the tight control exercised over the party organization by Taschereau and a few close colleagues. The leader of the A.L.N. was Paul Gouin, the son of a former
Liberal Prime Minister of Quebec and grandson of Honoré Mercier.
Gouin and his associates, like most of the younger generation, had
been influenced greatly by the nationalistic ideas of Bourassa, Groulx,
and members of L'Action Nationale (formerly L'Action Française).
As a consequence, they were alarmed at the threat which industrialism
presented to the survival of the traditional French-Canadian culture
and were critical of the close ties which existed between the Taschereau administration and the foreign capitalists.[1]

The original plan of the A.L.N. was to reform the Liberal party from
within by forcing it to shift to the left in its economic and social
policies and by persuading it to adopt a more nationalistic philosophy.
However, within a short time the Gouin group became convinced of
the futility of trying to reform the party or break the control of the
ruling oligarchy. As a result, the A.L.N. severed all connections with
the Liberals shortly before the provincial election of 1935 and set itself

[1]Many of Gouin's ideas are to be found in a number of speeches which he
delivered to various groups in the 1930's and which are collected in his *Servir,* I,
La Cause nationale (Montreal, 1938).

up as a separate political party. Aside from Gouin, other key figures in the A.L.N. at that time were Oscar Drouin, who was to become chief organizer of the new party, J. E. Grégoire, mayor of Quebec City, and Dr. Philippe Hamel, a dentist by profession, also from Quebec City. Both Grégoire and Hamel were bitter enemies of what they termed "the electricity trust" and for some years had been campaigning for the nationalization of the power companies.

When the A.L.N. was launched it met with a favourable response from many sections of the population since its ideas conformed with the nationalist ideology then sweeping the province. It was endorsed by the influential L'Action Nationale,[2] and was looked upon favourably by the Union Catholique des Cultivateurs[3] and other Catholic Action groups. The new party had one handicap, however: most of its key figures had had little practical experience in politics. Very few of them had ever been candidates in either provincial or federal elections or played any kind of active political role before. In contrast, their Liberal opponents were skilled politicians, strongly entrenched in office, and with a powerful and well-financed political machine. Moreover, in a province where traditional habits of voting were an important factor in politics, the Liberals had been looked upon as the party of the French Canadian ever since 1897. In many families, particularly in the rural areas, political affiliation was inherited with the family farm, and a large number of people were Liberal for no better reason than the fact that their fathers had always voted that way. It was only too apparent that Taschereau's administration was not going to be easily dislodged by a new and untried party, led by a group of young men who, however idealistic and enthusiastic, had little knowledge of the "know how" of the political game. For all these reasons there were obvious advantages for the A.L.N. in making an alliance with some other group equally opposed to the Liberal administration, but with more political experience and with a better electoral organization. The only group which could meet these requirements was the provincial Conservative party. A brief look at the political history of that party will indicate why it might be receptive to such an alliance.

The Conservative party had been the official opposition in the Quebec Legislature ever since its defeat at the polls in the election of 1897. From that time onward it was only on a few occasions that the party had been able to capture sufficient seats to present the Liberals with any kind of challenge. It suffered from its close association with the federal Conservative party which was, of course, looked upon by

[2]Mason Wade, *The French Canadians, 1760–1945* (Toronto, 1955), p. 906.
[3]See statement of A. Rioux, president of U.C.C., *Le Devoir*, 7 août 1934.

the average voter as the party of "British Imperialism," and, above all, as the party which had imposed conscription in 1917.

The leader of the Quebec Conservative party during the greater part of the 1920's was Arthur Sauvé, member of the Legislative Assembly for the electoral district of Deux Montagnes, who had become party leader in 1916. Acutely aware of the disadvantageous position in which his party was placed by its close connections with the federal Conservatives, Sauvé was determined to make every effort to dissociate the Quebec Conservative party from its federal counterpart. When the nationalist movement of Abbé Groulx and L'Action Française began to gain ground following the brief postwar depression of 1921 Sauvé adopted most of its ideas and slogans. He also gave his party a new orientation in matters of economic and social policy. Although the Conservatives, like the Liberals, had been staunch supporters of laissez-faire capitalism during most of their history, the party now took a turn to the left. Sauvé began to criticize the role of foreign capital in the industrial development of the province and to attack the Liberals for their generous concessions to the business interests. In one election speech he made this statement: "Our natural resources must serve not only the ends of speculators, but the welfare of contemporary classes and of the generations to come. . . . The government . . . has sold our wealth to foreigners who shared with ministers and politicians, while our own people emigrated from the province." Sauvé proposed "that we develop, as far as possible, our natural resources by our own people and for our own people."[4]

Sauvé's attempt to dissociate his party from the federal Conservatives was only partly successful. It is true that the new orientation which he gave the Quebec Conservative party won it the editorial support of *Le Devoir* and *L'Action Catholique*,[5] and that it was soon on friendly terms with such groups as the U.C.C. whose agitation for a government-sponsored scheme of low-cost rural credit had been turned down by the Liberals. Sauvé was not able, however, to convince the vast majority of voters that the Quebec Conservatives were completely independent of the federal organization.[6] The reason for this failure

---

[4]*Montreal Star*, May 10, 1927.

[5]Robert Rumilly, *Histoire de la Province de Québec*, XXVI, *Rayonnement de Québec* (Montréal, 1953), p. 157.

[6]This was an important factor in the Liberal victory over the Conservatives in the provincial election of 1927. See Jean Hamelin, Jacques Letarte, and Marcel Hamelin, "Les Elections provinciales dans le Québec," *Cahiers de Géographie de Québec*, 7 (oct. 1959–mars 1960), 39. See also, "L'Election provinciale de 1927: les conservateurs de Québec battus par les conservateurs d'Ottawa," *Le Devoir*, 11 fév. 1950.

is not hard to find. Sauvé's party still contained a strong right wing which was closely associated with the business interests and had strong ties with the federal Conservatives. This right wing had always been critical of his policies. In giving up the leadership shortly after the defeat suffered by his party in the 1927 election Sauvé attacked this group for its hostile attitude:

> Une fraction du parti conservateur fédéral a toujours été hostile à ma direction. On m'accuse de nationalisme. Le nationalisme que j'ai prêché et pratiqué est celui de Cartier, c'est le conservatisme intégral et foncièrement national. . . . Mes efforts n'ont pas été couronnés de succès. Il convient donc que je laisse le commandement du parti. . . .[7]

In 1929 Camillien Houde, mayor of Montreal and member of the provincial legislature for Montreal-Ste Marie, succeeded Sauvé as party leader. Houde was a colourful politician who was to play an important role in municipal and provincial politics for the next twenty years. In the eastern and working class section of Montreal where he had been brought up Houde was affectionately known as "le petit gars de Ste Marie." Like Sauvé, Houde was a nationalist with radical ideas, but he showed a greater readiness to compromise on policy if the situation demanded it. Moreover, he was a much more dynamic and hard-hitting politician than his predecessor.

In the election campaign of 1931 Houde followed the same line of attack as Sauvé. His main accusation against the Liberals was that they had turned over the natural resources and wealth of the province to foreign capitalists, and he referred to them as "a nest of traitors to their race and their province."[8] His platform consisted of a number of social reforms which the trade unions, the farmers' organizations, and other groups had been demanding for a long time: government pensions for widows and the aged, a reduction in electricity rates, an intensified programme of colonization, the establishment of a Ministry of Labour, and a government-sponsored scheme of low-cost rural credit.[9] Houde waged a vigorous campaign in all parts of the province and hopes were high in the ranks of the party that it would be able to defeat the Liberals. However, the latter emerged victorious once more and Houde himself lost his seat in the Assembly. When he resigned from the leadership a year later the party decided to call a convention made up of delegates from all parts of the province for the purpose of selecting a successor.

[7]Robert Rumilly, *Histoire de la Province de Québec*, XXIX, *Vers l'âge d'or* (Montréal, 1956), p. 98.
[8]*Montreal Star*, July 6, 1931.
[9]*Canadian Annual Review*, 1932, p. 165.

The Quebec Conservative party's convention of 1933 was one of the most famous in the history of the province. Before the convention met, the name most prominently mentioned for the leadership was Maurice Duplessis. The son of a judge and a lawyer by profession, Duplessis had started his career in politics when he was elected as Conservative member to the Legislative Assembly from the electoral district of Three Rivers in 1927. (He was to be returned to the legislature by that constituency in every election from that time until his sudden death in 1959.) Duplessis soon built up a reputation in the Assembly as a clever debater and able parliamentarian. He was also adept at those skilful manœuvres which are an asset in rising to the top in the field of politics. A short while after Houde lost his seat in the Legislative Assembly in the election of 1931, Duplessis was chosen as temporary leader of the party in that House.

When the Conservative convention started its proceedings in the city of Sherbrooke on October 3, 1933, the delegates were divided into two factions.[10] One of them supported Duplessis as leader, and the other supported Onésime Gagnon, a Conservative member of the federal Parliament. The Gagnon faction has been organized by Camillien Houde, who was determined to block Duplessis' bid for the leadership. Houde's antagonism towards Duplessis arose out of a disagreement which had developed between these two forceful personalities shortly after the 1931 election over matters of party strategy. But Houde was not successful in his attempt to prevent Duplessis from capturing the leadership. While the latter had been temporary leader of the party in the Assembly he had built up a considerable following within the party ranks, and, as a result, he had control of the party machine by the time the convention was called. The chairman of that convention was one of his supporters. Moreover, he had the influential backing of most of the Conservative members of the federal Parliament from Quebec, and these federal Conservatives participated in the convention as voting delegates. When the time came for the balloting Duplessis was elected leader by 334 votes to 214 for his opponent.

Although it was not apparent at the time, the political ideas of the new Conservative leader differed from those of Sauvé and Houde in one very important respect. Duplessis was certainly a nationalist, but he was by no means a radical. As subsequent events were to show, he was a "practical politician" whose main objective was to defeat the Taschereau government and put the Conservative party in its place

[10]A detailed description of the organization and proceedings of the convention is to be found in *La Presse*, 30 sept.–5 oct. 1933. See also Pierre Laporte, "Il y a 25 ans, la convention de Sherbrooke," *Le Devoir*, 1–3 oct. 1958.

rather than to bring about sweeping economic and social reforms. However, it was only after the Union Nationale's victory over the Liberals in 1936 that the economic conservatism of Duplessis was to be fully revealed.[11]

When Duplessis took over the Conservative leadership he inherited a party which had won only fourteen out of ninety seats in the previous election,[12] a party whose chances of defeating the Liberals did not appear to be any brighter than they had been at any other time during the preceding thirty-five years. There were obvious advantages, with little to lose, in making an alliance with another group, such as L'Action Libérale Nationale, which was equally opposed to the Liberals. If the Conservative party could supply the practical knowledge of the techniques of politics and some of the financial backing, the A.L.N. could provide new men, new ideas, and considerable popular support.

Thus, a short while before the provincial election of November 25, 1935, Duplessis and Gouin entered into negotiations with a view to forming a united front against the Taschereau administration. These negotiations were successful and on November 8 the two leaders issued a joint statement announcing that their respective parties had joined forces against the Liberals. This statement read in part, "Répondant au désir de l'électorat du Québec, le parti conservateur provincial et L'Action Libérale Nationale déclarent par leurs représentants attirés qu'aux élections du 25 novembre, ils présenteront un front uni contre l'ennemi commun du peuple de la province de Québec: le régime Taschereau."[13] The new coalition was to be known as the Union Nationale Duplessis-Gouin.

The Duplessis-Gouin combination was soon joined by a number of independent nationalists who had hitherto taken little or no active part in politics, although many of them were leaders of various Catholic Action and patriotic organizations. The outstanding figures among these independents were Albert Rioux, a former president of the U.C.C., and René Chaloult, a Quebec City lawyer who was one of the directors of L'Action Nationale.

Undoubtedly one of the most important aspects of the Union Nationale was the nature of the programme which it presented to the electorate. This programme was significant in two respects: for the first time in the history of the province a political movement presented to the electorate a clear-cut and comprehensive set of proposals for

[11]See infra, pp. 73–5.
[12]See Appendix A, Table VII.
[13]Le Devoir, 8 nov. 1935.

economic, social, and political reform; secondly, this programme was to lay down the basic principles which were to be followed by all reform movements in the province for the next decade or so. It is essential, therefore, to understand just how this programme originated, and the particular proposals for reform it put forward.

As pointed out in the last chapter, the nationalist intellectuals of the twenties, in spite of their campaign against the industrial system, had never formulated any concrete and coherent programme of social reform and had not been in agreement as to how the industrialists were to be curbed. In other words, their critique of the economic system was stronger than their positive suggestions for its transformation. With the spread of nationalistic sentiments to the masses of the people in the early thirties it soon became apparent that such a constructive programme was urgently needed. It was the Roman Catholic hierarchy which provided the nationalists with the positive proposals for which they had been looking, proposals which were the result of a new orientation taking place in the social thinking of the Church after 1930.

Any discussion of the social philosophy of the Roman Catholic Church, whether in Quebec or elsewhere, must start with the encyclical letter, *Rerum Novarum*, of Pope Leo XIII, which appeared in 1891. This encyclical set forth the basic principles which were to underlie the Church's approach to labour and social problems, principles which to a very large extent still determine Catholic thinking. In his encyclical Leo XIII rejected both socialism and economic liberalism as solutions to the problems of an industrial society. The rejection of socialism, it should be emphasized, was not merely because it involved the abolition of all right to private property and proposed the establishment of a completely collectivized economy, but also because the continental socialism of Leo's day, under the influence of Marxist doctrines, was strongly anti-religious and sometimes militantly atheistic. The consistent opposition of the Church to socialism since that time cannot be fully understood unless this vital point is kept in mind.

In opposition to the philosophy of economic liberalism, the Pope insisted that the state had a special obligation to intervene in the economy and protect the standard of living of the wage earner and other depressed classes. He criticized the treatment of labour as a mere commodity which is bought and sold in the market, and condemned the exploitation of workers by employers. He also defended the right of workers to organize into associations to promote their interests.

Although *Rerum Novarum* was, of course, not unknown to the Church in Quebec, Leo's critique of industrial capitalism and his call for reform had comparatively little impact on Catholic thought in that province until the depression decade. Even in the 1920's, when the Church had become aware of the challenge which the industrial system presented to the religious and cultural values of French Canada, it still showed comparatively little grasp of the serious social problems resulting from that system, and particularly of those which affected the urban worker. It is true, of course, that the Catholic trade union movement and other Catholic Action organizations founded in the 1920's were to a certain extent inspired by *Rerum Novarum*. It has been pointed out above, however, that the primary concern of the hierarchy in setting up these organizations was to promote the religious and moral advancement of their members rather than their economic well-being, although the latter objective was not altogether overlooked.[14]

There were a number of reasons for this neglect of the social problems of a capitalist civilization on the part of the Church in Quebec, but the most important one was the predominantly "ruralistic" character of the clergy's thinking—their preoccupation with the problems of a rural society and their strong belief that the trend towards industrialization could be reversed. In so far as the clergy did become aware of some of the problems faced by the urban worker, such as unemployment, the remedy suggested was more likely to be a return to the land than the introduction of unemployment insurance.

In the early thirties a change took place in the social thinking of the Quebec hierarchy and it was prompted to put forward a programme of reform which would come to grips with the problems of an urban and industrial society. An immediate reason was that the breakdown of the capitalist system in the depression focussed attention on certain social problems arising out of that system which could no longer be ignored. Even more persuasive was the appearance in 1931 of the encyclical, *Quadragesimo Anno*, of Pope Pius XI. This encyclical was the most important papal pronouncement on social questions since *Rerum Novarum*, and had a tremendous influence on Catholic thought in all parts of the world, including Quebec. Its purpose was to re-affirm the basic principles laid down in the earlier encyclical and to clarify and re-interpret those principles in the light of the changes which had taken place in industrial capitalism since the 1890's. Like his predecessor, Pius rejected both laissez-faire capitalism and socialism, although recognizing that one wing of the latter movement, democratic socialism, had moved away from the more extreme position

[14]See *supra*, pp. 40–1.

of the Marxists. The Pope's critique of capitalism was expressed in statements such as this: ". . . the immense number of propertyless wage earners on the one hand, and the superabundant riches of the fortunate few on the other, is an unanswerable argument that the earthly goods so abundantly produced in this age of industrialism are far from rightly distributed and equitably shared among the various classes of men."[15] As a remedy for this situation, he called for a re-distribution of private property.

A related consideration, nearer to home, also prompted the Quebec hierarchy to take a particular stand on the problems arising from the industrialization of that province. The depression had resulted in wide-spread dissatisfaction with the capitalist system, and unless the Church put forward a programme of reform within the framework of Catholic social philosophy it was quite conceivable that it would be faced by the growth of a socialist or communist movement which might very well be not only secularistic but even militantly atheistic. The need to take some positive action seemed all the more imperative to the hierarchy when the Co-operative Commonwealth Federation (C.C.F.), an avowedly socialist party, was formed in western Canada in 1932 and announced its intention of spreading its doctrines to all provinces. An eminent theologian who had been assigned the task of making a careful study of the social philosophy of the new party came to the conclusion that the C.C.F. "did not merit the support of Catholics" because of its promotion of the class war, its extensive programme of socialization, and "its materialistic conception of the social order."[16] A different solution to the problems of the day was imperative.

The responsibility for the formulation of the Church's programme of reform was entrusted by the hierarchy to an organization sponsored by the Jesuit Order in Montreal called the Ecole Sociale Populaire. This was not actually a school in the ordinary sense but an organiza-tion which had been set up before the First World War for the purpose of studying and propagating the teachings of the Church on a wide range of moral, educational, and social problems.

The Montreal Jesuits did not themselves draw up the proposed

[15]Pope Pius XI, *Quadragesimo Anno* (London, 1931), 29.

[16]R. P. Georges Levesque, O.P., "La Co-operative Commonwealth Federation," *Pour la restauration sociale au Canada* (Montréal, 1933). An even stronger con-demnation of the C.C.F. was made a year later by Archbishop Georges Gauthier of Montreal. See *Montreal Gazette*, Feb. 26, 1934. This ban on the party was not to be lifted until the bishops of Canada, both English and French, issued a joint statement in 1943 declaring that Catholics were free to support any Canadian party except the Communists. See *Canadian Register* (Kingston), Oct. 23, 1943.

programme. Instead they called together a group of prominent Catholic laymen and gave them the assignment of outlining a set of proposals which would be a concrete application of the principles put forward in *Quadragesimo Anno* to the specific conditions and problems peculiar to Quebec. This group of laymen was composed of individuals playing a leading role in all phases of French-Canadian life: the Catholic trade unions, the farmers' organizations, the co-operatives and credit unions, the patriotic and professional societies, the universities. The most prominent members of the group were Albert Rioux, president of the Union Catholique des Cultivateurs; Alfred Charpentier, one of the leaders of the Catholic unions; Wilfrid Guérin, secretary of the Caisses Populaires, or credit unions, in the Montreal area; Esdras Minville, a professor at the Ecole des Hautes Etudes Commerciales in Montreal; and Dr. Philippe Hamel and René Chaloult of Quebec City. Most of these people were also directors of L'Action Nationale.

The Ecole Sociale Populaire published the conclusions arrived at by this study group in a pamphlet entitled *Le Programme de restauration sociale* which appeared in the fall of 1933.[17] This pamphlet contained proposals for reform in four different areas. "Rural Reconstruction" suggested the steps which should be taken to strengthen and even extend the agrarian sector of the economy; "The Labour Question" put forward an extensive scheme of labour and social legislation which would raise the incomes and provide greater economic security for the working class; "Trusts and Finance" dealt with measures which should be taken to curb the power of the public utilities and other large business enterprises; and, "Political Reforms" called for legislation which would eliminate patronage politics and electoral and administrative corruption.

We come now to the immediate background of the programme of the Union Nationale. The relationship of this programme to the proposals of the Ecole Sociale Populaire can be traced back to the formation of L'Action Libérale Nationale. Paul Gouin, its leader, had not been a member of the group of Catholic laymen who had drawn up and formally affixed their signatures to *Le Programme de restauration sociale,* but he was in general sympathy with the ideas put forward for he had participated in some of the discussions leading up to the final proposals. It was not too surprising, therefore, that when he launched the A.L.N. a short while later he adopted the Ecole Sociale Populaire

[17]A. Rioux, *et al., Le Programme de restauration sociale* (Montréal, 1933).

document as the basis for his own programme.[18] He did, however, make some minor changes, and included a few additional proposals of his own. When the alliance with Duplessis was arranged the following year one of the basic conditions which Gouin insisted upon was that the Conservative leader accept the complete A.L.N. programme. In the light of later developments it is important to make it quite clear that Duplessis agreed to this condition at the time.[19] One of the clauses in the joint statement issued by the two leaders announcing the formation of the Union Nationale states this firmly:

> Après la défaite du régime anti-national et trustard de M. Taschereau, le parti conservateur provincial et L'Action Libérale Nationale formeront un gouvernement national dont le programme sera celui de l'Action Libérale Nationale, programme qui s'inspire des mêmes principes que celui du parti conservateur provincial.[20]

One other significant aspect of the Duplessis-Gouin programme should be mentioned here. The fact that the reforms proposed by the two leaders were based on *Le Programme de restauration sociale* was a decisive factor in winning the support of such influential figures as Rioux, Hamel, and Chaloult, all of whom had participated in the drawing-up of the Jesuit-inspired programme.

A brief summary of the more important proposals put forward in the programme of the Union Nationale Duplessis-Gouin of 1935 is now in order.[21]

AGRARIAN REFORMS

Reforms in the field of agriculture were given top priority in the Union Nationale's plan of action. They included a government-sponsored scheme of agricultural credit at low rates of interest, the extension of rural electrification, subsidies for certain types of farm products, government assistance in marketing, development of small and medium-size industries in rural regions which would be complementary to the farm economy. The monopolistic control exercised by "the milk trust" over the processing and market-

---

[18]Gouin acknowledged his debt to the Ecole Sociale Populaire in a speech which he delivered in August, 1934: "Nous avons pris comme base d'étude et de discussion, pour préparer notre manifeste, le programme de Restauration sociale publié sous les auspices de l'Ecole sociale populaire. . . . ce document reflétait de façon assez juste non seulement l'opinion de nos esprits les plus avertis mais aussi les sentiments, les aspirations et les besoins populaires." *Le Devoir,* 13 août 1934.

[19]See *infra,* chap. v.

[20]*Le Devoir,* 8 nov. 1935.

[21]This programme first appeared in *Le Devoir,* 28 juillet 1934, when it was the programme of L'Action Libérale Nationale. A few weeks later Gouin delivered a speech in the town of St Georges de Beauce in which he provided further amplification and explanation of his proposals. See *Le Devoir,* 13 août 1934. The full text of the programme, together with the text of Gouin's speech at St Georges de Beauce, is to be found in Appendix B.

ing of dairy products was to be destroyed through the organization of farmers' co-operatives. Emphasis was placed on an extensive back-to-the-land and colonization programme under which the government would spend large sums of money in building roads, schools, and churches and in draining the land. A special commission made up of independent experts and government officials would be set up to organize this programme.

LABOUR AND SOCIAL REFORMS

In this area it was proposed that the laws governing minimum wages, hours of work, and industrial hygiene be strengthened and extended. A Labour code was to be drawn up which would bring together and clarify all existing labour legislation. The Workmen's Compensation Act was to be revised so as to give the workingman greater security and indemnity in case of injury. Industry would be compelled to give priority to wages over dividends and to provide the worker with an income which would not only give him a fair standard of living, but also enable him to acquire property. The social legislation proposed included health insurance, pensions for needy mothers (that is, married women with children whose husbands had died or deserted them), old age pensions, and a slum clearance programme.

INDUSTRIAL AND FINANCIAL REFORMS

The programme called for "the destruction, by every possible means, of the stranglehold which the large financial institutions, the electricity trust, and the paper industry trust have over the Province and the municipalities." Aside from the pulp and paper and power companies, the "trusts" which were singled out for particular attention were the coal, gasoline, and bread companies. It was proposed that a publicly-owned hydro-electric system be established as a solution to the problem of high electricity rates. Its first task would be to develop all the unexploited water power resources of the Province. At the same time a special commission would be appointed to investigate the feasibility of the government gradually taking over all privately-owned companies engaged in the production and distribution of electric power. The commission woud be asked to determine whether the cost to the government of such a takeover would still permit a reduction of rates. The coal, gasoline and bread companies would be subjected to competition from state-owned enterprises in these fields if such a step was felt to be necessary in order to reduce prices. A thorough investigation would be made of the structure and methods of financing of all public utility companies in order to determine the extent of such abuses as watered stock and doctored financial statements. There would be a reduction in the rate of interest charged by banks on loans. The Companies Act would be more rigidly enforced.

GOVERNMENTAL AND ELECTORAL REFORMS

Under this heading it was suggested that cabinet ministers be prohibited from becoming shareholders or having any other form of financial interest in any company receiving contracts from the government. In addition, ministers would be barred from serving on the directorates of banks, insurance companies, financial houses, railways, or any company exploiting the province's water power or forest resources. Compulsory voting would be introduced, and a limitation would be placed on the amount of money which individuals or business concerns could contribute to the electoral funds of any political party. All voters in cities with a population over 10,000 would be required to have identification cards.

One of the most important features in this section of the programme was the suggestion that Quebec's upper house, the Legislative Council, be abolished and replaced by an economic council which would act as an advisory body to the Legislative Assembly on all economic matters. This proposal was a step in the direction of the corporative system advocated by Pope Pius XI in his encyclical, *Quadragesimo Anno*. Under this system employers and employees in each industry would be organized into a professional association or corporation, which would have considerable authority to make decisions regarding prices, wages, and general policy for that industry. All corporations would be joined together in an economic council at the top which would formulate policy for the economy as a whole.[22]

The comprehensive programme summarized above indicates the wide extent of the economic, social, and political changes which the Union Nationale proposed to introduce. It also provides us with some valuable insights into the nature of the assumptions and basic principles underlying the whole approach of both the nationalists and the Church in the 1930's to the question of social reform.

In the first place, it is evident that the nationalists, like the Church, still idealized the rural way of life and were not yet fully reconciled to the new industrial society. They still hoped to maintain, or even to expand somewhat, the relative importance of the agrarian sector of the province's economy.

Secondly, their avowed aim of breaking the domination of foreign capital over the economy and bringing about French-Canadian participation in the wealth and natural resources of the province was to be accomplished by five different methods: (*a*) A policy of social legislation and higher wage scales which would enable the wage earner to acquire property; (*b*) The formation of co-operatives which would compete with the large monopolies in some fields and thus curb their power; (*c*) Encouragement and assistance to small- and medium-scale

[22]Pius XI, *Quadragesimo Anno*, pp. 36–44. The "professional corporatism" advocated in the encyclical is not the same as the "state corporatism" of Mussolini's Fascism. The latter system involves the total elimination of parliamentary democracy; the former merely suggests that some of the functions of government concerned with regulation and control over the economy should be entrusted to associations of employers and employees in each industry. The Church's corporatism finds its inspiration in the craft guilds of the Middle Ages and proposes to establish a system of self-government in industry similar in some respects to Roosevelt's N.R.A. codes of the early thirties. For a very brief but accurate description of the differences between Catholic and Fascist corporatism, see Ernest Barker, *Principles of Social and Political Theory* (London, 1961), pp. 39–40.

French-Canadian business establishments; (*d*) Government regulation and control of public utilities and other large-scale business enterprises; (*e*) Government ownership of certain industries, but only as a last resort, and provided that such a step was deemed absolutely necessary for the well-being of the community as a whole.

Finally, it can be said that the programme taken as a whole, and following the inspiration of *Quadragesimo Anno* and other papal encyclicals, attempts to pursue a middle road between laissez-faire capitalism and socialism. Its objective is the redistribution of private property rather than its elimination. It is also interesting to note that in many respects Union Nationale's proposals were similar to those being incorporated about the same time in Roosevelt's New Deal in the United States.[23]

The formation of the Union Nationale meant that for the first time since the days of Honoré Mercier in the 1880's a powerful nationalist movement had arisen to play an important role in provincial politics. Like Mercier's party, the Union Nationale was determined to maintain all those traditional values and rights which had always been considered essential for cultural survival. It differed, however, in that it was also concerned with a problem which, in the nature of things, Mercier did not have to contend with. This was the Union Nationale's determination to raise the economic status of the French Canadian by bringing about extensive reforms in the system of industrial capitalism. For this reason the Duplessis-Gouin coalition must be described, not merely as a nationalist movement, but as a radical nationalist movement.[24]

Perhaps the greatest source of strength of the Union Nationale was the fact that it had the unofficial, but nevertheless effective support of all the various Catholic Action and patriotic organizations across the province: the Catholic trade unions, the farmers' organizations, the co-operatives and the credit unions, the youth organizations, the associations of French-Canadian businessmen and merchants. All of these organizations were supposed to be neutral in politics, but as pointed out earlier, they were all strongly nationalistic and therefore opposed

[23]When Paul Gouin formed his Action Libérale Nationale in 1934 he pointed out the similarity between his ideas and those of Roosevelt. See *Le Devoir*, 28 juillet 1934. There were, however, important differences between the two programmes as well, such as the emphasis placed by Gouin on the agrarian sector of the economy.

[24]In applying the term "radical" to the Union Nationale I mean only, of course, that its approach to economic policy was considered to be radical at the time. Many of its proposals for reform would not be considered very radical today.

to the Liberal party's policy towards the industrialists.[25] Moreover, many of the leaders of these organizations had participated in drawing up the programme of the Ecole Sociale Populaire which the Union Nationale had adopted. Needless to say, the new movement also had the enthusiastic backing of such nationalist publications as *L'Action Nationale* and the Montreal daily, *Le Devoir*. There was little doubt too that, although the hierarchy was careful that the Church as such should not become directly involved on one side or the other in the political struggle, most of the clergy were sympathetic towards the political movement which had adopted its programme of social reform.

As a result of the wide support behind the Union Nationale the Liberals, for the first time in nearly forty years, were presented with a real challenge to their continued control over the provincial administration. The seriousness of this threat was to become apparent in the election of 1935, the first test of strength of the Duplessis-Gouin combination.

THE UNION NATIONALE COMES TO POWER

When Paul Gouin and a few other young Liberals formed L'Action Libérale Nationale in 1934 and began to attack the policies of the Liberal "old guard," neither Taschereau nor any of his colleagues took the new movement very seriously. It was only when the Gouin group began to win wider support, and then joined forces with the Liberals' traditional enemy, the Conservative party, that Taschereau slowly began to recognize the serious nature of the challenge with which he was faced. He was still confident, however, that his party would be able to weather the storm and retain control over the provincial administration as it had done so often in the past.

There were several good reasons for Taschereau's confidence. Although many Quebec voters might be dissatisfied with Taschereau's economic policies, the Liberal party was still looked upon as a staunch defender of the Quebec point of view on such vital issues as provincial autonomy and relations with Britain. Another factor was that the party's control over the provincial administration placed it in the advantageous position of being able to spend government money and give out government jobs in a purely partisan fashion. When the budget was drawn up each year the administration made sure that a good

---

[25]The leaders of the U.C.C. had always been close to the old provincial Conservative party. Albert Rioux, president of the association until 1936, resigned his post to run as Union Nationale candidate in the election of that year. Several leaders of the Catholic unions supported Union Nationale candidates on the platform in the same election.

portion of the allocations to each department could be spent at the discretion of the minister, that is, in those ways which would be of most benefit to the party. Since the province lacked a non-partisan, competitive system for the selection of governmental personnel the way was left open for all sorts of patronage. The Liberals held a further advantage in that their huge majority in the legislature enabled them to manipulate the electoral machinery along lines which would provide the greatest handicap to the opposition forces. This can be illustrated by a bill which the party put through the legislature in 1931. Shortly after the election of that year a large number of defeated Conservatives contested the election of their Liberal opponents before the courts. The Conservatives sought to nullify the election of these Liberals on the grounds that they had been guilty of fraudulent practices on polling day. While litigation was still under way the Liberal majority in the legislature pushed through a law, popularly known as the Dillon Act (after the name of its sponsor) and applying retroactively to the 1931 election, which removed all such cases from the jurisdiction of the courts.[26]

When the election of 1935 was called, Taschereau toured the province denouncing the Union Nationale coalition as "un mariage qui va se terminer par un désastreux divorce."[27] He accused Duplessis of abandoning the principles for which the Conservative party stood and attacked Gouin for betraying the ideals of his father, Sir Lomer Gouin, who had preceded Taschereau as leader of the Liberal party. Taschereau also defended the policies which his administration had pursued in the past and contended that these policies had been of immeasurable benefit to the farmer, the worker, and other sections of the population. Although the Liberals had never shown much enthusiasm for the Ecole Sociale Populaire programme,[28] Taschereau promised to introduce some of the reforms which it put forward, such as old age pensions and a government-sponsored scheme of low-cost farm credit.

However, the Liberals did not rely solely on the introduction of a few reforms to win the support of the electorate. They had even more tangible benefits to offer. As in the past the government embarked on an extensive programme of public works several months before the election. New roads, public buildings, and bridges were built, or at least started, in all parts of the province. Some of these projects were

[26]See *Canadian Annual Review*, 1932, p. 171.

[27]*Le Devoir*, 11 nov. 1935.

[28]When the programme appeared Olivar Asselin, a prominent Liberal, stated, "It bears a greater resemblance to a 'bleu' [Conservative party] pamphlet than to a work of social apostolacy." *Montreal Gazette*, Nov. 21, 1933.

discontinued the day after the election. The public works programme provided additional, if temporary employment, and meant sizable government orders for local hardware merchants and shopkeepers in various towns and villages. Whenever the government provided a community with some badly needed public facility it was able to present itself as a "benefactor" which had "done something" for that particular town or district. This was an important consideration for the average Quebec voter when he was trying to decide which party to vote for. Government candidates in most electoral districts also spent fairly large sums of money on the distribution of drinks of "whisky blanc" and handed out other gifts and favours which might help to convince the voters that the Liberals were "des bons garçons."

The willingness of the Liberal party to use any and all methods to win an election is exemplified in the operation of its well-oiled electoral machine in the Montreal area on polling day. When the polls opened it soon became apparent that the names of many voters who were known to be opponents of the régime had been left off the voting lists. At the same time hundreds or even thousands of fictitious names might have been added to these lists in a particular electoral district. Impersonation of voters, or "telegraphing," was carried out on a large scale, and in certain polls where the party might be expected to do poorly some of the ballot boxes disappeared altogether. In several constituencies "strong arm" squads went from poll to poll intimidating voters, and then proceeded to smash up the committee rooms of the opposition. These activities were often carried out under the eye, and sometimes with the tacit approval, of election officials and the provincial police.[29]

The well-entrenched position of the Liberals, and their readiness to use all kinds of questionable tactics, obviously placed the Union Nationale in a disadvantageous position in the election campaign of 1935. However, shortly after the date of the election had been announced, the new coalition entered candidates in every electoral district and proceeded to wage a vigorous campaign in all parts of the province. Its appeal to the electorate was for the most part based on the comprehensive programme of economic and social reform summarized above. The Union Nationale leaders also made strong attacks on the administrative and electoral abuses of the Taschereau government. In spite of the many handicaps under which it fought the election, the Duplessis-Gouin combination succeeded in capturing a total

[29]The activities of the Liberal electoral machine in some of the Montreal constituencies in the election of 1935 are described in a series of articles in *Le Devoir*, 25 nov.–10 dec. 1935.

of forty-two seats, almost four times the number of seats held by the Conservative opposition in the previous legislature.[30] Although the Liberals, with forty-eight members elected, still maintained control over the administration, they had only a narrow margin of six seats—five after the Speaker had been selected.

The results of the election were a serious setback for the Taschereau régime. The gains made by the Union Nationale coalition completely changed the situation in the legislature where the Liberals had always had an overwhelming majority and had thus been able to put their legislative programme through with a minimum of obstruction. After the 1935 election the government was not only faced by a large and vigorous opposition, but one of the leaders of that opposition, Maurice Duplessis, was an astute politician who knew all the tricks of the parliamentary game.

When the 1936 session of the legislature was called, Duplessis used the many delaying tactics of the experienced parliamentarian to hold up the passing of the budget until such time as the government agreed to enact some of the proposals outlined in the Union Nationale programme. The result was that as time went on the government found itself in increasing financial difficulties. The most telling blow struck by Duplessis, however, and the one which was to sound the death knell of the Taschereau régime, was the information he was able to bring to light concerning the administration's handling of public funds.

Ever since the early 1920's, the Conservative party had been accusing the Liberals of graft, corruption, and inefficiency in the administration of government departments. Owing to the weakness of the party in the legislature, however, it had never been able to coerce the government into setting up a parliamentary inquiry to investigate these alleged irregularities. The Public Accounts Committee, which was supposed to maintain a close check on how public money was being spent, had not met for a long time. Even if it had been called into session at any time before the election of 1935, the huge Liberal majority would have been able to dominate proceedings and prevent any serious investigation from taking place. In the legislature of 1936, however, the Liberals no longer enjoyed this strategic advantage. The opposition was not only successful in bringing the Public Accounts Committee back to life, but the strength of its forces in that Committee made it difficult for the Liberals to control the inquiry.

The Public Accounts Committee was in session from May 5 to June 11, and under the skilful probing of Duplessis it quickly brought to

[30]See Appendix A, Table VII.

light a picture of patronage, nepotism, and the squandering of public funds which involved most government departments.[31] It was dis-covered that members of the administration, from cabinet ministers down to the lowest level of the civil service, were using the contacts and influence which they had as government officials to increase their private incomes and those of their friends and relatives. Certain offi-cials made a substantial income by selling materials of all kinds to various government departments at very high prices. One such case involved the director of the government-run School of Fine Arts who made sizable profits from the sale of automobile licence plates to the government.[32] The Treasury lost many thousands of dollars every year through the inflated travelling expenses of ministers and other indivi-duals; this was especially true of the expenditures of the Department of Colonization.[33] One of the most startling discoveries was that a brother of the Prime Minister, who was the accountant of the Legis-lative Assembly, had been putting the interest on bank deposits of government money into his own personal account. His only defence was that all his predecessors in the position of Assembly accountant had done the same thing.[34]

Another case investigated by the Committee concerned certain acti-vities of the Assistant Attorney General. When the latter was ques-tioned by Duplessis as to whether he had from time to time received fees for legal counsel from companies exploiting the province's natural resources he refused to answer.[35] A few days later he resigned from his government position. It should be mentioned here that for many years it had been common practice for the Prime Minister himself, as

[31]Although a stenographic report was made of the proceedings of the Public Accounts Committee, this report was never published. Consequently the discussion here of the evidence presented before the committee has had to be based on newspaper reports. For each case at least two sources have been referred to in order to make sure of the accuracy of the reporting. One of the main sources has been Montreal's La Presse, a newspaper which has usually been a strong sup-porter of the Liberal party. Another important source has been a series of articles published in Le Devoir shortly after the sessions of the committee had ended and entitled, "M. Godbout était ministre au temps des scandales révélés au comité des comptes publics." Le Devoir was anything but friendly towards the Liberals at the time, but these articles are well documented and contain verbatim reports of many of the sessions.

[32]See reports in La Presse, 13 mai 1936; Le Devoir, 23 juillet 1936; Canadian Annual Review, 1935–6, p. 283.

[33]See La Presse, 9, 14, 29 mai and 2, 3, 4 juin 1936; Canadian Annual Review, 1935–6, pp. 282–3.

[34]See La Presse, 5, 6, 9, 10 juin 1936; Le Devoir, 6 août 1936; Sherbrooke Daily Record, June 12, 1936.

[35]See La Presse, 15, 26 mai 1936; Le Devoir, 30 juillet 1936; Sherbrooke Daily Record, June 12, 1936.

well as a good number of his ministers, to accept appointments to the board of directors of many of these companies. Although there was nothing illegal in this practice, it is obvious that it could result in a serious conflict of interests and loyalties when these companies came to the government for some new concession. Taschereau had always justified his acceptance of these directorships by arguing that, "the head of a government should meet business men around a directors' table, learn about business, and give the province the benefit of it."[36]

The Public Accounts Committee also found a good number of instances where unsuccessful Liberal candidates and other friends of the party had been put on government payrolls at unusually high salaries or had been paid some kind of commission or fee without having to do much work.[37] In some cases special positions or assignments were created for these individuals. The Prime Minister himself had no less than forty-five of his relatives employed in various government departments.[38]

One other interesting aspect of the committee's investigations was that they showed how the Liberals used their control over the provincial administration to build up a powerful political machine. In colonization regions, for instance, government subsidies and other forms of financial assistance to new colonists were not sent to the latter directly, but were turned over to the Liberal member or local organizer in that district, who saw to it that the money was distributed in ways which would be of greatest benefit to the party.[39] The government indirectly bought the support of a number of newspapers in the province by handing out sizable printing contracts at generous prices and by spending large sums of money on publicity and advertising for the various government departments.[40]

The revelations of the Public Accounts Committee created a sensation throughout the province and completely discredited the Taschereau administration. Around the beginning of June, when the commit-

[36]*Canadian Annual Review*, 1928–9, p. 381.

[37]For reports of some of these cases, see *La Presse*, 29, 30 mai 1936; *Le Devoir*, 13 août 1936.

[38]Although this information is not directly based on evidence presented before the committee, it is nevertheless reliable. The Union Nationale organization made its own investigation into the Public Accounts and came up with a list of the names, occupations, and salaries or fees of these forty-five relatives. See the party's booklet, *Le Catéchisme des électeurs* (Montréal, 1936), pp. 74–80. This publication is obviously partisan, but it is well documented.

[39]See *La Presse*, 7, 14 mai 1936; *Le Devoir*, 4, 13 août 1936.

[40]See the case of the Quebec City newspaper, *Le Soleil*, as reported in *La Presse*, 29 mai 1936. *Le Catéchisme des électeurs*, pp. 119–27, makes an analysis based on the Public Accounts for 1935 of the money paid out by the government to various newspapers in the province.

tee was still in the midst of its deliberations, Taschereau suddenly announced his resignation as Prime Minister and recommended to the Lieutenant Governor that Adelard Godbout, Minister of Agriculture, be appointed in his place. At the same time the Legislative Assembly was dissolved and a new election was called for the following August.

Godbout was a logical choice for Prime Minister, for he was one of the few members of Taschereau's cabinet who had not been involved, either directly or indirectly, in the scandals of the administration. In selecting his cabinet the new Liberal leader reduced the number of ministers from fourteen to ten, and appointed only four members from the previous government.[41] Like Godbout himself, these men had not been involved in the investigations of the Public Accounts Committee. The strategy of the Liberals was to go before the electorate with "a government of new men," as they termed it. In an attempt to dissociate himself from the Taschereau régime, Godbout did not try to defend the policies of his predecessor, but instead promised that a Royal Commission of Inquiry would be set up to investigate every aspect of the provincial administration.

Godbout appeared determined to set up a government, not only of new men, but also of new policies, for he recognized the extent of the dissatisfaction throughout the province with the economic system and the widespread desire for social reform. When the election campaign of 1936 got under way he put forward a programme which was similar in many respects to that of the Union Nationale. The main proposals in that programme were: an extension of rural credit facilities, a programme of rural electrification, and the provision of subsidies on certain farm products; an intensified colonization programme; a sweeping reduction of electricity rates throughout the province; a public works programme to solve the problem of unemployment; a minimum wage scale for industrial workers not covered by collective labour agreements, and the introduction of certain amendments to the Workmen's Compensation Act requested by the trade unions; the establishment of a system of needy mothers' allowances; and the elimination of the practice of cabinet ministers accepting directorships from companies doing business with the government.[42]

The most important difference between Godbout's appeal to the electorate and that of the Union Nationale was that the Liberal leader refrained from making a direct attack on the large corporations and business interests, and there was no attempt to stir up the nationalistic

[41]See *Sherbrooke Daily Record*, June 28, 1936.
[42]These proposals were put forward by Godbout in a radio address. See *La Tribune* (Sherbrooke), 6 juillet 1936.

sentiments of the Quebec voter. Moreover, the Prime Minister, himself a farmer, tended to concentrate his efforts on winning the support of the rural rather than the urban voter. When announcing his programme he stressed the vital role of agriculture in the economy: "Restaurer l'agriculture pour restaurer toute notre vie économique; c'est le fond même de notre politique."[43] There was a very practical aspect to this strategy of emphasizing the concern of the Liberals for the interests of the farmer. Although the farm population of the province had been declining for many years, the rural vote was still the decisive factor in elections. This was because of the distorted nature of the electoral system, which gave the rural areas approximately 63 per cent of the seats in the legislature in spite of the fact that by 1931 only 37 per cent of the people of Quebec lived in rural districts.[44]

The Union Nationale entered the election campaign under the leadership of Maurice Duplessis. Paul Gouin had had a disagreement with the former Conservative leader and had quit the coalition shortly after the dissolution of the legislature. The reasons for this split between the two leaders, and the way in which Duplessis subsequently succeeded in making the Union Nationale a unified party under his control, will be dealt with in the next chapter. What needs to be mentioned here is that Gouin's defection had little immediate effect on the strength of the Union Nationale as most of his Action Libérale Nationale followers, including such prominent figures as Oscar Drouin, Dr. Philippe Hamel, and J. E. Grégoire, remained in the coalition with Duplessis.

The election of 1936 was to demonstrate that the deathbed conversion of the Liberal party to social reform and honest administration had come too late. All through the election the opposition forces attacked the Liberals for the administrative and political corruption of the Taschereau régime and refused to absolve the Godbout government from the sins of the previous administration. They strongly denied that it was "a government of new men." As stated by Duplessis, "M. Godbout est l'héritier de M. Taschereau. . . . En politique comme ailleurs, l'héritier d'un régime assume la responsabilité des dettes et des méfaits de son auteur. . . ."[45] In another speech later in the campaign he repeated the charge that there had been no real change of direction: "Le gouvernement Godbout est une nouvelle pousse des

[43]Ibid.
[44]In 1936 there were 90 seats in the legislature. They are listed in Quebec, Legislative Assembly, Report on the General Election of 1936 (Quebec, 1936), Appendix I, pp. 3–4. According to the 1931 census figures, 57 of these electoral districts were predominantly rural, and 33 were predominantly urban. Of the latter, 5 were in Quebec City, and 16 were in the Montreal metropolitan area. See Census of Canada, 1931 (Ottawa), II, Table 16.

branches décrépites du gouvernement Taschereau. . . . Pouvez-vous avoir confiance en un régime qui refuse de punir les voleurs d'élections en favorisant des lois électorales malhonnêtes? Lorsqu'un régime refuse de protéger la source même de la démocratie, on ne peut avoir confiance en lui."[46] Duplessis promised that if the Union Nationale was elected to office it would continue the investigations begun by the Public Accounts Committee into the administrative practices of the Taschereau régime, and all those found guilty of misusing public funds would be punished. A clean sweep would be made of the whole administration, graft and corruption would be eliminated, and an end would be put to the squandering of government money.

The Union Nationale also attacked the Liberals for promoting the interests of the large business corporations while ignoring the serious predicament of the unemployed and neglecting the needs of the common people. The administration was referred to as "ce régime de véritable trahison nationale" because of the extensive concessions it had granted to the companies exploiting the province's natural resources.[47] In a radio address one prominent Union Nationale candidate stated, "Ce mot 'Union' signifie la solidarité entre tous les gens de bonne volonté, afin de mettre à la raison les trusts et les monopoles qui ont été protégés jusqu'ici par le régime Taschereau-Godbout-Bouchard et qui ont travaillé dans l'intérêt des financiers et des capitalistes, au détriment du peuple et de la masse des électeurs."[48] The trusts which were usually singled out for attack were the pulp and paper, timber, mining, coal, gasoline, and power companies. The opposition to the power companies was particularly strong as this industry was considered to be the most important single factor in "la dictature économique" which controlled the province.

Perhaps one of the most telling aspects of the Union Nationale's campaign was its appeal to the nationalistic and anti-English sentiments of the French-Canadian population. Antagonism towards the English reached a peak as Union Nationale orators, in meeting after meeting, warned the people of Quebec that their cultural values and their traditional way of life were threatened by the dominant role played by the British, American, and English-Canadian industrialists in the economic life of the province. The strong feelings of the nationalists towards "les étrangers" were forcibly expressed in a speech delivered at a mass meeting in Montreal by Dr. Philippe Hamel, the

[45]*Le Devoir*, 24 juin 1936.
[46]*La Tribune*, 6 août 1936.
[47]See Union Nationale advertisement, *Le Devoir*, 15 août 1936.
[48]*Le Devoir*, 15 août 1936.

outstanding opponent of the large corporations, and particularly of "le trust de l'électricité":

> Or notre patrie, notre foi, nos traditions, nos libertés, tout cela est menacé. Nos ressources naturelles, elles ont été vendues par le régime pour un plat de lentilles aux étrangers. Vos foyers, ouvriers, on est en train de vous les arracher et déjà la lutte s'organise contre votre clocher par de sourdes menées anticléricales qui se font plus audacieuses et violentes.[49]

At another meeting Hamel's close associate, J. E. Grégoire of Quebec City, spoke in similar vein of the the usurpations of "les étrangers":

> . . . une calamité nous étreint de toutes parts. Chacun est exploité, l'épicier canadien-français, le bûcheron, le petit propriétaire. Les meilleures places sont prises par des étrangers. . . . Les usines sont fermées, parce que notre province a été vendue aux étrangers. Les produits agricoles ne se vendent pas, parce que l'on a fermé nos débouchés.[50]

On every possible occasion Duplessis and other prominent figures in the Union Nationale expressed their determination to take whatever steps were necessary to protect the interests of the small-scale French-Canadian business enterprise engaged in a life and death struggle with the larger and more firmly entrenched English-owned corporations. This meant the small independent grocer in competition with the large chain stores, the small insurance broker against the large companies, and the small manufacturing concern against the larger establishments. It was also promised that legislation would be enacted compelling the large corporations controlled by foreign capital to hire more French Canadians in the higher supervisory and managerial positions.

The Union Nationale's appeal to the nationalistic sentiments of the French Canadian, and its promises of economic, social, and administrative reform, met with an unequivocal response from the electorate. When the time came for the balloting the people of Quebec turned the Liberal party out of office and elected the nationalist movement led by Maurice Duplessis. The Union Nationale won seventy-six out of the ninety seats in the legislature, while the Liberals with only fourteen seats were now in the novel position of being the official opposition.[51]

The chain of events leading to the Union Nationale victory of 1936 shows two things. First of all, the Quebec voter seemed to be convinced that the time had come for a government housecleaning, the

[49]*Ibid.*, 13 août 1936.
[50]*La Tribune*, 5 août 1936.
[51]Appendix A, Table VII.

elimination of graft and corruption, and the introduction of extensive reforms in administrative and electoral practices. Even more important, the success of this new nationalist movement was a clear indication of the strong opposition which had developed to the Liberal party's policy of promoting the industrialization of the province through the intervention of foreign capital. The defeat of the Liberals was a protest, not only against an economic system which had changed the traditional way of life and brought economic insecurity in its wake, but also against the dominant role played by English-speaking industrialists in that system. This protest was accompanied by a demand that the new capitalist economy be reformed and modified and that positive steps be taken to enable the French Canadian to regain control over the wealth and natural resources of his province. The direction these reforms were to take was to be determined by the principles of social Catholicism as laid down in the encyclicals of Pope Leo XIII and Pope Pius XI.

CHAPTER V

The Economic Policies of the Union Nationale in Two Administrations

AFTER ITS VICTORY in 1936 the Union Nationale was to remain in office until 1939. Defeated by the Liberals in the election of that year, the party returned to power in 1944 and maintained control over the Quebec administration until it was defeated a second time by the Liberals in 1960. In other words, during most of the twenty-four-year period between 1936 and 1960 the Union Nationale was the dominant force in Quebec politics. This was an important period, not only in the political, but also in the economic life of the province, characterized as it was by an intensification of the trend towards industrialization and urbanization which began after the First World War.

When the Union Nationale won the election of 1936 the people of Quebec had every reason to believe that it would inaugurate a new era in Quebec politics by destroying the control which the English-speaking industrialists exercised over the economy and by enacting comprehensive economic and social reforms. However, the direction which the economic policies of the Union Nationale were to take, once the party was in firm control of the administration, turned out to be of quite a different nature. The explanation of this sudden reversal of policy is to be found in a struggle for power within the party, which began even before the 1936 election, and to this struggle we turn now.

It will be remembered that the Union Nationale started out in 1935 as a coalition between Maurice Duplessis, the leader of the provincial Conservative party, and Paul Gouin, leader of a group of young left-wing Liberals who called themselves L'Action Libérale Nationale. One of the terms of this agreement was that Duplessis would accept the complete A.L.N. programme of reform.[1] Another very important stipulation was that power in the coalition was to be shared equally between the two leaders. They had agreed that if the Union Nationale took office, "Ce Gouvernement national Duplessis-Gouin aura comme premier ministre, M. Maurice Duplessis, et la majorité des ministres sera choisie par M. Paul Gouin, parmi les membres de L'Action Libérale Nationale."[2]

In spite of this arrangement to share control in the coalition, and to put into effect the A.L.N. programme, there appears to be little doubt that at a fairly early date Duplessis had become determined to dominate the Union Nationale and pigeonhole most of Gouin's proposals for reform. In this aim he had a decided advantage, for Duplessis was an experienced politician and skilled parliamentarian and Gouin had little knowledge of either parliamentary tactics or the intricate manœuvres which so often characterize party politics. While Gouin was busy attacking the trusts during the pre-election legislative session of 1936 Duplessis made a name for himself and strengthened his position in the coalition by the skill with which he obstructed the Liberal's legislative programme and by the important role he played during the sessions of the Public Accounts Committee in bringing to light the many abuses of the Taschereau régime.

Duplessis' opportunity came just before the election of 1936 when Gouin, having finally become convinced that his partner in the coalition could not be depended upon to live up to the terms of their agreement, broke suddenly with Duplessis. He accused the latter of trying to dominate the Union Nationale and revive the old Conservative party under a new name. In a statement to the press Gouin said, "Il est évident que M. Duplessis et certains de ses partisans, contrairement à l'entente du 7 novembre, et contrairement à l'intérêt de la province, cherchent à reconstituer le parti conservateur tory sous l'étendard de l'Union Nationale."[3] This break with Duplessis turned out to be an unfortunate move on Gouin's part, for he had assumed that when he left the coalition he would be followed by all of his A.L.N. group and by most of the independent nationalists. Contrary to his expectations, practically all his original followers, including such close associates and radical nationalists as Dr. Philippe Hamel, J. E. Grégoire, René Chaloult, and Oscar Drouin refused to join him. Instead they strongly denounced his action and reaffirmed their confidence in the leadership of Duplessis, for they were still convinced that

[1]See supra, p. 58.
[2]Le Devoir, 8 nov. 1935.
[3]La Tribune (Sherbrooke), 19 juin 1936.

the latter would live up to his commitment to curb the trusts and carry out the party's programme of reform. A statement of solidarity was issued by Drouin and Hamel at the time: "L'Union Nationale durera en dépit des défections. Nous resterons jusqu'à la fin avec Duplessis, le héros de la dernière session, le chef de L'Union Nationale."[4] Grégoire attacked Gouin's move as "trahison envers un allié loyal."[5] This support from the radicals was an important asset to Duplessis in the electoral campaign of 1936. It was perhaps significant, in the light of subsequent developments, that while Hamel and other left-wing elements concentrated their attacks on the trusts and their English owners, Duplessis for the most part emphasized the scandals and corruption of the Liberal administration.[6]

By the time the Union Nationale took over the provincial administration it had thus been transformed from a coalition into a unified party under the leadership of Duplessis. It was a party, however, with a strong left wing which had put its confidence in Duplessis that all aspects of the announced programme would be quickly implemented. The left-wingers were soon to be disillusioned. Although the radicals had played a vital role in the Union Nationale's victory, Duplessis decided that the time had come to curb their influence within the party. This became apparent when the Union Nationale leader announced the membership of his cabinet. To the complete surprise of the radicals, eight out of the fourteen cabinet ministers were former Conservatives,[7] in spite of the fact that the A.L.N. wing of the original coalition had been by far the stronger one.[8] Most important of all, the two leading radical nationalists and main opponents of the trusts, Dr. Philippe Hamel and J. E. Grégoire, were not included in the cabinet. Hamel immediately denounced the composition of the cabinet as "une autre victoire pour les trusts."[9] A short time later he, together with Grégoire and Chaloult, broke away altogether from the Union Nationale. Within the next year or so they were followed by Oscar Drouin and about a dozen other leading figures among the radical

[4]*La Tribune*, 20 juin 1936.
[5]*Ibid.*
[6]This is readily apparent when one studies the newspaper reports of the speeches made by Duplessis during the 1936 campaign. See for instance, *Montreal Gazette*, July 13, 1936; *La Tribune*, 20, 27 juillet, 6 août 1936; *Le Devoir*, 24 juin, 13, 16 juillet 1936.
[7]*Canadian Annual Review*, 1935–6, p. 285.
[8]In the election of 1935, when the Union Nationale was still a coalition between Duplessis and Gouin, L'Action Libérale Nationale elected twenty-six members to the legislature as compared to sixteen seats won by its Conservative allies. See Appendix A, Table VII.
[9]*La Tribune*, 27 août 1936.

nationalists in the Assembly. Duplessis succeeded, however, in retaining the support of most of the former members of the A.L.N. who had seats in the legislature.

With the departure of Gouin, Hamel, Grégoire, and the other radicals comprising the left wing of the original coalition, the Union Nationale had undoubtedly been weakened to some extent, since this group, though small, constituted the leading intellectuals in the movement. However, Duplessis had now achieved complete personal domination of the Union Nationale, and his leadership was never again to be challenged. From that time on he ruled the Union Nationale in an authoritarian manner and never called a provincial convention at which the rank and file of the party would have an opportunity to discuss policy and demand an accounting of his leadership. During the long period between his election as leader of the old provincial Conservative party in 1933 and his death in 1959 Duplessis never had to face any kind of party gathering to seek a renewal of his mandate.[10]

Once the radicals had been eliminated and Duplessis had undisputed control of the Union Nationale he was in a position to mould its policies in accordance with his own particular economic philosophy. That philosophy turned out to be closely akin to the economic liberalism of Taschereau. It was based on the strong conviction that individual initiative and private enterprise were progressive forces whose full freedom to develop and expand were essential for the prosperity of the province. The role of government was not to regulate or control business, but rather to encourage and co-operate with private enterprise in every way. Government ownership of industry, or anything which even remotely smacked of socialism, was to be absolutely rejected. This economic philosophy illustrates one of the paradoxical aspects of the personality of Duplessis: although the Union Nationale leader was in most respects a very devout Catholic, there was little indication during his long career that he had ever been influenced by the proposals for the reform of capitalism put forward in the encyclicals of Leo XIII and Pius XI. Duplessis took from the papal encyclicals their rejection of socialism but ignored their critique of economic liberalism.

In view of the nature of Duplessis' economic philosophy it is not surprising that the Union Nationale had not been in office very long before it became apparent to the industrialists that they had little to

[10]The way in which Duplessis ran the Union Nationale is described in Pierre Laporte, *Le Vrai Visage de Duplessis* (Montreal, 1960). See also Gérard Bergeron, "Political Parties in Quebec," *University of Toronto Quarterly*, XXVII (April, 1958), 356–9.

fear from the new régime in the way of government intervention or radical experiments in labour and social legislation. Duplessis soon made it quite clear that, although he was determined to clean up the abuses and corruption of the Taschereau administration, he had little intention of making widespread economic changes or carrying out the more radical aspects of the original A.L.N. programme on which his party had been elected to office. The party's pledge to the electorate to destroy "la dictature économique" and to bring about greater participation in and control over the Quebec economy by the French Canadian was quickly forgotten. Much lip service was paid to the principle that the growth and development of small-scale French-Canadian enterprise must be encouraged, but the large English-owned manufacturing plants, chain stores, and insurance companies continued to dominate. Nor were any steps taken by the government to compel these enterprises to employ a larger number of French Canadians in the higher managerial and supervisory posts. As in the past, the French Canadian continued to occupy the subordinate and lower-paid positions in every industry. Very little was done to eliminate abuses in the financing of large corporations, and the world of big business continued to be characterized by interlocking directorates, holding companies, watered stock, and a control exercised by a minority of the stockholders.

The most important single reversal in party policy towards the industrialists concerned the promise made all through the election campaign that, if elected to office, the Union Nationale would take immediate steps to regulate and control the activities of the larger power companies and would establish a provincially owned hydro-electric system. When Dr. Hamel, shortly after the election, asked that the Beauharnois Light, Heat, and Power Company be nationalized, Duplessis refused to take any action on the grounds that the government was not in a financial position to undertake such a move. In rejecting the ideas of the radicals he stated: "Je ne me suis jamais laissé conduire par des extrémistes et je ne le ferai pas non plus à l'avenir. Je ne me suis jamais soumis au chantage et à l'intimidation, et je ne m'y soumettrai pas maintenant."[11] As a result of Duplessis' attitude the privately owned power companies continued to exploit this important natural resource with a minimum of government regulation.[12]

[11]*La Tribune*, 27 août 1936.

[12]In 1937 a Provincial Electricity Board was set up to regulate the power companies, but its control over the hydro-electric industry turned out to be weak and ineffective. See J. H. Dales, *Hydroelectricity and Industrial Development: Quebec, 1898–1940* (Cambridge, Mass., 1957), p. 32.

In regard to social legislation, it is true that the Union Nationale did put into effect some minor reforms such as pensions for the blind and government allowances for destitute mothers. Certain changes were also made in the Workmen's Compensation Act. However, most of the social and labour planks in the party's original programme, such as the elimination of slums, health insurance, a labour code, and other measures to strengthen the economic position of the worker, were never enacted. Nothing was done by the government to compel industry to give prior consideration to wages rather than dividends. The proposed Economic Council which would act as an advisory body to the government, and which was supposed to replace Quebec's upper house, the Legislative Council, never materialized. Duplessis continued to fill vacancies in the upper house as they occurred and twenty-four years later it was still in existence. Nor did the Union Nationale take any steps towards establishing the corporative system favoured by the Church and many nationalists.

The only important labour legislation enacted during the first Union Nationale administration was two measures, known as Bills 19 and 20, which were more beneficial to the employers than to the workingman, and as a result met with a storm of protest from the whole trade union movement.[13] One of these bills gave the government power to abrogate or modify at will collective labour agreements freely arrived at between employers and employees without any consultation with the interested parties. Inasmuch as the government's sympathy tended to lie with the business interests, this legislation could mean the loss of wage scales won by the unions after hard collective bargaining. The other measure was a Fair Wage Act which empowered the government to step in and establish wages and working conditions in any industry or trade. Although on the surface this appeared favourable to labour, in practice the Fair Wage Board often set wages at a lower level than the unions could obtain through collective bargaining. Moreover, many employers cut down higher wages to the level fixed by the Board. One of the most objectionable features of both acts from the point of view of labour was that no government department, nor any contractor working for the government (which often meant a friend of the party), was bound to observe the terms of any collective agreement or any order of the Fair Wage Board.

In the field of political and administrative reforms, again very little

[13]A good summary of the main features of these bills is to be found in the *Canadian Annual Review*, 1937–8, p. 230. In regard to the attitude of the trade unions towards this legislation, see Henri St. Pierre, "Godbout Will Change Labor Laws," *Montreal Star*, Nov. 2, 1939.

was done, although the government did pass a law forbidding cabinet ministers from becoming members of boards of directors of business corporations. The Duplessis administration also made a thorough investigation into the civil service and discharged many individuals doing superfluous jobs or receiving excessive salaries. For a while it was also careful to eliminate undue expenditure in the granting of government contracts.

In spite of the startling reversal of policies of the Union Nationale once it had come under the control of Duplessis, there was one important section of the party's original programme which was carried out almost to the letter—the different measures which the party had promised to take in order to assist and raise the standard of living of the farmer. One of the first acts of the party after coming to power was to establish a system of agricultural credit at low rates of interest. This brought considerable relief to debt-ridden farmers for it enabled them to stay on the land and even to modernize their farms. In addition, a considerable number of agricultural schools were established, legislation was passed which set a minimum wage for forest workers, and large sums of money were spent on rural roads. The government also expanded the Liberals' back-to-the-land and colonization programme and in the three years between 1936 and 1939 spent around double the amount of money on colonization projects that the Taschereau administration had spent in the previous six years.[14] These projects took the form of financial assistance to farmers' sons to enable them to settle on new farm land, the opening-up of new areas by clearing and draining the land, and the expenditure of large sums of money to assist new communities in establishing schools, hospitals, and health services, and in building roads.

There were two important considerations behind Duplessis' solicitude for the welfare of the people in the rural areas. First of all, in spite of the fact that his general economic policies gave every encouragement to the foreign industrialists who were changing the face of Quebec, he still idealized the rural way of life and looked upon the farmer as the most stable, industrious, and law-abiding social type, "the true French Canadian." The other consideration was that under the electoral system inherited from the Taschereau régime, which Duplessis had no inclination to change, the political importance of the rural voter was out of all proportion to his numbers.[15]

---

[14]For figures on governmental expenditures on colonization, see Esdras Minville, "La colonisation," in E. Minville, éd., *L'Agriculture* (Montréal, 1944), p. 306n.
[15]See *supra*, p. 69.

By the time of the election of 1939 Duplessis had succeeded in eliminating practically all of the radical aspects of the party's original programme and had gone a long way towards transforming the Union Nationale from a party of social reform into a party of economic conservatism. This drastic reversal of policy was one of the reasons, although not the main one, for the party's defeat at the polls that year. (The other factors in that defeat together with the reasons for the party's return to power in 1944 will be dealt with in the next chapter.)

But the rejection of the Union Nationale by the Quebec voter in the election of 1939 did not bring about any alteration in Duplessis' economic policies. During the years in opposition between 1939 and 1944 the party continued to move to the right, and the second Union Nationale administration which took office following the party's victory in the election of 1944 was to be characterized by a strengthening and consolidation of its ties with the foreign industrialists.

When the Union Nationale returned to power Quebec's industrial revolution, which had slowed down during the depression years, had already entered upon a second and even more intensive phase.[16] The dynamic factor in getting this second phase under way was the outbreak of war in 1939, which resulted in enormous demands for the products of Quebec's mines and forests and for manufactured goods of all kinds. This development involved the expansion of existing industries and the establishment of scores of new ones. A good deal of this economic expansion took place in industries closely connected with the war effort—aircraft, shipbuilding, and munitions.

In the postwar period this increased tempo of industrialization was maintained, and even accelerated. The province of Quebec rapidly became a major Canadian producer of such manufactured products as electrical apparatus, transportation equipment, iron and steel, newsprint, textiles, and aluminum. The most spectacular development was the increased production of minerals of all kinds, and particularly the start which was made in the exploitation of the rich iron ore deposits of northern Quebec. As a result of the latter development some economists now began to refer to the valley of the St. Lawrence as a future Canadian Ruhr. By the middle of the 1950's there was little doubt that Quebec could be described as a mature industrial economy in which the vast majority of the people lived in urban areas and

[16]The rapid pace of industrial development between 1939 and 1950 is described in O. J. Firestone, "Recent Industrial Growth," in Jean-C. Falardeau, éd., *Essais sur le Québec contemporain* (Québec, 1953), pp. 45–54.

depended upon manufacturing, mining, and related industries for
their livelihood.[17]

The accelerated rate of Quebec's industrialization, at least during
the postwar years, can to a very large extent be attributed to the
economic policies pursued by the Union Nationale. The groundwork
for these policies had been laid during Duplessis' first administration
when he discarded the party's programme of reform and emerged as
a staunch champion of industrial capitalism. Even this reversal of
economic policy, however, could hardly have led one to expect that
when the Union Nationale leader returned to power in 1944 he would
adopt identically the same attitude as Taschereau in regard to the
role of foreign capital in the industrial development of the province.
Like the former Liberal leader, Duplessis was convinced that the
prosperity of the province and the well-being of its people were dependent on the exploitation of Quebec's natural resources and the
expansion of its manufacturing industry. He was also convinced that
such industrial development was the function of private rather than
public enterprise. In the Speech from the Throne opening the 1948
session of the Legislature he expressed his confidence in the efforts of
private individuals: "Nous sommes d'opinion que le paternalisme
d'état est l'ennemi du progrès véritable. Nous croyons que la province
de Québec sera développée plus rationnellement et plus rapidement
par l'initiative privée bien comprise, c'est-à-dire saine et juste. . . ."
Inasmuch as the amount of domestic capital available for investment
was not much greater than it had been in Taschereau's time, it was
obvious that the large sums of money required for industrial expansion
still had to come from outside the province.

From the beginning of his second administration Duplessis was to
pursue a policy of encouragement of and collaboration with American
and other foreign capitalists who might be interested in investing in
the province. As in the past, government legislation, or sometimes the
lack of it, permitted these interests to exploit the natural resources of
the province under the most favourable circumstances. Large areas of
Crown land were leased to pulp and paper companies on generous
terms. The royalties paid by mining companies were kept at a nominal

[17]Between 1941 and 1951 the urban population increased from 63 per cent to
67 per cent. Quebec, Department of Trade and Commerce, *Statistical Year Book*,
1953, p. 65. During the same period the proportion of gainfully occupied males
engaged in agriculture dropped from 27 per cent to 17 per cent. Nathan Keyfitz,
"Population Problems," in Falardeau, éd., *Essais sur le Québec contemporain*, p.
89.

level. The Union Nationale also continued the old Liberal policy of granting tax exemptions to manufacturing concerns willing to open branch plants in various parts of the province. At the same time the régime adopted a discriminatory policy towards organized labour which, as we shall see, provided the Quebec employer with certain advantages in dealing with his labour force which were not to be found in most provinces in Canada.

The strong ties existing between the administration and the industrialists were particularly evident in the more remote parts of the province, such as northern Quebec and the Gaspé Peninsula. These were regions where a good deal of the postwar development took place. As a result of certain privileges granted by the government to industries in these areas many towns were company-dominated. They may be described as "industrial fiefs," where the word of the company was law, where the employees lived in company houses and bought at company stores, and where the company, either directly or indirectly, controlled the municipal government. If any trade unions existed in these towns they were invariably management-dominated.[18] In return for these privileges the company worked closely with the Union Nationale party organization in the area and endeavoured to see that its employees voted the "right way" in every election.

The most controversial concession made to foreign capital was in regard to the province's huge resources of iron ore. It had been known for a number of years that there were iron deposits, perhaps the richest on the continent, in the far northern region of the province called "Nouveau-Québec." These resources had never been exploited because their remoteness from industrial centres, and the lack of transportation facilities, would have made such exploitation a hazardous business venture. During the war years, however, American steel companies started to become interested in Quebec iron ore because existing supplies in the Lake Superior region were running out. Shortly after the war one of these companies approached the Union Nationale government with a project for exploiting these resources in an undertaking involving the expenditure of some $200,000,000. It was successful in persuading the government to grant it rights in return for the payment of a royalty which amounted to about one cent on every ton of iron ore extracted. Just how generous this arrangement was is indicated by the fact that the province of Newfoundland at about the same time collected thirty-three cents per ton for the exploitation of similar iron

[18]For some examples of these "closed towns" see "Nouvelles Concessions," *Le Devoir*, 28 oct. 1955.

ore resources in Labrador.[19] During the 1950's additional concessions were extended by the Quebec government to other American concerns interested in the iron ore deposits of Nouveau-Québec.[20]

The Union Nationale's policy of encouragement to private enterprise in the industrial development of the province was accompanied by uncompromising hostility to all proposals for government ownership of public utilities or other monopolistic enterprises. This was particularly true in regard to the electric power companies, despite their vital role in the Quebec economy as the major source of industrial energy. When the Liberal administration of 1939–44 had taken a first step in the direction of a publicly owned hydro-electric system by nationalizing the Montreal Light, Heat and Power Company, the Union Nationale had strongly opposed the move and denounced it as "bolshevistic."[21] In spite of this attitude, when the party returned to office in 1944 it made no attempt to abolish Hydro Quebec, as the government-owned power project was called. Aside from the technical difficulties involved in de-nationalization, Duplessis was too astute a politician not to realize that the action of the Liberal party had widespread popular support. However, the Union Nationale leader showed no inclination to follow the example of Ontario and other provinces by expanding the scope of Hydro Quebec and establishing a province-wide government monopoly in this field. Throughout most of the province electric power production and distribution continued to be the preserve of private enterprise.[22]

Quebec's industrialists also had an ally in Duplessis in his strong opposition to the high level of federal taxation in the postwar years, and in his constant attacks upon the programme of social legislation introduced by the Ottawa government after 1940, including such services as unemployment insurance, old age pensions, family allowances, and hospital insurance. Duplessis' argument was that Ottawa's monopolization of the most lucrative types of taxation deprived the province of adequate sources of revenue, while the federal programme of social legislation constituted an invasion of a field in which the

[19]See "Combien la tonne?" *Le Devoir*, 16 sept. 1955; and "Nouvelles Concessions," *Le Devoir*, 28 oct. 1955.

[20]There is a rather interesting contrast between the welcome and encouragement that American capital has found in Quebec and the hostility and tough bargaining it has had to contend with from nationalist and socialist governments in other underdeveloped areas.

[21]*Montreal Gazette*, Dec. 11, 1944.

[22]In 1955 privately owned central electric stations generated almost three times as much electric energy as those which were publicly owned. Dominion Bureau of Statistics, *Canada Year Book*, 1957–8, pp. 574–5.

provinces had prior rights under the constitution.[23] The reasons underlying the opposition of the industrialists to the central government's
policies were much less complex. A high level of federal taxation to
finance social legislation was a form of redistribution of wealth under
which the business community footed most of the bill. It could hardly
be expected that the average businessman would be particularly enthusiastic about such a policy.

If Duplessis was strongly opposed to the growth of federal social
services because they infringed upon the rights of the province, this
did not mean that he was in favour of the rapid expansion of such
services at the provincial level. Although it would not be true to say
that the second Union Nationale administration introduced no social
legislation, the general attitude of Duplessis was that the social welfare state was a form of "paternalism" to be avoided at all costs. When
a trade union delegation made a request for the expansion of the
existing system of government old age pensions, Duplessis rejected it:
"Le meilleur système est encore celui qui dépend le moins de l'Etat."[24]
He also expressed strong opposition to proposals put forward for a
comprehensive health insurance scheme, stating that "no country or
province can get good medical attention with assembly line doctors."[25]
Although the administration made fairly substantial grants to all levels
of education every year, the general approach of the party in this area
was that there was a limit to what the state could do and that private
individuals and private enterprise must step in to fill the gap.[26] When
the Liberal party began a campaign in the 1950's for increased social
services, Duplessis accused them of being unrealistic, ". . . de créer
des appétits, de faire des promesses irréalisables, d'oublier que les
gouvernements administrent avec les argents qui proviennent des
taxes. . . . Le gouvernement ne peut remplacer la charité et la phi-
lanthropie."[27]

Aside from large-scale industrial capitalism, there was one other
form of private enterprise which received the same preferential treatment from the second Union Nationale administration as it had from
the first one. This was the agricultural sector of the economy. In The
Speech from the Throne opening the 1949 session of the legislature
the government reaffirmed its dominant place: "Parmi les entreprises

[23]The struggle between Duplessis and Ottawa is described more fully in chap. VI.
[24]Le Devoir, 12 jan. 1951.
[25]Montreal Star, Dec. 10, 1952.
[26]This attitude ignored the fact that it was precisely because private individuals
and private enterprise were unable, or unwilling, to make adequate contributions
to education that additional state aid was needed.
[27]La Presse, 19 nov. 1952.

privées, aucune n'est plus importante que l'agriculture à laquelle revient une place prépondérante dans notre économie." If we bear in mind that during this second stage of industrialization the farm population was declining even more rapidly than it had done during the first stage,[28] it is at once obvious that this statement was economic nonsense. However, Duplessis still looked upon the farmer as the most stable and law-abiding element in the population: "In the rural class we find the stable element which can counteract the spirit of disorder which is being found in some urban areas these days."[29] It has to be remembered in this connection too that although important shifts in population had taken place from rural to urban areas, very little had been done in the way of redistribution of electoral seats. By 1951, the rural population of the province had fallen to 33 per cent, but the rural areas still had 55 per cent of the seats in the legislature,[30] and as a consequence continued to have a disproportionate influence in politics.

The Union Nationale's policy of assistance to the farmer took several forms. Shortly after the party's return to power in 1944 the amount of money available for farm loans was increased and the rate of interest was reduced. Millions were spent by the government on the drainage of lands, the establishment of sons of farmers on new farm land, the building of agricultural schools and colleges, and the provision of sewage systems for small municipalities in rural areas. Legislation was passed which placed a ban on the production and sale of margarine in order to protect the dairy farmer's sale of butter, a step which resulted in higher food costs for the urban population. The government also established a Rural Electricity Office for the purpose of providing financial and technical assistance to farming communities interested in forming co-operatives for the distribution of electric power. As a result of the growth of these co-operatives, together with the extension of the power lines of the large privately owned companies, electrical facilities were available for farm families even in the most remote parts of the province by the 1950's.[31]

[28]See *supra*, p. 81n.

[29]*Montreal Star*, July 15, 1952.

[30]In 1952 there were 92 seats in the legislature. They are listed in Quebec, Legislative Assembly, *Report on the General Election of 1952* (Quebec, 1952), Appendix I, pp. 3–4. According to the 1951 census figures, 51 of these electoral districts were predominantly rural, while 41 were predominantly urban. Of the latter, 5 were in Quebec City, and 16 were in the Montreal metropolitan area. See *Census of Canada*, 1951 (Ottawa), I, Table 14.

[31]A description of the various measures taken by the Union Nationale to assist the farmer during the first and second Duplessis administrations is to be found in Paul Bouchard, *L'Administration de la Province de Québec: 1936–1939, 1944–1952* (Québec, 1952), pp. 11–37.

If the industrialists and the farmers were treated by the Union Nationale as privileged classes, the attitude of the party was quite different towards another important occupational group in the province, the industrial workers. This became apparent when the second phase of industrialization resulted in the rapid growth, for the first time in the history of the province, of a powerful and militant trade union movement. The reaction of the Union Nationale to this new development was to provide the strongest evidence of the party's rightward orientation in economic policy under the guiding hand of Duplessis and of the closeness of the ties which bound the party to the industrialists.

During the first phase of industrialization in Quebec there had been comparatively little trade union organization. In 1935, just before the Union Nationale first came to power, trade union membership stood at approximately 50,000,[32] which was only about 9 per cent of industrial wage earners.[33] At that time most unions were affiliated with either the church-sponsored Confédération des Travailleurs Catholiques du Canada (C.T.C.C.), or the Trades and Labour Congress of Canada (T.L.C.). The latter organization was made up for the most part of craft unions affiliated with the American Federation of Labor in the United States.

The expansion of the labour movement in Quebec only really began in the late thirties. The most important single factor in this growth was the C.I.O.'s invasion of Canada with its industrial brand of trade unionism. For the first time, important sections of the working class which had been neglected by the old craft unions were organized. Canadian locals of the C.I.O. unions, together with a number of purely Canadian unions, came together in 1940 to form a third central labour organization, the Canadian Congress of Labour (C.C.L.).

The war years, which had seen an acceleration of the industrialization process, had been an important period of trade union growth. By 1946 membership in trade unions had increased to 208,000,[34] which was four times greater than in 1935. In the steady industrial expansion of the postwar period membership continued to grow, although at a slower pace, and by 1951 there were 260,000 trade unionists in the province.[35] This constituted approximately 32 per cent of industrial

[32]Appendix A, Table X.
[33]According to the 1931 Census there were about 550,000 industrial wage-earners in the province. See Appendix A, Table IX.
[34]Appendix A, Table X.
[35]*Ibid.*

wage earners,[36] and thus an appreciable section of the working class in Quebec. The breakdown of this trade union membership among the three central labour organizations, in approximate percentages, was C.C.L. 20 per cent, C.T.C.C. 34 per cent, and T.L.C. something over 40 per cent.[37] (The T.L.C. had maintained its position as the largest central labour organization in the province ever since the early years of the war.)

The increasing importance of the trade union movement as a social force in Quebec was not due solely to the rapid growth in membership. An even more telling factor was the greater militancy accompanying this growth. Until the late thirties such trade unionism as existed in Quebec could not be described as particularly aggressive in making its demands on management. The C.T.C.C. had always shown as much interest in fighting the international unions as in fighting the employers. During most of its history it had followed a rigidly conservative interpretation of Catholic social philosophy, adopting the view that, although formed primarily for the purpose of defending the interests of the workers, it must never lose sight of the rights of the employer. Socialism and the doctrine of the class war were absolutely rejected and the strike weapon was to be used only as a very last resort.[38] Nor could the T.L.C. unions be considered very radical, except perhaps by comparison. Like its American counterpart the T.L.C. lacked any clear-cut social and economic philosophy and was more interested in obtaining immediate gains for its members in the way of higher wages and better working conditions than in promoting radical changes in the structure of the capitalist system.

The greater militancy which began to develop in the Quebec trade union movement in the late thirties can be attributed largely to the activity of the C.C.L., the Canadian counterpart of the C.I.O. The C.C.L. had introduced into Canada the same high pressure tactics of organization as those used by the steel and automobile workers in the United States during the same period. Moreover, the C.C.L., unlike the T.L.C., was not concerned solely with wage increases and better working conditions. It had adopted the philosophy of democratic socialism, allied itself with the C.C.F. party, and called for far-reach-

[36]Appendix A, Table IX.
[37]These percentages are based on rough estimates given the writer by a trade union official and are therefore subject to a margin of error. The federal Department of Labour does not have a breakdown of the membership of central labour organizations by provinces.
[38]The aims, principles, and policies of the C.T.C.C. in its early days are described in H. A. Logan, *Trade Unions in Canada* (Toronto, 1948), chap. xxv.

ing changes in the economic system, including government ownership of the more important industries.[39] It thus represented an uncompromising type of trade unionism which set the pattern for the whole trade union movement in the province.

As a result of the activities of the C.C.L., the T.L.C. had been forced to adopt a more aggressive type of unionism in the late thirties. It became more radical, not only in its organizing tactics and in its willingness to call strikes, but also in its attitude towards the economic system. In addition to the usual demands for better wages and working conditions, it now called for important changes in the structure of the economy through the introduction of government planning and the nationalization of certain key industries.[40] Aside from the necessity of competing with the C.C.L., another factor in the new aggressiveness of the T.L.C. was the more radical leadership which developed after the Communists captured control of some of the more important unions during the war years.[41]

In spite of this leftward orientation in the tactics and policies of the international unions, surprisingly enough it was not the T.L.C., or even the C.C.L., but the Catholic unions which were to emerge in the postwar period as the most dynamic trade union movement in Quebec. This startling transformation was brought about by the serious predicament in which the C.T.C.C. found itself in the early forties. From 1935 onward the Catholic trade union movement had been losing ground steadily to the more militant international unions, and particularly to the T.L.C. By 1943 the proportion of trade unionists in Quebec who belonged to the Catholic organization had fallen to 28 per cent, as compared to 74 per cent in 1935,[42] and it appeared that these unions were facing extinction.

Indeed the C.T.C.C. might very well have disappeared from the labour scene in the province but for the sweeping changes made in the leadership of the movement shortly after the war, and the adoption of a more radical interpretation of Catholic social philosophy. In 1946, Alfred Charpentier, the conservative and cautious head of the C.T.C.C., was replaced by Gérard Picard, a journalist by profession who turned out to be a hard-hitting trade union leader very similar to

[39]*Ibid.*, pp. 554–60.

[40]See the Post-War Reconstruction Programme of the T.L.C., in *ibid.*, pp. 550–4.

[41]In regard to Communist infiltration of the Canadian trade union movement during the 1940's, see Don Cameron, "Communism in Canada: Labor is Fighting the Threat of Moscow Rule or Ruin," *Montreal Star*, March 15, 1948; also Blair Fraser, "The Commies Muscle in," *Maclean's Magazine*, Jan. 15, 1947.

[42]Appendix A, Table X.

Walter Reuther of the United Automobile Workers. Picard was surrounded on his executive by a group of brilliant young intellectuals who had come under the influence of the Catholic social movement in France, which at that time leaned more towards the left than similar movements in many other countries.[43] Under its new leadership the C.T.C.C. embarked upon a vigorous organizing campaign and fought even harder than the international unions for better wages and working conditions. The preoccupation of the former leadership with "the rights of employers" gave way to an emphasis on the interests of the workers, and the old reluctance to use the strike weapon was discarded.

The most important aspect, however, of the new orientation of the Catholic unions was the adoption, as part of their programme, of one of the more radical suggestions for reform of the economic system put forward by Pope Pius XI in his encyclical, *Quadragesimo Anno.* The reform in question was the recommendation that wherever possible the wage contract should be modified by a contract of partnership, so that "wage earners are made sharers of some sort in the ownership, or the management, or the profits."[44] Following this suggestion, the C.T.C.C. now began to press for a radical reform of the structure of private industry itself, so that the workers, through their unions, would become partners in the enterprise with all the rights and privileges such a partnership involved. In his presidential address to the 1949 convention of the C.T.C.C. Gérard Picard quoted with approval the view of the well-known French jurist, Georges Ripert, on this subject: "Pourquoi ne pas avoir accordé à la collectivité ouvrière un véritable pouvoir de décision sur certaines questions? Il y a des modifications de l'entreprise qui ne peuvent être décidées sans l'accord du capital. Il doit y en avoir qui ne peuvent l'être sans l'accord du personnel."[45] The C.T.C.C. proposals for "co-partnership" in industry meant that the workers would not only share in profits but would also participate in making decisions concerning many aspects of the enterprise concerned,

[43]See statements made in 1944, shortly after the Liberation, by Cardinal Suhard of Paris and other members of the French hierarchy, concerning the urgent need for "structural reform of the social order." *Canadian Register* (Kingston, Ont.), Dec. 30, 1944.

[44](London, 1931), p. 31.

[45]Georges Ripert was a professor in the Faculty of Law at the University of Paris. For text of Picard's address, see *Le Devoir*, 23 sept. 1949. A more extensive discussion of the principles underlying these suggestions for "co-partnership" in industry is to be found in P. E. Bolté *et al.*, *Structural Reforms in the Enterprise* (Quebec, 1949). It is rather interesting to note that the ideas presented here are basically the same as those put forward in Germany after the Second World War under the name of "co-determination in industry."

such as the introduction of new methods of production, which up to now had always been looked upon as the sole prerogative of management. The new dynamism of the C.T.C.C. halted its decline[46] and made it the most vigorous champion of the rights and interests of the Quebec worker.

This rapid growth of a powerful trade union movement in Quebec during the second phase of industrialization presented the province's industrialists with an entirely new and serious situation. No longer could they depend on a plentiful supply of cheap and docile labour; they were now faced in many key industries by an aggressive trade unionism which, in its demands for wage increases and fringe benefits and in its readiness to use the strike weapon to back up these demands, was obviously determined to obtain a greater share of the income from production. During the period from 1940 to 1949 there were about three times as many workers involved in strikes as there had been during the period from 1930 to 1939.[47] The militant attitude of the trade unions not only constituted a threat to the profits of private enterprise, but, in the case of the proposals of the C.T.C.C. for the participation of the workers in management, also threatened the absolute control which the entrepreneur had hitherto exercised over his business establishment. In the face of these developments the industrialists might well consider themselves fortunate that they had in the Union Nationale administration a powerful ally which seemed to need little urging to take whatever steps were necessary to protect their interests.

The reaction of Duplessis to the development of the trade union movement as a new social force in Quebec was determined by the nature of his economic philosophy. His attitude towards organized labour may be described as one of toleration, but never of enthusiasm. Moreover, the condition of such toleration was that the trade unions "respect the rights of the employer" and "maintain law and order." This meant in effect that they should not be too aggressive, but preferably docile, and that they should not press too vigorously their demands for higher wages and better working conditions. Such demands, by impairing profits, would undermine the proper functioning of the system of private enterprise. Strikes were looked upon as generally undesirable, not merely because they affected the stability of the economy, but above all because they were a form of disorder. With an attitude of this nature, Duplessis could hardly be expected to look

[46]By 1951 the Catholic unions constituted about 34 per cent of the total trade union membership in the province. See Appendix A, Table X.

[47]Quebec, Department of Trade and Commerce, *Statistical Year Book*, 1953, p. 585.

upon the growing strength and militancy of the trade union movement in Quebec with a favourable eye.

The full significance of the labour policies to be pursued by the second Union Nationale administration, can be appreciated only with an understanding of the nature of the legislation concerning trade unions and collective bargaining which was on the Quebec statute books when the party returned to power in 1944. This was to be found in an act passed by the Godbout government just before it went out of office called the Labour Relations Act.[48] The main features of this act may be summarized as follows: (a) only certified unions have the right to bargain collectively, and the right to strike; (b) certification is granted by a three-man Labour Relations Board appointed by the government, if it is satisfied that the union applying for certification represents 60 per cent of the employees (later changed to 51 per cent by the Union Nationale); (c) there must be no coercion by unions or employers in regard to either joining a union or refraining from doing so; (d) employers must recognize any certified union and attempt to negotiate a collective labour agreement with it; (e) if the attempt of the two parties to draw up a collective agreement is unsuccessful, the dispute must be turned over to a government-appointed Board of Arbitration; (f) neither party is compelled to accept the decision of the Board, but no strike or lockout can be called until fourteen days after the arbitrators have handed down their recommendations.

During the first few years after the Union Nationale returned to power, it made no attempt to revoke or revise the Labour Relations Act; nor did it take any particularly drastic steps to control the activities of the trade unions. The party's lack of sympathy towards organized labour was indicated, however, by the fairly consistent policy it pursued of interpreting the Act in such a way as to favour the employer. Sometimes the Act was ignored altogether. For instance, the government often did nothing to compel employers to negotiate with a certified union. Although company-dominated unions were illegal, the Labour Relations Board certified a sizable number every year. Many trade union leaders who had been dismissed by their employers for trying to organize the workers found it almost impossible to get remedial action by the Board. Certification of unions was sometimes withdrawn without any other justification than the claim of the employers that such unions no longer represented a majority of the employees. Applications for certification were frequently held up in the Department of Labour for months, a delay which provided the em-

48Statutes of Quebec, 8 Geo. VI, c. 30.

ployers with plenty of opportunity to intimidate or bribe employees into leaving the union. Government boards of arbitration set up to settle a dispute might take a year or more to make their report. Meanwhile no strike could be called.[49]

In spite of this rather one-sided interpretation, or perhaps misinterpretation, of the Labour Relations Act, the trade union movement continued to increase in strength, and in the late forties was involved in some long and bitterly fought strikes. As a result Duplessis apparently became convinced that existing legislation, however interpreted, was inadequate to meet the threat which the trade union movement presented to the province's private enterprise economy, and that stronger measures were called for. He thereupon embarked upon a policy towards the labour movement which had two aspects: the enactment of legislation which would seriously curtail the activities of the unions; and the dispatch of the provincial police to any area where a strike was in progress in order to protect the interests of the employers.

The determination of Duplessis to place more stringent governmental controls over the trade union movement became apparent during the 1949 session of the Legislative Assembly. At that time the government introduced a bill, known as Bill No. 5, whose purpose it was to establish a comprehensive labour code.[50] The proposed code barred union security provisions, such as the closed and union shop; it stipulated that unincorporated, as well as incorporated unions, could be summoned before the provincial courts as a body, or their officers could be summoned individually; before any strike could be called the Labour Relations Board must arrange for a secret strike vote among the employees, a majority of whom must approve; sympathy strikes and slowdowns were prohibited; policemen and firemen could only join a local union which could not affiliate with similar unions in other cities and towns; disputes between policemen, firemen, and school teachers on the one hand, and municipal and school corporations on the other, must be submitted to a government-appointed arbitration board whose decision would be binding on both parties.

[49]A careful analysis of the various ways in which the government violated the spirit and intention of the Labour Relations Act is to be found in H. A. Logan, *State Intervention and Assistance in Collective Bargaining: The Canadian Experience, 1943–1954* (Toronto, 1956), pp. 70–1. See also L. J. Rogers, "Duplessis and Labor," *Canadian Forum*, Oct., 1947, pp. 151–2; Fernand Dansereau, "Il n'y a plus de modérateur impartial," *Le Devoir*, 29 avril 1953.

[50]For a summary of the main clauses of the bill, see Maritime Labour Institute, Dalhousie University, "The Quebec Labour Code," *Labour and Learning*, Feb., 1949.

The most important and most controversial part of the Bill was a clause which prohibited unions from having officers, or representatives, who were "Communists or Marxists," or who belonged to any organization "which co-operates with the Communists." Any union whose officers fell into any of these categories could be refused certification by the Labour Relations Board and thus lose its right to engage in collective bargaining. This anti-Communist clause had serious implications for the whole trade union movement. It meant that if a union had even one Communist or Marxist on its executive the whole union would lose its bargaining rights. The threat which this clause constituted for organized labour was accentuated by the fact that Duplessis, and other members of the administration, tended to use the label "Communist" very loosely and often applied it to trade union leaders who happened to be rather critical of governmental policies.

The Union Nationale's labour code, and particularly its anti-Communist clause, raised a storm of protest throughout the province. The three large labour confederations, the T.L.C., the C.C.L., and the C.T.C.C., as well as a number of independent unions, denounced it as a threat to the basic rights of organized labour and immediately formed a coalition to fight the passage of the Bill through the legislature.[51] Perhaps more important, from the point of view of the government, the Catholic hierarchy intervened and let it be known that it was opposed to several aspects of the code as being contrary to social justice.[52] In the face of this widespread opposition, Duplessis retreated and announced that the labour code would be withdrawn until there had been an opportunity for further study of the matter.

The withdrawal of Bill No. 5 turned out to be only a temporary retreat. It soon became apparent that the government was still determined to enact legislation to curb the unions, although its strategy now was to use more piecemeal methods in achieving its aims. Over the next five years a number of bills were passed which gradually put into effect practically all of the provisions of the original labour code. In 1949, an Act Respecting Municipal and School Corporations and Their Employees[53] established a system of compulsory arbitration for any dispute between these corporations and the professional associations representing the employees. In 1950, an Act Respecting Public Order[54] broke up provincial federations of policemen and firemen and prohibited these two categories of public employees from belonging to

[51]*Montreal Gazette*, Feb. 2, 1949.
[52]*Montreal Star*, Feb. 3, 1949.
[53]13 Geo. VI, c. 26.
[54]14 Geo. VI, c. 37.

any union other than a purely local one. Probably the two most important pieces of labour legislation passed by the Union Nationale were enacted in 1954, and were known as Bills 19 and 20. The first one, an amendment to the Quebec Labour Relations Act,[55] decertified unions which "tolerated Communists" among their officers or organizers. The second one, an amendment to the Public Services Employees Disputes Act,[56] provided for the decertification of any union engaged in, or even threatening to call, a strike in any public service. Both these bills were made retroactive to 1944 in order to control some of the more radical unions which had been involved in strikes years earlier. The retroactive clause of Bill 20 enabled the Labour Relations Board to decertify the Catholic Teachers' Alliance of Montreal which had called a strike of short duration five years previously.[57]

In pursuing his objective of restricting the activities of the trade unions Duplessis did not rely solely on the enactment of more rigorous labour legislation. He also had at his disposal, in the form of the provincial police force, a more direct method of curbing the unions. Although in theory the police were above politics, in practice they had always been used by the party in power, whether Union Nationale or Liberal, for all sorts of partisan purposes. The head of the force, as well as the higher officials, were political appointments, and therefore staunch adherents of the party which happened to be in office.[58]

The tactics of the Union Nationale were to send a large number of provincial police into any town or area as soon as a strike broke out. On many occasions this action was taken, not at the request of the local municipal authorities, the only ones who legally had the right to ask for such assistance, but at the request of the company involved in the industrial dispute. The official reason which was always given by the government for the intervention of the provincial police was that their presence was necessary for the maintenance of law and order. To a certain extent this was undoubtedly true. More often than not, however, the police were used for the purpose of intimidating strikers, arresting their leaders, carrying strikebreakers through picket lines, and doing everything possible to break the strike. Needless to say these tactics of the police were resisted by the striking unions, and pitched battles often took place between the two groups.[59]

The best illustration of these more direct methods used by the

[55]2–3 Elizabeth II, c. 10.
[56]2–3 Elizabeth II, c. 11.
[57]See Logan, *State Intervention and Assistance in Collective Bargaining*, p. 72.
[58]See evidence presented before the Royal Commission which investigated the provincial police force in 1944. *Montreal Gazette*, April 20, 1944.
[59]See editorial, *Le Devoir*, 13 déc. 1952.

government in its relations with the trade unions is to be found in a strike which took place in 1949 in a mining town in the Eastern Townships, close to the American border, called Asbestos. This particular strike turned out to be one of the most dramatic episodes in the history of the Canadian labour movement, and, before it was over, it had taken on all the appearances of a miniature civil war.[60]

The Asbestos strike arose out of an industrial dispute between several thousand asbestos miners belonging to a Catholic union affiliated with the C.T.C.C. and the Canadian Johns-Manville Company, an American-owned concern. It began after several months of negotiations between the union and the company had failed to result in any agreement on a new contract. The walkout was illegal as the Labour Relations Act stipulated that such disputes must go to a government-appointed board of arbitration before a strike could be called—a procedure which union leaders knew from previous experience could involve a delay of a year or more.

Shortly after the strike broke out the Duplessis government, at the request of the company, sent a force of about one hundred provincial police into the town to maintain order. This action was taken against the opposition of the town council which felt that the presence of the police would only aggravate the situation.[61] However, the strike went on without incident until a couple of months later when the company suddenly announced that it proposed to re-open the plant by bringing in workers from other towns to take over the strikers' jobs. In reaction to this announcement the strikers immediately threw a picket line around the plant—an illegal action as the strike itself was contrary to the law. They then blocked all roads leading into the town to keep out the strikebreakers. This led to a clash with the provincial police who used tear gas on the strikers. In retaliation, several of the policemen were disarmed and beaten up, and their cars were overturned. The police called for reinforcements, and early the next morning a large number of men from the nearby city of Sherbrooke, armed with rifles and tear gas, converged on the town. Upon the arrival of the reinforcements the police called a meeting of the townspeople in front of the church and the Riot Act was read. They then proceeded to inaugurate a veritable reign of terror in the town for the next few days. Wholesale arrests were made in restaurants, on the streets, in

---

[60]For an exhaustive study of all aspects of the strike, see Pierre-Elliott Trudeau, éd., *La Grève de l'amiante* (Montréal, 1956). See also Jacqueline Sirois, "Asbestos Strike," *Montreal Standard*, May 28, 1949; "The Facts of the Asbestos Strike," *Ensign* (Montreal), May 28, 1949.

[61]See Trudeau, éd., *La Grève de l'amiante*, p. 176.

the church hall, in stores, and in private homes. Many did not know why they were arrested as they had not been present at the reading of the Riot Act. Although there were few cases of resisting arrest, some of the strikers were beaten up with a violence which shocked newspapermen.[62] Others were taken to police headquarters and given a "going over" in the form of punches and kicks.[63]

The activities of the police were characterized by many other flagrant violations of the law they were supposed to uphold. People were arrested and held for over forty-eight hours without any charge being brought against them. Those arrested were prevented from seeing their lawyers for several days. Reporters and photographers taking pictures of strikers who had been badly beaten up by the police were molested, and one was arrested. The calling of a meeting for the purpose of reading the Riot Act was itself completely out of order for, as is well known, the real purpose of the Act is to disperse a crowd already in a state of riot.[64]

The drastic measures used by the Union Nationale against the trade unions, as illustrated by the Asbestos strike, together with its restrictive labour legislation, aroused the antagonism of all sections of the labour movement in the province. This antagonism was particularly strong in the case of the C.T.C.C. The latter was to become involved in other clashes with the provincial police aside from the one arising out of the strike in Asbestos.

The most serious of these clashes took place in 1952 during a strike in a small textile town outside of Montreal called Louiseville. The tactics of the government in the Louiseville strike followed the same pattern as in the case of Asbestos; the intervention of the provincial police against the wishes of the municipal council, reading of the Riot Act, police violence, arbitrary arrests, and other illegal actions.[65] The temper of the C.T.C.C. was indicated by the fact that for a while it contemplated calling a general strike of all its unions throughout the province as a protest against the way in which the government handled the situation.[66] This was the first time in the history of the province that a central labour organization had ever put forward the idea of a general strike. Although the plan was discarded later, it drew from

[62]Photographs of some of the strikers who were beaten up are to be found in Sirois, "Asbestos Strike."

[63]Trudeau, éd., La Grève de l'amiante, p. 200.

[64]A list of the many illegal actions committed by the police is to be found in ibid., pp. 380–1.

[65]See Montreal Star, Dec. 12, 1952; Le Devoir, 12 déc. 1952; Montreal Gazette, Dec. 12 and 17, 1952.

[66]See Montreal Star, Dec. 12, 1952.

Duplessis the charge of Communist influence: "certains chefs ouvriers suivent consciemment ou inconsciemment le programme de Tim Buck et de Fred Rose."[67] This estrangement between the C.T.C.C. and the Union Nationale was all the more unexpected because there had always been a fairly close relationship between the two groups from the earliest days of Duplessis' party.

Probably the most important result of the government's attitude towards the trade unions was that it brought about a greater feeling of solidarity among the different sections of the labour movement in the province. The formation of a coalition of all three central labour organizations to fight Bill No. 5 was one of the rare occasions in the history of the Quebec labour movement when all unions were solidly united on any one particular policy. The same organizations came together again on several other occasions for the purpose of lodging a united protest against certain aspects of the Union Nationale's anti-labour policy.[68] During the Asbestos strike both the C.C.L. and the T.L.C. gave solid support to the Catholic unions, not only in the form of resolutions of solidarity, but also by contributing truckloads of food to the families of the strikers.

The policy of collaboration between the C.T.C.C. and the C.C.L. in opposition to Union Nationale tactics was to continue and to be strengthened in the years to come, but the same cannot be said for the T.L.C. As we shall see, the co-operation of the latter with the two other confederations was not to last very long.

In concluding this chapter on the economic policies of the Union Nationale it will be useful to try to evaluate the extent of the transformation which took place in the party once it was firmly under the control of Duplessis, and to consider the question of what effect this transformation may have had on the party's electoral support.

We have seen that the party which was elected to office in 1936 on a pledge to destroy the power of foreign industrialists over the economy quickly became a staunch ally of these same industrialists; that the party which had promised to reform the capitalistic system and introduce economic and social reforms was transformed into the greatest defender of that economic system; and that the party which had promised to enact legislation which would strengthen the position of the working class ended up by becoming a bitter opponent of the whole trade union movement, and particularly of the Catholic unions,

[67] *Le Devoir*, 15 jan. 1953. The reference here was to Tim Buck, leader of the Labour Progressive party, and Fred Rose, a former L.P.P. member of Parliament.
[68] See Trudeau, éd., *La Grève de l'amiante*, p. 363.

even though the support of the latter had been an important factor in the electoral victory of 1936. In spite of this complete reversal of economic policy, the Union Nationale not only succeeded in returning to power in 1944 after its defeat of 1939, but was also successful in winning the subsequent elections of 1948, 1952, and 1956. Although the party won only forty-eight out of the ninety-one seats in the legislature in the election of 1944, in the other three contests it captured eighty-two, sixty-eight, and seventy-two seats respectively.[69]

In view of the Union Nationale's consistent policy of promoting the interests of the farm population, and the fact that the latter was over-represented in the provincial legislature,[70] one might be led to assume that the large number of seats won by the party in the elections of 1948, 1952, and 1956, was due solely to the support of the rural voters. Although this is far from being the whole answer, it is nevertheless true that the rural areas constituted the most dependable source of Union Nationale support. In all three elections Duplessis' party captured a large majority of the fifty-one seats in the legislature which were predominantly rural.[71] The largest number of rural constituencies won by the Liberals in any one of these elections was the six seats captured by that party in the election of 1956.[72] It should be pointed out, however, that this does not mean that Liberal strength in the rural areas was negligible; there were a good number of rural seats in the 1956 election which the party lost by a fairly narrow margin.[73]

The most important question raised by the Union Nationale's electoral victories concerns the extent of the support the party received from the urban areas. This support was greater than one would anticipate, taking into consideration Duplessis' economic policies. In Table I we find the popular vote polled by the Union Nationale in cities of 20,000 and over, in the elections of 1948, 1952, and 1956. Even a cursory glance at this table indicates that Duplessis' party consistently received substantial backing from the urban voter. This support was particularly strong in those cities which are usually referred to as regional capitals, Chicoutimi, Hull, Sherbrooke, and Three Rivers. In Greater Quebec, which is second in importance to Greater Montreal from the point of view of population, the party was not quite as strong, although it received a comfortable majority in the 1956 election. In the French-speaking section of Greater Montreal the party

[69]Appendix A, Table VII.
[70]See *supra*, p. 85.
[71]In regard to the breakdown of rural and urban seats in the legislature, see *supra*, p. 85n.
[72]See *infra*, p. 174.
[73]*Ibid.*

obtained a slight majority of the vote in the elections of 1948 and 1956, and about half of the vote in 1952.

TABLE I

PERCENTAGE OF POPULAR VOTE POLLED BY THE UNION NATIONALE
PARTY IN CITIES OF 20,000 AND OVER,
ELECTIONS OF 1948, 1952, 1956

City	Population (1951)	Elections		
		1948	1952	1956
Chicoutimi	23,216	64.76%	73.99%	68.49%
Granby	21,989	46.09	46.73	48.05
Hull	43,483	65.60	60.73	53.28
St. Hyacinthe	20,236	44.85	52.12	44.93
Valleyfield	22,414	60.78	60.37	56.64
Shawinigan Falls	26,903	47.95	36.97	43.61
Sherbrooke	50,543	57.06	54.69	54.99
Three Rivers	46,074	76.66	60.51	61.73
Greater Montreal	1,395,400			
French Districts[a]		56.26	49.31	51.53
English Districts[b]		26.60	23.99	23.68
Greater Quebec[c]	274,827	40.84	46.26	57.53

SOURCES: for population of cities, Quebec, Department of Trade and Commerce, *Statistical Year Book*, 1953, p. 62; popular vote percentage have been calculated from official figures published in Quebec, Legislative Assembly, *Report on the General Election*, 1948, 1952, 1956; party affiliation of candidates has been checked in *Canadian Parliamentary Guide*, 1949, 1953, 1957. The votes received by candidates who called themselves "independent Union Nationale" have been included in the above percentages.

[a]Includes electoral districts of Chambly, Jacques Cartier, Jeanne Mance, Laval, Laurier, Mercier, Ste. Marie, St. Henri, St. Jacques, Maisonneuve.

[b]Includes electoral districts of Notre-Dame-de-Grâce, Outremont, Ste. Anne, St. Louis, Verdun, Westmount-St. George.

[c]Includes electoral districts of Quebec Centre, Quebec County, Quebec East, Quebec West, St. Sauveur, Lévis.

One of the most interesting aspects of Table I is the indication that the only urban area in the province where the Union Nationale was really weak was in the predominantly English-speaking electoral districts located in the western section of Montreal Island.[74] These districts include such diverse income groups as the working class voters of Ste. Anne and Verdun and the upper class residents of Westmount and Outremont. This strong opposition to the Union Nationale on the part of the English voter made the western part of Montreal a Liberal stronghold. The main reason for this antagonism towards Duplessis'

[74]It is important to note that this section of Montreal contains the most important concentration of English-speaking voters to be found in the province.

TABLE II

PERCENTAGE OF POPULAR VOTE POLLED BY THE UNION NATIONALE PARTY IN
FRENCH WORKING CLASS ELECTORAL DISTRICTS IN MONTREAL AND
QUEBEC CITY, AND IN SELECTED INDUSTRIAL TOWNS IN
ELECTIONS OF 1948, 1952, 1956

Working Class Districts and Industrial Towns[a]	Elections		
	1948	1952	1956
MONTREAL			
St. Henri	54.33%	41.02%	47.54%
St. Jacques	60.56	54.08	62.36
Ste. Marie	55.48	44.89	54.80
Maisonneuve	52.70	48.11	53.25
MONTREAL PLAIN[b]			
St. Hyacinthe	44.85	52.12	44.93
St. Jean	64.80	61.29	55.66
Valleyfield	60.78	60.37	56.64
Sorel	46.83	46.37	53.02
EASTERN TOWNSHIPS[c]			
Drummondville	60.96	48.67	53.03
Granby	46.09	46.73	48.05
Magog	43.64	35.39	36.70
Thetford Mines	50.28	50.61	52.32
QUEBEC CITY			
Quebec East	54.17	48.34	55.47
St. Sauveur	46.48	57.01	68.77
NORTH SHORE OF ST. LAWRENCE			
Arvida	40.70	45.25	37.73
Cap-de-la-Madeleine	69.74	60.71	57.46
Grand'Mère	49.42	44.05	48.82
Shawinigan Falls	47.95	36.97	43.61

SOURCES: As for Table I.

[a]The working class electoral districts of Montreal and Quebec City listed here comprise those sections of these two cities which sociologists refer to as "zones of workingmen's homes." See Carl A. Dawson and Warner E. Gettys, An Introduction to Sociology (rev. ed.; New York, 1935), pp. 129–31 and 145–56. The industrial towns selected are urban communities throughout the province where manufacturing is the main type of economic activity. These towns are described in D. F. Putnam, ed., Canadian Regions (2nd ed.; Toronto, 1954), chap. IX.

[b]This is the term used by geographers to describe the lowlands surrounding Montreal.

[c]The region southeast of Montreal bordering on the State of Vermont and part of the State of Maine.

party was the attitude which that party adopted towards the question of participation in the war of 1939, as described in the next chapter. Although the English-speaking minority in Quebec would strongly object to any suggestion that it is "nationalistic," it is obvious that this group, like the French minority in Canada, closes its ranks and presents a united front whenever it feels that its point of view or interests as an ethnic group are challenged.

If the support which the Union Nationale received from the urban areas in the elections of 1948, 1952, and 1956 was greater than one would have expected, an even more surprising aspect of the party's performance in these three elections was the strength of the party among the working class section of the urban population. Table II provides an analysis of the popular vote polled by the Union Nationale in French working class constituencies in Montreal and Quebec City, and in the more important industrial towns throughout the province. We can see from Table II that Duplessis' party usually managed to obtain a majority or very close to a majority of the popular vote in working class districts in every election. Although the party lost a little ground in most districts in the election of 1952, following the Asbestos strike and the attempt of Duplessis to put through his labour code, it made a good comeback in 1956. In all three elections there were only a comparatively few instances of the party receiving less than 45 per cent of the popular vote. There were only three towns where party support at any time dropped below 40 per cent: the textile town of Magog in the Eastern Townships, the aluminum centre of Arvida in the Lac St. Jean area, and the chemical and pulp and paper manufacturing town of Shawinigan Falls, just north of Three Rivers. It is rather significant that in all three towns most of the workers belong to unions affiliated with the C.T.C.C.[75]

The preceding analysis presents us with a paradox: that in a highly industrialized and urbanized province like Quebec, with a steadily growing working class and a militant trade union movement, a party of unrestricted "free enterprise," openly collaborating with foreign industrialists and partial to the farming interests, was able to obtain the support of a majority of the voters in most French-speaking urban areas, including a large number of districts which were predominantly working class. The explanation for this rather perplexing aspect of Quebec politics lies in the fact that the Union Nationale under Duplessis, in spite of its economic policies, was not just another conservative

[75]In 1952 six out of the eight trade union locals in Magog were affiliated with the C.T.C.C.; in Shawinigan Falls, thirteen out of seventeen; in Arvida, three out of six. In the latter city the vast majority of trade union members belonged to the C.T.C.C. locals. A list of trade union locals affiliated with the C.T.C.C. and other central labour organizations is to be found in Canada, Department of Labour, *Labour Organization in Canada*, 1952, pp. 27–98.

party. It was also a nationalist party, and as such was to emerge during the 1940's as the uncompromising champion of the French-Canadian point of view on several issues of crucial importance to the people of Quebec—issues so vital to a very large number of voters, in urban as well as rural areas, that the whole question of economic policy tended to be pushed into the background until the late 1950's. These issues arose out of the strong opposition of the Quebec voter to three different aspects of federal government policy from 1939 onward: the decision to commit Canada to participation in World War II; the growing centralization of power in the hands of the federal authority at the expense of the provinces; and an attitude on the part of the Ottawa government towards the growth of Communist activities which many French Canadians considered to be complacent and negative.

CHAPTER VI

The Union Nationale and
the Federal Government

WHEN THE SECOND WORLD WAR BEGAN in the late summer of 1939 a
Liberal government led by Mackenzie King was in power at Ottawa.
The Liberals had won the previous election of 1935 by a large
majority, having captured 171 out of the 245 seats in the House of
Commons.[1] This large majority included a hard core of fifty-five
Quebec seats out of a total of sixty-five for that province.[2]

The outbreak of war presented King's government with an extremely
difficult problem, for the people of Canada were sharply divided on
the issue of participation. The situation was basically the same as
during the First World War; the average English-speaking Canadian
was as strongly for whole-hearted participation in 1939 as the French
Canadian was opposed to it. While the English section of the population adopted the attitude that Canada must be at the side of Britain
and her allies in what they considered to be a just cause, the French,
on the other hand, looked upon the war as just another incident in
European power politics in which the interests of Britain and France
were certainly involved, but those of Canada decidedly were not.[3]
Moreover, this cleavage within the country as a whole was reflected
within the ranks of the Liberal party, for the English and French

[1]*Canadian Parliamentary Guide*, 1936, p. 365.
[2]*Ibid.*
[3]A good analysis of the French-Canadian attitude towards the war is to be
found in Blair Fraser, "Crisis in Quebec," *Maclean's Magazine*, Aug. 15, 1944.
See also J. W. Pickersgill, *The Mackenzie King Record, I, 1939–1944* (Toronto,
1960), pp. 14–23.

wings of that party tended to adopt the same opinion as the rest of their respective language groups.

In view of these serious differences of opinion it was obvious that Mackenzie King's government would have to formulate a policy which would somehow reconcile the divergent views of the two groups, if the unity of the country, and of the Liberal party, was to be maintained. The policy which King finally decided upon was a compromise under which Canada would actively enter the war on the side of the Allies, but with a definite pledge on the part of the government that recruiting would be on a voluntary basis, and that under no circumstances would conscription for overseas service be introduced. In presenting the government's policy to the legislature the Prime Minister stated:

I wish now to repeat the undertaking I gave in Parliament on behalf of the Government on March 30th. last [1939]. The present Government believes that conscription of men for overseas service will not be a necessary or an effective step. No such measure will be introduced by the present Administration.[4]

Mackenzie King's compromise was successful, for it was accepted by Parliament with only two or three dissenting voices. It received the full support, not only of the Liberal party, including the vast majority of its Quebec members, but of all the opposition parties as well. It was a policy which was satisfactory to most English Canadians, because it appeared at that time that there would be sufficient volunteers to meet Canada's commitments overseas and conscription would not be needed. For the French Canadian it simply meant that, while anyone in Canada could volunteer if he wanted to, the people of Quebec were under no compulsion to fight in a cause which they saw in quite a different light from their compatriots.

The government's policy on participation did not, however, go entirely unchallenged. Although it was acceptable to most English and French Canadians, there were vociferous minorities on both sides who objected strongly to it for different reasons. The first and most serious attack upon it was to come from the province of Quebec in the person of Maurice Duplessis.

When the war broke out neither Duplessis nor any of his colleagues gave any indication that they were opposed to Canada's participation. The federal government was taken completely by surprise, therefore, when the Union Nationale leader suddenly dissolved the provincial legislature a few weeks after the declaration of war and called a

[4]Canada, *House of Commons Debates*, Special War Session, Sept. 8, 1939, p. 36.

general election in protest against King's policies. Duplessis contended that the federal government was using the sweeping powers it possessed under the War Measures Act as a pretext for curtailing the rights of the province under the British North America Act. In a keynote speech at the beginning of the election campaign he declared that the federal government would now push even further its efforts towards centralization:

Invoquant le prétexte de la guerre, déclarée par le gouvernement fédéral, une campagne d'assimilation et de centralisation, manifeste depuis plusieurs années, s'accentue de façon intolérable.

Des arrêtés ministériels ont été passés par Ottawa en vertu du *War Measures Act* ou *Mesure de Guerre*, avec le désir et l'effet de centraliser à Ottawa, pour des fins de guerre, toute la finance des particuliers, des municipalités, des provinces et du pays.[5]

The actual motives behind Duplessis' action in calling an election when only three years of his five-year term of office had elapsed have never been quite clear. It is possible that he saw in the issue of participation an opportunity for the Union Nationale to regain some of the ground it had lost owing to its shift to the right in economic policy. One thing which was quite clear was that, inasmuch as the prosecution of a war under modern conditions requires a considerable centralization of power in the hands of a central or federal government, Duplessis' stand on provincial rights could hardly have been interpreted otherwise than as a direct challenge to the war effort itself. It jeopardized the whole policy of compromise on the question of participation which had been so carefully worked out by Mackenzie King.

The federal Liberal party was not slow in taking up Duplessis' challenge. The French-Canadian members of King's cabinet—Ernest Lapointe, Minister of Justice; C. G. Power, Minister of Pensions and National Health; and P. J. A. Cardin, Minister of Public Works—intervened immediately in the Quebec election by throwing their whole-hearted support behind the provincial Liberal party led by Adelard Godbout. Like other Liberals, Godbout supported King's compromise policy. The main argument that the federal ministers presented to the voters during the electoral campaign was that their presence in Mackenzie King's cabinet was the only barrier to conscription for overseas service. As stated by Lapointe, "Nous sommes le rempart entre vous et la conscription. Nous sommes ia muraille qui

5"Manifeste de l'Union Nationale aux élections de septembre 1939," *Le Temps* (Québec) 26 mai 1944.

vous protège. . . ."[6] The Quebec ministers threatened that if Duplessis was not driven from office they would at once resign from the federal cabinet. Again quoting Lapointe, "Je ne resterai pas là malgré vous, mes collègues de Québec dans le cabinet ne resteront pas là malgré vous. . . . Si Québec ne veut pas de représentants dans le cabinet et surtout si Québec ne veut pas de nous, nous nous inclinerons."[7] It was pointed out that the resignation of the Quebec members of Mackenzie King's cabinet would result in the formation of a completely English-speaking Liberal or coalition government which would immediately introduce conscription.

Duplessis had made a bad miscalculation, for the argument of the federal Liberals was the most effective threat which could be made in anti-conscriptionist Quebec. Faced by the possibility of conscription if the Union Nationale were not defeated, the people of Quebec went to the polls and voted Godbout's Liberal party into office by a large majority.

The election of 1939 completely reversed the relative positions of the Union Nationale and Liberal parties in the Quebec legislature. The Union Nationale, which had won such a large number of seats in the election of 1936, was now reduced to an ineffective opposition of fourteen members out of a total number of eighty-six in the legislature.[8] Moreover, the party's chances of returning to power appeared to be extremely remote. There was, however, one aspect of the Union Nationale's position which was to play an important part in later developments. Duplessis' attacks on the policy of the federal government towards the war meant that the Union Nationale had become the party most closely identified in the mind of the French-Canadian voter with vigorous opposition to participation.

Although by a dramatic turn of events the Liberals were once more strongly entrenched in office with a large majority of sixty-nine seats,[9] it was obvious that their success at the polls had been due to the intervention of the federal wing of the party. In return for this support Godbout and his government felt compelled to co-operate in every possible way with the federal government, not only in the prosecution of the war, but in other matters as well. One of the most important aspects of this policy of co-operation was the strong efforts made by the provincial Liberals to convince the people of Quebec that they should give their full support to the war effort. Thus, in spite of

[6]*Le Devoir*, 10 oct. 1939.
[7]*Ibid.*
[8]Appendix A, Table VII.
[9]*Ibid.*

Godbout's firm control over the provincial administration from 1939 onward, there was this one potential source of weakness in the position of his party: the more the provincial Liberals co-operated with Ottawa, the more deeply their political fortunes became bound up with those of the federal party. The popularity of the latter with the Quebec electorate depended on Ottawa being able to maintain its policy of voluntary enlistment for the armed forces, and the maintenance of that policy was in turn dependent upon the flow of volunteers being sufficient to meet Canada's commitments overseas.

During the first year or two of the war the federal government maintained its compromise policy on participation without too much difficulty. It is true that in June, 1940, when the fall of France aroused considerable fear throughout Canada that the country was in danger of invasion, the government had put through a bill called the National Resources Mobilization Act, which provided for compulsory military service for all able-bodied males between the ages of 21 and 45, but these troops were to be used only for the defence of Canada and its territorial waters, and could not be sent overseas. The setting-up of this "home defence army" aroused comparatively little opposition in Quebec as French Canadians generally did not question the desirability of taking all steps necessary to defend Canadian territory effectively. It was not considered to be "conscription," as the meaning of that term in Quebec, and indeed in other parts of Canada as well, has always been limited to compulsory military service overseas.

Unfortunately for the federal government, as the war progressed and the Allies suffered one reverse after another, the demands on Canada for a steadily growing number of troops in Europe began to make it increasingly doubtful whether the voluntary method of recruitment would continue to provide the necessary manpower. As a result, the question of conscription for overseas service became more and more a subject of public discussion, and by 1942 had become the major political issue of the day.

From the beginning of the war until the spring of 1942 Prime Minister King had always expressed his opposition to conscription under any circumstances. However, in the face of the growing pressure from the daily press throughout the country, from the Conservative party, and even from within his own party, he came to the conclusion that some sort of action must be taken. He announced, therefore, that a national plebiscite would be held in April of that year, in which the people of Canada would be asked whether they were willing to release the government from its pledge of "no conscription."

During the campaign preceding the plebiscite King and all members of his cabinet, including the French Canadian ministers, asked for a "Yes" vote.[10] The leaders of the other parties in Parliament also asked the electorate to give an affirmative answer.[11] The only real opposition came from Quebec where an organization was hastily formed called La Ligue pour la Défense du Canada whose purpose it was to make a last-ditch stand against any attempt on the part of the government to escape from its pledge. The moving force behind the organization of this League was the nationalist intellectuals who belonged to L'Action Nationale,[12] but the anti-conscription campaign was also supported by prominent individuals from many other groups: the farmers' organizations, the Catholic trade unions, the patriotic and youth organizations.[13] It received the blessing of the veteran nationalist leader, Henri Bourassa[14] and was backed by the Montreal daily, Le Devoir. La Ligue pour la Défense du Canada waged an energetic campaign for a "No" vote, and achieved a high measure of success within Quebec. When the results of the plebiscite were announced it was found that Quebec had voted 72 per cent "No," while the other provinces, taken as a group, had voted 79 per cent "Yes." The national percentages were 64 per cent "Yes" and 35 per cent "No" (1 per cent of the ballots were spoiled).[15]

The outcome of the plebiscite presented Mackenzie King with something of a dilemma. On the one hand the people of Quebec had indicated quite clearly that they would never accept conscription no matter how serious the war situation became. The vast majority of English Canadians, on the other hand, had not only agreed to release King from his "no conscription" pledge, but also now began to demand that the government take immediate action in the direction of compulsory service for overseas. Even more important, these demands

[10]Le Devoir, 25 avril 1942.

[11]See the speech delivered over the C.B.C. network by R. B. Hanson, Conservative leader, entitled, "Your Duty," April 20, 1942; and that of M. J. Coldwell, C.C.F. leader, entitled, "Go to the Polls," April 21, 1942. (Ottawa, 1942).

[12]For the names of the leading figures in the League and an outline of its objectives, see the Montreal Star, Feb. 8, 1942.

[13]In regard to the attitude of the Union Catholique des Cultivateurs, see Firmin Létourneau, L'U.C.C. (La Trappe, Qué., 1949), p. 156. The Catholic trade unions had been in favour of a policy of neutrality for Canada from the beginning of the war. See Alfred Charpentier, "Historique de la C.T.C.C.," Programme-Souvenir, Congrès annuel, et vingt-cinquième anniversaire de la Confédération des Travailleurs Catholiques du Canada (Québec, 1946), p. 34.

[14]See his speech at a mass meeting in Montreal organized by La Ligue pour la Défense du Canada, Le Devoir, 12 fév. 1942.

[15]See Chief Plebiscite Officer, "Statement of the Results of the Plebiscite Held on the 27th. Day of April, 1942," Canada Gazette, LXXV, 413 (June 23, 1942).

found some support within the ranks of Mackenzie King's own cabinet.[16] The Prime Minister felt compelled, therefore, in spite of the attitude of the Quebec voters, to present a bill to Parliament which would empower the government to introduce conscription at any time it thought such a step necessary merely by passing an order-in-council. This bill, commonly known as Bill 80, bore the title, "An Act to Amend the National Resources Mobilization Act." As a concession to his French-Canadian supporters, King went out of his way to emphasize that the passing of the bill did not mean that conscription would be put into effect immediately, and indeed it might never be necessary to do so. It merely meant that if the war situation became so serious that the government felt it had no alternative but to introduce conscription it would have a free hand to do so. The policy of the government King described as "not necessarily conscription, but conscription if necessary."[17]

Although Bill 80 was supported by most Liberals and by the Conservative party and passed Parliament by a large majority, it created a serious crisis within the ranks of the federal Liberal party. When King had first announced his intention of introducing the bill, P. J. A. Cardin, Minister of Public Works, and one of the influential members of the cabinet from Quebec, submitted his resignation. Most of the French-Canadian members of the Liberal party voted against the bill. They did, however, continue to support the government on all other issues.

The reaction of the people of Quebec to the enactment of Bill 80 could have easily been foreseen. While the bill was still being debated in Parliament a resolution had been introduced in the Quebec Legislative Assembly calling upon the federal government to maintain the voluntary system of recruiting under all circumstances. This resolution was proposed by a Liberal and supported by most members of that party, as well as by the Union Nationale opposition. It passed by a vote of sixty-one to seven.[18] When Bill 80 was finally passed there was widespread resentment throughout the province. Even if it did not mean the immediate introduction of conscription, most French Canadians considered that the King government had broken its pledge. From that time onward Canada's policy of participation in the war

[16]There were two ministers who were particularly dissatisfied with the voluntary system of recruitment, J. L. Ralston, Minister of National Defence, and Angus L. Macdonald, Minister of National Defence for Naval Services. The problems faced by King in holding his cabinet together during the conscription controversy of 1942 are described in Pickersgill, *The Mackenzie King Record*, I, chap. xiv.

[17]Canada, *House of Commons Debates*, June 10, 1942, p. 3236.

[18]*Montreal Gazette*, May 21, 1942.

met with increasing opposition from French Canada. This opposition was intensified by the heavy income taxes, shortages of goods, rationing and wage controls, all of which had been introduced in the first few years of the war and were steadily extended as the war progressed. These various restrictions were irksome enough for those who wholeheartedly supported the war effort; they were doubly irritating for those who were opposed to participation in the first place.

Needless to say, the conscription crisis of 1942 had important repercussions on Quebec provincial politics. With the breakdown of King's compromise policy the provincial Liberal party began to find itself in a difficult position. The Union Nationale, on the other hand, was provided with the opportunity it had been waiting for.

At the time of the plebiscite Duplessis had adopted the popular position of announcing publicly that he was voting in the negative, and called upon all other voters to do likewise.[19] Premier Godbout, for his part, attempted to sidestep the issue by taking the stand that the plebiscite had nothing to do with provincial politics. When Bill 80 was passed Duplessis was quick to capitalize on the bitter resentment of the Quebec voter by stressing on every possible occasion the close ties existing between the federal and provincial wings of the Liberal party. He accused the provincial Liberals of being subservient to Ottawa and contended that they must bear equal responsibility for the policies of the federal government. The strength of this argument lay in the fact that Godbout had gone out of his way to give the central government every possible assistance in the prosecution of the war. Another argument which met with a ready response from the average French-Canadian voter was Duplessis' contention that, although the provisions of Bill 80 had not as yet been put into force, the government was using an indirect and "hypocritical" form of conscription by exerting various kinds of pressure on the men in the home defence forces to "go active," that is, to volunteer for overseas service.[20]

In the face of the Union Nationale attacks it soon became apparent to Godbout that his close association with the federal Liberals, which had been such an asset in 1939, had now become a serious liability. By the time that the provincial election of 1944 was called the Liberals had quite definitely been thrown on the defensive. During the election campaign the Liberal leader, although never missing an opportunity to emphasize his opposition to conscription, tried to have the election

[19]*Le Devoir*, 25 avril 1942.

[20]See Maurice Duplessis, "J'ai sacrifié le pouvoir à l'accomplissement de mon devoir," *L'Œil* (Montréal), II, 11 (15 juin 1942), 11–16.

fought on purely provincial issues.[21] This attempt to dissociate the policies of the provincial government from those of the federal wing of the Liberal party failed. Duplessis succeeded in making the federal government's policies towards the war and conscription the main issue of the election. The electorate expressed their strong opposition to these policies by turning the provincial Liberal party out of office and returning the Union Nationale to power.

The significance of the 1944 election was that, by another unexpected turn of events, Duplessis' opposition to the war policy of the federal government, which had resulted in the defeat of the Union Nationale in 1939, made it possible for this party of conservative nationalism to return to power five years later. It was true that the Union Nationale's majority in the legislature was not very great, as the party had won only forty-eight seats as against thirty-seven for the Liberals.[22] This was owing largely to the fact that the nationalist and anti-Liberal vote was split because of the participation in the election of a newly formed party of radical nationalism called the Bloc Populaire.[23] This party, like the Union Nationale, was anti-war and anti-conscription, but in addition it had a programme of economic and social reform.[24] The Bloc Populaire did not last very long, however; it disintegrated shortly after the 1944 election, leaving the Union Nationale as the only nationalist party in the field.

Aside from the disappearance of the Bloc Populaire as a rival nationalist party, there was another development which increased the strength of the Union Nationale with the electorate. In November, 1944, the serious shortage of reinforcements for Canadian army units in Europe compelled the federal cabinet to implement the provisions of Bill 80 by an order-in-council conscripting 16,000 men from the home defence army for service overseas. In spite of the fact that the total number of conscripts sent overseas before the war ended in 1945 was relatively insignificant, the dissatisfaction of the people of Quebec with the Liberals, both federal and provincial, reached an all-time high. In March, 1945, a resolution was introduced in the Legislative

[21]See Adelard Godbout, *Notre Maître l'avenir* (Montréal, 1944).

[22]Appendix A, Table VII.

[23]The Bloc Populaire won only four seats, but polled approximately 15 per cent of the popular vote, as compared to 37 per cent for the Union Nationale, and 40 per cent for the Liberals. Canadian Press dispatch, *Montreal Gazette*, Aug. 17, 1944. A good deal of the Liberal support came from the English-speaking minority in the province who were solidly behind the war effort.

[24]A brief description of the history and policies of the Bloc Populaire is to be found *infra*, pp. 153–4.

Assembly by René Chaloult, independent nationalist, censuring the federal government for enforcing conscription, and expressing regret that "M. Mackenzie King ait renié ses engagements les plus sacrés à ce sujet." Even the Liberals felt compelled to support the resolution, and it passed by a vote of sixty-seven to five.[25] The latter party and its leader, Adelard Godbout, were now completely discredited in the eyes of the electorate. Moreover, this antagonism was to continue long after the war was over and prove to be a continuing stumbling block to the provincial Liberal party. Nevertheless, most Quebec voters continued to vote Liberal in federal elections for other and rather complex reasons, which we need not go into fully here. There is, however, one point which might be mentioned. In provincial elections the Quebec voter can support either of two parties, both of which are predominantly French Canadian. At Ottawa he must choose between several parties, all of which are predominantly English-speaking. The Liberals were supported as the lesser evil compared with the Conservatives who were even more strongly pro-war and pro-conscriptionist.

However, the steadily growing strength of the Union Nationale during the 1940's was not due solely to the policies adopted by the party on the war and conscription issue. An increasingly important factor, once the war was over, was the party's stand on the question of provincial rights, and to it attention must now be given.

Ever since the Dominion of Canada was established in 1867 all of the provinces comprising this federal state have usually indicated a readiness to resist any attempt on the part of the central government to restrict their autonomy or invade their fields of jurisdiction. It has been the province of Quebec, however, which has always been most insistent on maintaining intact every one of those areas of legislation guaranteed to the provinces under the British North America Act. The reason for this uncompromising stand has been outlined in some detail earlier in this study,[26] but the basic principle involved bears repeating at this point. The province of Quebec is the only political unit in the Canadian federal system which the French Canadians control, the only place where they can enact the type of legislation which conforms to their Roman Catholic scale of values and their interests as a minority ethnic group. They are convinced that any legislative powers ceded to the federal authority are powers ceded to a government which will always be predominantly English and Protestant, and which therefore cannot be expected to appreciate fully or

[25]*Le Devoir*, 2 mars 1945.
[26]See *supra*, pp. 6–7.

understand the French-Canadian's system of values or his particular point of view.

During the period from 1867 until 1939 the province of Quebec was highly successful in maintaining almost unchanged all those rights and prerogatives guaranteed in the British North America Act. An important factor in this success was the constant vigilance on the part of successive Quebec governments and their resistance to the slightest sign of encroachment by the federal authority. This was particularly true of the various Liberal régimes in control of the provincial administration between 1897 and 1936. Prime Ministers like Sir Lomer Gouin and L. A. Taschereau never hesitated to take a strong stand against the federal authority at the least hint that the latter might be planning an invasion of the provincial field.[27] Their task was considerably facilitated by the fact that, during the greater part of the period from 1896 onward, the central government was in the hands of the federal wing of their own party, which was equally concerned about maintaining the autonomy of the provinces.

The ability of Quebec, as well as the other provinces, to maintain intact their fields of jurisdiction was to be sharply challenged in the late thirties. This challenge, the most serious one since Confederation, began to develop with the outbreak of World War II, when the federal Liberal party, in complete reversal of its traditional attitude, started to pursue a consistent policy of increasing the powers of the central government at the expense of the provinces.

There were several aspects to this new orientation of Liberal policy. First of all, under pressure from all parts of the country, and particularly from the economically depressed provinces, the federal government began to introduce various forms of social services, a field of legislation which was essentially the responsibility and within the jurisdiction of the provinces. Furthermore, as one might anticipate in any federal state, Canada's entry into the war necessitated a tremendous increase in the powers of the central authority and compelled it to legislate in many areas which ordinarily were under the control of the provinces. This was much more true of the Second than of the First World War when the government adopted more of a laissez-faire attitude towards the economy. Finally, in its search for the money to finance both the war and its programme of social services, the federal government found it necessary to monopolize the most lucrative sources of tax revenue, thus curtailing seriously the taxation resources of the provinces. This meant that the latter often did not have the

27In regard to Taschereau's attitude, see *supra*, p. 25.

financial means for putting into effect various forms of legislation which they had every constitutional right to enact.

Although the end of the war brought a relaxation or elimination of many of the controls over the economy exercised by the federal government, and the latter withdrew from some fields of legislation such as labour relations, the trend towards centralization was by no means completely reversed. In two areas particularly, the Ottawa government continued to press forward: it continued to expand its programme of social services; and to monopolize the major sources of tax revenue at the expense of the provinces. The justification now for the large proportion of the tax dollar which still found its way into the federal treasury was that, aside from the steadily increasing cost of social services, large sums of money were required for rearmament as the cold war began.

Whatever the necessity for the increased powers of the federal government during the war and the cold war, whatever the merits of its programme of social legislation, or whatever might be the justification for the monopolization of tax revenue, there was little doubt that these policies threatened to alter radically the constitutional arrangements of 1867 by relegating the provinces to an essentially minor and subordinate role within the Canadian federal system.[28] A matter of serious concern for all of the provinces, this issue was particularly crucial for the province of Quebec because of the close relationship between provincial autonomy and cultural survival. It was not surprising, therefore, that the most vigorous and effective opposition to the federal government's centralizing policies was to come from that province. It was also inevitable that such opposition would be spearheaded by the Union Nationale, rather than by the provincial Liberal party, since the latter had now lost a good deal of its independence and freedom of movement in dealing with its federal counterpart.

Although Duplessis had on several occasions during the late 1930's emphasized the determination of his party to defend the autonomy of the province against the federal authority, it was not until the outbreak of war that the question of provincial rights became a controversial issue between the Union Nationale and the Liberal party. During the election campaign of 1939, as we have seen, the main argument used by Duplessis was that the federal government was using its extensive powers under the War Measures Act as a pretext for destroying the rights of the provinces under the British North America Act. This

[28]This problem is discussed in H. F. Angus, "Two Restrictions on Provincial Autonomy," *Canadian Journal of Economics and Political Science*, XXI (Nov. 1955), 445–46.

continued to be one of the main accusations made against the Liberals all during the war years. When Godbout's provincial administration, in line with its policy of co-operation with Ottawa, agreed in 1942 that the province would step out of the important taxation fields of succession duties and personal and corporation income taxes for the duration of the war in return for annual lump sum grants from the federal authority, it was denounced by Duplessis for betraying the true interests of the province. The Union Nationale also attacked the Quebec Liberals for agreeing to an amendment to the British North America Act in 1940 establishing a federal system of unemployment insurance, a move which Duplessis had opposed when he was in office between 1936 and 1939.[29] As a result of this intransigent attitude towards the federal government, there is little doubt that by the time the election of 1944 was called, the Union Nationale party had become identified in the mind of the Quebec voter, not only with opposition to the war, but also with a vigorous defence of the rights of the province under the constitution.

When the Union Nationale returned to office in 1944 Duplessis soon made it quite clear that the greatest concern of his government would be to oppose, by every legal means, the centralizing policies of the federal authority. The maintenance of the autonomy of the province was, he said, essential for the survival of the French-Canadian way of life. In one by-election campaign Duplessis made the statement: "Il y a un autre point important. C'est le droit d'être maître chez soi. . . . L'Autonomie, c'est le droit . . . de faire des lois pour nous et par nous, de faire régler les questions qui regardent Québec par Québec, plutôt que de les faire régler par Ottawa."[30]

In line with these objectives, the second Union Nationale administration was to reverse completely the policy of co-operation with the federal authority which had characterized Godbout's régime. The whole programme of social legislation introduced by the Ottawa government now met with relentless opposition from the province of Quebec. The federal scheme of family allowances established in 1944 was criticized as unconstitutional, and Duplessis endeavoured to have it revised along lines which would "respect the rights of the provinces."[31] Just as the Union Nationale had opposed the inauguration of a federal system of unemployment insurance, it now opposed the

[29]The correspondence exchanged between Duplessis and the federal Prime Minister on this question is to be found in *Documents instructifs et inattaquables qu'il faut lire et faire lire* (Québec, n.d.).

[30]*Le Devoir*, 19 nov. 1945.

[31]*Montreal Gazette*, Feb. 3, 1945.

proposal for a national scheme of hospital insurance based on co-operation between the Dominion and the provinces.[32] The provincial government compelled Quebec universities to turn down fairly substantial yearly grants from the federal government on the grounds that such grants constituted an invasion of the exclusively provincial field of education. It refused to co-operate with Ottawa in many other areas, such as a federal proposal for the construction of a Trans-Canada highway.[33] In his self-appointed role as defender of the rights of the provinces under the constitution, Duplessis also stoutly rejected all suggestions that the federal authority could unilaterally amend the British North America Act, contending that the Act was a compact between the different provinces and that, as a consequence, it could not be modified without their unanimous consent.[34]

The most important aspect of the Union Nationale's struggle with the central government concerned the question of taxation. This struggle began to develop shortly after the end of the war when the federal government began to exert pressure on the provinces to renew the wartime taxation agreements under which the provinces refrained from collecting succession duties and personal and corporation income taxes, in return for yearly lump sum grants from the central authority.[35] This whole idea was resisted strongly by Duplessis, who argued that if the provincial government should ever become dependent on federal grants rather than its own tax resources for the financing of its day-to-day activities, the ultimate result would be complete federal domination and the end of provincial autonomy.[36] The reasoning behind this contention was that any governmental authority which makes a grant of money is bound sooner or later to lay down the conditions under which such money is to be spent.

Not only did Duplessis refuse to relinquish any of these taxation fields but he also put forward a rather questionable constitutional

---

[32]Maurice Duplessis, *Mémoire du gouvernement de la Province de Québec présenté à la conférence fédérale-provinciale* (Québec, 1946), p. 21.

[33]The various areas in which Quebec refused to co-operate with Ottawa are described in Maurice Lamontagne, *Le fédéralisme canadien, evolution et problèmes* (Québec, 1954), p. 90.

[34]Duplessis, *Mémoire du gouvernement de la Province de Québec . . .*, pp. 3–6. For a criticism of this "compact theory of Confederation," see R. MacGregor Dawson, *The Government of Canada* (1st ed.; Toronto: 1947), pp. 143–47. The various arguments for and against this theory are fully described in Paul Gérin-Lajoie, *Constitutional Amendment in Canada* (Toronto, 1950).

[35]See the proposals put forward at the Dominion-provincial conference of 1945–46, Dawson, *The Government of Canada*, pp. 131–5.

[36]Duplessis, *Mémoire du gouvernement de la Province de Québec . . .*, pp. 19–20.

theory concerning the taxation powers of the province in these areas. According to the British North America Act, Section 91, the Dominion has power to raise money "by any mode or system of taxation," while the provinces, under Section 92, have authority to impose "direct taxation within the province in order to the raising of a revenue for provincial purposes." Duplessis contended that the real meaning of these taxation clauses was that the provinces had rights prior to those of the federal government in the field of direct taxation.[37]

In spite of the strong stand taken by the Duplessis government on the taxation issue, it was slow in taking any concrete steps towards exercising the rights it claimed. The chief reason here was that the federal government had already entered the fields of personal and corporation income taxes, and succession duties, with such a high level of assessment that there was very little potential revenue left for the provinces. In a surprise move in 1954, however, Quebec introduced a personal and a corporation income tax with rates of assessment which amounted to 15 per cent of the federal tax in these fields. This step was successful in wringing from the central government the concession that residents of Quebec, and companies doing business in that province, could reduce their federal income tax by 10 per cent.

In this whole controversy one of the most frequent accusations made by Duplessis was that the federal government's invasion of the strictly provincial field of social legislation was only made possible by using tax revenue which rightfully belonged to the provinces. On occasion, Duplessis also used the argument that the lack of certain social services at the provincial level was due to the federal government's monopolization of tax revenue. It is highly questionable, however, whether he was really interested in introducing such social services, since, as was pointed out in the last chapter, he was opposed to the social welfare state as a form of "paternalism."

The importance of this struggle for provincial rights in Quebec politics after 1944 is indicated by the fact that the Union Nationale was successful in making it the dominant issue in every election until that of 1960. In the elections of 1948, 1952, and 1956, the main argument of Duplessis for the return of his party to power was that it constituted the sole bulwark against complete domination by the federal government and loss of provincial autonomy, with all that that implied from the point of view of cultural survival. The nature of the Union Nationale's appeal to the electorate in this regard can be readily illustrated. In the 1948 election campaign Duplessis stated: "La légis-

[37]*Ibid.*, p. 8.

lature de Québec, c'est une forteresse que nous devons défendre sans défaillance. C'est elle qui nous permet de nous construire des écoles qui nous conviennent, de parler notre langue, de pratiquer notre religion, de faire des lois applicables à notre population."[38] In 1952 he emphasized this point again: "La défense de nos droits, c'est la question de l'heure. Voulons-nous vivre et survivre. C'est là le point important. . . . Il faut absolument que Québec administre ses propres affaires. Nous n'avons pas de directives à prendre d'ailleurs."[39] Basically the same argument was used once more in the 1956 campaign: "Nous sommes engagés dans une lutte de vie ou de mort. Il s'agit de savoir si Québec doit survivre comme province, comme province distincte, possédant non seulement des droits, mais aussi les sources de revenus nécessaires pour les faire valoir. Le seul parti qui offre des garanties dans cette lutte, c'est l'Union nationale."[40]

There were certain other aspects of Ottawa's policies which were seized upon by the Union Nationale as additional evidence that the federal Liberals not only were unconcerned with the interests and attitude of the people of Quebec, but that their real intent was to destroy the identity of the French Canadians as a distinct cultural group. Ottawa's postwar policy of encouraging immigration, particularly from the British Isles, was described as a Liberal plot to increase the English-speaking proportion of the population and thus decrease the French influence.[41] A chance statement by Mr. Louis St. Laurent, shortly before he became Prime Minister, that it was constitutionally possible for the federal Parliament to abolish the French language (although he did not suggest that anyone seriously considered doing so) was used by the Union Nationale's propaganda machine as positive proof of Ottawa's plans to make Canada a purely English-speaking country.[42] The policy of the federal government during the war years of making grants and loans of several billion dollars to England, as part of Canada's contribution to the war effort, was made an important issue in the election of 1948. The party's slogan in that election was, "Les libéraux donnent aux étrangers; Duplessis donne à sa province," and a pamphlet distributed by the party at the time made the following appeal to local interest: "Un vote pour DUPLESSIS, c'est un vote pour votre province, pour votre comté, pour votre

[38]*Le Temps* (Québec), 16 juillet 1948.
[39]*La Presse*, 4 juillet 1952.
[40]*La Presse*, 19 juin 1956.
[41]See Union Nationale advertisement, *Le Temps*, 16 juillet 1948; also Pierre Morin, "Causons d'autonomie," *Renaissance* (Québec), juillet 1948, p. 23.
[42]For Mr. St. Laurent's statement, see Canada, *House of Commons Debates* (unrevised), June 18, 1946, pp. 2696–97.

localité, pour votre famille; c'est un vote pour vous! car DUPLESSIS n'a pas donné aux étrangers."[43] The Union Nationale used the same strategy to arouse the people of Quebec against the Liberals when the latter committed Canada to a policy of financial and technical assistance to underdeveloped countries under the Colombo Plan. The slogan now was, "Pourquoi tant d'égards pour les pays asiatiques, et si peu pour les droits du Québec?"[44]

The strength of Duplessis' appeal to the Quebec voter to support his party as the only guarantee that the rights of the province would be respected is not too difficult to understand if we bear in mind the crucial role that provincial autonomy has always played in French-Canadian thinking. This autonomist sentiment was intensified by the antagonism which developed towards the federal government during the war years. Although the average French Canadian might know very little about the fine constitutional points at issue in this controversy over Dominion-provincial relations, he did know that he was opposed to increased legislative power being extended to a federal government which had once more involved him in a war in which he was not interested in participating. Nor could he be expected to accept readily the high level of federal taxation which accompanied that war and the postwar rearmament programme. As a result of his isolationism and his preoccupation with his own affairs, he found it difficult to see the sense of grants and loans to England or to underdeveloped countries of which he had never heard. Although there is no need for us to accept Duplessis' contention that a federal government, with a French-Canadian prime minister and several cabinet ministers from the same language group, was planning to anglicize Canada and destroy French-Canadian culture, it is easy to see how such an argument would find ready acceptance when public opinion in Quebec was already aroused over the participation issue. From the point of view of many a French Canadian, any government which was so unconcerned about his interests and attitudes as to enforce conscription might very well be capable of doing anything.

Perhaps one of the most important aspects of the Union Nationale's struggle with Ottawa over provincial rights was that it enabled the party to win a considerable measure of support in several elections from the radical nationalists and the trade unions, the two influential groups in the province who were most strongly opposed to Duplessis' economic policies. When the Bloc Populaire, the party of radical nationalism which had been formed in the early forties, began to

[43]*Duplessis donne à sa province* (Québec, 1948), p. 32.
[44]*Le Temps,* 17 mai 1956.

disintegrate around 1945, many of its organizers and local leaders swung over to the Union Nationale. In the general election of 1948 a good number of former Bloc Populaire candidates supported the party on the platform and over the radio.[45] René Chaloult, one of the left-wing nationalists who had broken with Duplessis in 1936 because of the latter's economic policies, joined forces once more with the Union Nationale, and in the elections of 1948 and 1952 ran as an independent nationalist with the party's backing.[46] Most of the members of L'Action Nationale supported the Union Nationale, and until the late 1940's it was looked upon favourably by the nationalist daily, Le Devoir. Duplessis also succeeded in winning over his old political rival, and predecessor as leader of the provincial Conservative party back in the early thirties, Mayor Camillien Houde of Montreal. Houde had his own personal quarrel with Ottawa for he had been interned in 1940 for his opposition to the war. Shortly after his release from confinement about the end of the war he was re-elected mayor of Montreal. In throwing his support behind the Union Nationale, Mayor Houde denounced Prime Minister St. Laurent and stated that he was in the electoral fight "parce que je veux démasquer les renégats qui nous ont trahis à Ottawa."[47] Houde's support was particularly helpful to the party in the Montreal area, for he had a strong following in the French working-class constituencies.[48] The basic position of most of these individuals and groups was that, although they might disagree with the economic policies of Duplessis, they felt that the maintenance of provincial autonomy was the paramount issue of the day. They therefore threw their support behind the only party which presented effective opposition to Ottawa's centralizing policies.

The attitude of the trade unions was somewhat similar to that of the radical nationalists. Quebec's industrial workers had no more enthusiasm than any other group in the province for Canada's participation in the war and the centralization of powers in the hands of the federal government. In the 1942 plebiscite on conscription the "No" vote in predominantly French working-class districts in Montreal such as

[45]Duplessis was not too successful, however, in winning over the leading figures in the Bloc Populaire. Some of them retired from politics when the party broke up. Others were to play a prominent role in various organizations and political movements opposed to the Union Nationale. See infra, p. 154n.

[46]Chaloult's reasons for supporting the Union Nationale and opposing the Liberals were outlined in an advertisement published during the 1948 election campaign. See "J'accuse!" Montreal-Matin, 27 juillet 1948.

[47]Ibid.

[48]While Houde was in the internment camp many trade union leaders in the Montreal area carried on a continuous agitation for his release. See report of mass meeting in Le Devoir, 21 juillet 1944.

Hochelaga, St. Jacques, and Ste Marie had run as high as 75 and 80 per cent.[49] Thus, in spite of Duplessis' unfriendly attitude towards the trade unions, the fact that the Union Nationale was the outstanding antagonist of Ottawa's policies tended to divide the labour movement and made it difficult for it to present any kind of united opposition to the party. Moreover, the Union Nationale's skilful distribution of patronage, to be described in the next chapter, won over many trade union leaders to the party's cause.

This lack of a solid trade union front in the face of the Union Nationale's anti-labour policies can be attributed to a very large extent to the Trades and Labour Congress (T.L.C.), the largest and most powerful of the three central labour organizations in the province. While it is true that the Congress had formed a coalition with the other labour organizations at the time of the Asbestos strike and Duplessis' restrictive labour code, this co-operation did not last very long. Shortly after these events it quickly forgot its pledge of union solidarity and uncompromising opposition to the Union Nationale. This was not too surprising for the radicalism which characterized the T.L.C. during the war years was essentially temporary in nature. Even before the Asbestos strike it had pretty well pigeon-holed all its proposals for sweeping reforms and had returned to its old pattern of business unionism and ready acceptance of the capitalist system as long as it provided the workers with fair wages and working conditions. When all Communists were expelled from affiliated unions around 1949 the Congress lost whatever dynamic leadership it had ever had. During the greater part of the next decade the T.L.C. was not only the largest, but also the most conservative, central labour organization in the province.[50]

As a result of this rightward orientation, most of the leaders of the T.L.C. in the province were on friendly terms with the Union Nationale, and by 1950 had formed the same close relationship with the party as the leaders of the Catholic unions had had in earlier times.[51] When the Canadian Congress of Labour (C.C.L.) and the Confédération des Travailleurs Catholiques du Canada (C.T.C.C.) organized a march on Quebec in 1954 as a protest against some of the government's labour legislation, the T.L.C. refused to join them. This attitude won it the warm praise of the Minister of Labour.[52] Although

[49]For an analysis of the plebiscite vote in Quebec, see F.-Albert Angers, "Un vote de race," L'Action Nationale, XIX, 4 (mai 1942), 299–312.

[50]See Réginald Boisvert, "La grève et le mouvement ouvrier," in Pierre-Elliott Trudeau, éd., La Grève de l'amiante (Montréal, 1956), pp. 362–64.

[51]Ibid., p. 363.

[52]See Montreal Gazette, June 14, 1954.

the T.L.C. was officially neutral in politics, in most elections between 1944 and 1956 the Union Nationale could depend on the open support of a certain number of the leaders of its affiliated unions, some of whom held important posts in the Congress.[53] These leaders usually avoided any reference to the Union Nationale's restrictive labour legislation, but supported other aspects of party policy, such as opposition to Ottawa's centralizing tendencies and Duplessis' war on Communism.[54] As a reward for this collaboration the T.L.C. unions now received preferential treatment from the government in jurisdictional disputes with unions affiliated with the other two central labour organizations.[55]

While the T.L.C. was on the most friendly terms with the Union Nationale, this does not mean that the membership of the C.C.L. and the C.T.C.C. were solidly united in their opposition to the party. There was never any question of the strong antagonism towards the Union Nationale, on the part of the top leadership in these two organizations, but this was not necessarily true of all the minor leaders, or of all the rank and file, except perhaps for a short period following the Asbestos strike. In regard to the C.T.C.C., it must be remembered that although its economic policies had shifted to the left in the 1940's, it was still strongly nationalistic; it was therefore not too difficult to convince a good number of its members that they should support the party which presented the most effective opposition to Ottawa's policies.[56] Even the top leadership of the C.C.L. and the C.T.C.C., and particularly of the latter, were in general agreement with the Union Nationale that the autonomy of the province must be maintained, although they did believe that Duplessis was exploiting this issue for his own purposes. In 1954 a meeting of leaders of the C.C.L. unions in Quebec passed a resolution which gave qualified support to the Union Nationale in its

[53]Paul Fournier, the President of the Montreal Trades and Labour Council during the greater part of the 1940's, was a well-known Union Nationale supporter. Joseph Matte, a prominent labour leader in Quebec City, ran as Union Nationale candidate in the 1948 election. During the 1956 election campaign a good number of trade union officials connected with the T.L.C. unions openly supported the party. See advertisement, "Real Labour Leaders Back National Union," *Montreal Gazette*, June 19, 1956.

[54]Duplessis' anti-Communist campaign is described below.

[55]See the accusations levelled against the Quebec section of the T.L.C. at the 1954 convention of the Canadian Congress of Labour, *Montreal Gazette*, Sept. 28, 1954.

[56]One unsuccessful Social Democratic (C.C.F.) candidate in the 1956 election admitted that union members will only follow the advice of their leaders when union affairs are being discussed. "It is clear that they won't stand for union leaders telling them who to vote for." *Montreal Gazette*, June 22, 1956.

tax dispute with Ottawa.[57] The same year the annual congress of the C.T.C.C. went on record that "le droit à l'impôt direct pour les provinces est incontestable et doit être respecté par le gouvernement canadien."[58]

The dilemma in which the trade union movement was placed by these conflicting attitudes towards the Union Nationale was very well illustrated by the experience of the C.T.C.C. when it formed a Political Action Committee to fight the party in the provincial election of 1952. The committee threw its weight behind a number of Liberal candidates and succeeded in electing about a half dozen of them in spite of strong Union Nationale opposition; but these activities created such dissension within the movement, and aroused such opposition from some of the leaders of affiliated unions, that in the following election of 1956 the C.T.C.C. remained aloof and refused to endorse any particular candidate or party.[59]

The stand taken by the Union Nationale on the important issues of provincial autonomy and of participation in the war goes a long way towards explaining the party's victories at the polls from 1944 to 1956. There was, however, one other aspect of Union Nationale policy during this period which cannot be overlooked for it was also a factor in the support the party received from the electorate: this was the attitude adopted by Duplessis and his party towards "the menace of Communism."

As with the question of provincial autonomy, the importance of the issue of Communism in Quebec politics during the last twenty-five years can only be understood by keeping in mind the basic characteristics of the society which we are studying. In this context the particular characteristic that is influential is that the people of Quebec constitute a strongly Roman Catholic society in which a large majority of the people adhere to the doctrines and social philosophy of the Church, as interpreted by the hierarchy.

The fact that the Roman Catholic Church, whether in Quebec or elsewhere, is strongly opposed to Communism in all its aspects is quite well known. The main reason for this opposition, however, is not

[57]*Montreal Gazette*, June 1, 1954.
[58]*Le Devoir*, 22 sept. 1954.
[59]In regard to the controversy within the C.T.C.C. over the question of political action, see the report of the discussions on this subject at the 1954 convention in Fernand Dansereau, "Gérard Picard et Jean Marchand interviennent en faveur d'une action politique plus poussée," *Le Devoir*, 24 sept. 1954.

always fully appreciated. The Church's aversion to Communism is not based primarily on economic and political grounds, but rather on religious and philosophical ones. Communism is opposed, not so much because it is anti-democratic, anti-liberal, and anti-capitalistic—although these factors carry a certain weight—but because it is a materialistic philosophy of which a systematic and militant atheism is an essential ingredient. As such it is diametrically opposed to the Catholic philosophy of life with its emphasis on the primacy of spiritual goals. In Quebec the terms "Communism" and "atheism" are used interchangeably. Cardinal Villeneuve of Quebec City, in an important address delivered in 1938, clearly set forth the Church's views of the essential conflict between the principles of Communism and those of Christianity.

The attitude of the Church regarding Communism is well known. The reason why she is irreconcilably opposed to Communism is plain. The principles of Communism are diametrically opposed to those of Christianity. The Communists in Russia proclaim and teach that there is no God and persecute those who believe in Him. . . . As a matter of fact, a consistent Communist must necessarily be an atheist, . . . Lastly, I would remind you that Communism is not a social and political system, but a gigantic conspiracy organized throughout the world to wage war against all human and Divine laws and destroy Christian civilization.[60]

In spite of the strong opposition of the French Canadian to everything Communist, this particular issue did not arouse much interest on the part of the average voter until the outbreak of the Spanish Civil War in 1936. Shortly after the beginning of that conflict, however, the people of Quebec, and Catholics in other parts of the world as well, began to look upon it as a holy war in which the defenders of Spain's Christian heritage, led by General Franco, were locked in deadly combat with the forces of international Communism disguised as Republicans.[61]

The Spanish Civil War left the French Canadian with two very strong and lasting impressions. One was the identification of Communism with the burning of churches, the killing of priests and nuns, the destruction of the family as a social institution, the end of all morality, and the total elimination of all religious influences and

[60]*Montreal Gazette*, Nov. 30, 1938.

[61]The French Canadian's attitude towards the war was conditioned by the fact that the Quebec newspapers gave their readers a rather one-sided version of the conflict. See Michael Oliver, "Quebec and Canadian Democracy," *Canadian Journal of Economics and Political Science*, XXIII, 4 (Nov., 1957), 509.

practices under a governmental system inspired by the principles of militant atheism. The other lesson drawn from the Spanish conflict was that the extent of the threat which the Communist movement presents in any given area or country cannot be determined merely by calculating the number of people who are enrolled on membership lists. It was contended that if a handful of Communists could wield such power in Catholic Spain, they could do the same in Catholic Quebec. The fact, therefore, that the membership of the Communist party in the latter province was insignificant, and that it had never been able to elect a single member to the legislature, was considered completely irrelevant from the point of view of the danger which that group presented to the French-Canadian way of life.[62]

This hatred and fear of Communism on the part of the people of Quebec, although somewhat dormant during the war years, was to become intensified in the postwar period. The cause of this second and more intense wave of anti-Communism was the large number of arrests and executions of bishops, priests, and prominent lay leaders which followed the Russian occupation of such predominantly Catholic countries as Poland and Hungary. In a Gallup poll taken after the war it was found that 79 per cent of the people of Quebec considered that Communism was either "a very serious threat," or "a fairly serious threat" to the Canadian form of government.[63]

It is not our concern here to settle the question of the accuracy of the French-Canadian interpretation of the Spanish Civil War.[64] Nor is it the place to discuss fully whether the threat of Communism in Canada and in Quebec was ever as serious as the people of the latter province were led to believe. There does appear to be little doubt that this threat was greatly exaggerated by many French Canadians, but our purpose here is rather to describe the impact which this deep-seated antagonism towards the movement had on Quebec politics, and in particular how it affected the fortunes of the Union Nationale party.

[62]For a short history of the Communist party in Quebec up to the period immediately following World War II, see Gérard Dion, Le Communisme dans la province de Québec (Québec, 1949). Although Dion, unlike many French Canadians at the time, did not look upon the Communist movement as an immediate threat, he did point out a number of reasons why the party was a stronger political force than its small membership would have led one to believe. See p. 21.

[63]Montreal Star, Aug. 20, 1947.

[64]This writer certainly considers that the French-Canadian viewpoint on the Spanish Civil War was quite distorted, although this does not necessarily mean that he accepts the official version presented by the Loyalists.

The attitude which the Union Nationale was to adopt towards Communist activities in the province became apparent shortly after the party's electoral victory of 1936. Duplessis declared war on Communism and indicated that he was ready to take whatever measures he considered necessary to curb the activities of that movement. The most important step in this direction was the enactment in 1937 of a law entitled an Act Respecting Communistic Propaganda, but known in popular terminology as the "Padlock Law." Under this act Duplessis, as Attorney General, was given extensive powers to close, or padlock, any premises used for the purpose of "propagating Communism or Bolshevism." The law made no attempt to define the terms "Communism" or "Bolshevism," such definition being left to the discretion of the Attorney General. Although the Padlock Law met with a storm of protest from the English-speaking minority in Quebec, who looked upon its loose terminology and the sweeping powers it gave to the Attorney General as a threat to civil liberties,[65] it received the overwhelming support of the French Canadians. The act passed both houses of the legislature by a unanimous vote as it was supported by opposition as well as government members.[66] It did not, of course, by any means eliminate Communist activities in Quebec, but it did hamper considerably the functioning of the party in that province.[67] Even more important it enabled the Union Nationale to establish itself firmly in the eyes of the Quebec voter as a strong opponent of Communism.

When the Union Nationale returned to power in 1944 after five years in opposition, the postwar wave of anti-Communism was sweeping Quebec. Duplessis took advantage of the situation by intensifying his crusade against the movement. The Padlock Law was rigorously enforced and the Communist party, now known as the Labour Progressive party (L.P.P.), found its premises and those of its front organizations padlocked on many occasions. Large quantities of literature were seized by the government in repeated raids. The Union Nationale's war on the Communists also took the form of enacting legislation which restricted their activities in the trade union movement.[68] The government not only refused to certify trade unions in

[65]See statement made by R. L. Calder of the Montreal branch of the Civil Liberties Union, in "Letters to the Editor," *Montreal Gazette*, March 25, 1938.
[66]See G. A. Coughlin, *The Quebec Padlock Law*, L'Œuvre des Tracts, no 234 (Montréal, 1938).
[67]See Dion, *Le Communisme dans la province de Québec*, pp. 20–21.
[68]See *supra*, pp. 93–4.

which members of the L.P.P. played an active role, but also jailed these leaders on the slightest pretext.

The most important aspect of the Union Nationale's anti-Communist crusade, however, was the systematic campaign which was launched to convince the electorate that the Liberal party, both federally and provincially, was not only pursuing a policy of co-operation with the Communists, but also had a powerful left wing whose ideology was close to that of "the followers of Moscow." In this campaign the Union Nationale followed several lines of attack.[69] It was pointed out, for instance, that the Liberal party had always expressed the point of view that the threat of Communism was too remote to be given any serious consideration, and that when the party had been in control of the Quebec administration between 1939 and 1944, no attempt had been made to enforce the Padlock Law. There was the fact that during the war years the federal government had done everything it could to create a favourable impression of Russia on the part of the Canadian public, and had sponsored documentary films and radio broadcasts which presented a one-sided picture of the Soviet régime.[70] It was contended that the federal government had from time to time appointed Communists and fellow travellers to key positions in various governmental agencies, such as the National Film Board, and had used Communist lecturers on government-sponsored radio broadcasts.[71] As proof of its accusations, the Union Nationale was able to point out that the Royal Commission appointed in 1946 to investigate espionage in governmental agencies had found that the Communists had been fairly successful in infiltrating certain branches of the civil service during the war.[72] The Union Nationale also raised the question of why Canada had diplomatic relations with the Communist countries, but not with the Vatican. Certain trade agreements made by Ottawa with

[69]Many of the arguments used by the Union Nationale, as described below, are to be found in Noel Dorion, Le Communisme et le parti Libéral (Québec, 1948); also Pierre Vignon, "Qui nous protégera du communisme?" Renaissance (Québec, juillet 1948), pp. 38–52.

[70]This refers to the "honeymoon" period in the relations between Russia and the West, when the former country was looked upon as "our gallant ally." An example of the type of film used by the government was one called, "Our Northern Neighbour," which presented a rather uncritical and enthusiastic picture of developments in Russia.

[71]The names of some of these individuals are mentioned in Vignon, "Qui nous protégera du communisme?" p. 44.

[72]See Canada, The Report of the Royal Commission to Investigate the Facts Relating to and the Circumstances Surrounding the Communication, by Public Officials and Other Persons in Positions of Trust of Secret and Confidential Information to Agents of a Foreign Power (Ottawa, 1946).

countries behind the Iron Curtain were strongly attacked on the grounds that they were detrimental to the interests of the Quebec farmer and provided one more indication of the friendliness of the Liberal party towards the Communists.[73] As evidence of the sympathy existing between the left wing of the party and the "atheistic Communists," the Union Nationale cited the names of certain prominent Liberals who were known to be rather anti-clerical.[74] Perhaps the Union Nationale's strongest argument for the existence of close ties between the Liberals and the Communists was the fact that in every election the latter attacked Duplessis as their number one enemy, but supported the Liberals in every constituency where they had no candidates of their own, which meant in most constituencies.[75] This argument was further strengthened by the failure of the Liberals in many instances to repudiate such support in clear terms.[76]

Duplessis' anti-Communist campaign was also directly related to the question of provincial autonomy. The Union Nationale contended that the task of the Communists would be simplified considerably if all legislative power was centralized at Ottawa, for "il est plus facile pour les communistes de saisir le contrôle d'un pays lorsqu'ils ont affaire à un seul gouvernement au lieu de dix."[77]

Although the various arguments put forward by the Union Nationale would hardly be considered by an objective observer as conclusive proof that there was a close working alliance between the Communists and the Liberals, the party's campaign met with a considerable measure of success among the people of Quebec. In the aroused state of postwar public opinion over the Communist issue many voters were easily convinced that the Union Nationale was the only bulwark against "the forces of subversion," while the Liberals were "soft on

---

[73]In regard to one trade agreement under which a large quantity of eggs was imported from Poland, see Union Nationale advertisement, "Les Québecois forcés de manger des œufs communistes!" Le Temps, 7 juin 1956.

[74]Vignon, "Qui nous protégera du communisme?" p. 45.

[75]In 1944 the L.P.P., for devious reasons of its own, proposed a coalition with the federal Liberal party. See Tim Buck, What Kind of Government? Liberal–Labour Coalition vs. Tory Reaction (Toronto, 1944). In regard to the tactics of the party in Quebec, see Karl Gerhard, "Local Reds Intimate an Out-and-Out Struggle May Begin for Control of Province's Labour," Montreal Gazette, May 30, 1952.

[76]The Liberals tended to adopt the attitude that they welcomed support for their policies no matter where it came from. When the L.P.P. proposed the alliance with the Liberals in 1944, the head of the National Liberal Federation stated, "The Liberal party welcomes co-operation from everyone in Canada in putting into effect Liberal principles and policies . . ." Montreal Gazette, June 24, 1944.

[77]Vignon, "Qui nous protégera du communisme?" p. 45.

Communism." It was widely believed that a victory of the Liberal party would result in the rapid increase of Communist influence in Quebec. An indication of the effectiveness of the Union Nationale's campaign to link the Liberals and the Communists was the fact that, at the time of the 1956 election, Liberal leader Georges Lapalme was on the point of appealing to the hierarchy to intervene and assure the electorate that he and his party were not "militant atheists."[78]

Duplessis' vigorous anti-Communist crusade, his rigid enforcement of the Padlock Law, and his strategy of associating the Liberals with the Communists, played an important role in his electoral victories from 1944 onward. As one might anticipate, the Communist issue was useful to the party in winning support among the clergy, particularly in the rural areas, and among the teaching orders of nuns and brothers.[79] It also won support from many other groups as well, including a good section of the trade union movement. In the case of the C.T.C.C., while that body as a whole considered that social reform was the best antidote for Communism, there was a sizable minority who favoured repressive measures against the movement.[80] Duplessis' anti-Communist policies found even greater support among the unions affiliated with the T.L.C. Even before the latter had expelled the Communist unions in 1949 there was a powerful group within the Quebec section of this central labour organization which was as fully anti-Communist as Duplessis himself, and which was ready to support any steps taken to curb the movement.[81]

From the preceding analysis we can see how three main issues dominated the political struggle in Quebec during the period from 1939 to 1956. In the elections of 1939 and 1944 the question of participation in the war was the most important issue, but in the elections of 1948, 1952, and 1956 it was the Union Nationale's defence of provincial autonomy, and to a lesser extent its opposition to Communism,

[78]See Lapalme's statement, *L'Action Catholique*, 22 mai 1956.

[79]See Gérard Dion and Louis O'Neill, *Political Immorality in the Province of Quebec* (Montreal, 1956), pp. 10–15.

[80]At the 1953 convention this minority, led by the textile unions, tried unsuccessfully to have the C.T.C.C. pass a resolution calling for the outlawing of the Communist party in Canada. *Le Devoir*, 18 sept. 1953.

[81]The Montreal Trades and Labour Council was expelled from the T.L.C. in 1945 because of its attacks upon Communist unions in the latter organization. *Montreal Gazette*, May 15, 1945. The Council was reinstated a few years later when the T.L.C. itself finally turned against the Communists. During the 1956 election several leading figures in the Quebec section of the T.L.C. advised the membership, "Vote for whoever you please, but please don't vote for any Communist candidates." *Montreal Gazette*, June 18, 1956.

which had the greatest influence on the decision of the electorate. Yet reactions to political issues do not tell the whole story. Aside from the popular stand taken by the Union Nationale on these three issues, there was another factor of quite a different nature which contributed in some measure to each electoral victory of Duplessis' party, but which became increasingly important in the 1950's. This was the way in which the Union Nationale used its control over the administration and the legislature to build up its electoral strength, and at the same time to handicap seriously the Liberal and other opposition parties in their search for power.

CHAPTER VII

Administrative and Electoral Practices
under the Union Nationale

ONE OF THE PLEDGES on which the Union Nationale was first elected to office in 1936 was that it would eliminate the many different forms of administrative and electoral corruption characteristic of the Taschereau régime. During his first administration from 1936 to 1939, Duplessis did indeed eradicate some of the more important abuses of his predecessor.[1] This reforming zeal of the Union Nationale did not, however, survive the period when the party was out of office between 1939 and 1944, and shortly after it was returned to power it began to pursue a systematic policy of using its control over the administration and the legislature for partisan purposes in an even more compelling fashion than had been used under the old Taschereau administration. To understand how and why this was attempted, it will be helpful to recall one aspect of the general picture of public affairs in Quebec given earlier.

It has been explained that most of the people of Quebec have little real understanding of the theoretical principles underlying the democratic institutions of government, or of the specific practices and spirit which should characterize their day-to-day operation. Consequently the average voter tends to look upon government expenditures on such things as public works or social services, not as a right of the citizen whose taxes make such expenditures possible, but as a special favour or privilege granted by the party which happens to be in office. He is also left quite indifferent to and unconcerned over breaches of orthodox parliamentary practices which would arouse a

[1]See *supra*, p. 78–9.

public outcry in another province—the lack of proper budgetary procedures or partisanship on the part of the Speaker, for example.

As a result of these peculiarities in the functioning of parliamentary government in Quebec, a political party which is successful in winning an election in that province is immediately provided with three distinct advantages over its opponents. It is in a position to use the expenditure of public money and the appointment of government personnel as a means of building up its electoral support; it can tap lucrative sources of revenue for its election campaigns, sources which are not available to the opposition parties; and its dominant position in the legislature enables it to fashion the electoral machinery along lines which will be most disadvantageous to the opposition. Our first task, therefore, will be to show how the Union Nationale used its control over the administration to increase its electoral strength through the expenditure of government funds and the appointment of individuals to public office. In other words, we shall examine the Union Nationale's patronage system.

For any party in office, whether in Quebec or elsewhere, to be in a position where it can use the distribution of government money and jobs to win supporters, that party must, of course, be relatively free from the restraints of a non-partisan or merit system for the recruitment of government personnel. Another essential condition is that cabinet ministers and other high administrative officials must be left a wide area of discretionary power in the spending of the money voted by the legislature in the yearly budget.

In regard to the first factor, Quebec has never had any tradition that government personnel should be selected on the basis of competitive examinations under a merit system. It is true that in 1943 the Godbout administration set up a three-man Civil Service Commission whose function was to eliminate patronage in appointments to government positions. However, the Commission had little opportunity to make any basic changes in the existing system of selection before the Union Nationale returned to power in 1944. Although Duplessis had never been very favourable towards the idea of a Civil Service Commission, he nevertheless did not abolish it. Its powers and activities were simply curtailed, and as a result the Commission had relatively little control over the way in which the various government departments selected a good portion of their personnel.[2]

[2]See Taylor Cole, *The Canadian Bureaucracy* (Durham, 1949), pp. 185–96. Cole points out that although the Union Nationale made fewer dismissals after 1944 than it did after 1936, "it created an indeterminate number of new posts for National Union adherents." See p. 178n.

As for the second requirement for the establishment of an effective patronage system, it was the practice of the Duplessis administration in drawing up its yearly budget to make sure that a sizable proportion of the estimates for each department or agency were on a non-statutory basis and could be spent at the discretion of the minister or agency head. This was particularly true of the estimates for the Department of Education. On one occasion when the opposition suggested the introduction of a system of statutory grants for school commissions on some fixed basis, Duplessis replied that this would be an undue hindrance in administration: "Le gouvernement a été élu pour administrer et non pour être lié par des statuts. Il ne sera jamais 'statufié.' "[3] As a result of this unusual approach to budgeting, administrative officials had a fairly free hand to spend large sums of money in those ways which would be of most benefit to the party. When the budget was presented to the legislature the government could always depend on its large and docile majority to push it through without alteration. Moreover, departmental heads never felt themselves bound to limit their expenditures to the amount voted in the budget. In election years, when large amounts of money were needed for the purpose of patronage, some government agencies spent huge sums in excess of the appropriation voted in the legislature. In 1956 Liberal leader Georges Lapalme presented a detailed statement to the Legislative Assembly which showed that during the election year 1948–9 approximately $83,000,000 had been spent in excess of the $142,000,000 voted in the budget, and that during the election year 1952–3 expenditures had been around $61,000,000 in excess of the $261,000,000 voted.[4] These breaches of orthodox budgetary procedure were attacked continually by the opposition, but the latter was handicapped by the government's use of its control over the legislature to curb discussion and the Speaker was often partisan in the handling of debates.[5]

The Union Nationale's patronage system operated at two different levels—one individual, the other collective—that is, the party attempted to win the support not only of particular individuals, but also of whole communities, school districts, and religious institutions and organiza-

[3]*La Presse*, 18 jan. 1956.

[4]See *Le Devoir*, 8 fév. 1956. An excellent analysis of the Union Nationale's methods of financing is to be found in Roland Parenteau, "Finances provinciales, 1953," *L'Actualité Économique*, juillet-sept. 1953, pp. 343–51.

[5]The way in which Duplessis dominated the proceedings in the legislature is described in Harold H. Martin, "Quebec's Little Strong Man," *Saturday Evening Post*, Jan. 15, 1949. For examples of the partisanship of the Speaker, see reports of debates in the Assembly, *Le Devoir*, 26 fév. 1953; *Montreal Star*, Feb. 4, 1954.

tions.[6] In regard to the former group the objective was to get the backing of those key individuals in every community whose activities and interests had given them a certain pre-eminence and influence or whose occupations were of such a nature as to bring them into daily contact with large groups of people. It included doctors, lawyers, notaries, trade union leaders, salesmen, shopkeepers, mayors and municipal councillors, members of school boards, and the leaders of co-operative societies, farmers' unions, and patriotic associations. These people were important to the Union Nationale because their active support would result in blocks of voters swinging over to the party. For instance, if a mayor and a number of members of a municipal council could be induced to align themselves with the party, a good portion of the voters in that particular municipality would do likewise.

In line with this strategy, every year the administration handed out a large number of jobs, contracts, and orders to individuals in these categories, with the understanding that they would give open support to the Union Nationale. Lawyers and notaries were given some of the legal or notarial business of the various government departments, or were appointed to one of the many official boards and commissions; the leaders of rural co-operatives or farmers' organizations were offered part-time jobs or assignments by the Department of Agriculture; small retail merchants and hardware stores in every town throughout the province received orders for supplies from various government departments, in spite of the fact that such supplies could be bought more cheaply from wholesalers or manufacturers.[7] Whenever a mayor, municipal councillor, or school commissioner happened to own some kind of business establishment, he found that the government was always ready to place orders and contracts at very generous prices.

The distribution of government jobs and other favours was particularly effective in winning the support, or at least the neutrality, of

[6]Probably the best description of the Union Nationale's patronage system, as well as other aspects of its electoral machine, is to be found in a series of articles written by a reporter for Le Devoir shortly after the 1956 election. See Pierre Laporte, "Les Élections ne se font pas avec des prières," Le Devoir, 1 oct.–7 déc. 1956. These articles are well documented as Laporte gives names, places, and in many instances provides sworn affidavits from voters and election workers to support his statements. See also Gérard Dion and Louis O'Neill, Political Immorality in the Province of Quebec (Montreal, 1956); Stuart Keate, "Maurice the Magnificent," Maclean's Magazine, Sept. 1, 1948.

[7]This practice was criticized every year by the Auditor General in his report on the Public Accounts. See F. Zalloni, "De l'argent . . . oui, mais pas pour eux!" Le Devoir, 24 mars 1950.

trade union leaders. Patronage here took the form of government appointments to various boards and commissions dealing with labour matters or social welfare schemes. Until the Asbestos strike of 1949 most of these positions were given to leaders of either the Catholic unions or the Trades and Labour Congress. After 1949 only the leaders of the latter organization were looked upon favourably by the government.[8] There is little doubt that we have here one of the factors in the benevolent attitude adopted by the T.L.C. towards the Union Nationale during the greater part of the 1950's. It is also one of the reasons why the formation of a united labour front against Duplessis' party was so difficult to achieve.

Although the Union Nationale's patronage system was aimed primarily at the more influential individuals in every community, the rank and file voter was by no means neglected. His turn usually came, however, only when an election was called. Many voters were won over by being given part-time jobs building roads, government buildings, bridges, and other public works. It was a common practice for the Roads Department to move large quantities of equipment into an electoral district a few weeks before an election and busily start constructing and surfacing roads. The day after the election all work had stopped and the bulldozers, tractors, and other equipment had disappeared.[9] Where the government had no jobs to hand out individuals might be placed on the payroll of a government department for a few weeks without having to do any work at all. Just before the election of 1952 the Roads Department paid out cheques in one electoral district to a number of children between the ages of five and twelve.[10] Another practice which became widespread during the 1952 and 1956 election campaigns was to have the Department of Health pay the hospital bills of friends of the party out of a fund which was supposed to be used only for strictly indigent cases.[11] In short, the Union

[8]See Réginald Boisvert, "La Grève et le mouvement ouvrier," in P. E. Trudeau, éd., La Grève de l'amiante (Montréal, 1956), pp. 362–3.

[9]For a description of these tactics, see Jacqueline Sirois, "Beauce Battle Hotly Waged," Standard (Montreal), Nov. 17, 1945.

[10]Montreal Star, March 4, 1954. On one occasion a Liberal member of the provincial legislature was able to produce a cheque in the amount of $150.00 which had been paid by a government department to an individual who, so it was alleged, "had never done five minutes' work for the Province," Le Devoir, 26 nov. 1955.

[11]See Laporte, "Les Elections ne se font pas avec des prières," Le Devoir, 3–9 nov. 1956. Shortly after the 1956 election a Union Nationale member, acting as spokesman for the Minister of Health, admitted in a letter to a constituent that serious abuses had developed in regard to the payment of hospital bills, and that rich as well as poor had had their accounts paid by the government. For facsimile of the letter, see Le Devoir, 15 août 1956.

Nationale with the vast resources of the government at its disposal stood ready to offer some sort of benefit to almost any voter, whatever his occupation, sex, age, or particular economic interest.

In spite of the obvious advantages enjoyed by the Union Nationale through this ability to distribute patronage to thousands of voters in every electoral district, the most effective use of the taxpayer's money for the purpose of winning elections was to be found in the operation of the patronage system at the collective or group level. The main reason for its special success at this level was the unusual dependence of the municipalities, school districts, and religious institutions upon financial assistance from the provincial government. This dependence has a historical explanation.

In the past Quebec municipalities and school commissions have been expected to finance themselves from their own sources of revenue. These sources have to a large extent been limited to a tax on real estate and a sales tax. The revenue from these two taxation fields, however, is no longer adequate to provide for the varied municipal services and the extensive educational facilities required by the modern industrial community. As a result, these lower levels of government have had to depend more and more on financial assistance from the provincial government, or alternatively they have had to ask the latter to take over the responsibility of providing certain public services.

The many organizations and institutions sponsored by the Church have been faced by a similar financial problem. In Quebec the Church has always provided certain facilities, such as hospitals, homes for the aged, colleges and universities, and charitable institutions, which in other areas are usually considered the responsibility of the state. Until comparatively recently these religious institutions have been financed either by contributions from private individuals and business corporations or out of the revenues of the fairly extensive tracts of land acquired by the Church both before and after the English conquest. The demands on these institutions have multiplied so rapidly in the modern era, however, that many of them would have to curtail or discontinue their activities if they were not able to obtain additional financial assistance from the state. Successive Quebec governments going back as far as the Gouin and Taschereau régimes have recognized this need, and as a consequence have followed the practice of making special grants to these organizations from time to time.[12]

[12]It should be pointed out here that, unlike many other areas and countries, the question of state assistance to religious organizations has never been a controversial one in Quebec. Although there is no official union of Church and State

The dependence of the various municipalities, school commissions, and church organizations on the provincial government for financial assistance, or for the provision of facilities which they could no longer finance themselves, placed the Union Nationale in an excellent position to capture the support of large blocks of voters in every electoral district. In every election campaign prominent members of the party, including Duplessis himself, visited the many cities, towns, and villages throughout the province and bluntly told the voters in each community that they had to support the Union Nationale if they wanted a new road, bridge, sewage system, or a provincial grant to build a badly needed hospital or school. It was made quite clear that the failure of any community to give a majority to the party would mean that that community would be cut off from provincial grants and expenditures until the next election. In the election of 1952 Duplessis is reported as having made the following statement at a public meeting in one electoral district: "Je vous avais avertis en 1948 de ne pas élire le candidat libéral. Vous ne m'avez pas écouté. Malheureusement votre comté n'a pas obtenu les subventions, les octrois qui auraient pu le rendre plus heureux. J'espère que la leçon aura servi et que vous voterez contre le candidat libéral cette fois-ci."[13] Another illustration of the party's tactics is provided by a statement reported to have been made by the Union Nationale leader during the 1956 campaign: "If you do want government help to build the bridge, then all you have to do is to vote for Gaston Hardy [the Union Nationale candidate], because if Mr. Hardy asks for help he will get it. If on the other hand you vote for the Liberal candidate, René Hamel, then the government will respect your opinions."[14] On still another occasion when Duplessis was explaining the policy of the government in regard to grants for school commissions he stated quite frankly, "It is our principle—and I'm not hiding it—that when there are two school commissions asking for grants and one is friendly, we take care of the friends first; when there is enough to take care of opponents we do so generously without political considerations."[15]

When the administration did make a grant to some municipality or school commission, it was not sent directly to the recipient, but channelled through the Union Nationale member for the district, or

in that province, the general feeling has always been that there should be close co-operation between these two bodies rather than rigid separation. Moreover, the provincial government has always followed the practice of giving financial assistance to Protestant as well as Catholic organizations.

[13]Pierre Laporte, *Le Vrai Visage de Duplessis* (Montreal, 1960), p. 86.
[14]*Montreal Gazette*, June 13, 1956.
[15]*Ibid.*, Feb. 24, 1954.

the local dispenser of patronage. However, if it was an important grant, the cheque was handed over to the proper municipal or school official with considerable fanfare at some public meeting, either by a cabinet minister or by Duplessis himself. It was also a common practice for Union Nationale candidates to present to the electors a long list of expenditures made in their particular constituency by all government departments during the previous four years. This included even those expenditures which were completely unavoidable if the government was to provide any services at all. The purpose behind all these tactics was to impress upon the voters the wide range of benefits bestowed on them because of the generosity of the party, and to build up in the public mind the image of Duplessis as a benefactor "qui donne à sa province."

In dealing with the various church organizations seeking financial assistance the Union Nationale could not afford to be quite as blunt, nor could it expect these organizations or their leaders to align themselves openly with the party, owing to the rule laid down by the hierarchy that members of the clergy must not become directly involved in politics. However, when the government made a grant to one of the church's charitable institutions, to a youth centre, or to one of the many parochial activities, there was usually a tacit understanding that the priest or religious authority involved would discreetly let it be known to his parishioners that they should support the party which had been so generous to them.[16] Government grants were also used to exert pressure in other ways. Whenever a college or university seeking financial assistance from the government had one or two professors, or perhaps a student body, who were critical of some aspects of the Union Nationale régime, the latter was not slow to hint that grants would be forthcoming more quickly if such critics were silenced.[17] Another practice, quite common in the rural areas and small towns, was for the Roads Department to make a detour from the highway in order to pave the road and the walk leading right up to the doors of a church. This was only done, of course, in those towns and villages where the parish priest was co-operative and his parishioners voted "the right way." (In these tactics the party showed no religious discrimination. The Roads Department was just as ready to pave the road and walk leading up to a Protestant church, always

---

[16]One priest is quoted as saying, "Vote for whoever you like, but when we have a good government we keep it." Another is reported to have made the statement, "Before going to vote, don't forget to look at our nice new school." See Dion and O'Neill, *Political Immorality in the Province of Quebec*, p. 16.

[17]See Roger Lemelin, "The Silent Struggle at Laval," *Maclean's Magazine*, Aug. 1, 1952.

provided that the congregation of that church was friendly towards the party.[18])

There is little doubt that the Union Nationale's "carrot and whip" technique was highly effective. There were large numbers of voters in all parts of the province whose lack of understanding of the democratic process made them quite ready to accept the party's argument that an administration which provides public works and hands out grants and jobs is a benefactor whose generosity should be rewarded by voting it back into office. Such voters obviously failed to grasp the fact that the money a government spends comes from the taxes which the citizen pays, and that these expenditures should be based on the needs of a particular community, not its political affiliation.

Perhaps the most interesting aspect of these unorthodox tactics used by the Union Nationale was that they enabled the party to obtain a certain amount of support even from those voters who were strongly opposed to its policies and indignant at its political blackmail, but who did not want to deprive their community of some badly needed public facilities.[19] This may not have been a very heroic attitude to adopt, but it was to some extent understandable, particularly in the frontier regions of the province where communities had heavy financial charges to bear but little revenue with which to carry them.

One other aspect of the Union Nationale's ability to spend government money for partisan purposes should not be overlooked. This was the opportunity it provided the party to win the support of a good section of the daily and weekly press across the province. Many newspapers, and particularly those weeklies published in the small towns and rural areas, found it difficult to survive on the income from the sale of their papers and from commercial advertising. As a consequence, they had to find additional sources of revenue wherever they could. At this point the government was always ready to come to the rescue. For those newspapers which were willing to support the Union Nationale sizable government printing contracts were available at good prices. The various government departments from time to time had a certain amount of advertising to place in daily and weekly newspapers. In addition, the party spent huge sums of money on full-page advertisements during every election campaign. One other way in which the Union Nationale created a favourable press was by

[18]See Laporte, "Les Elections ne se font pas avec des prières," *Le Devoir*, 10 oct. 1956.

[19]When the writer visited various parts of the province during the election campaign of 1952, he found this attitude quite common among the voters in small towns and rural areas.

giving fairly generous gifts to editors, members of the legislative press gallery, and reporters covering Duplessis' electoral campaigns.[20] If we take all these factors into consideration, it is not surprising that by the 1950's the Union Nationale had the support, or at least the benevolent neutrality, of most of the large dailies in Montreal and Quebec City, and had the overwhelming support of the small weeklies throughout the province.[21]

In addition to the establishment of a patronage system which was instrumental in gaining the support of a large number of voters in different parts of the province, the Union Nationale used its control over the administration to provide itself with an adequate supply of funds to finance its election campaigns by exerting various forms of pressure on certain individuals and business concerns to contribute to the party. The need for a large campaign chest was due to the fact that even under the conditions prevailing in Quebec in Duplessis' day there still were many types of expenditure during an election which could not very well be charged up to some government department or agency. Examples of such expenditure would be the large sums of money required for advertisements in newspapers, radio and television broadcasts, the printing and distribution of leaflets and pamphlets, the hiring of scrutineers and impersonators on polling day.

The first and undoubtedly the most lucrative source of revenue for the Union Nationale was the many different companies doing business with the various government departments, including such concerns as the manufacturers of trucks, tractors, and other automotive equipment, construction companies, paint, chemical, lumber and paper companies, and the distributors of hardware and metal products. These firms did not necessarily contribute to the party out of choice, but because they had to if they wanted to get any government business. A construction company, for instance, which wanted to obtain an important contract to build a road, a bridge, or some public building, was not likely to be too successful unless it was willing to make a donation to the party. The methods used by the Union Nationale in collecting the money from all these companies had some

[20]See Keate, "Maurice the Magnificent," p. 71.

[21]In Montreal the party had the enthusiastic support of the *Star*, the *Gazette*, and *Le Matin*. *La Presse*, the French language newspaper with the largest circulation in North America, was staunchly Liberal in federal politics, but for a while during the 1950's adopted a policy of neutrality in provincial politics. *Le Devoir*, however, became increasingly hostile towards the Union Nationale after 1949. In Quebec City, the influential *L'Action Catholique* usually gave strong support to the party's policies. *Le Soleil*, a Liberal newspaper, was critical.

novel features. Whenever a government department awarded a contract or placed an order for material there was an understanding that the business concern involved would give a certain sum of money to a party representative whose name was provided by the party treasurer or the chief organizer. The amount of the money requested might be a few hundred dollars, or several thousand, depending on the size of the contract or order. This arrangement was accepted by most firms seeking government business without too much protest as they could add the amount of the "kickback" to the price of the contract or material purchased by the government. In other words, it was the taxpayer who ultimately footed the bill.[22] Moreover, construction companies which were regular contributors to party funds benefited from the fact that whenever the government made a grant to help defray the cost of building a school, a hospital, or other institution, it usually insisted that the contract be given to "a friend of the party" at a high bid.[23]

A second source of funds for the Union Nationale arose out of the wide discretionary power possessed by the administration in the granting or renewing of several thousand licences every year for the sale of beer, wine, and hard liquor. The party required every person who held a permit to sell these alcoholic beverages, whether he was the owner of a tavern, grocery store, restaurant, night club, or hotel, to make an annual contribution to the party fund.[24] The amount of the contribution was determined by the party's estimate of "what the traffic would bear." The failure of any of these establishments to "cooperate" meant the loss of their licences on one technicality or another, or the refusal of the Quebec Liquor Commission to renew the licences the following year.[25]

[22]The way in which the "kickback" system worked has been described by witnesses appearing before a Royal Commission appointed by the Lesage government shortly after it came to power in 1960. This commission was headed by Mr. Justice Elie Salvas, and was assigned the task of investigating the purchasing methods of the Duplessis administration. At the time of writing (August, 1961) no official report of the findings of the Salvas Commission has yet been published. However, all the daily newspapers in the province carried fairly complete reports of the proceedings. See in particular: *Montreal Star*, May 10, 11, 17, 25, June 21, 22, 29, 1961; *Montreal Gazette*, May 25, June 29, 30, 1961; *La Presse*, 11 mai 1961; *Le Devoir*, 30 juin 1961.

[23]See editorial, *L'Action Catholique*, 28 juin 1947.

[24]A description of these tactics is to be found in Blair Fraser, "Shakedown," *Maclean's Magazine*, Nov. 15, 1945.

[25]On one occasion when a Liberal member of the Assembly stated that tavern keepers in Quebec City had to pay the party $500.00 per year, or risk losing their licences, Duplessis replied, "It cost more when the Liberals were in power." *Montreal Star*, March 6, 1947.

Still another source of income which Duplessis' party could count on was the large corporations exploiting the natural resources of the province, such as the mining, power, timber, pulp and paper companies, and other business concerns which were the recipients of some favour from the government. It must be admitted that it is rather difficult to obtain factual and reliable evidence as to the nature and extent of the contributions from these sources, as there is no requirement in the Quebec Election Act that candidates or parties must make public the source of their funds. However, many Union Nationale officials would admit privately that some of these concerns either made a direct contribution to the party or financed the election campaigns of particular candidates. An important factor in the ability of the Union Nationale to obtain contributions from many of these industries was that their profitable operation depended upon government concessions in the way of timber-cutting rights, mining and water power rights, and exemptions from certain types of taxation. The industrialists were fully aware that if they refused to co-operate with the party, either financially or otherwise, the latter could penalize them by eliminating tax exemptions or other concessions, or by rigidly enforcing the labour laws to their disadvantage.[26]

There is little question that these various sources of revenue were extremely productive for the Union Nationale. The party never made a public appeal for funds, never took up a collection at a political meeting, had no revenue from membership fees or the sale of party literature, and yet was able to spend an estimated three to four million dollars in every election campaign.[27] This sum was undoubtedly much greater than that spent by any party in the neighbouring province of Ontario which had approximately the same number of electors. It was roughly equivalent to the amount spent by the Progressive Conservative party in the country as a whole during the federal election of

[26]On occasion Duplessis indicated his readiness to adopt drastic measures against any industrialist who dared to cross him. When the president of one of the largest pulp and paper companies in the province chose to ignore the suggestion of Duplessis that special price concessions should be granted to the company's Quebec customers, the Premier went to the trouble of having a special bill passed by the legislature doubling the valuation for tax purposes on the company's property in Quebec City. *Montreal Gazette*, Feb. 2, 1956.

[27]According to one analysis of the various types of propaganda media used by the Union Nationale in the 1956 election, the party spent around $2,000,000 on publicity alone. See Pierre Laporte, "Les Elections ne se font pas avec des prières," *Le Devoir*, 1–6 oct. 1956. As we shall see shortly, the money spent on publicity was only one of the many types of expenditure made by the party, although it was probably the costliest one. The estimate of $3,000,000 to $4,000,000 does not, therefore, appear to be too high.

1949.[28] It was probably five or six times the amount of money at the disposal of the provincial Liberal party in every election after 1944.[29]

The huge electoral fund accumulated by the Union Nationale was useful to the party in many different ways.[30] For one thing it enabled it to get its message over to every elector in a highly effective manner by using the various propaganda media to the point of saturation. During the last two or three weeks preceding every election, the Union Nationale had large full-page advertisements almost every day in all of the fifteen daily newspapers in the province. Similar advertisements were published in the approximately 175 weekly newspapers to be found in different regions and in certain sections of the larger cities. There were daily broadcasts over all of some thirty-five radio stations in the province, and in the closing days of the campaign the party almost drowned out the opposition. Posters, billboards, banners, and even neon signs were placed in prominent places in every electoral district. Tons of leaflets and pamphlets were distributed, and during the 1956 election campaign some 45,000 copies of a book outlining the accomplishments of the Union Nationale régime, and costing about $1.00 per copy, were handed out free to important individuals in each community.[31] Each one of the ninety-two Union Nationale candidates sent out at least one, sometimes two or more, letters or "manifestos," to all the electors in his district, who might number as high as eighty thousand. Hundreds of meetings were organized at which well-known speakers were paid sums of money ranging from $25 to $100 for singing the praises of the party. Overlooking nothing, the Union Nationale even distributed calendars and booklets of matches which carried a picture of Duplessis.

[28]The finances of the Progressive Conservative party are discussed in John R. Williams, *The Conservative Party of Canada: 1920–1949* (Durham, 1956), p. 143.

[29]The Liberal party claimed that it spent only $275,000 on publicity in the 1956 election. Laporte, "Les Elections ne se font pas avec des prières," *Le Devoir*, 1 oct. 1956. Although this figure is probably too low, it has been fairly obvious to anyone who has followed Quebec election campaigns since the end of World War II that the Liberals have not had anything like the financial resources of the Union Nationale.

[30]The description below of the different ways in which the Union Nationale disposed of its electoral funds is based to a considerable extent on *ibid.*, 1–8 oct. and 27–30 oct. 1956. It is also based on the experiences of the writer when he visited different parts of the province during the election campaign of 1952. For a good description of an election campaign in a rural area, see Marcel Rioux, "L'Election, vue de l'Anse-à-la-Barbe," *Cité libre*, II, 3 (déc. 1952), 47–52.

[31]In one town where a number of workers were on strike at the time of the 1956 election the party provided their families with a weekly supply of meat. Laporte, "Les Elections ne se font pas avec des prières," *Le Devoir*, 29 oct. 1956.

The party's well-filled campaign chest also enabled it to obtain the support of large numbers of voters through gifts, handouts, or other benefits. In many electoral districts youth organizations, social and athletic clubs, and parochial organizations received donations of anywhere from $200 to $2,000 from the party. Influential individuals in every community who could not be looked after by giving them a government job, commission, or contract, were sometimes given gifts of a hundred dollars or more to induce them to come out openly for the party. The smaller fry were given presents as varied as sacks of potatoes, nylon stockings, hams, bags of flour, and pairs of shoes.[31] Owners of cars were offered up to $25 for their participation in one of the innumerable parades organized through various towns. Following the good old Roman custom of providing circuses, as well as bread, the party organization offered free entertainment in many constituencies in the form of wrestling matches, night club shows, movies, band concerts, and bingo games at which handsome prizes were provided by the party candidate. These different forms of entertainment were often timed to coincide with an important mass meeting called by the Liberal party in that particular town.

The distribution of beer, whisky, and other kinds of alcoholic beverages played an important role in "softening up" the electorate in the two or three weeks immediately preceding polling day. This practice did not originate with the Union Nationale, for it had always been characteristic of Quebec elections. As in other matters, however, Duplessis' party was able to provide these inducements on a much grander scale. In the rural areas gifts of cases of beer, or bottles of whisky, were handed out in large quantities. In many towns and villages beer parties were organized at which everyone was welcome and could drink to his heart's content. In the larger cities like Montreal representatives of the party went from tavern to tavern and provided a round of drinks with the compliments of the local candidate. Union Nationale committee rooms were usually well stocked, and anyone could have a drink for the asking.[32] Sometimes one was even able to obtain his favourite brand. Thanks to the Union Nationale no one needed to go thirsty during a Quebec election campaign.

On polling day the Union Nationale was able to place paid scrutineers, or party agents, in every one of the approximately eleven thousand polls in the province. In every electoral district dozens of automobiles and taxis were hired for the purpose of bringing voters to the polls. In some districts the party paid out thousands of dollars to "telegraphers," individuals who went from poll to poll voting under

[32]*Ibid.*, 30 oct. 1956.

fictitious names. In the larger urban areas, like Montreal, squads of strong-arm men were hired to smash up the committee rooms of Liberal candidates and intimidate their supporters on their way to the polling station.[33]

The ability of the Union Nationale to make these huge expenditures in every election gave it a tremendous advantage over its opponents. The Liberal party was able to spend only a fraction of the money spent by the government party on the different types of propaganda media; it could not possibly match the tangible benefits in the way of gifts and handouts distributed by the Union Nationale; it did not have the same facilities for the protection of its interests on polling day.

As if these disadvantages were not enough, there was still another handicap faced by the opposition in its struggle with the Union Nationale. It was the fact that the latter's control over the legislature enabled it to fashion the electoral machinery along lines which would be most disadvantageous to the opposition parties.

In Quebec, as in the other Canadian provinces and at the federal level, any changes in the electoral system concerning such matters as qualifications for voting, organization of the balloting, or redistribution of seats, are brought about through a bill introduced in the legislature by the government. This means in effect that the dominant party is always in a position to make such modifications in the electoral machinery as will be to its advantage. In most of the provinces, however, as well as at Ottawa, strong sentiment has developed over the years against the government using its control over the legislature to make changes in election procedure which would be grossly unfair to the opposition parties.

This feeling that a government should adopt an attitude of fair play towards its opponents in matters concerning the electoral system has never made much headway in Quebec. If we go back to the Liberal administrations prior to 1936 we find that they seldom hesitated to use their control over the legislature to weight the electoral system against their opponents.[34] One of the most serious abuses under the Taschereau administration was the discrimination in the distribution of seats in the Assembly in favour of the rural areas, that is, of the particular areas where the Liberal party found its greatest support.[35]

[33]These tactics are described more fully later in this chapter.

[34]See, for instance, the Dillon Act passed by the Taschereau administration, supra, p. 63.

[35]See supra, p. 69.

When the Union Nationale came to power in 1936 it made a few reforms in the Quebec Election Act, but did nothing about giving the urban voters more equitable representation in the legislature. The reason for this lack of interest in redistribution was that shortly after the 1936 election the rural areas began to give the Union Nationale the same solid type of support that they had given to the Liberals in the past. The second Union Nationale administration had even less incentive to change the electoral map of the province. After the Liberals were defeated in the election of 1948, such strength as the party retained was concentrated largely in the Montreal area.[36] That area contained about a third of the population of the province, but had only one-sixth of the seats in the Assembly.[37] Any redistribution would merely strengthen the position of the Liberals.

In spite of the many handicaps under which the Liberals had to operate, the party began to revive in the early fifties, and in the election of 1952 succeeded in increasing its representation in the legislature from eight to twenty-three seats. This resurgence of the opposition party as a political force in the province apparently convinced the government that some drastic changes had to be made in the Election Act if Liberal growth was to be halted. Accordingly, a bill was put through the legislature in 1953 which provided for sweeping alterations in electoral procedure. This measure, commonly known as Bill 34, was one of the most glaring examples in the history of the province of a party using its control over the legislature for the purpose of weakening the electoral strength of a political opponent.[38]

The main characteristics of the voting procedure in Quebec elections prior to the introduction of Bill 34 may be summarized briefly. Every Canadian citizen domiciled in the province, twenty-one years of age and over, had the right to vote; a list of voters was prepared by enumerators who went from door to door in each constituency about four weeks before polling day; enumerators worked in pairs, one of them being appointed by the government party and the other by the official opposition; the enumerators gave each voter a slip which had to be brought to the poll on election day for identification purposes; only those people whose names were on the voting list had the right to vote; the organization of the polling in each electoral

[36]Six out of the eight seats won by the Liberals in the election of 1948 were in the Montreal area. See *Montreal Star*, July 29, 1948.

[37]Greater Montreal had sixteen seats out of the ninety-two in the Legislative Assembly. According to the 1951 census, the population of Greater Montreal was 1,395,400, while the population of the province was 4,055,681. Quebec, Department of Trade and Commerce, *Statistical Year Book*, 1953, pp. 61–3.

[38]See *Statutes of Quebec*, 1–2 Elizabeth II, c. 32.

district was under the supervision of a returning officer appointed by the cabinet; the returning officer appointed a deputy returning officer and a clerk for each poll in the electoral district; the deputy was appointed from a list provided by the government party organization, while the poll clerk was appointed from a list provided by the opposition.[39]

It is not proposed here to describe in detail the various aspects of Bill 34, but merely to point out a few of the more controversial changes it introduced in election procedure.[40] The first and most important of these changes was the elimination in all urban areas of the practice of enumerators working in pairs in the preparation of the voting lists.[41] Henceforth there would be only a single enumerator going from door to door in each poll, and he would be appointed by the returning officer for the district. Inasmuch as the latter official was appointed by the cabinet, and was therefore a close friend of the government, this would mean in practice that practically all enumerators would be provided by the local Union Nationale organization. Such a change in procedure left the door open to all kinds of irregularities and illegalities. The most obvious one was that the single enumerator, with no representative of the opposition to check his work, would have the sole responsibility of deciding what names were to be put on the voting lists, and what names were to be left off. He would be in a position, therefore, to eliminate the names of those people who he had reason to believe were planning to vote against the government. It is true that a person whose name had been left off the voting list could apply to the Board of Revisors in his electoral district to have it put back on. The function of this Board was to correct the lists after the enumerators had finished their work. The average urban voter, however, knew little about the technicalities of the electoral process, he usually did not bother checking the voting lists during the period of revision, and even if he had found that his name had been left off he probably would not have done anything about it.

Another important alteration in election procedure was the elimination of the restriction laid down in the original act that enumerators must not in any way become involved in the election campaign, even

[39]The Quebec Election Act, 1945 (9 Geo. VI, c. 15, and amendments thereto; 11 Geo. VI, c. 21; 15–16 Geo. VI, c. 19).

[40]For a critical analysis of the Bill, see Lorenzo Paré, editorial, *L'Action Catholique*, 20 déc. 1956.

[41]The second enumerator had been eliminated in rural electoral districts in 1945.

after they had completed their work of compiling the lists. It would now be possible for the enumerator upon the completion of his task to accept a well-paid, if temporary, job in the Union Nationale electoral organization. As an election worker he would be a great asset to the party for he would be able to place at its disposal whatever information he had picked up as an enumerator, such as the way in which certain electors planned to vote. This information would be extremely valuable on polling day, and would facilitate an abuse, common enough in the past, under which the deputy returning officer would challenge, on some technicality, the right to vote of people he believed to be against the government.

Bill 34 introduced one other amendment to the Election Act which had serious implications for the opposition party. In the past whenever a candidate had reason to believe that enumerators, deputy returning officers, or other election officials had exceeded their authority, or were guilty of irregularities, he could take immediate legal action to rectify the situation. A special clause in the revised act, however, stipulated that all these individuals, while acting in their official capacity, had immunity before the courts. This meant that where such officials were guilty of some illegal action prejudicial to the interests of a candidate the latter could do absolutely nothing about it at the time.

The favourable position in which the Union Nationale was placed through its control over the electoral machinery can be illustrated by describing the tactics of the party in the provincial election of 1956, the first election to be called after the enactment of Bill 34. This election was to be characterized by activities seldom seen before, even in a province which has always shown a considerable amount of toleration towards questionable electoral practices. Many of these practices may be directly attributed to Bill 34. Others were merely an extension and perfection of tactics followed in the past. It should also be pointed out that the irregularities outlined below were not as common in the rural districts as in Montreal and other urban areas.

The irregularities began with the preparation of the voting lists. As anticipated by the opponents of Bill 34, the single enumerator appointed from the Union Nationale organization used his official position to promote the interests of the party. In strongly Liberal areas dozens of voters might be left off the voting lists in a single poll.[42] There were apartment buildings and whole streets where the

---

[42]At an air force base just outside Montreal where the men were known to be strongly Liberal no enumeration was taken. As a result approximately five hundred voters were denied the right to vote. Laporte, "Les Élections ne se font pas avec des prières," Le Devoir, 23 nov. 1956.

people never saw an enumerator. At the same time the lists were padded with fictitious names, and with the names of voters who had left the district or who had died. Even the names of children between the ages of two and six were sometimes listed.[43] In several electoral districts the enumerators turned their lists over to a Union Nationale organizer who in turn was supposed to deliver them to the returning office.[44] This gave the party organization an opportunity for unofficial revision. In addition to their official work, enumerators often asked questions concerning the party affiliation of voters, suggested to the voters how they should cast their ballot, and distributed party literature.

The abuses which characterized the preparation of the voting lists were followed by even more serious irregularities on polling day. Impersonation, or telegraphing, was carried out on a large scale, particularly in Montreal.[45] The telegraphers used the fictitious names, the names of dead people, and others illegally added to the lists by the enumerators. In certain districts where the election was likely to be close the party organization was willing to pay voters from $5.00 to $10.00 for their voting slips, as the possession of such slips facilitated impersonation. There was little doubt that large numbers of blank ballots had found their way into the hands of the Union Nationale organization several days before the election. In one electoral district a number of men dumped three hundred ballots already marked in favour of a Union Nationale candidate into a sewer in an attempt to get rid of them before the arrival of the police.[46] In some cases where ballot boxes were carefully inspected on the morning of the election they were found to contain ballots already marked for the Union Nationale candidate.[47]

Another practice which was fairly common in polls which were known to be strongly Liberal was for the deputy returning officer to

---

[43]In the electoral district of Quebec County, for instance. *Ibid.*, 12 oct. 1956.

[44]In the electoral district of Montreal-Jeanne Mance practically all of the enumerators turned their lists over to the local Union Nationale headquarters for "transcribing" before they were handed in to the proper authorities. *Montreal Gazette*, May 19, 1956.

[45]For a description of the operations of the Union Nationale electoral machine in the Montreal area, see René Montpetit and G.-R. Côté, "La Police municipale a fait échec à de nombreux coups de force," *La Presse*, 21 juin 1956; also Laporte, "Les Elections ne se font pas avec des prières," *Le Devoir*, 13, 16, 24 nov., 4 déc. 1956.

[46]See Montpetit and Côté, "La Police municipale a fait échec à de nombreux coups de force." For other cases of a similar kind, see Laporte, "Les Elections ne se font pas avec des prières," *Le Devoir*, 14 nov. 1956.

[47]This happened in the electoral district of Chambly. *Ibid.*, 20 nov. 1956.

invalidate dozens of ballots by neglecting to initial them properly.[48] Many voters whose names had originally been on the voting list arrived at the poll only to find that they had been taken off for some technical reason.[49] In at least one electoral district the ballot boxes were turned over at the end of the day to Union Nationale workers who delivered them a short while later to the central returning office.[50] Some ballot boxes disappeared altogether after the polling.

The Union Nationale electoral machine also resorted to more direct and drastic tactics. In a number of constituencies in the east end of Montreal squads of strong-arm men drove around in automobiles intimidating voters and smashing up Liberal committee rooms.[51] In one constituency they entered a number of polls armed with guns and stuffed the ballot boxes with ballots for the government candidate, or took the boxes away with them and returned them some time later.[52] Strangely enough some of the ballots which were stuffed in the boxes were found to be properly initialed by the deputy returning officer for that poll.[53]

Although the representatives of the Liberal candidate in each poll were sometimes successful in preventing irregularities of the nature being described, it was almost impossible to control the situation. Many of these representatives were housewives and other political amateurs whose main concern was making a few extra dollars for the day. They had no knowledge of the detailed procedure and technical aspects of an election and were easily hoodwinked and intimidated by the deputy returning officer in charge of the poll. Some of these representatives, for instance, were easily lured away on the pretext that they were needed immediately at Liberal headquarters.

It would be impossible to say with any precision just how many seats the Liberals lost in the election of 1956 owing to the activities of Duplessis' electoral machine. There were, however, about half a dozen urban constituencies, and also a few rural ones, where the party lost by a very narrow margin and probably should have won. In

[48]According to one Liberal party official this practice was widespread in the electoral district of St. Maurice, a district where the Union Nationale was particularly determined to defeat the opposition candidate. *Le Devoir*, 30 juin 1956.

[49]This happened to the provincial leader of the Social Democratic (C.C.F.) party. *Montreal Star*, June 20, 1956.

[50]This was the electoral district of Jonquière-Kénogami, *Le Devoir*, 30 juin 1956.

[51]*Montreal Star*, June 20, 1956.

[52]This was the electoral district of Montreal-Laurier. Laporte, "Les Elections ne se font pas avec des prières," *Le Devoir*, 16, 17, 19 nov. 1956.

[53]*Ibid.*

another half dozen urban seats where the Liberals should have been easy victors they just managed to squeeze through.

At this point one might ask why those Liberal candidates whose victory had been snatched from them through such questionable methods did not contest the election before the courts as they had every right to do. The answer lies in the fact that, just before the enactment of Bill 34, the Union Nationale had put another bill through the legislature which placed election contestation cases under the jurisdiction of the Magistrates Court, rather than the Superior Court, as heretofore.[54] The judges in the Superior Court are appointed by the federal cabinet, but the judges in the Magistrates Court are appointed by the provincial government, and such appointments were usually made from members of the legal profession who were close to the Union Nationale party. Defeated candidates saw little point in contesting elections under these circumstances. The following statement made by an unsuccessful Liberal candidate is revealing:

Si les causes en contestation d'élections étaient entendues devant un juge de la Cour supérieure, j'aurais contesté immédiatement. Mais je n'irai certainement pas risquer $5,000 ou $10,000 devant la Cour de magistrat. Les juges de cette cour sont nommés par M. Duplessis; je n'ai aucune confiance en eux.[55]

Such were the handicaps faced by the Liberal opposition in the closing years of the Duplessis administration.

[54]See Statutes of Quebec, 1–2 Elizabeth II, c. 31 (1953).

[55]Laporte, "Les Élections ne se font pas avec des prières," Le Devoir, 7 déc. 1956.

CHAPTER VIII

The Growth of Opposition
to the Union Nationale

THE ELECTION OF 1956 was Duplessis' last victory. In September, 1959, on a tour of northern Quebec, the Union Nationale leader suffered a heart attack and died shortly afterwards. In the election of the following year the Union Nationale was defeated by a narrow margin of seats and the Liberals were returned to power after sixteen years in the political wilderness.

Although the death of Duplessis less than a year before the election of 1960 was certainly a factor in the defeat of the Union Nationale, this single incident does not provide anything like a complete explanation of the victory of the Liberals. The loss of a party leader, even one who dominated his party as Duplessis did, does not usually result in disaster for that party unless political conditions are ripe for such a development and there is a strong opposition party ready to take over. As we shall see, conditions were indeed approaching this readiness and it is quite possible that the Union Nationale would have been defeated even if Duplessis had not died.

In seeking a fuller explanation of the defeat of the Union Nationale in 1960 two aspects of the political situation in Quebec in the 1950's warrant analysis: the gradual development of strong opposition to the Union Nationale's policies from a number of economic, religious, and political groups within the province; and the nature of the policies and strategy of the Liberal party which enabled it to capture the support of these discontented elements in the Quebec electorate.

The various groups whose opposition to the Union Nationale was to play a leading role in the ultimate defeat of that party fall into four categories: a small but influential group of radical nationalists; the greater part of the trade union movement; important sections of the Roman Catholic Church; and two minor political movements, the Union des Electeurs and La Ligue d'Action Civique. In most cases this opposition can be traced back to the 1940's; in other words, dissatisfaction with the policies of the Union Nationale had been slowly developing even while the party was winning its most spectacular electoral victories.

THE RADICAL NATIONALISTS

When Duplessis eliminated the left wing of the Union Nationale in 1936 and transformed it into a party of conservative nationalism, he weakened considerably but did not destroy radical nationalism as a force in Quebec politics. On the contrary, during the whole period from 1936 onward there always were a number of individuals and groups who were as nationalistic as Duplessis but were radical in their ideas concerning economic and social reform. As a consequence, they were opposed to the economic conservatism of the Union Nationale and its alliance with the industrialists, although they agreed with the party's policy on the issues of the war and provincial autonomy. On several occasions during the 1930's and 1940's these left-wing nationalists launched political movements which, even if they were not very successful, did help to keep the radical tradition alive as an alternative to the Union Nationale's conservative brand of nationalism.

The most ambitious attempt to organize a political party which would bring together all radical nationalists was the formation of the Bloc Populaire in 1942. It included Paul Gouin, René Chaloult, Dr. Philippe Hamel, and other left-wing nationalists who had been associated with the Union Nationale before Duplessis captured the party; a small group of federal Liberals who had broken with their party over the conscription issue; and a third group of young nationalists who had hitherto taken no active part in politics and whose leader was André Laurendeau, editor of the review *L'Action Nationale*. The policies of the Bloc Populaire combined opposition to the war and to federal centralization with a programme of economic and social reform based on the papal encyclicals and similar in many respects to the Action Libérale Nationale proposals of the early thirties. The programme stressed the importance of destroying "la dictature économique" resulting from the control exercised over the wealth and natural resources of the province by foreign capital. This was to be accomplished mainly through extensive government regulation of the larger industrial enterprises, the development of the co-operative movement, and strong encouragement and assistance from the government for small-scale French-Canadian business enterprises. Certain trusts, such as the electric power, gas, and telephone companies, would be nationalized. Special attention would be given to the rural sector of the economy. The government would expand its colonization programme, extend rural electrification, and provide more adequate credit facilities for farmers. The Bloc Populaire further advocated the introduction of family allowances, action to eliminate slums, and the enactment of labour legislation which would strengthen the economic position of the industrial worker.[1]

Although the Bloc Populaire won a certain amount of support, particularly among the youth of the province, during the first few years of its existence, it was not successful in dislodging the Union Nationale as the outstanding exponent of the nationalist ideology. It waged a vigorous campaign in the provincial election of 1944, but won only four out of the ninety-one seats in the legislature. It did, however, succeed in polling around 15 per cent of the popular vote,[2] and showed considerable strength in certain areas such as the Eastern Townships, the Lac St. Jean and Abitibi regions, the St. Maurice industrial region, the northeastern section of Montreal, and some of the industrial towns surrounding that city. Shortly after the end of the war the Bloc began to disintegrate owing to internal dissensions, shortage of funds, and lack of political experience among its leaders. Its disappearance from the Quebec political scene again left the Union Nationale as the only important nationalist party in the field.

The rise and fall of the Bloc Populaire was nevertheless a significant development in the political history of Quebec. Although the party broke up, its supporters continued to represent sizable pockets of discontent in those areas where it had been particularly strong, and in later years many of its leading figures were to take an active part in various organizations and political movements opposed to the Union Nationale.[3]

[1] See Maxime Raymond in *Programme provincial du Bloc* (Montreal, 1943).

[2] Canadian Press figures, *Montreal Gazette*, Aug. 17, 1944.

[3] André Laurendeau, provincial leader of the Bloc, became one of the editors of *Le Devoir*; and thus assumed a key post; Jean Drapeau, a Bloc candidate in 1944 for one of the Montreal constituencies, became leader of La Ligue d'Action Civique and eventually mayor of Montreal; Michel Chartrand, a party organizer, became provincial leader of the Social Democratic (C.C.F.) party; René Hamel and Emilien Lafrance joined the Liberals and were appointed to the cabinet of Premier Lesage after his victory in 1960.

For several years after the disappearance of the Bloc Populaire very little was heard in Quebec about radical nationalism, either as an ideology or as a political force. This situation began to change slowly in the early fifties, however, with the appearance of a new school of nationalist thought whose adherents called themselves "social nationalists," or sometimes, "independent nationalists," but who were in the radical nationalist tradition as it has been described here. Like La Ligue d'Action Française in the 1920's, the social nationalists did not constitute an organized mass movement, much less a political party. They were rather an *élite*, drawn largely from the intelligentsia, whose only bond was a common approach to the problems facing French Canada in the mid-twentieth century. A few of the more important figures in this group, such as André Laurendeau and René Chaloult, had been active in politics at one time or another: Laurendeau had been provincial leader of the Bloc Populaire; Chaloult had run as an independent nationalist with Union Nationale support in the elections of 1948 and 1952, but had broken with Duplessis' party shortly after the latter election. Most of the social nationalists, however, were young intellectuals who had never been affiliated with any political party.

This new school of nationalist thought found some support in the Catholic unions, among university students and other youth groups, and among the younger members of the clergy and of La Ligue d'Action Nationale. It appeared to have the blessing of Abbé Groulx, the outstanding theoretician of Quebec nationalism in an earlier day but now retired from public life.[4] The rallying point and most aggressive exponent of social nationalism was Montreal's *Le Devoir*.

The social nationalists were in full agreement with the Union Nationale's opposition to the federal government's monopolization of tax revenue and invasion of the provincial field of social legislation. They had become convinced, however, that the cultural survival of the French Canadian faced as serious a threat from Duplessis' economic and social policies as from the federal policy of centralization. For this group the problems confronting the people of Quebec in the mature industrialized economy of the 1950's called for a new nationalist ideology which would place the emphasis on the social question. The French Canadians must regain control over the wealth and natural resources of their province, and raise their incomes and standards of living through the introduction of economic and social

[4]See interview given by Groulx to a reporter of *Le Devoir*, 25 avril 1957.

reforms. In the words of René Chaloult, "L'indépendance politique est une utopie sans l'indépendance économique."[5]

Like previous radical nationalist movements such as the Bloc Populaire, the specific measures proposed by the social nationalists for the economic emancipation of the French Canadian found most of their inspiration in the Catholic social thought of postwar western Europe.[6] Their ideas differed from those of earlier radical nationalist movements, however, in several important respects. There was no longer any nostalgia for the old rural society and all suggestions for a return to the land had disappeared. In contrast to the Bloc Populaire, greater emphasis was placed on the necessity of introducing legislation which would provide more adequate protection to the urban worker in his right to organize, to bargain collectively, and to strike. Much more consideration was given to the various forms of social legislation, the contention being that federal invasion of this particular field in the past had been due to the inadequacy of provincial legislation. It was particularly significant that the old emphasis on the desirability of fostering the growth of small-scale French-Canadian business enterprises had been discarded. Public ownership also played a more important part in the proposals of the social nationalists, and some of them went so far as to suggest that the government take over all public utilities and natural resources of the province. This was a much wider interpretation than had usually been given in Quebec to the directive in the encyclical *Quadragesimo Anno* of Pope Pius XI which stated, "certain forms of property must be reserved to the state, since they carry with them an opportunity of domination too great to be left to private individuals without injury to the community at large."[7]

The social nationalists differed from earlier radical nationalists in still one other important respect. They were deeply concerned about the proper functioning of democratic institutions and were aroused over the electoral abuses, misuse of public funds, breaches of the spirit of parliamentary procedure, and other practices characteristic of the Union Nationale administration.

[5]*Le Devoir*, 12 mars 1956.

[6]The ideas of this new school of nationalist thought are to be found here and there in articles published by various individuals. See editorial, *Le Devoir*, 27 juin 1953; Jean-Paul Robillard, "Pour un nationalisme social," *L'Action Nationale*, XXXI, 4 (avril 1948), 284–96; Gérard Dion and Joseph Pelchat, "Repenser le nationalisme," *L'Action Nationale*, XXXI, 6 (juin 1948), 403–12; Jean-Marc Léger, "Aspects of French-Canadian Nationalism," *University of Toronto Quarterly*, XXVII, 3 (April, 1958), 310–29.

[7]Pius XI, *Quadragesimo Anno* (London, 1931), p. 51.

Although the social nationalists were small in numbers, the fact that they combined social reform with nationalism made them the most dangerous opponents on the ideological level with which the Union Nationale had to contend. Duplessis fully realized the nature of this threat for his most bitter denunciations and most biting invectives were aimed, not at the Liberals or the Social Democratic (C.C.F.) party, but at *Le Devoir*, the voice of the social nationalists. In one speech delivered in the legislature he referred to it with the strongest epithet in his vocabulary: "*Le Devoir* est un journal bolsheviste."[8] The role of these nationalists amidst the growing opposition to the Duplessis administration in the 1950's was to provide the arguments, the ammunition which other groups as well could use to attack the Union Nationale régime.

THE TRADE UNION MOVEMENT

In chapter v the conflict which developed in the late forties between the Union Nationale and the trade unions was described in some detail. A later chapter pointed out that while the top leadership and a certain portion of the membership of the unions affiliated with the Canadian Congress of Labour and with the Confédération des Travailleurs Catholiques du Canada were strongly anti-Union Nationale,[9] the largest trade union movement in Quebec, the Trades and Labour Congress, was favourable towards the party. As a result of this split in the ranks of organized labour it was difficult for it to present any kind of united front to the Duplessis régime.

Shortly after the 1956 election the Union Nationale began to find it increasingly difficult to play off one union against another and to get trade union leaders to support the party openly. The most important reason for this new development was the national merger of the Trades and Labour Congress of Canada and the Canadian Congress of Labour in 1956 to form the Canadian Labour Congress. In Quebec all trade unions formerly affiliated with the T.L.C. and the C.C.L. were united into the Quebec Federation of Labour (Q.F.L.), and negotiations were entered into with the Catholic unions with a view to bringing them into the C.L.C. and thus establishing a completely unified labour movement.

In its demands for social legislation and in its criticisms of the government's labour policies the Quebec Federation of Labour soon

[8]*Le Devoir*, 14 jan. 1954.
[9]See *supra*, pp. 121–3.

showed a militancy which was not to be found in the old T.L.C. This militancy was to some extent due to the inclusion of the old C.C.L. unions which had always been aggressive labour organizations. However, there was also a changed attitude on the part of those trade unions which had formerly been affiliated with the T.L.C. A number of the leaders of these trade unions, who had supported the Union Nationale in the past, or at least had not actively opposed it, had finally become disillusioned with that party's economic and labour policies. The most persuasive factor, however, in turning the Q.F.L. into a bitter foe of the Duplessis administration was the way in which the latter handled a strike which broke out in 1957 in a mining town in the Gaspé peninsula called Murdochville. This strike was to turn into the most serious industrial conflict that the province had seen since the Asbestos strike of 1949.[10]

The Murdochville strike involved the Gaspé Copper Mines Ltd. and the United Steel Workers of America, an affiliate of the C.L.C. The U.S.W.A. had begun to organize the workers at Gaspé Copper in 1952. These organizational activities were carried out under difficult conditions for the company was determined to keep the union out of the mines. However, an investigation made by the Labour Relations Board in 1956 showed that around 80 per cent of the workers had been signed up by the union. The latter thereupon filed an application with the Board requesting certification as official bargaining agent for the workers. The company succeeded in blocking all certification proceedings, however, by obtaining a writ of prohibition against the Board on a legal technicality. In March, 1957, the company fired the president of the U.S.W.A. local and a number of other employees who were key men in the union. A few days later the union called the men out on strike.

From the very beginning of the strike the miners at Murdochville had the solid support of the trade union movement in Quebec, for the Catholic unions supported the strikers just as strongly as the Q.F.L. Shortly after the strike began Claude Jodoin, president of the C.L.C., and Roger Provost, president of the Q.F.L., wrote letters to Duplessis requesting that he intervene in order to bring about a quick settlement of the dispute. Similar requests were made to the government by municipal councillors, mayors, school commissioners,

[10]A description of the various developments in the strike is to be found in *Montreal Gazette*, May 24, Aug. 20, 27, 1957; *Montreal Star*, Aug. 20, 1957; *Le Devoir*, 17, 26 août 1957; *Le Social Démocrate* (Montréal), août 1957. The latter gives the most detailed account of the strike, but is biased in favour of the trade unions. For the company point of view, see its advertisement, *Montreal Gazette*, Aug. 23, 1957.

and parish priests in the Gaspé region, and by the Gaspé section of the Union Catholique des Cultivateurs. All these requests were ignored by the Prime Minister, the Minister of Labour, and other members of the government. The administration adopted the same position as that of the company. It contended that inasmuch as the union was not certified as bargaining agent, the strike was illegal, and the strikers should therefore return to work.

As the strike dragged on through the summer of 1957 the antagonism between the company and the strikers increased and there were sporadic acts of violence on both sides, including the dynamiting of some company installations by the strikers. The bitterness of the trade unionists towards the company became especially strong with the decision of the latter to bring in workers from other parts of the province and from Ontario to take over the strikers' jobs. Around the middle of August the strikers began to find themselves in a precarious financial position with no end of the strike in sight. At this point the leaders of the various sections of the Quebec trade union movement decided to organize a "march on Murdochville" as an indication of their solidarity with the men on strike, and in the hope of arousing public opinion in the province over their serious plight. The march on Murdochville consisted of a motorcade of three buses and seventy carloads of trade unionists who converged on the town from various parts of the province. It was led by such prominent labour leaders as Claude Jodoin of the C.L.C. and Gérard Picard of the C.T.C.C.

The arrival of the motorcade in Murdochville was the signal for an outbreak of violence reminiscent of the Asbestos strike. When the trade unionists set up a picket line in front of the company property, the men who had been hired by the mine to replace the strikers attacked the pickets with heavy stones and several of them were injured. A pitched battle then took place between the opposing groups until the provincial police on the scene finally decided to intervene. Later the same day the non-striking employees of the mine ran wild in the streets of the town, ransacking the office of the U.S.W.A. local, turning over any cars they could find belonging to trade unionists, slashing tires and destroying upholstery. The mayor of Murdochville imposed a curfew on the town and threatened to read the Riot Act if there was any further violence. Mr. Jodoin sent a telegram to Duplessis in which he lodged a strong protest against the attacks on the trade unionists, and accused the provincial police of idly standing by while the attacks were being made. The most important effect of Murdochville's day of violence was that Duplessis finally

decided to intervene in the strike and attempt to bring about a settlement. Shortly afterwards the strikers went back to work even though
they had not succeeded in their original aim of getting the U.S.W.A.
recognized as official bargaining agent.

The dilatory way in which the provincial government responded to
the Murdochville strike was not the only reason for the growing
antagonism between Duplessis and the Q.F.L. The latter organization
was also aroused over the government's consistent refusal to give
serious consideration to its recommendations concerning unemployment, education, and health insurance. The general attitude of the
Q.F.L. towards the Duplessis régime was expressed in a statement
issued during its 1958 convention which accused the government of
favouring management consistently:

> Dans notre province, le gouvernement est carrément favorable à la cause
> du patronat et tolère à peine le syndicalisme. . . . Le premier ministre n'a
> reconnu le bien-fondé d'aucune requête et a mis en doute la véracité de
> nos assertions.[11]

This attitude of the Q.F.L., coupled with the consistent opposition of
the C.T.C.C. unions to the Union Nationale administration, meant
that by the time Duplessis died in 1959 the Quebec trade union movement was more solidly united in its opposition to his party than it had
been at any other time since 1949.

THE ROMAN CATHOLIC CHURCH

A third source of opposition to the Union Nationale party was found
in certain sections of the Roman Catholic Church. A word of caution
is in order here. In the description which follows of the attitude of the
Church, the reference on any given matter is usually to a trend or
prevailing current of opinion within that body rather than to a hard
and fast attitude on which the whole clergy is in agreement. The
reason is that, although all members of the Church adhere to the
same basic theological and philosophical doctrines, there may be
wide differences of opinion, either within the hierarchy or between the
hierarchy and the lower clergy, on specific economic, social, and
political questions. Like other organizations, the Church has its right
and left wings, its conservatives and its radicals, as well as a good
number of members, the "neutralists," who have no strong opinion one
way or the other on a given question.[12]

[11]*Le Devoir*, 21 nov. 1958.
[12]The position of the Church in Quebec is similar to that of the Church in
France as described by a well-known French political scientist: "Des esprits peu
familiers des réalités ou des institutions religieuses s'imaginent parfois l'Eglise

Until about 1949, the year of the Asbestos strike, the Church in Quebec was on fairly friendly terms with the Union Nationale régime. In one respect this was not surprising, for it had been the policy of the hierarchy, at least since the turn of the century, to co-operate with the party which happened to be in power, whatever its political complexion. The ties between the Church and Duplessis' régime were strengthened, however, by the Union Nationale's policy of opposition to federal centralization and by its war on communism.

After 1949 these close relations between the Church and the pro-vincial administration began to deteriorate and there were some sharp clashes between Duplessis and the hierarchy. A strong opposition developed among a large section of both the higher and the lower clergy towards the Union Nationale's policies in three different areas: the party's ultra-conservative economic and social policies, and its hostile attitude towards the trade unions; the administrative and electoral abuses which characterized the Duplessis régime, and the widespread "political immorality" it had fostered; the attempts of the party to increase its influence and even gain control over the Church's charitable and educational institutions.

The attitude of the Church in Quebec on the social question had passed through several stages since the early 1930's. During the first stage there had been a shift to the left in social thinking and some attempt had been made to come to grips with the problems of an industrial civilization, although the nostalgia for a return to the old rural society was still very strong. This leftward trend had expressed itself in the programme of social reform put forward by the Ecole Sociale Populaire in 1933.[13] However, about 1936 the Church as a whole had turned back to its more conservative views in social matters. The most important factor in this retreat was the world-wide ideological conflict which grew out of the Spanish Civil War, and the fear which that conflict had aroused in Church circles over the spread of the "atheistic doctrines" of communism and socialism. The third stage, and the one we are particularly concerned with here, began around the end of World War II when a turn to the left once more took place in the attitude of important sections of the clergy.

There were a number of factors responsible for this most recent change in the Church's approach to the social problem. One was that,

comme une grande armée, manœuvrant avec ensemble, et n'ayant qu'une pensée: la réalité est moins sommaire. Le catholicisme, en France tout au moins, est un monde aux multiples nuances de pensée. . . ." René Rémond, "La Fin de la Troisième République," *Revue française de science politique*, VII, 2 (avril-juin 1957), 269.

[13]See *supra*, pp. 56–7.

like the social nationalists, many of the Quebec clergy had come under the influence of the more radical Catholic social thought of postwar western Europe.[14] Another was the steady pressure from the Catholic trade unions, engaged in a struggle for survival with the international unions, and increasingly insistent that the Church take a more positive stand in the defence of the interests of the working class. There was also the fact that a growing number of priests came now from an urban rather than a rural background and had a better understanding of the problems of the urban masses.

This new orientation in the social thinking of the Church made it more sympathetic to the grievances and demands of the working class and at the same time more critical of the Union Nationale's economic and labour policies. When Duplessis proposed his famous labour code in 1949, as part of his campaign against the trade unions, the hierarchy criticized certain aspects of it as "contrary to social justice," and Duplessis felt compelled to withdraw it.[15] During the Asbestos strike of the same year the bishops resisted government pressure to have "certain priests" silenced for their support of the strikers and instead ordered special collections taken up in all parish churches for the purpose of helping the families of the men on strike. The total amount of money collected in the twelve dioceses of the province was over $167,000.00.[16] The action taken by the bishops in support of the strikers was denounced by the government as "church interference," and according to one report, Premier Duplessis went so far as to make an unsuccessful attempt to have one of the bishops take the matter up with the Vatican in the hope that the latter would compel the Quebec hierarchy to withdraw from the whole affair.[17]

Perhaps the clearest evidence of the change taking place in the attitude of the Church on the labour question was to be found in a

[14]See the joint letter issued by the French cardinals in 1949 which not only condemned the Communist movement, but also attacked the abuses of capitalism and called for a reform of "social structures," La Croix (Paris), 15 sept. 1949.

[15]See supra, p. 93.

[16]The role of the Church in the Asbestos strike is described in Gérard Dion, "L'Eglise et le conflit de l'amiante," in P. E. Trudeau, éd., La Grève de l'amiante (Montréal, 1956), pp. 239–62.

[17]The source of this report was the Montreal English Catholic weekly, The Ensign, May 21, 1949. There has been some disagreement as to whether Duplessis was as unsuccessful as this report would indicate. About half a year after the events we have been describing, Archbishop Charbonneau of Montreal, who had played a leading role in support of the strikers at Asbestos, resigned from his office "for reasons of health." There has always been a widespread belief among trade unionists and other groups that the Archbishop did not resign voluntarily but was relieved of his duties by the Vatican because of the displeasure of the Quebec government over his stand on the Asbestos strike. Although there is a good deal of evidence to support the view that Charbonneau did have to yield

pastoral letter issued by the bishops in 1950 and entitled, *Le Problème ouvrier en regard de la doctrine sociale de l'Eglise*.[18] This letter was the most important pronouncement made by the hierarchy on this particular subject since the beginning of Quebec's industrial revolution. Its basic theme was that, in spite of the improvement in economic conditions since the 1930's, the wealth and resources of the province were still far from being equitably distributed, and large numbers of workers lacked economic security and proper housing conditions. The letter outlined in detail the various measures which should be taken to remedy the situation. Many of these proposals had been put forward in previous statements of the hierarchy: the payment of "a just wage" by industry; better hygienic conditions in factories; more effective legislation to protect the stability and economic security of the family; the promotion of co-operatives of various kinds. There were, however, three aspects of the letter which had a new and impressive emphasis. One was the recognition that the workers had not only the right, but actually the duty to organize into trade unions for the purpose of bargaining collectively with their employers and thus raising their economic status. On this particular point of collective bargaining the bishops indirectly criticized the inadequacy of the guarantees provided the workers in existing provincial legislation. The second major point, and the most radical aspect of the pastoral letter, was the official sanction which it gave to the demands of the Catholic unions that the structure of private enterprise be gradually reformed so that the workers would participate in the management, profits, and ownership of the industry in which they worked.[19] Finally, the

---

to pressure from the Vatican, it nevertheless seems likely that the main reason for this action on the part of the Church authorities was the deep personal antagonism existing between Duplessis and the Archbishop rather than the latter's social views. Bishop Desranleau of Sherbrooke, a strong critic of industrial capitalism and of the government's labour policies and the real radical among the hierarchy, was not compelled to resign. On the contrary, he was raised to the office of Archbishop about a year after the strike. Moreover, the pastoral letter issued by the bishops in 1950 on the labour question, described below, would hardly seem to indicate that the Vatican had placed restraints on the freedom of the Quebec hierarchy to criticize the capitalist system. A good description of the various aspects of "the Charbonneau affair" is to be found in, "Mgr. Charbonneau et l'opinion publique dans l'Eglise," *Cité Libre*, jan.-fév. 1960, 3–7.

18(Québec: Service extérieur d'éducation sociale, Université Laval, 1950). The letter was praised by the Vatican authorities and translated into English, Italian, Spanish, and Dutch. See Dion, "L'Eglise et le conflit de l'amiante," pp. 261–2.

19These ideas of the Catholic unions are discussed *supra*, pp. 89–90. Here is a good illustration of the extent of the influence which the Catholic trade unions and some of the lower clergy were able to exert on the hierarchy. In spite of the Church's formal organizational structure with authority flowing downward from the bishop to the priest to the layman, it is obvious that the hierarchy cannot altogether ignore strong pressures from below.

bishops' statement indicated that they had at last abandoned their old ideas in regard to a return to the land and had accepted the fact that the industrialization of the province was irreversible.

The publication of the bishops' pastoral letter widened the rift between the leaders of the Church and the Duplessis government. Antonio Barrette, Minister of Labour, in an obvious reference to the recommendations of the bishops, stated in the legislature: "It is here in the Province of Quebec that true social and Christian justice finds its application. We give lessons, and let no one give us any."[20] Duplessis for his part commented some while later in regard to the proposals for profit sharing, "Unless there is sharing in the debts and losses, there can be no share in benefits. That is common sense."[21]

One of the most significant aspects of the pastoral letter was the indirect support it gave to those members of the lower clergy whose interest in economic and social reform had made them critical of Union Nationale policies. After the publication of the letter these critics became considerably more vocal. The most outspoken attacks on government policy came from members of the Faculty of Social Sciences at Church-controlled Laval University. The Dean of that faculty at the time was Rev. Georges H. Levesque, a prominent member of the Dominican Order, whose social views were diametrically opposed to those of the provincial administration.[22] A second source of opposition was the monthly review, *Relations*, published by the Jesuit Order in Montreal. Although the French-Canadian Jesuits had usually been associated with the conservative wing of the Church in Quebec, in the late 1950's *Relations* began to publish articles attacking the Union Nationale for its handling of labour disputes and accused the party of consistently favouring the interests of the employer.[23] The author of a good many of these articles, Father Jacques Cousineau, was labelled a "Bolshevist" by Duplessis.[24]

In addition to being dissatisfied with Duplessis' economic and social policies, many of the hierarchy and lower clergy were also aroused over the electoral abuses and widespread "political immorality" which had characterized Quebec politics since the Union Nationale returned

[20]*Montreal Star*, March 23, 1950.

[21]*Ibid.*, Nov. 6, 1952.

[22]In regard to the conflict between the Faculty of Social Sciences at Laval and the administration, see Roger Lemelin, "The Silent Struggle at Laval," *Maclean's Magazine*, Aug. 1, 1952.

[23]See, for instance, editorial, *Relations*, no 198, (juin 1957), 141–2; also Jacques Cousineau, S.J., "Une Modèle de règlement de grève," in *Relations*, no 200, (août 1957), 208–9.

[24]*Montreal Star*, Jan. 25, 1958.

to power in 1944. While recognizing that there had always been a considerable amount of political corruption in the past, they were alarmed at the extent to which such practices as impersonation of voters, false oaths, dishonest tactics of election officials, and misuse of public funds had become a commonplace under the Duplessis régime. That régime was held largely responsible for the fact that many of the people of Quebec had come to adopt a standard of morality in political matters which was entirely different from the one which they followed in private life. It was observed that a large number of voters, who in everyday life were honest and law-abiding and adhered to rigid moral principles, accepted with complacency these different forms of electoral corruption and were quite ready to sell their vote for a government job, the payment of their hospital bills, or the promise of a new school building in their community.

The Union Nationale was also held responsible for the rapid growth of the drinking problem and the spread of alcoholism. This was attributed to the readiness of the party to hand out liquor licences to its friends and financial supporters, with the result that taverns, cabarets, night clubs, and cafés mushroomed in all parts of the province. The régime was criticized for the policy of "toleration" pursued by the provincial police which permitted these establishments to remain open many hours after the closing time decreed by law.

These strong feelings on the part of the clergy towards the administrative and electoral abuses of the Union Nationale administration found dramatic expression shortly after the 1956 election when two priests connected with Laval University, Fathers Gérard Dion and Louis O'Neill, published a pamphlet entitled *L'Immoralité politique dans la province de Québec*, and in the English version, *Political Immorality in the Province of Quebec*.[25] This document was a sharp indictment of political practices in the province and outlined in detail the nature of the threats, false accusations, impersonation of voters, and dishonesty of election officials which had characterized the 1956 election. Although the two priests did not mention any specific party, there was little doubt that their attack was directed primarily at the activities of the Union Nationale.

The appearance of the priests' pamphlet created a sensation throughout the province and it received widespread publicity in the press. Duplessis and his colleagues, obviously embarrassed, made no

25(Montreal, 1956). Although this document could not be considered an official statement of the Church in Quebec, the fact that it was not repudiated by any member of the hierarchy was a fairly good indication that the latter were in agreement with the views expressed therein.

comment and simply ignored the priests' accusations, no doubt hoping that the whole affair would soon blow over. Instead the Dion-O'Neill statement opened up an active public discussion of Quebec's political mores for the first time in the history of the province. It also gave an impetus to the organization of "public morality leagues" whose purpose it was to clean up Quebec politics. Their first target was the Union Nationale party.

The third area of conflict between the Church and the Duplessis administration arose, as has been mentioned above, out of the deep concern of the higher clergy about the influence which the Union Nationale was beginning to exert over the policies of the Church's charitable and educational institutions. This influence was achieved through the government's tactics of making financial grants to these hard-pressed institutions dependent on their willingness to "co-operate" with the party. In the terminology of the Union Nationale, "co-operation" meant that the institutions had to silence or fire any member of the staff who was particularly critical of the Duplessis government, that contracts for new buildings and orders for new equipment had to go to firms designated by the party, and that during elections such institutions had to promote, directly or indirectly, the interests of "their benefactors."[26]

Perhaps the best illustration of the practices of the government along these lines was to be found in its attitude towards Laval University. As we have seen, the Faculty of Social Sciences at that university was one of the more influential centres of opposition to the economic and labour policies of the administration. Because the authorities at Laval refused to silence these critics of the government they found that badly needed grants were either drastically reduced or delayed for long periods of time.[27] Under the circumstances it is not surprising that one of the reforms considered to be most needed by the leaders of the Church was the replacement of the existing system of discretionary grants to religious institutions by statutory grants, which would be based on the relative needs of such institutions rather than on their political reliability.

As a result of the conflict in these various areas between the Union Nationale and important sections of the clergy, by the 1950's the Duplessis government was confronted by a serious challenge from this source. This challenge was not a direct one, for the Church as

[26]Fathers Dion and O'Neill, pp. 15–16, describe how these tactics of the Union Nationale enabled the party to obtain the indirect support of a number of parish priests.
[27]See Lemelin, "The Silent Struggle at Laval."

a whole showed little intention of declaring open war on the Union Nationale party, such a step being already precluded by the policy of the hierarchy of maintaining officially correct relations with the government in power, whatever its political complexion. There is also good reason to believe that Duplessis still had friends among both the higher and the lower clergy. It was rather in those more subtle and indirect ways, arising out of the great influence which the Church had always exercised over the thinking of the average French Canadian, that the opposition to the Union Nationale from this direction began to make itself felt.

MINOR POLITICAL MOVEMENTS

Although there were a number of minor political movements during the 1950's which were bitter foes of the Union Nationale, the only ones of any real significance were the Union des Electeurs and La Ligue d'Action Civique.[28]

The Union des Electeurs was in many ways a rather curious political movement. It was formed just before World War II and combined social credit theories with an intransigent nationalism. Like other Quebec nationalist movements it was opposed to participation in the war and was a strong advocate of provincial autonomy. The whole economic programme of the Union des Electeurs was based on one principle: unemployment, low standards of living, and other social problems were due to the fact that the masses of the people did not have the purchasing power to buy all the goods and services produced. The remedy was for the federal government to provide the provincial governments with sufficient money to pay regular social dividends along the following lines: $20 per month for every citizen from the cradle to grave, a pension of $60 per month to every person over sixty years of age, a bonus of $100 to parents on the birth of each child. These payments were to be made without any increase in taxation; in fact, all income taxes were to be reduced and eventually eliminated. The federal government would finance the whole scheme by printing more money, the theory being that the total amount of money in circulation should equal the value of all goods and services produced in the economy.[29]

In spite of its rather naive economic theories, its lack of any well-

[28]Popular support for the Social Democratic (C.C.F.) party was negligible. It polled less than 1 per cent of the popular vote in the 1956 election. See Canadian Press figures, *Montreal Star*, June 21, 1956.

[29]*Programme de l'Union des Electeurs* (Montréal, 1946). See also Herbert F. Quinn, "The Social Credit Movement in Quebec," *Canadian Forum*, March, 1947.

known political figures, and a shortage of funds which prevented it from using the usual channels of propaganda, the Union des Electeurs began to acquire some strength in the early 1940's among voters who were dissatisfied with the old parties. Although originally formed as a pressure group rather than a political party, it was encouraged enough to decide to enter candidates in every electoral district in the provincial election of 1948. It was not successful in winning a single seat, but it captured around 9 per cent of the popular vote[30] and showed considerable strength in certain areas, mainly the electoral districts around Quebec City, the industrial towns in the Eastern Townships and the Lac St. Jean district, and the mining towns in the Abitibi region. The party also had a certain number of supporters in the subsistence farming areas of the lower St. Lawrence below Quebec City.

Shortly after the 1948 election the Union des Electeurs decided to retire from direct participation in elections and revert to its previous practice of organizing groups of voters in each electoral district for the purpose of exerting pressure on governments at both the federal and the provincial level to adopt social credit theories. However, the collapse of the Union des Electeurs as a political party, like the break-up of the Bloc Populaire, left behind pockets of discontented voters in certain parts of the province—voters who could be classified as "independents," since they were not satisfied with the policies of either of the major parties.

The other minor political movement, La Ligue d'Action Civique, was formed in 1954 by a group of Montreal citizens closely associated with *Le Devoir* who were interested in reforming the Montreal civic administration. The reformers proposed to eliminate graft and corruption among municipal officials and put an end to the policy of civic "toleration" of gambling houses, "blind pigs," and other establishments operating outside the law. The members of the L.A.C. chose as their first leader, Jean Drapeau, a former member of the Bloc Populaire. In the municipal elections of 1954 La Ligue d'Action Civique won control over the Montreal administration and Drapeau was elected mayor. The reforming activities of the League, however, aroused the opposition of influential groups in the city which were closely connected with the Union Nationale. In the municipal elections of 1957 the latter party threw its weight against Drapeau, with the result that he was ousted from office and the L.A.C. lost control over the administration.

[30]Canadian Press figures, *Montreal Star*, July 29, 1948.

This intervention of the Union Nationale in Montreal municipal politics turned the L.A.C. into a bitter enemy of the provincial government. In August, 1958, it announced that it was expanding its activities, and planned "to extend to the whole of Quebec a campaign for political reform, restoration of democracy and administrative honesty."[31] Its programme also called for the nationalization of certain natural resources and public utilities, the "liberation" of all levels of education from political control and interference, and a more positive approach to the problem of provincial autonomy than that pursued by the Union Nationale.[32]

In spite of the expansion of its activities to other parts of the province the strength of La Ligue d'Action Civique continued to be centred in the Montreal area, or more specifically, in the eastern and French-speaking section of the city. However, its opposition to the Union Nationale meant that when the next provincial election was called the latter party would have a difficult fight on its hands in Montreal's east end.

Our analysis of the attitudes of the radical nationalists, the trade unions, members of the Church, and other groups towards the Union Nationale indicates the widespread opposition which faced that party by the middle 1950's. However, its ability to capture a large proportion of the seats in every election was still largely unimpaired, and this was due not only to the popularity of certain aspects of the party's policies and the efficiency of its electoral machine, but above all to the lack of unity and co-ordination among its many opponents. The Union Nationale's strongly entrenched position could not be seriously challenged unless a united front was formed of all opposing groups. The only political force in the province which had the organization, finances, and political experience to organize such a united front was the Liberal party.

[31]*Montreal Star*, Aug. 19, 1958.
[32]See *Le Devoir*, 14 fév., 8 juin 1959.

CHAPTER IX

The Election of 1960

A DESCRIPTION of the policies and strategy which enabled the Liberals to capture the support of the various groups opposed to the Union Nationale and thus bring about the defeat of that party in 1960 must begin with an outline of the developments within the Quebec Liberal party after 1936. When the Liberal government was turned out of office in the election of that year, the party was completely discredited in the eyes of the average Quebec voter because of the graft and corruption which had characterized the Taschereau régime and because its alliance with the industrialists had resulted in foreign domination of the province's economy. Under Adelard Godbout, who had become leader just previous to the 1936 election, certain steps were taken to reform the party, and in 1939 when the conscription issue was much to the fore it defeated the Union Nationale and returned to power. As a result of Godbout's efforts the Liberal administration from 1939 to 1944, while not completely free from patronage and electoral abuses, was a considerable improvement over the old Taschereau régime and had a better record than the Duplessis administration from 1944 to 1959.

The Liberals when in office remained staunch defenders of private enterprise and had close ties with the business interests, but they did put through several popular reforms, some of which had been part of the original Action Libérale Nationale programme. The most important of these reforms was the nationalization of the Montreal Light, Heat and Power Company in 1944. Godbout's government also set up a Superior Council of Labour as an advisory body on labour matters, extended the right to vote to women, established a system of compulsory education with free text-books, and appointed a Civil Service

Commission whose function it was to eliminate patronage in the selection of government personnel.

In spite of the considerable popular support for certain aspects of his administration, Godbout was handicapped by his close association with the federal Liberals, and by the strong support which he gave the Ottawa government in its prosecution of the war and in its policy of centralization. This co-operation with the federal Liberals led to the downfall of his government in the election of 1944, and to the even more disastrous defeat in the election of 1948 when the Liberals won only eight out of the ninety-two seats in the legislature and polled only 36 per cent of the popular vote.[1] Shortly after the election of 1948 Godbout resigned as party leader and a provincial convention was called in May, 1950, to appoint his successor. Georges E. Lapalme, a Liberal member of the House of Commons, was chosen as the new leader.

Mr. Lapalme inherited a political movement which was seriously weakened and demoralized. Under his leadership, however, the Liberal party was rejuvenated and strengthened, and steps were taken to infuse some elements of democracy into its organizational structure. Following along these lines, Liberal adherents in each electoral district were organized into constituency associations, which in turn were united into a Provincial Liberal Federation. The ultimate goal was for the Federation to take over the full direction of the party. A drive was started to collect campaign funds from rank and file members of the party in order to decrease dependence on business and financial interests.

The Liberal party also took a turn to the left in economic and social policies. Lapalme set himself the task of enlisting under the Liberal banner all the forces of discontent within the province by associating the party with most of the grievances and proposals for reform put forward by the social nationalists, the Church, the trade unions, and other groups.[2] Under the slogan of "social justice" he called for revision of existing labour legislation to raise minimum wage scales, provide the worker with stronger guarantees of his right to organize and bargain collectively, outlaw company unions, and eliminate political

[1]Canadian Press figures, *Montreal Star*, July 29, 1948.

[2]Lapalme's various proposals for reform are to be found in a number of pamphlets, advertisements in newspapers, and other literature published by the party during the 1952 and 1956 election campaigns. See *Le Parti libéral provincial s'engage* . . . (Montreal, 1952); *Le Digeste de la justice sociale* (Montreal, 1952); "Against you Duplessis—For you Lapalme," advertisement, *Montreal Star*, June 19, 1956. The official programme of the party in 1956 is to be found in the weekly newspaper, *La Réforme*, 6 juin 1956.

influence from the Labour Relations Board. As the first step towards giving the people of Quebec a more equitable share of the income from the wealth of their province foreign companies exploiting natural resources would be compelled to pay higher royalties. Various types of social legislation were to be introduced, such as health insurance, maternity allowances, additional aid to education at all levels, and increased allowances to invalids, the blind, the aged, and to widows in financial need. For the farmer, the Liberals proposed an increase in the maximum amount of the loans made available by the Farm Credit Bureau and extensive governmental assistance in the marketing of farm products.

Mr. Lapalme made a particularly strong campaign against the Union Nationale's patronage system, its misuse of public funds, its electoral tactics, and the abuses concerned with the granting of liquor licences. He pledged his party to put an end to all these practices, and also promised to set up a system of statutory rather than discretionary grants for school commissions, municipalities, universities, and hospitals. The Liberals also proposed changes in the electoral laws which would eliminate the single enumerator system set up by Bill 34 and give the urban areas more equitable representation in the legislature. A limitation would be placed on the amount of money candidates could spend on election campaigns.

On the controversial question of provincial autonomy Lapalme's programme indicated that the Liberals had taken an obvious swing in the direction of the nationalist position. A firm commitment was given that if the party were elected to office it would oppose strongly all attempts of the federal government to infringe upon the rights of the province or deprive it of any of its taxing powers. The Liberals' strongest argument against the Union Nationale on this point was that the refusal of Duplessis' party to introduce various forms of social legislation provided the federal government with an excuse to invade these particular fields of legislation. The position of the Liberals on the question of provincial autonomy was expressed clearly in a statement issued by the party in 1956 outlining its programme:

Une véritable autonomie provinciale exige une autonomie fiscale, c'est-à-dire le droit et le pouvoir de la législature provinciale de fixer ses propres impôts selon ses besoins, dans toute la mesure permise par la Constitution canadienne. . . .

La question de l'autonomie ne se limite pas aux impôts. Elle implique le droit et le devoir de la province d'avoir et de mettre en œuvre une politique précise dans toutes les matières que la Constitution canadienne lui attribue:

richesses naturelles, éducation, agriculture, relations ouvrières, santé et bien-être social, etc. L'absence de politique provinciale constructive et progressive dans ces domaines met gravement en danger l'autonomie provinciale.[3]

Mr. Lapalme's strategy of uniting behind the Liberal party "toutes les forces de l'opposition," that is, all the various groups and movements dissatisfied with the policies of the Union Nationale, was to a certain extent successful. He won over a good number of the radical nationalists, and several former members of the Bloc Populaire ran as Liberal candidates or supported the party on the platform in the elections of 1952 and 1956. In the 1956 election René Chaloult and Pierre Laporte, a Montreal newspaperman, ran as independent nationalists with Liberal backing. *Le Devoir*, the spokesman of the social nationalists, although still critical of the Liberals in some respects, backed the party in both elections. The party succeeded in obtaining the unofficial but nevertheless effective support of a good number of Catholic trade unions in various industrial areas.[4] The Liberals also found another ally in the Union des Electeurs, and several members of that group ran under the Liberal banner in the 1956 election. This support from Quebec's Social Crediters was given because the Liberals agreed to insert a clause in their programme reading. "Le Parti libéral provincial considère que tout ce qui est physiquement exécutable dans la province doit être rendu financièrement possible selon les besoins de la population, des municipalités, des commissions scolaires et des autres corps publics de cette province."[5] This rather vague statement was looked upon as an endorsement of the financial theories of the Union des Electeurs.

As a result of Mr. Lapalme's efforts, by the middle 1950's the Liberal party was better organized and much stronger than it had been just after its disastrous defeat of 1948. In the 1952 election the party succeeded in increasing its representation in the legislature from eight to twenty-three seats. This was only about a quarter of the total number of seats, but the party's popular vote of approximately 46 per cent was only slightly lower than that of the Union Nationale, which had polled just over 50 per cent.[6] It compared favourably with the 36 per cent polled by the Liberals in the 1948 election. In the election of 1956 the

[3]"Programme du parti libéral," *La Réforme*, 6 juin 1956.

[4]This was particularly true of the 1952 election. See Confédération des Travailleurs Catholiques du Canada, *Procès-verbal: Trente-et-unième session du Congrès de la C.T.C.C., Shawinigan Falls, P.Q., 1952* (Québec, 1952), pp. 79–94. The Liberals did not receive as much support from the C.T.C.C. in the 1956 election. The reasons for this have been pointed out *supra*, p. 123.

[5]"Programme du parti libéral," *La Réforme*, 6 juin 1956.

[6]Canadian Press figures, *Montreal Star*, July 17, 1952.

Liberals lost a little ground as their representation in the legislature dropped to twenty seats, and their popular vote to 44 per cent.[7] This slight setback was probably due to the disadvantageous position in which the opposition was placed by the changes made in the electoral system when Bill 34 was passed in 1953.

A clearer picture of the nature of the challenge which the rejuvenated Liberal party presented to the Union Nationale can be obtained from an examination of the type of electoral district where the party was successful either in winning the seat or in making a good showing in the election of 1956. Of the twenty seats won by the Liberals in 1956 seven were in the western and predominantly English-speaking section of Montreal; seven were industrial constituencies scattered throughout the province; and six were rural electoral districts.[8] In addition to these twenty seats there were a good number of other constituencies where the party displayed considerable strength. If we can assume that any Liberal candidate who won 80 per cent or more of the vote of his successful Union Nationale opponent had made a good showing, we find that there were fifteen rural seats and eleven urban ones in this category.[9] The significant point here is not merely that the Liberals fought a strong battle in twenty-six electoral districts, but that slightly over half of them were rural. As we have pointed out before, the rural vote is extremely important in Quebec elections for it controls a majority of the seats in the legislature.

Between the elections of 1956 and 1960 several developments further strengthened the position of the Liberal party and weakened that of the Union Nationale. One of them was, strangely enough, the successive victories of the Conservative party in the federal elections of 1957 and 1958. With the Conservatives in control of the federal administration the Union Nationale had lost one of its strongest arguments against

[7]Canadian Press figures, *Montreal Star*, June 21, 1956.

[8]The Montreal seats were Jacques Cartier, Notre-Dame-de-Grâce, Westmount-St. George, Verdun, St. Henri, St. Louis, Outremont; other urban and industrial ridings were Chambly, St. Hyacinthe, Richmond, St. Maurice, Hull, Rouyn-Noranda, Quebec West; the rural seats were Compton, Brome, Rivière-du-Loup, Rimouski, Bonaventure, Abitibi West. See maps in *Montreal Star*, June 21, 1956, showing regional distribution of seats.

[9]The rural seats were Abitibi East, Argenteuil, Gaspé-Nord, Huntingdon, Lac St. Jean, L'Assomption, L'Islet, Matapédia, Napierville-Laprairie, Roberval, Rouville, Témiscamingue, Vaudreuil-Soulanges, Verchères, Wolfe; the urban seats were Arthabaska, Drummond, Jonquière-Kénogami, Laval, Lévis, Maisonneuve, Mégantic, Jeanne Mance, Richelieu, Shefford, Stanstead. The votes received by each candidate in the electoral districts shown here are to be found in Quebec, Legislative Assembly, *Report on the General Election of 1956* (Quebec, 1956). As this report does not indicate party affiliation of candidates, one must refer to the *Canadian Parliamentary Guide*, 1957, for this information.

the provincial Liberal party—the accusation made by Duplessis so often in the past that if the Liberals came to power in Quebec they would immediately surrender the rights of the province to their "friends" at Ottawa. Moreover, although it would be erroneous to look upon the Union Nationale as merely the Quebec branch of the federal Conservative party, Duplessis and his colleagues had close ties with the Conservatives and now found it difficult to use the old slogan that the Union Nationale was the province's last line of defence against "les centralisateurs d'Ottawa." There was also one side effect to the Conservative sweep of Quebec seats in the federal election of 1958 which was helpful to the provincial wing of the Liberal party: that sweep resulted in considerable unemployment among experienced and well-known Liberal politicians in the field of federal politics. These politicians became available as candidates in the provincial election of 1960.

Undoubtedly the most important change in the Quebec political situation between 1956 and 1960 resulted from the sudden death of Maurice Duplessis in September, 1959, just a little less than a year before the election of 1960. This unexpected event was a serious blow to the Union Nationale in several ways. Although Duplessis had many enemies, he also had a large and devoted popular following. He was an extremely clever politician and an experienced parliamentarian, who dominated his party and his cabinet as few Canadian political leaders have ever successfully done.[10] He not only made the major decisions concerning the over-all policy of the government, but also made policy for many of the government departments. He never hesitated to intervene in the administration of a department whenever he thought such a step necessary. He decided on party strategy and supervised party organization. Above all, it was his driving energy and forceful personality which held together the many divergent elements making up the Union Nationale. Senator C.G. Power, a prominent Liberal member of the federal upper house who comes from Quebec City, and who knew Duplessis well, has said of the Union Nationale leader:

. . . Maurice Duplessis . . . was able to establish over his compatriots a domination based on such opposing factors as affection, esteem and fear, to such an extent that it was difficult to assess just which of these motives moved his devoted supporters in their almost frenzied loyalty. It must never be forgotten that Duplessis built a tremendously effective political machine out of the most diverse elements. He had support from the greedy and the unselfish, from the sinful and the righteous, from labour and from management, from the settler and from the lumberman. All these, mostly with

---

[10]In regard to the relationship between Duplessis and his cabinet, see Pierre Laporte, *Le Vrai Visage de Duplessis* (Montréal, 1960), chaps. vi and ix.

opposing interests, rallied to his banner, and he molded them all into an almost perfect electoral machine, and with all that, in my own personal view, he was a genial and consistent friend.[11]

Shortly after the death of Duplessis the Lieutenant Governor consulted with the members of the provincial cabinet with a view to appointing a successor. This was not a very difficult decision to make. The cabinet was unanimous in submitting to the Lieutenant Governor the name of Paul Sauvé, Minister of Youth and Social Welfare in the Duplessis cabinet and son of Arthur Sauvé, leader of the provincial Conservative party in the 1920's. Sauvé was the only outstanding figure in the cabinet who had any chance of receiving the solid support of all sections of the party. Like Duplessis he was a skilful politician and experienced parliamentarian, and had built up a reputation as a capable administrator. It has been said that he was the only member of the cabinet who had the complete confidence of Duplessis.[12] He was probably the only minister who dared to stand up to the Union Nationale leader or disagree with him in public.[13] To an experienced Quebec politician is credited a particularly apt statement concerning Sauvé's unique position in Duplessis' cabinet: "Il y a dans le gouvernement de la province trois sortes de ministres: ceux qui son assez intimes pour dire 'Oui, Maurice,' ceux qui disent 'Oui, Chef,' et il y a Paul Sauvé!"[14]

Under Sauvé's leadership it appeared that the Union Nationale would recover from the loss of Duplessis. The new Union Nationale leader was apparently convinced that the time was long overdue for the introduction of extensive administrative reforms and that many of Duplessis' policies must be discarded. Sauvé entered into negotiations with the federal government with a view to finding some formula which would enable Quebec universities to receive the same annual grants as those in other provinces. Bill 34 which had established the single enumerator system in urban constituencies was revoked. A new spirit prevailed in the legislature as the Speaker became more impartial and the Liberal opposition was provided with greater opportunity to debate and criticize government policies. Steps were taken to modify, if not eliminate completely, some of the abuses of the patronage system, and public works were no longer denied to any constituency merely because it had voted Liberal. The Labour Relations Act was revised along lines which the trade union movement had been suggesting for years. The provin-

[11]Personal communication.
[12]Laporte, *Le Vrai Visage de Duplessis*, p. 101.
[13]*Ibid.*, p. 22.
[14]*Ibid.*, p. 65.

cial police were ordered by the government to be impartial in labour disputes.

Just as the Union Nationale under Sauvé's leadership began to recover from the loss of Duplessis the party received another blow when Sauvé himself died suddenly from a heart attack on January 2, 1960, about three months after the death of his predecessor. The situation in which the Union Nationale found itself this time was quite different from that following the death of Duplessis. Sauvé had been looked upon by everyone as the obvious successor to Duplessis. When he died there was no longer any prominent figure who had the unquestioned support of every section of the party. A week later a caucus of all Union Nationale members of the legislature was called for the purpose of selecting a new leader. Before the caucus met the two names which were most often mentioned as possible leaders were Daniel Johnson, Minister of Hydraulic Resources, and Yves Prévost, Provincial Secretary. The man who emerged as the new leader, however, was Antonio Barrette, who had been Minister of Labour since 1944. Barrette had not sought the leadership and had been thinking of retiring from politics.[15] It seemed obvious that his selection was a compromise appointment in an attempt to maintain the unity of the party for the forthcoming election which was only a few months away.

Barrette was not a strong leader like Duplessis or Sauvé. He did not have their dominating personality and lacked their political flair and skill in manœuvring. Although well liked and respected by all those who had ever been associated with him, he was not as well known as his predecessors and did not have their popular following. There was little likelihood that he would dominate the party in the same fashion as the other Union Nationale leaders had done. During the brief period between his appointment as leader and the election of June, 1960, Barrette continued to carry out the reforms introduced by Sauvé, although at no time did he openly repudiate the policies of Duplessis.

As a result of the important changes which had taken place in the Quebec political situation after 1956 the Union Nationale entered the election campaign of 1960 with some serious handicaps. For one thing, in spite of all the attempts to maintain party unity there were some serious differences within the party over the question of Barrette's leadership. Although it was not apparent at the time, Barrette did not enjoy the full confidence and co-operation of two leading figures in the party organization, J. D. Bégin, chief organizer, and Gérald Martineau, party treasurer. (In fact, when Barrette resigned as party leader in

[15]See his statement in *Montreal Star*, Oct. 15, 1960.

September, 1960, just three months after the defeat of the Union Nationale, he gave as his reason for doing so the strong opposition he had had to contend with from these two key individuals in the party organization, and stated that this opposition had developed several months before the 1960 election.[16]) During the course of the election campaign a good number of local leaders and organizers in various parts of the province deserted the Union Nationale and swung over to the Liberals.[17] It was also significant that the Union Nationale was not successful in this election in getting a number of prominent labour leaders to come out in open support of the party. Both the Quebec Federation of Labour and the Catholic unions adopted a policy of official neutrality in the election, and merely asked their members to get out and vote. Such a policy was likely to benefit the Liberals more than the Union Nationale.

One of the most serious handicaps faced by Mr. Barrette's party was the campaign which Fathers Gérard Dion and Louis O'Neill had waged ever since 1956 against the "political immorality" of Quebec politics.[18] This campaign aroused considerable opposition to the electoral tactics pursued by the Union Nationale in the past, and an increasing number of voters were no longer willing to tolerate these practices. A month before the election the two priests published another booklet entitled *Le Chrétien et les élections*.[19] Its effectiveness lay in its timing rather than its contents for it consisted mainly of an amplification of the criticisms made against Quebec's political mores in the priests' earlier publication. In addition, a Catholic Action organization called Fédération Nationale des Ligues du Sacré-Cœur, with branches in all dioceses in the province, embarked upon a crusade for honest elections and asked that both political parties and all candidates refrain from "insults, fraud, evil-minded insinuations, violence and abuse of liquor."[20] This crusade had the endorsement of Cardinal Léger, Archbishop of Montreal.

In view of these developments it was perhaps not surprising that the Union Nationale's electoral campaign, although not completely free from certain abuses and illegalities, was a considerable improvement over the tactics used by the party in the past. There were not the same irregularities in the preparation of voting lists, nor the same lavish expenditure of government money to influence voters through such

[16]See *La Presse*, 15 sept. 1960.
[17]A list of these individuals is to be found in *Le Devoir*, 20 juin 1960.
[18]See *supra*, pp. 165–6.
[19](Montreal: Les Editions de l'Homme, 1960).
[20]*Montreal Gazette*, June 3, 1960.

means as payment of their hospital bills, putting them on government payrolls, and so on. There were very few cases of voters being threatened that if they did not support the party their village or town would be cut off from all government expenditures and grants for the next four years. Although the Communist issue was not absent from the campaign, there was little in the way of a concerted effort to link the Liberals with that group. In all fairness, too, it should be pointed out that the improved tone of the Union Nationale electoral campaign can to some extent be attributed to Mr. Barrette. He was a different type of political leader from Duplessis and refused to adopt some of the latter's questionable practices.

The most important argument presented by Mr. Barrette to the electorate as a reason for returning his party to power was that the policies of Duplessis and Sauvé, which he promised to continue, were responsible for the prosperity of the province and the well-being of its people. An advertisement in an English language newspaper carried the slogan, "Three Leaders . . . One Policy . . . A Singleness of Purpose."[21] In numerous speeches throughout the election campaign the Union Nationale leader stressed the good things which had been enjoyed by all sections of the public: "Nous n'avons pas honte de notre passé. C'est un passé chargé de réalisations en faveur des cultivateurs, des colons, des ouvriers, des vieillards, de la jeunesse. Il n'aurait pas été possible de faire autant et aussi bien en aussi peu de temps."[22] There was, of course, an element of the defensive in all this, and a further indication of the defensive nature of the Union Nationale campaign is that Barrette's speeches devoted a good deal of time to answering Liberal attacks on his party's record.

Mr. Barrette also emphasized the role played by the Union Nationale in defence of provincial autonomy and seldom lost an opportunity to denounce the Liberals as "the party of federal centralization." He was not successful, however, in making the question of provincial autonomy a dominant issue in the election as Duplessis had done so often in the past. One of the reasons for this was, of course, the changed political situation arising out of the Conservative victory in the federal elections of 1957 and 1958. Furthermore, many voters felt that Quebec's struggle against the expansion of federal powers had largely been won. Most important of all, ever since Adelard Godbout had relinquished the leadership of the provincial Liberal party in 1950 that party itself had moved steadily towards a more autonomist and nationalist position.

---

[21]*Montreal Star*, May 21, 1960.
[22]*Le Devoir*, 20 juin 1960.

Although the Liberals, like the Union Nationale, entered the election campaign of 1960 with a new leader, this change in leadership had not weakened the party. In 1958 Mr. Lapalme had resigned as head of the Quebec Liberal party and had been succeeded by Jean Lesage, former Minister of Northern Affairs and National Resources in the federal cabinet of Louis St. Laurent. Lapalme had decided to resign because he realized that certain sections of the party, although appreciative of what he had done to build up its strength, had begun to feel that after two straight electoral defeats it was time to look for a new leader—the usual reaction in Quebec to the failure of a leader to get quick results. (It will be remembered that Godbout had also resigned after losing two elections.) Mr. Lapalme had stayed on, however, as leader of the Liberal opposition in the Legislative Assembly and had soon become the right-hand man of Lesage. This was fortunate for both Mr. Lesage and the party, for although the new leader was an able politician and administrator he had had little experience in the field of provincial politics up to this time.

Lesage adopted Lapalme's programme of administrative, electoral, and social reform, and pursued the same strategy of winning the support of all those individuals and groups who were opposed to the Union Nationale. He also continued Lapalme's policy of giving the party a more nationalist orientation. Organizational activities were expanded and long before election day candidates had been selected in all the various constituencies.

In his appeal to the electorate Mr. Lesage followed two main lines of attack: he criticized the administrative and electoral corruption of the Union Nationale, and he emphasized the urgent need for certain social reforms. In his speeches the Liberal leader referred to the Union Nationale administration as "un gouvernement corrumpu." A typical newspaper advertisement published by the party read, "Le régime actuel de l'Union Nationale est devenu un gouvernement usé et cynique, qui parle de plus en plus et agit de moins en moins. L'Union Nationale? L'Union des Scandales!"[23] Mr. Lesage promised that if his party was elected to office the civil service would be reformed, the patronage system eliminated, and rigid controls placed over the spending of government money. A thorough investigation would be made of all aspects of the Union Nationale administration and all those found guilty of illegal activities would be punished with the full force of the law.

The strongest feature of the Liberal party's electoral campaign was

[23]La Presse, 21 juin 1960.

its proposal to introduce an extensive programme of social and labour legislation.[24] Although this programme was similar in most respects to those put forward in the election of 1952 and 1956, there was a difference of emphasis. Two reforms were particularly stressed in the speeches made by Mr. Lesage and in the literature distributed by the party. One, the immediate introduction of a hospital insurance plan which would provide the people of Quebec with the same security and benefits as those enjoyed by the people of the other provinces; the other, an ambitious programme of government aid to education which would establish a system of free schooling at all levels, including university, provide free text-books in all public schools, and make living allowances available for all students in financial need. The party's social security proposals also included increased benefits for invalids, the blind, and the aged.

There were two other aspects of Lesage's programme which, although they did not receive as much attention in the election campaign as those mentioned above, represented significant departures from traditional Liberal policy. One of them was the establishment of a Department of Cultural Affairs for the purpose of maintaining and fostering all those traits and characteristics of the people of Quebec as a distinct cultural group on the North American continent. The other one was the creation of an Economic Planning and Development Council which would have the responsibility of providing the government with a planned programme of economic and industrial development. Such planned development would ensure that the exploitation of the province's natural resources would primarily benefit the people of Quebec. The party's programme stated: "The general improvement in living standards which should result from an expanding economy, will continue to pass us by, so long as we fail to exercise adequate control and sound management. . . . Scientific developments no longer permit government by improvisation."[25]

As the election campaign drew to a close both parties made the usual predictions of a sweeping victory for their forces. It is probable, however, that the Union Nationale really expected to lose a number of seats, and that the Liberals would have considered themselves fortunate if they could have increased substantially their representation in the legislature. Most political commentators anticipated a Union Nationale victory with a reduced majority. A few hours after the polls closed on election day, however, it became apparent that Mr. Lesage

[24]See infra, Appendix C, for 1960 Political Manifesto of the Quebec Liberal Party.
[25]Ibid., p. 9.

would be called upon to form the next Quebec government. The Liberals captured fifty-one sets to the Union Nationale's forty-three, with a popular vote of approximately 51 per cent as compared to 47 per cent for their opponents.[26]

Again, an adequate understanding of the various factors which entered into the Liberal victory of 1960 requires a careful analysis of the type of electoral district and geographic region in which the party was successful in winning seats. This is to be found in Table III. Out of the fifty-one seats captured by the Liberals, twenty-nine were predominantly urban and twenty-two were predominantly rural. Thus, although the urban areas still constituted the most important source of Liberal support, the trend towards increased support from the rural voters, which we had noted in our earlier analysis of the 1956 election, had obviously continued to develop. The regional breakdown is even more significant than the urban-rural distribution of seats. The vast majority of Liberal seats were in five fairly distinct regions: the Montreal metropolitan community, the Montreal Plain, the Eastern Townships, the Lower St. Lawrence, and Northern Quebec.

In Montreal the Liberals won ten seats. The first seven shown on the table were in the western and predominantly English-speaking section of the community, which had been strongly Liberal ever since the beginning of the Second World War.[27] The other three were in the eastern and French-speaking part of Montreal, a section of the city where La Ligue d'Action Civique had usually received strong support in municipal elections, and where the Bloc Populaire had had a large number of supporters in the provincial election of 1944.[28] There were three other seats in eastern Montreal, Jeanne Mance, Mercier, and Maisonneuve, where the Liberals lost by a very narrow margin.[29]

The nine electoral districts won by the Liberal party in the Montreal Plain were either industrial seats or rural constituencies containing a large number of people who commuted to Montreal daily for work.

[26]See Canadian Press figures, *Montreal Star*, June 23, 1960.
[27]See *supra*, pp. 99–100.
[28]In 1944 the Bloc Populaire succeeded in electing its candidate in Laurier, and received between 25 and 30 per cent of the popular vote in a number of other electoral districts in eastern Montreal, namely, Ste. Marie, Jeanne Mance, Mercier, Maisonneuve, and Laval. At that time Laval included what is now known as the electoral district of Bourget. See *Report on the General Election of 1944* and *Canadian Parliamentary Guide*, 1945.
[29]In Jeanne Mance the Liberal party received 35,548 votes to the Union Nationale's 38,015, in Mercier, 15,494 to 16,423, and in Maisonneuve, 20,552 to 22,682. See *Report on the General Election of 1960* and *Canadian Parliamentary Guide*, 1961.

TABLE III

ELECTORAL DISTRICTS WON BY THE LIBERAL PARTY, RURAL AND URBAN,
BY GEOGRAPHIC REGIONS, IN THE QUEBEC ELECTION OF 1960

Montreal		Montreal Plain[a]		Eastern Townships[b]	
Jacques Cartier	U	Vaudreuil-Soulanges	R	Drummond	U
Notre-Dame-de-Grâce	U	Deux-Montagnes	R	Brome	R
Outremont	U	Terrebonne	U	Stanstead	U
Westmount-St. George	U	St. Jean	U	Richmond	U
St. Henri	U	Iberville	R	Sherbrooke	U
Verdun	U	Chambly	U	Mégantic	U
St. Louis	U	Verchères	R	Arthabaska	U
Laurier	U	Richelieu	U	Wolfe	R
Laval	U	St. Hyacinthe	U	Beauce	R
Bourget	U				
		TOTAL	5 U	TOTAL	6 U
TOTAL	10 U		4 R		3 R

Lower St. Lawrence[c]		Northern Quebec[d]		Other regions[e]	
Bellechasse	R	Duplessis	U	Quebec West	U
Montmagny	R	Saguenay	R	Quebec County	U
L'Islet	R	Jonquière-Kénogami	U	Lévis	U
Rivière-du-Loup	R	Lac St. Jean	R	Portneuf	R
Rimouski	R	Roberval	R	St. Maurice	U
Matapédia	R	Abitibi East	R	Hull	U
Matane	R	Abitibi West	R		
Bonaventure	R	Rouyn-Noranda	U	TOTAL	5 U
Gaspé-Nord	R				1 R
		TOTAL	3 U		
TOTAL	9 R		5 R		

SOURCES: for seats won by the Liberals, *Canadian Parliamentary Guide*, 1961;
for rural-urban characteristics of electoral districts, *Census of Canada*, 1951
(Ottawa) I, Table 14. It is possible that the 1961 census figures will show that
a few of the seats listed here as rural now have a small urban majority. The
Montreal Star, June 23, 1960, contains a number of maps showing regional distribution of seats won by both the Liberal and the Union Nationale parties.
    [a]This is the term used by geographers to describe the lowlands surrounding
Montreal.
    [b]The region southeast of Montreal bordering on the state of Vermont and part
of the state of Maine.
    [c]The south shore of the St. Lawrence River between Quebec City and Gaspé.
    [d]The far northern section of the province between the Abitibi and Saguenay
regions.
    [e]Quebec West, Quebec County, Lévis, and Portneuf are in the Quebec City
region. St. Maurice is located just north of the St. Lawrence River halfway
between Montreal and Quebec City. Hull is opposite the City of Ottawa in the
western part of the province.

The Liberals had always had a considerable amount of support in this
area in the past. In the election of 1952 the party had won in Verchères
and Richelieu. Although these seats were lost in the election of 1956,

two other constituencies in the Montreal Plain, Chambly and St. Hya-cinthe, went Liberal in that election, and the party fell short of victory in Vaudreuil-Soulanges by only a few hundred votes.[30]

It was not the support which the Liberals received in the Montreal and surrounding areas, however, which was the most decisive factor in the victory of the party. It was rather its ability to capture twenty-six seats in the three other regions, the Eastern Townships, the Lower St. Lawrence, and Northern Quebec.

All three regions have certain characteristics in common, although the Eastern Townships differ in some respects.[31] Northern Quebec and the Lower St. Lawrence are frontier and colonization areas of the prov-ince, remote from the large urban centres, where the influence of the clergy is particularly strong. However, they are quite unlike other rural areas in the province. One of the differences is their large working class population. Here one finds some of the more important manu-facturing, mining, and power developments of Quebec, the aluminum manufacturing centre of Arvida, the iron ore mines of Ungava, the copper mines of Rouyn-Noranda and the Gaspé peninsula, the huge power developments around the Gulf of the St. Lawrence. In addition, there are a large number of pulp and paper industries scattered throughout both regions. Farming in these areas is a much more hazard-ous enterprise than in the fertile valley of the St. Lawrence around Montreal. Owing to climatic and other geographic conditions sub-sistence farming is common and the farmer's income must be supple-mented by working in the logging camps in the winter, in nearby in-dustrial centres, or by fishing and trapping.

The Eastern Townships is also a frontier area of the province, but differs from the other two in that it is predominantly urban. There is, however, a very large rural population. Although agricultural condi-tions are generally favourable, there is a certain amount of subsistence farming. This region constitutes the second most important manufac-turing area in the province after Montreal. The production of textiles leads, but there are also a large number of lumber and pulp and paper plants, and the mining of asbestos is a major industry.

[30]The Liberal candidate in Vaudreuil-Soulanges was Paul Gérin-Lajoie, who later became Minister of Youth in Lesage's cabinet. He received 7,311 votes to 7,681 for his Union Nationale opponent. See *Report on the General Election of 1956.*

[31]The description which follows is to a considerable extent based on Benoit Brouillette, "La région des Appalaches," and Pierre Dagenais, "La région des Laurentides," in Esdras Minville, éd., *Notre Milieu* (Montréal, 1946), chaps. III and IV. The characteristics of Quebec's regional economies are also dealt with in Canada, *Report of the Royal Commission on Dominion-Provincial Relations* (Ottawa, 1940), Book I, pp. 190–3.

The similarities between the three regions are more important than their differences. They all have economies which tend towards instability. In times of recession, such as in the late 1950's, there is an unusually high level of unemployment, because their economic activities are based on either the exportation of raw materials, like minerals and forest products, which are subject to wide fluctuations in demand on world markets, or on manufactured goods, such as textiles, which have to face stiff competition from imports. It is in these regions rather than in Montreal and Quebec City that the presence of the foreign industrialist is most obvious. Many towns have only one large industry, whose ownership and management are English-speaking, and which is usually engaged in the processing of some important natural resource. A fall-off in production in that particular industry immediately endangers the standard of living of the whole community, and of the surrounding countryside as well. Some of the most bitterly fought strikes in the history of the province have occurred in these areas. The two most notable examples are the Asbestos strike of 1949 in the Eastern Townships, and the Murdochville strike of 1958 in Gaspé.

As a result of these factors nationalistic sentiments have been stronger in these regions than in many other parts of Quebec. It is here, rather than in the Montreal area, that the Catholic unions have always been most successful in organizing the workers.[32] It was also in these areas that the smaller nationalist parties found a good deal of their support in the 1940's. In the provincial election of 1944 two out of the four electoral districts captured by the Bloc Populaire were Beauce and Stanstead in the Eastern Townships. Although the Union des Electeurs never succeeded in winning a seat in the provincial legislature, it always had a large number of followers in the Northern Quebec region. In the election of 1948 it polled around 30 per cent of the popular vote in Jonquière-Kénogami, Rouyn-Noranda, Abitibi East, and Abitibi West.[33]

It should also be pointed out that Quebec County, Portneuf, and St. Maurice, three of the constituencies shown in Table III under the heading, "Other Regions," have some of the same characteristics as the

[32]In many of the industrial towns in these regions, such as, Arvida, Jonquière, Rimouski, Asbestos, Magog, Thetford Mines, Drummondville, and Sherbrooke, practically all of the unions are affiliated with the C.T.C.C. It is only in the mining towns in the Abitibi district that the Catholic unions are weak or nonexistent. See Canada, Department of Labour, *Labour Organization in Canada*, 1958, pp. 76–83.

[33]See *Report on the General Election of 1948* and *Canadian Parliamentary Guide*, 1949. It should be noted that in 1948 the area which now constitutes the electoral district of Jonquière-Kénogami was still part of the electoral district of Chicoutimi.

areas we have been discussing. In these electoral districts we find large chemical and pulp and paper industries whose ownership and management are English-speaking; many towns have only one large industry; farming is mainly of the subsistence type; nationalistic sentiments are strong; most workers belong to the Catholic unions; and parties of protest have always had a considerable following. St. Maurice was one of the two seats won by the Bloc Populaire in the federal election of 1945. Quebec County was represented in the provincial legislature by René Chaloult, a left-wing nationalist, during the period from 1944 to 1952.

This analysis of the regional distribution of seats won by the Liberal party in the Quebec election of 1960 indicates two important facts: first, the Liberals were able not only to retain, but also to expand their popular support in their traditional strongholds in and around Montreal; and second, and much more significant, the party was able to break new ground and capture a large number of seats in the frontier regions of the province, regions where the clergy were particularly influential, farming conditions were poor, economic unrest was widespread, trade unions were militant, nationalistic sentiments were very strong, and where the disappearance of parties of protest, such as the Bloc Populaire and the Union des Electeurs, had left behind pockets of discontent in certain districts. Thus, although there were many factors responsible for the Liberal victory of 1960, including the sudden death of Duplessis, the most important one was the ability of Mr. Lesage to carry to a successful conclusion the strategy of Mr. Lapalme of uniting behind the Liberal party "toutes les forces de l'opposition," all those individuals and groups throughout the province which had become dissatisfied with the policies of the Union Nationale.

CHAPTER X

The Rejuvenation and Recovery of
the Union Nationale

ALTHOUGH THE LIBERAL VICTORY OF 1960 was a severe defeat for the Union Nationale, it did not destroy the party. It still remained strong in the legislature, and under the leadership of Daniel Johnson was to slowly recover and return to power in 1966, although with diminished popular support. After the death of Johnson in 1968, however, the party rapidly declined and in the election of 1973 it completely disappeared from the legislature. The history of the Union Nationale after 1960 therefore falls into two parts: the various factors which enabled the party to return to power in 1966, and the policies it pursued in office; and secondly, the reasons for its rapid deterioration and decline after 1968.

In the first period the major challenge which the Union Nationale had to meet was the widespread changes in the traditional structure of Quebec society introduced by the Lesage administration in the early sixties; these have come to be known as "the Quiet Revolution." A brief description of the policies of the Liberals which were to result in these changes is essential for an understanding of the formidable nature of the challenge with which the opposition was faced.

THE LIBERAL PARTY AND THE QUIET REVOLUTION

Like the Union Nationale in 1936, the Quebec Liberal party came to power in 1960 as a party of reform. Unlike Duplessis' party, however, the Liberals not only carried out their promised reforms but in most respects went far beyond them. During the period between 1960 and

1966 they put through sweeping educational, economic, and administrative reforms which had a profound impact on the modernization and democratization of Quebec society. Although the extensive changes we will be describing must for the most part be credited to the initiative of the Lesage government, at the same time they were also a response to pressures and demands which had been building up for some time from various segments of Quebec society and which had been held in check by the restrictive policies of the Duplessis regime. Like any revolution, the one we are discussing did not start from scratch in 1960; it had been slowly developing since the end of the Second World War. The Lesage regime acted as the catalyst which set it in motion.

The ability of any leader to undertake widespread changes in a province's institutions is dependent not only on that leader's personal inclinations and convictions, but also on the availability of a sizable number of dedicated and capable innovators among the party's elite. In this respect Lesage was particularly fortunate that when he formed his cabinet he could call upon a hard core of unusually talented and imaginative politicians from within party ranks; they formed an unusual combination of men of ideas who at the same time had the administrative ability and political "know-how" to put their ideas into effect.

Although the cabinet put together by Lesage after his victory included some old-line politicians, the most influential group surrounding the Prime Minister was a dynamic group of a half-dozen people or so who played the key role in the Quiet Revolution and dominated the decision-making process, sometimes in opposition to the more cautious policies that Lesage himself would have followed. The main members of this group, whom the press referred to as the "Equipe du Tonnerre," were: Georges-Emile Lapalme, Lesage's predecessor as party leader, who was in many ways the architect of the Liberal victory of 1960, Attorney-General and Minister of Cultural Affairs; René Lévesque, journalist and popular C.B.C. political commentator, Minister of Natural Resources and later Minister of Social Affairs; Paul Gérin-Lajoie, an outstanding authority on the Canadian constitution, Minister of Youth and later Minister of Education; Pierre Laporte, a former journalist with Le Devoir and harsh critic of the Union Nationale's patronage system, entered the cabinet in 1962 to become Minister of Municipal Affairs; Eric Kierans, economist and former head of the Montreal Stock Exchange, appointed Minister of Revenue in 1963 and later Minister of Health. Two other less prominent members of this dynamic group should be mentioned: Claire Kirkland-Casgrain, appointed Minister of State in 1962, later Minister of Transport, was the first female member of a Quebec cabinet; Gérard D. Lévesque, lawyer and businessman from the Gaspé region, Minister of Commerce and Industry, was a young politician with considerable promise.[1]

The magnitude of the task facing the Liberal party when it came to power lay in the fact that the Duplessis era had left Quebec in the contradictory position of being an advanced industrial society with institutions, ideologies, and attitudes which were largely pre-industrial. This contradiction was to be found in the educational system, the attitude of the government toward the economy, the administrative and electoral systems, labour legislation, and social welfare services.

Although some advances had been made in the educational system since the Second World War, when the Liberals came to power it still was deficient both quantitatively and qualitatively, and it was almost entirely under the control of the Church. For financial or other reasons too many young people dropped out of the school system too early and without the adequate intellectual and specialized skills which one Quebec educationist called, "la clé de la société moderne."[2] As stated in an earlier chapter,[3] in higher education the system of classical colleges was geared to turning out priests, doctors, and lawyers, rather than the engineers, accountants, and technicians needed in an industrial society; furthermore, these colleges were beyond the reach of those who could not afford the fees.

After education, the area in which the policies of governments in the past had been most inadequate was in regard to the economy and the development of natural resources. We have seen that both the Taschereau and Duplessis administrations, with their strong commitment to private enterprise, had a restricted and negative attitude towards the intervention of the state in the economy. This led to the uncontrolled activity of the large multinational corporations and the wasteful exploitation of natural resources, and it did little to increase the participation of the French Quebecer in the English-dominated economy of the province.

The shortcomings of the province's electoral system and civil service have often been touched on before. The electoral map, a carry-over from the days when Quebec was a predominantly agrarian society, was heavily weighted in favour of the rural areas with gross under-representation of urban areas. The civil service was riddled with patronage and inefficiency and thus unable to meet the requirements of a modern state.

[1]For brief biographies of the ministers mentioned here see Thomas Sloan, *Quebec: The Not-So-Quiet Revolution* (Toronto, 1965), pp. 64–77.

[2]Paul-Emile Gingras, "L'Ecole des technocrates," *Relations*, no. 344 (déc. 1969), p. 337.

[3]See *supra*, chap. I, p. 13.

Quebec also had the anachronism of an upper house (the Legislative Council), which had long since been abolished in the other provinces.

Social welfare services were outdated and inferior compared to other provinces, and like education, were almost entirely in the hands of the clergy. The Church's hospitals, orphanages, homes for the aged, and other charitable institutions had performed a useful service in the heavily agrarian society of the past, but its human and financial resources were no longer adequate to meet the needs of an urbanized and industrialized state. Moreover, many of the religious principles underlying the provision of these social services were being increasingly questioned by the growth of secular values.

In its goal of bringing about the modernization of Quebec, undoubtedly the most important and lasting reforms introduced by the Lesage government were the revolutionary changes in the educational system. From the outset it was recognized that if the people of Quebec were to participate fully in the industrial society in which they lived they must acquire the necessary technical, managerial, and administrative skills required by that society. Paul Gérin-Lajoie, Minister of Youth, and the major driving force behind the province's educational revolution stated: "L'éducation est devenue pour le citoyen le premier des besoins et pour l'état le premier des devoirs sociaux. Elle forme la base même d'une politique de bien-être."[4] As an indication of the high priority it was giving to this question, the government in 1961 set up a royal commission of inquiry, headed by Msgr. Alphonse-Marie Parent, Vice-Rector of Laval University, with a mandate to study all aspects of the organization and financing of education.

Without waiting for the findings of the Parent Commission, a number of important educational reforms were introduced in the early sixties by Gérin-Lajoie under the heading of "la Grande charte de l'éducation."[5] The underlying principle of this "Grande charte" was that in a democratic society all children, irrespective of the level of income of their family, had a right to education at all levels in accordance with their aptitudes and capabilities. The more important of these reforms were: the raising of the compulsory school leaving age from fourteen to fifteen with the understanding that it would later be raised to sixteen; the establishment of a network of comprehensive high schools in various regions throughout the province with school commissions being required to provide free schooling up to the eleventh year; parents of children still attending school at the ages of sixteen and seventeen were given grants of $10.00 a month; large-scale increases were made in

[4]Paul Gérin-Lajoie, *Pourquoi le bill 60* (Montreal, 1963), p. 33.
[5]*Ibid.*, chap. VII.

government loans and bursaries for university students from lower-income families, particularly those students entering the teaching profession.[6]

The revamping of the educational system undertaken by the government also necessitated reform of educational structures. In what was known as "Operation 55" the large number of school commissions in small towns and cities throughout the province were reorganized into 55 regional school commissions, and parents were given the right to vote in the election of school boards, a right which had hitherto been restricted to property owners. All of these changes resulted in rapidly growing expenditures and the provincial government had to step in with large subsidies to school commissions. It also set up a system of yearly grants to universities to meet both operating and capital expenditures.

In 1964 in accordance with one of the first recommendations of the Parent Commission, a Ministry of Education was established with Gérin-Lajoie as the first incumbent. This was a highly controversial measure because for the first time it effectively took control over all education out of the hands of the Church and put it under the control of the state.[7] Although the public school system still remained divided along confessional lines, the curriculum in the Catholic schools began to slowly change as less emphasis was placed on classical and religious studies and more on the subjects characteristic of an industrial and secular society.

The groundwork was also laid for the implementation of another recommendation of the Parent Commission: the establishment in all regions of the province of "Colleges of General and Professional Education," commonly known as CEGEPs. These colleges would introduce a new, two-year level of education between high school and university. Students in CEGEPs would be offered the alternative of a terminal programme leading to a diploma in some professional or technical subject, or they could follow a pre-university programme. The colleges were to be non-denominational and free.[8]

Aside from the extensive reorganization of the educational system,

[6]For a summary of these reforms see, *Annuaire du Québec*, 1964–65, pp. 256–7. As a result of these changes, 80 per cent of young people between the ages of 13 and 16 were in secondary schools in 1965 as compared to 57 per cent in 1960. See Jules Leblanc, "En Education ça ne va pas trop vite!" *Le Magazine Maclean*, sept. 1966, p. 24.

[7]The controversy over this particular recommendation of the Parent Commission is described in Jules Leblanc, "L'Education au Québec," *Canadian Annual Review*, 1963, pp. 369–79.

[8]For a brief survey of educational reforms between 1960 and 1969 see Gingras, "L'Ecole des technocrates," pp. 337–40.

the most important item on the agenda of the Lesage administration was the active intervention of the government in the economy with the goal of bringing about greater participation and control by the people of Quebec over the economic development of their province; in the terminology of the time, they must become "Maîtres chez nous." In one speech Lesage summed it up, "la racine du mal, c'est que notre économie ne nous appartient pas . . . C'est aussi simple que cela, mais c'est aussi grave que cela."[9]

There were actually two aspects to this problem of foreign domination of Quebec's economic life: one was that American and English-Canadian capitalists owned and controlled most of the large industries; the other was that the middle and upper levels of management in these industries were almost completely English-speaking. In contrast, although the neighbouring province of Ontario also had an economy which in many areas was owned and controlled by American capital, the upper-level personnel in that province was almost completely English-Canadian.

In its plans to bring about Quebec's "libération économique" the government used two main approaches: the establishment of public enterprises to exploit and develop the natural resources of the province; and secondly, government assistance to strengthen small and medium-sized Quebec-owned firms. Except in the case of electric power, the Liberals did not propose to nationalize any of the existing foreign-owned companies but rather to regulate them more closely in such matters as royalties paid to the province for exploiting natural resources.[10] Even the government-sponsored enterprises in many cases were not to be completely state-owned, but "mixed enterprises" with both public and private funding—in Lesage's words, "a happy alliance between private enterprise and the state."[11]

In its drive to "emancipate" the economy the most important step taken by the Lesage government was the decision to call an election in 1962 to seek a mandate for the nationalization of all power companies which were still privately owned, which meant the majority of them.[12] The man who masterminded the project was René Lévesque, the strongest nationalist in the cabinet and one who also had leanings towards socialism. The importance of the role which hydro-electric power played in the economy of the province had often been emphasized before. As the major source of energy it was seen as the basis of all industrial development: government control over this important natural re-

[9]Address to the Quebec Liberal Federation, Montreal, Sept. 30, 1962 (mimeographed).
[10]See Lesage's statement, *Montreal Star*, June 5, 1961.
[11]*Ibid.*
[12]See *supra*, p. 83, n22.

source was an important first step towards control over the whole economy. According to one election slogan, it was, "la clé du royaume qui nous rendra tous maîtres chez nous."[13]

During the election campaign a number of other arguments were put forward in support of the government's policy of nationalization: the profits of the power companies could be used to lower rates and provide better service; it would enable the government to decentralize industry to more remote areas of the province; the province would receive the tax revenues which the private companies were paying to the federal government; and finally, it would provide the opportunity for university-trained Quebecers to move into managerial jobs in an industry operating completely in French.[14] Although there was undoubtedly a good deal of exaggeration in all these claims, they were convincing enough for the electorate and the Liberals were easily returned to power.

Another ambitious project undertaken by the government to further its goal of "Maîtres chez nous" was the establishment in 1964 of a government corporation, La Sidérurgie du Québec (SIDBEC), which was to set up a fully integrated steel complex on the St. Lawrence River near Montreal, thus breaking Quebec's dependence on the Ontario steel industry in the Hamilton area. There were some who dreamed that, with the combination of the steel complex, cheap electric power, and the iron ore of northern Quebec, the valley of the St. Lawrence could become an industrial area like the valley of the Ruhr in Germany. Liberal hopes for SIDBEC were soon dashed, however: the project involved larger sums of money than were anticipated, there were management problems, and the government was divided whether it should be completely state-owned or a mixed enterprise with some participation of private capital. The Liberals were out of office before the project could be fully implemented.[15] Aside from SIDBEC, there was one other less spectacular public enterprise created by the Lesage administration: La Société Québécoise d'Exploration Minière (SOQUEM), whose purpose it was to involve the government in the discovery and exploitation of mineral resources.

The proposal of the Lesage government to give various forms of assistance to strengthen small and medium-sized Quebec-based firms was not an original one; in one form or the other it had been in the programme of every Quebec party since the nineteen-thirties. In pursuit of this goal yet another crown corporation was set up in 1962 called

[13]Liberal Party advertisement, *La Presse*, 16 oct. 1962.

[14]*Ibid.*; see also Lesage statement, *La Presse*, 1 oct. 1962; Lévesque's statement, *Montreal Star*, Nov. 8, 1962.

[15]On the problems surrounding SIDBEC see, Richard Jones, *Community in Crisis: French-Canadian Nationalism in Perspective* (Toronto, 1972), pp. 136–7.

La Société Générale de Financement (S.G.F.). The S.G.F. was to be financed not only by government funds but also by participation of the private investor. Its purpose was to provide financial assistance, as well as managerial and technical expertise where needed, to those Quebec firms with modest capitalization, often family-owned, which were struggling for survival. It was hoped that these firms would prosper and develop into larger corporations which would some day challenge the dominant position of the large foreign-owned companies in the same field.

Probably one of the most important and least publicized aspects of the modernization process undertaken by the Lesage government was its "bureaucratic revolution," involving the complete reform and rationalization of the public service. In one respect some such reform could have been expected, for one of the major proposals of the Liberals in the election campaign was the elimination of the patronage and political corruption of the Duplessis regime. An even more important factor was that the large increase in the activities of the state and the complex nature of its undertakings called for a much more efficient public service than could be obtained under a system of appointment and promotion based on political favouritism.

Although political patronage was not completely eliminated, the emphasis in the hiring policies of government departments and agencies was on competence and expertise, not political affiliation. The Civil Service Commission, set up in 1944 but with little power during the Duplessis regime, was revitalized and given a greater role in recruitment and promotion, and a new system of scientific personnel management was introduced. Public servants were given the right to organize, to bargain collectively, and to strike.[16]

The "bureaucratic revolution" was not only characterized by the dwindling influence of political patronage but also by a spectacular increase in numbers, technical skill, and influence of the new class of bureaucrats.[17] The increase in numbers was the natural result of increased state activity and the creation of new departments, public enterprises, and other governmental agencies. The technical skill of the new public service was due to a well-planned campaign to recruit a brilliant group of administrators and specialists from the universities, the federal public service, and the business world. These specialists

[16]See André Gelinas, "The Quebec Public Service," in Dale C. Thomson, ed. *Quebec Society and Politics: Views from the Inside* (Toronto, 1973), pp. 96–7.

[17]Between 1960 and 1965 the number of employees in the public service, including government-owned enterprises (but excluding the personnel of Hydro-Québec and Société des Alcools) increased by 53 per cent. See Daniel Latouche, "Le vrai nature de la Révolution tranquille," *Canadian Journal of Political Science*, VII, 3 (Sept. 1974), p. 532.

quickly moved into the senior posts in all branches of the administration, while positions at the junior level were filled by graduates fresh from the universities.[18] With its high level of professional competence the Quebec bureaucracy, like bureaucracies everywhere, had its own conception of the policies which should be pursued. Although the public no doubt exaggerated its influence, there is no question of the importance of its role in the decision-making process during the Quiet Revolution—a role it continued to play long after the Lesage government was out of office.

Closely connected with the Liberal Party's drive to eliminate patronage, other reforms were introduced in regard to the financing of elections and some changes were made in the electoral map. In an attempt to decrease the influence of business firms and other special interests in the electoral process a bill was passed limiting campaign expenditures of candidates as well as parties. A modest system of state subsidies was also introduced under which the government reimbursed candidates for part of their election expenses.[19] One other important change in the Election Act was the reduction of the voting age from 21 to 18.

The distortions in Quebec's electoral map which gave gross over-representation to the province's rural population in the legislature was a matter of considerable concern for the government. The basic problem was the urgent necessity to give Montreal and other urban areas more seats, and to eliminate many of the rural or semi-rural electoral districts with dwindling population. The major obstacle to eliminating the rural seats was Section 80 of the British North America Act which protected a group of thirteen electoral districts in the western and southern part of the province from alteration without the consent of a majority of their sitting members. This was an archaic provision intended to protect the representation of the predominantly English-Protestant population in these areas at the time of Confederation. In order to eliminate Section 80 a bill would have to be passed by both houses of the provincial legislature which would almost certainly be blocked by the Union Nationale–dominated Legislative Council.[20] In the face of this obstacle the government had to remain content with a limited reform by giving the Montreal

[18]For a description of the new public service see Peter Desbarats, *The State of Quebec* (Toronto, 1966), chap. VIII. A by-product of the increase in governmental personnel was that it provided additional opportunities for many of the graduates of Quebec's French universities who were unable to find, or were not interested in finding, positions in the large English-dominated business corporations.

[19]Harold M. Angell, "The Evolution and Application of Quebec Election Expense Legislation, 1960–66," *Report of the Committee on Election Expenses* (Ottawa, 1966).

[20]In regard to the problems surrounding Section 80 see James Stewart, "First Step: Repeal Law on Fixed Ridings," in *Election Analysis Pinpoints Reform Need* (reprinted from *Montreal Star*, May 30–June 5, 1970).

area eleven additional seats and adding two others in the Lac Saint-Jean area.

The intervention of the Lesage government in the fields of health, welfare, and labour legislation equalled that of its active role in educational reform and economic development. Shortly after coming into office the Liberal government introduced a comprehensive hospital insurance plan; in 1964 it set up a universal, compulsory, and contributory pension plan. It also began to exercise more control and intervene more actively in the regulation of private welfare agencies which were still largely under the control of the Church. These institutions had to conform to standards and procedures established by the government and they increasingly depended on the government for their financing. In the field of labour legislation the most important move was the enactment of a Labour Code in 1964 which eliminated the one-sided and discriminatory legislation of the Duplessis era against the trade unions.

The modernizing policies of the Quiet Revolution which we have been describing had a significant impact on the relations between Quebec and the federal government. Those relations were usually as strained under the Lesage administration as they had been during the Duplessis regime, but not for quite the same reasons. The Union Nationale as a nationalist party had been a fervent defender of provincial autonomy on principle, but was satisfied merely with opposing the intervention of the federal government in areas of provincial jurisdiction under the constitution. The Quebec Liberal Party, on the other hand, became a proponent of provincial autonomy by necessity as its concept of a dynamic, interventionist state, legislating in many different fields, put it in conflict with the federal government which had already entered these fields or was about to do so. The Lesage administration's ambitious legislative programme also called for increasingly large sums of money and resulted in a continual struggle with Ottawa over a larger share of the tax dollar.

A major source of disagreement between Quebec and Ottawa, and one which was the subject of considerable debate at every federal-provincial conference in the early sixties, was the federal government's shared-cost programmes. This type of programme was an arrangement under which the federal government offered to make a grant to the provinces for the introduction of a certain service, such as hospital insurance, provided that the province set up a plan which conformed to certain standards set by Ottawa, and that it paid a certain proportion of the total cost.[21] These shared-cost programmes were the most frequent

[21]See R. MacGregor Dawson, *The Government of Canada*, revised by Norman Ward (5th edition, Toronto, 1970), p. 105.

method used by the federal government to intervene indirectly in areas such as health, welfare, and education which were under provincial jurisdiction. Since the war Ottawa had argued that such intervention was necessary in order to equalize services and opportunities available to every Canadian citizen regardless of the part of the country in which he lived.

Whatever the merits of these programmes from the federal point of view, they constituted an invasion of provincial jurisdiction under Section 92 of the B.N.A. Act and as such ran headlong into the opposition of the Quebec government, and to a lesser extent the governments of the other provinces. The provinces argued that shared-cost programmes compelled them to conform to Ottawa's priorities rather than their own, but if they refused to go along with the central government's proposals they would sacrifice sizable federal grants. The Lesage government presented the additional argument, which was essentially the same as that of the Duplessis administration, that Quebec linguistically and culturally was not the same as the other provinces, and that that province's government was the one which was in the best position to decide on priorities to meet its people's cultural and material aspirations.

The solution to this problem proposed by Lesage, with some support from the other provinces, was that a province would have the right to "contract out" of federal programmes involving conditional subsidies whenever it felt it necessary to do so, and at the same time receive adequate compensation from Ottawa so that it would not suffer financially compared to the other provinces. This proposal ultimately won the reluctant agreement of Ottawa, and shortly afterwards the Quebec government announced its withdrawal from a large number of existing shared-cost programmes.[22]

Although the federal government of Lester B. Pearson, which came to power in 1963, was generally sympathetic to Quebec's special position, there was one notable exception. For some years the central government had been planning to establish a Canada-wide, universal, contributory pension scheme. Just as it was about to launch it, Lesage stunned the delegates to the 1964 federal-provincial conference by unexpectedly announcing that Quebec intended to go ahead with its own plan. After lengthy and involved negotiations between the Quebec and federal governments, the latter agreed that the Canada Pension Plan would not apply within Quebec.[23] There was incidentally much more than

[22]For a description of the dispute over shared-cost programmes see Donald V. Smiley, *Canada in Question: Federalism in the Seventies* (2nd ed., Toronto, 1976), pp. 134–40; and Jones, *Community in Crisis*, pp. 97–9.

[23]The negotiations between the two governments are described in Desbarats, *The State of Quebec*, chap. IX.

provincial rights involved in this incident. The fact that Quebec would have its own pension plan meant that it would have full control over the large sums of money in the plan's investment fund which could be used as a source of financing for provincial and local governments.

Another major grievance of the Lesage government against the federal authority also originated with the Duplessis administration: the federal government's monopolization of the taxation fields of personal and corporation income taxes and succession duties. As the costs of the province's modernization programme steadily escalated, the Lesage administration increased its pressure on the federal authority to reduce its level of taxation in these fields so that the province could move in. In 1963 Lesage demanded that Ottawa vacate the field of corporation taxes by 25 per cent, personal income tax by 25 per cent, and succession duties by 100 per cent. With considerable support from the other provinces he gradually obtained some, but not all, of his demands. By 1966 Ottawa was turning over to the provinces 24 per cent of the personal income tax and 75 per cent of the succession duties. Although these concessions were welcomed, they failed to satisfy the appetite of the Lesage or succeeding Quebec administrations.[24]

There was one other controversy between the Quebec and federal governments during Lesage's term of office which should be mentioned, one which up to then had not been very much to the fore. It arose out of the contention of the Lesage government that Quebec had the right to sign international agreements with the governments of other countries on certain matters. The Quebec argument was that Section 92 of the B.N.A. Act, in giving the provinces authority to legislate in such matters as education and cultural affairs, also gave it the authority to make international agreements or treaties in these areas.[25] This argument was vigorously contested by the federal government whose general position was that, although the provinces could negotiate agreements with other countries, they must advise the federal government, and that such agreements were only valid when they were concluded under the authority of the federal power.[26] This issue was to be an increasing source of friction in the relations between Quebec and Ottawa.

In spite of the often acrimonious debate between Quebec and the federal government during the Lesage administration, the Quebec Lib-

[24]In regard to the dispute with Ottawa over taxation see Jones, *Community in Crisis*, pp. 111–14; and Dawson, *The Government of Canada*, pp. 112–14.

[25]For a scholarly presentation of the Quebec argument see Jacques-Yvan Morin, "The Treaty-Making Power of Quebec," in Frederick Vaughan *et al.*, *Contemporary Issues in Canadian Politics* (Scarborough, Ont., 1970), pp. 128–38.

[26]See Jones, *Community in Crisis*, p. 108; and Gilles Lalande, "Quebec and International Affairs," in Thomson, *Quebec Society and Politics*, pp. 243–5.

eral party remained staunchly federalist at a time when an increasing number of individuals and groups in Quebec, "the separatists," were attracted by the idea of Quebec breaking away from Canada and becoming an independent state. Speaking in the National Assembly in June, 1965, Lesage stated: "nous vivons dans un pays qui s'appelle le Canada. Nous sommes des Québécois mais nous sommes aussi des Canadiens. Cela, on ne me l'ôtera pas de l'idée."[27] Although strongly rejecting separatism, the Quebec Liberal party increasingly pressed for wide-sweeping changes in the Canadian constitutional structure which would give the province some form of special status.[28]

Before turning to the Union Nationale and its reaction to the Quiet Revolution, there are a few brief observations which must be made concerning the record of the Lesage administration between 1960 and 1966. Although Lesage's Liberal party did not carry through with all of its ambitious plans, and in the view of some critics was not vigorous enough in certain directions, it nevertheless was a government which left a strong imprint on Quebec society. It developed a public service conforming to the needs of the modern industrial state, it took the first steps in the regulation and subsidization of election funds, it set up a system of health and social services comparable to or better than most industrial states, it vigorously defended Quebec's special position in the Canadian constitutional system while still remaining staunchly federalist—a difficult balancing act.

There are two areas where the Liberal record deserves special attention: the educational revolution for which the Lesage administration was responsible; and the initiative it took in bringing about for the first time the active intervention of the state in the province's economy. By expanding and modernizing the educational system the people of Quebec became increasingly qualified to take over some of the key positions in the industrial system which had escaped them up to then. The activity of the state in the economy, particularly in the natural resource industries, meant that the people of the province, through their government, were at least beginning to have some control over their foreign-dominated economic system. Accomplishments in both areas, particularly the latter, fell short of expectations, but they were a strong beginning.

Perhaps the most important aspect of Lesage's Quiet Revolution was not so much what it accomplished, although that was not negligible, but what it set in motion, the innovations it introduced, the new ground it broke. Subsequent Quebec administrations all continued to a greater or lesser extent policies for which the Quiet Revolution had prepared

[27]*Le Devoir*, 25 juin 1965.
[28]See speech at Ste. Foy, Qué., *Le Devoir*, 15 déc. 1965.

the way. It is for this reason that the Lesage administration from 1960 to 1966 was one of the most outstanding periods in Quebec's history.

DANIEL JOHNSON AND THE OLD GUARD

The ability of the Union Nationale to recover and return to power in 1966 was not only unexpected, but it was also no small achievement if we consider the difficult situation in which the party found itself after the 1960 defeat, and the sharp challenge it faced from the popular reforms of Lesage's Quiet Revolution. That achievement must be attributed mainly to the perseverance and political skill of a rather unusual politician by the name of Daniel Johnson. Johnson was elected leader of the Union Nationale at its convention of 1961 and remained in that post until his sudden death in 1968. In seeking an answer to the question of how he succeeded in staging a comeback for his party we must direct our attention to the internal problems of the Union Nationale in the early sixties, examine the proceedings of the party convention of 1961, and finally, have a close look at the changing and often contradictory policies pursued by Johnson which enabled the party to win the election of 1966.

Although the Union Nationale remained a sizable opposition in the legislature after its defeat of 1960, the Liberal victory had left it disorganized, badly divided, and suffering from a low level of morale. Its future looked uncertain and it seemed that the party which had been so closely associated with one man, Maurice Duplessis, would not survive the loss of its powerful leader. The troubled situation of the party was aggravated further when the Liberals, shortly after they came to power, set up a commission of inquiry known as the Salvas Commission, with a mandate to investigate the rather questionable purchasing methods of the former administration and inquire into alleged irregularities in its sale of Hydro-Quebec's natural gas system to the Quebec Natural Gas Corporation, a private company. As the Commission's hearings day after day brought out mounting evidence of favouritism, patronage, and political corruption, the Union Nationale's public image deteriorated further.[29]

During the first few months of this difficult period for the Union Nationale, the leader was still Antonio Barrette, who had led the party in the disastrous election campaign of 1960. Barrette's tenure as leader

[29]For official report of the commission's findings, particularly as they affected Martineau and other Union Nationale notables, see *Memoire à la Commission Royale d'Enquête sur les méthodes d'achat utilisées au Département de la Colonisation et au Service des Achats du gouvernement* (Québec, 1963), Deuxième Partie; see also comments, *supra*, p. 141.

was an unhappy one because, as mentioned in the last chapter, his authority from the very beginning had been consistently challenged by the manœuvres behind the scenes of Gérald Martineau, party treasurer, and J. D. Bégin, provincial organizer.[30] These two powerful politicians, whom Barrette denounced as "les éminences grises," had great influence over the rank and file members of the Union Nationale because one controlled party finances and the other party organization. As party treasurer, Martineau was heavily implicated in the investigations of the Salvas Commission. Making no attempt to repudiate the charges of patronage made against the party, Martineau defended these practices with the argument, "As long as there is poverty to be relieved, as long as there are family problems to be resolved, I will not hesitate to reduce the profits of companies and distribute them among hundreds and hundreds of people."[31]

In an attempt to eliminate Martineau's control over party funds Barrette tried to get support from influential members of the party for a plan whereby finances would be turned over to a three- or five-man committee rather than being in the hands of one man. When this attempt failed, Barrette resigned suddenly in September, 1960, with bitter denunciations against his opponents. He was succeeded by Yves Prévost, former provincial secretary, who became parliamentary leader while plans were being made for a leadership convention to be held the following year. When he too resigned a short while later for health reasons, he was succeeded by Antonio Talbot, former Minister of Roads, who carried on as interim leader until the convention.

The Union Nationale convention in Quebec City in September, 1961, was the first one in the history of the party.[32] The task facing the approximately 2,000 delegates who attended was not only to choose a permanent party leader, but also to rebuild the party structure and draw up a programme. Although there were a number of candidates in the running, there were only two who really counted, both of whom had been in the Duplessis cabinet: Jean-Jacques Bertrand, former Minister of Lands and Forests, and Daniel Johnson, former Minister of Hydraulic Resources.

Even before the convention had met it was fairly obvious that it would result in a power struggle between two bitterly opposed factions

[30]See *supra*, pp. 177–8; for a detailed account of the internal party struggle see Antonio Barrette, *Mémoires* (Montréal, 1966), chaps. XIII–XV.

[31]*Gazette*, July 11, 1961; *Montreal Star*, July 11, 1961; see also editorial, *Le Devoir*, 12 juillet 1961.

[32]Although Duplessis had been elected leader of the Quebec Conservative party at its convention of 1933, no convention was held when he became leader of the Union Nationale. See *supra*, pp. 73–5.

whom we will refer to as "the reformers" and "the old guard."[33] Bertrand was the candidate of the reformers, while Daniel Johnson had the support of the old guard, that is, of those who were satisfied with the *status quo* within the party. Bertrand was in the tradition of Paul Sauvé, while Johnson was in that of "le Chef." Bertrand's supporters came mainly from the younger members of the party, some of whom were Conservatives in federal politics. He also had the open support of Madame Sauvé, the widow of the late premier. Johnson was backed by the more influential members of the party in the legislature and also had many of the local organizers at the constituency level working for him.

In his campaign for the leadership Bertrand called for major reforms and renovation of the party from within which would eliminate patronage, end the influence of business and financial interests over party affairs, and make the party structure more democratic. On the subject of patronage, although not denouncing any particular persons, he stated, "there should be no question of dismissing lighly certain practices which are contrary to the common good of the province." He also rejected "this dependence of public men on big financial interests," and proposed that legislation be enacted limiting election expenses and providing government subsidies for all candidates.[34] Party funds should be placed in the hands of a trust company rather than being under the control of one person. Bertrand made a particularly strong plea for a more democratic party structure with the leadership fully accountable to the membership. He called for the establishment of strong party associations in each electoral district which would play the dominant role at the local level instead of leaving all political activities in the hands of a small privileged clique surrounding the deputy. Provincial conventions should be called not only for the purpose of selecting a new leader, but also to provide an opportunity for the rank and file to participate in the formulation of party programmes and policies.[35]

Johnson did not openly reject Bertrand's proposals for reform and the elimination of patronage, but tended rather to ignore these issues whenever possible. On the rare occasion when he did make some comment he argued that whatever reforms the party might have needed had already been accomplished, and that the Salvas Commission was not

---

[33]For a brief description of the convention and the struggle for the leadership see, *Canadian Annual Review*, 1961, pp. 51–3; Christian Vien and Dominique Lapointe, *L'Union Nationale: Son Histoire, ses chefs, sa doctrine* (Québec, 1969), pp. 91–5.

[34]*Gazette*, Aug. 14, 1961.

[35]*Le Devoir*, 18 sept. 1961.

only useless, but designed to cause injury to French Canadians and the Union Nationale. Most of Johnson's campaign speeches focused on the policies of the Liberal administration which, it was contended, would result in the increased socialization of the economy and constituted a threat to the confessional school system. Above all, Johnson's campaign literature stressed his qualities as the party's "best fighter," the candidate whom Lesage feared the most, and presented him as "the only one who can give us back power quickly."[36] This argument, together with the superior organization and finances of Johnson's campaign undoubtedly played an important role in the final results. When the ballots were counted Johnson had won by a narrow margin of 1,006 votes to 912 for Bertrand. The surprising thing was not that Johnson had won, but that the reform wing of the party had shown such strength. The party remained badly divided, however, for although Bertrand offered the new leader his collaboration, his supporters refused to accept their close defeat which they attributed to irregularities in the balloting procedure.[37]

The Union Nationale convention of 1961 not only selected a leader, but also drew up a programme and made some changes in the party structure. This programme was based on resolutions passed by a number of policy committees and then passed on to the general assembly for final consideration. Most of the resolutions were quickly pushed through by the convention organizers with practically no opportunity for debate or amendment. Although this dubious procedure does not say much for the democratic processes in the party, the programme is nevertheless of some importance for the clues it gives us as to the goals and political philosophy of the dominant faction in the party behind Johnson.[38]

As one might have anticipated, the Union Nationale programme put great emphasis on the continuing struggle for provincial autonomy and the recovery of the constitutional rights which had been lost to the federal government. These "droits sacrés" were essential to ensure "le rayonnement d'une civilisation française et catholique sur le territoire québécois."[39] Specifically, the party demanded the elimination of all shared cost programmes, and the withdrawal of the federal government from all fields reserved exclusively for the provinces in the B.N.A. Act

[36]For Johnson's policies and strategy see *Le Devoir*, 25 sept. 1961; *Montreal Star*, Sept. 23, 25, 1961.

[37]*Le Devoir*, 25 sept. 1961; *Gazette*, Sept. 25, 1961.

[38]The main resolutions of the convention as described below are summarized in *Le Devoir*, 25 sept. 1961; see also *Montreal Star*, Sept. 23, 1961; *Gazette*, Sept. 25, 1961.

[39]*Le Devoir*, 25 sept. 1961.

so that Quebec could immediately occupy these fields; the province must have priority in direct taxation and be given the entire field of succession duties.

With an eye on the party's traditionally strong support in small towns and rural areas the programme called for the increased autonomy of municipal governments and school commissions and the provision of new sources of revenue for these lower levels of government. The provincial government should provide subsidies to municipalities for public works and build more rural roads. As "l'agriculture familiale" must remain one of the principal bases of the provincial economy, government assistance must be given to the farmer to lower costs of production and to market his produce.

In the area of economic and social policy we find the usual proposal of Quebec parties for governmental assistance to small and medium-sized business firms, strong support for the principle of private enterprise, public works for the relief of unemployment, the raising of the basic income tax exemption, a provincial pension plan, adoption of a policy of "achat chez nous," and enactment of a Labour Code which, among other things, would abolish company unions. The hospital insurance plan being introduced by the Lesage government was rejected on the argument that it would result in "the socialization of hospitals and the medical profession." Instead it was proposed to introduce a complete health insurance scheme in co-operation with private insurance companies and other organizations.

In the controversial realm of education the party came out in strong defence of the confessional school system in which the continued participation of the clergy and religious orders was absolutely essential. Free schooling was accepted in principle provided that the costs of education were equitably shared among those who were really able to pay them. Nothing must be done to destroy the fundamental values on which the existing educational system rested.

A close scrutiny of the Union Nationale programme of 1961 summarized above indicates that, with a few exceptions, it could have been drawn up by the Duplessis administration. The party was proposing to answer the modernizing challenge of the Quiet Revolution with the policies and political style of another era: it was planning to fight a modern war with the obsolete weapons of yesterday. If further evidence was needed that the Union Nationale of the early sixties was still under the spell of the ultra-conservative and authoritarian tradition of Duplessis we need only look at the attitude of the convention towards party reorganization and finances and the problem of patronage.

Although a resolution was passed to establish permanent local party associations in each electoral district, a proposal to form a provincial federation of these associations which could express the collective will of the membership was rejected.[40] Instead, a permanent secretariat was to be established, headed by a director-general appointed by the leader, which would direct and co-ordinate the activities of the local associations. The convention also decided that three key committees should be set up to advise the leader on matters of political organization, parliamentary strategy, and finance. These committees would each have three to five members, all of them appointed by the leader. The proposal for a finance committee meant one important change: the control of party funds was to be taken from Gérald Martineau, the party treasurer, and turned over to this committee which would be made up of non-parliamentarians. On the question of patronage a resolution was passed giving the leader authority to appoint a committee "to study the problem." At no point during the convention was there any question of censuring either Martineau or Bégin who had been so heavily involved in the Salvas inquiry.

The emphasis which the resolutions above put on "the leadership principle" indicated that the Johnson-dominated convention was not seriously interested in injecting democratic processes into party structures.[41] This left the Union Nationale in much the same position as under Duplessis, with all the major policy decisions and levers of power in the hands of the leader. There was, however, one important difference which should not be overlooked: unlike Johnson, "Le Chef" never had to face a strong reformist faction within the party.

When a political party gives its leader the sweeping authority which the Union Nationale gave to Daniel Johnson, the political views and personality of the leader become an extremely important factor in the direction that party takes, for there is a difference between the possession of power and the way in which it is exercised. In attempting to make an evaluation of Johnson as a political leader we are faced by a difficult task, for he was a complex person and there has always been considerable controversy regarding his personal qualities and the nature of his political convictions.[42]

[40]In reply to a question from a journalist Johnson is reported to have answered, "As far as I am concerned the party is made up of the leader and the ninety-five county associations and nothing more." Montreal Star, Sept. 27, 1961.

[41]For a strong criticism of the party in this respect see Editorial Le Devoir, 25 sept. 1961.

[42]Although there is no adequate biography of Johnson there have been a number of short studies and brief commentaries which provide some insights into his record as a political leader: see Vien and Lapointe, L'Union Nationale, chaps. VIII–IX; Gérard Bergeron, Du Duplessisme à Trudeau et Bourassa, 1956–1971 (Montréal, 1971), pp. 491–501; Jérôme Proulx, Le Panier de crabes: Un Témoignage vécu sur

Daniel Johnson was a lawyer by profession and had served in the Duplessis administration as Minister of Natural Resources. He was not usually looked upon as an intellectual, but no one questioned his intelligence. Although his position as Union Nationale leader gave him great authority, he did not have the authoritarian personality of Duplessis. He was not an orator in the classical style of Lesage, but was still a good platform performer with a sense of humor and informality which gave the impression of "the common touch" which was lacking in the more reserved approach of the Liberal leader. He liked meeting people, moved easily in a crowd, and was perfectly at home sitting around with a group of men in a tavern drinking beer.

The Union Nationale leader was rarely presented in a particularly favourable light in the press or by political commentators who questioned his sincerity or looked upon him as an opportunist with no real convictions. He was often attacked as a demagogue and accused of promoting contradictory policies. The Liberals in an attempt to portray him strictly as a lightweight politician often referred to him as "Danny Boy."[43]

Some of the criticisms of Johnson were justified, some were exaggerated, others were simply mistaken; but the most important failure of his critics was their inability to understand his conception of politics and how he visualized his role as a party leader. Johnson could adhere rigidly to a particular policy then suddenly change it if he thought that position was leading the party nowhere. Although this could be interpreted as opportunism or lack of sincerity, it could also be interpreted as a shrewd appreciation of the difference between the politically desirable and the politically possible.

The criticism that Johnson did not hold any strong convictions was not quite true. Johnson was a Quebec nationalist and a conservative in that order. There can be no question of his life-long commitment to the nationalist cause, although he could be flexible in the means to achieve his goals.[44] Although instinctively conservative on economic and social

---

l'Union Nationale sous Daniel Johnson, Montréal, 1971), pp. 76–107; Richard B. Holden, Election 1970: Le Point Tournant (Montréal, 1970), pp. 10–17; Jean-Louis Laporte, Daniel Johnson, cet inconnu (Montréal, 1968). It should also be mentioned that this writer was personally acquainted with Johnson and some of the comments made here are based on impressions gained from occasional chats with him about Quebec politics.

[43]Newspaper cartoonists at the time often featured Johnson dressed in a cowboy outfit with two guns shooting in all directions.

[44]Around 1939–40 both Johnson and the writer were active in a Canada-wide student body called the Canadian Student Assembly. While the English-speaking students were mostly socialist, the French students were all Quebec nationalists, and

questions, he could compromise on some of his beliefs if he thought the interests of the party demanded it.

Perhaps the answer to the enigma of Johnson is the recognition that he was above all a politician—one hundred percent a politician—who saw his essential role as a leader getting his party into power and keeping it there. If this required some twists and turns in his political position or involved contradictions in policies proposed at different times this had to be done (this attitude was not altogether unique to the Union Nationale, but that party was more obvious). The greatest error of the Liberals, which they were to discover in due time, was to underestimate the abilities of Johnson as a politician. Like his mentor, Duplessis, the Union Nationale leader was an able debater, an aggressive fighter, and above all, a superb political strategist.

In spite of what has just been said here about Johnson's qualities as a political leader, it must be admitted that they were not particularly evident in the first test of his leadership when the Liberals suddenly called an election in 1962. It was a difficult test, however, for the Union Nationale went into the election with three handicaps: the party was under the cloud of the adverse publicity it had received from the procedings of the Salvas Commission; it was still split between the Johnson and Bertrand factions; and above all, the Liberals had made the election a referendum on the nationalization of the power companies, an issue which was bound to have wide popular appeal.

Although Johnson no doubt would have preferred to have the election fought on other issues than the nationalization of power, he was compelled to take a position. That position was a rather ambiguous one, for he proposed that only two small power companies which had been losing money be immediately nationalized, and that a referendum be held after the election to decide on the fate of the other larger and more prosperous companies.[45] It was noteworthy that Bertrand in his election speeches adopted a different position: he agreed in principle that all the power companies had to be nationalized, but criticized the Liberals for the way they were going about it.[46]

In his attempt to steer the election campaign away from the nationalization issue, Johnson made a strong attack on the government accusing at least some of the ministers of favouring the elimination of religion from the educational system and the establishment of neutral

Daniel Johnson was the most intransigent nationalist of them all. Jean-Jacques Bertrand was also active in the C.S.A., but even then he was a moderate nationalist.

[45]*La Presse*, 24 sept. 1962.
[46]*Le Devoir*, 20 oct. 1962.

or secular schools. This met with a vigorous denial from Lesage, and such adverse reaction in the press that Johnson realized he had made a mistake and quickly shifted his criticisms to other aspects of government policy.[47] One particular subject which was consistently referred to by the Union Nationale was the heavy increase in taxation resulting from the government's "politique de grandeur." Johnson referred to the Prime Minister as "Jean La Taxe," and never missed an opportunity to provide a detailed list of new taxes introduced by the government.[48] Another theme was the threat which the private enterprise system faced from some members of the cabinet and particularly René Lévesque. Lévesque was singled out for attack because of his left-wing views and his role in the nationalization of the power companies. On one occasion Johnson was reported to have referred to him as "a semi-Castro and half-baked dictator."[49]

The Union Nationale campaign, however, did not consist only of attacks on government policies. The party also stressed some of the reforms it would introduce if elected to power. Three of these were particularly emphasized at every opportunity: reduction in taxes for low-income groups by raising the level of basic exemptions for single people as well as families; the introduction of a universal portable pension plan; and a substantial raise in the minimum wage. The party's programme also promised increased financial aid to municipalities and the re-establishment of the financial independence of school commissions.[50]

In spite of the Union Nationale's attack on the government's taxation policies and the reforms it proposed to introduce if elected, it was unable to shift the focus of the political debate away from the issue of nationalization of the power companies. The popularity of that issue, together with the split between Johnson and Bertrand, which was obvious throughout the campaign,[51] combined to defeat the Union Nationale. The Liberals were returned to power with an increased majority: 63 seats to the opposition's 31.

[47]For the controversy over the educational issue see, *Montreal Star*, Oct. 12, 1962; *Le Devoir*, 13 oct. 1962; *La Presse*, 15 oct. 1962.

[48]One of the questions asked in a full-page newspaper advertisement was, "Où va notre argent?" *Le Devoir*, 6 oct. 1962; see also speeches by Johnson, *Le Devoir*, 8 oct. 1962; *Montreal Star*, Nov. 1, 1962; and in television debate, *Gazette*, Nov. 12, 1962.

[49]*Gazette*, Oct. 13, 1962.

[50]For summary of Union Nationale programme see, *Gazette*, Nov. 13, 14, 1962; also party pamphlet, *Action Plan for a Young Nation* (Quebec, 1962).

[51]A sensation was caused when Bertrand, under prodding from a student audience, admitted that Johnson as well as Lesage could be considered a demagogue. See *Le Devoir*, 17, 18, 19 oct. 1962.

The defeat of 1962 did not change Johnson's political style or methods of operation. For the first two years or so after that defeat he followed the same practices and policies he had pursued since his appointment to the leadership. Although usually not challenging directly the broad general objectives of the Quiet Revolution, he attacked many of the government's specific policies and methods of achieving them. Johnson's tactics were the sharp thrust here and there, where Liberal mistakes or short-comings left the party vulnerable: a form of guerrilla warfare rather than an all-out frontal attack on the administration's long-term aims.

The favorite topics of the Union Nationale leader in his campaign against the government were pretty much the same as in the 1962 election: high taxation, defence of private enterprise, criticism of the lack of autonomy of municipalities and school commissions, the threat of socialism and secularization in some Liberal programmes, and the "scandal" of a social security system in which benefits went to millionaires as well as to those in need. Johnson was rarely concerned with inconsistencies or in making contradictory statements. He could, for instance, attack state intervention in the economy one day and a short while later demand that the government put large amounts of money into establishing some state-run enterprise.[52]

The Union Nationale devoted a considerable amount of attention to the constitutional question. Johnson called for Quebec's right to self-determination, and put forward a theory which he was to enlarge upon later, that Canada was made up of two sovereign nations which must come together on a basis of equality to remake the constitution. He continually brandished the threat of separatism if self-determination for Quebec was not forthcoming and never ceased to insist that Ottawa must turn over to the province a larger share of the tax dollar.[53]

Johnson's hit-and-run tactics against the Liberals were not particularly successful. By 1964 his general failure to make headway or score points which would embarrass the Lesage administration began to increase the strains within the party, which was still split between the Johnson and Bertrand factions. Johnson was criticized by a party newspaper for giving his followers rhetoric rather than substance, and at the same time dissatisfaction was expressed with the excessively strong agricultural orientation of the Union Nationale. A number of the younger members who had been elected to the legislature in 1962 agitated for

[52]For a rather critical description of Johnson's policies and tactics in the early sixties see Jacques Guay, "Johnson par lui-même," *Le Magazine Maclean*, oct. 1966, pp. 11–13, 26, 28, 30–2; for a more detached view, Thomas Sloan, *Quebec: The Not-So-Quiet Revolution* (Toronto, 1965), pp. 78–80.

[53]See *Le Devoir*, 17, 18 sept., 4 oct. 1963.

structural reforms which would give the party a new and more democratic look. Without rejecting the priority of private enterprise, they
also wanted a more positive attitude adopted towards the role of the
state in the economy. On the far right of the Union Nationale Johnson's
leadership was criticized as ineffective by Yves Gabias, member for
Three Rivers, who had the support of Gérald Martineau, still an influential member of the party with a seat in the upper house.[54]

On top of all these internal problems the Union Nationale lost four
by-elections to the Liberals in August, 1964, in Dorchester, Matane,
Montreal-Verdun, and Saguenay. The Liberal victories in Verdun and
Saguenay could have been expected, but Dorchester and Matane in the
lower St. Lawrence area were strongly rural and the Union Nationale
could have been expected to do better, particularly as the Liberals were
beginning to experience some difficulties with the rural voters, who
were beginning to clamour for more patronage.[55]

In the face of the discouraging situation in which the party found
itself in the fall of 1964 Johnson suddenly decided to make one of those
dramatic reversals of policy of which he was capable: he discarded most
of his old tactics and political style and set himself the task of rejuvenat-
ing the party, democratizing party structures, and reformulating party
doctrines in the general spirit of the Quiet Revolution. In speculating
about the reasons for this turn-about in attitudes, one might ask if Daniel
Johnson, like Saul of Tarsus on the road to Damascus, experienced a
sudden conversion. Or was it his perception as a practical politician
that if the Union Nationale was to have any chance of challenging the
Liberals in the next election the unity of the party must be restored, and
it would have to present to the voters a dynamic programme which
would capture their imagination? Whatever the motivation of the Union
Nationale leader in his sudden change of direction, it was soon obvious
that Daniel Johnson, the spokesman of the Old Guard, had been transformed into Johnson the Reformer.

DANIEL JOHNSON THE REFORMER

There were two aspects to Johnson's drive to rejuvenate and modernize the party. The first one was to recapture the initiative on the constitutional question by coming forward with a bold new set of proposals
concerning the future of Quebec in the Canadian federal system. The
second one was to call a party convention to reorganize party structures,

[54]The unrest within the party is described in Le Devoir, 17 nov. 1964.
[55]In at least one electoral district the Liberals tried hard to meet these demands;
see Brian Upton, "The Pork Barrel in Dorchester," Montreal Star, Oct. 1, 1964.

reappraise the party's traditional policies, and lay the groundwork for a new programme to be presented to the voters in the next election.

The urgency for the Union Nationale to present a fresh and original contribution to the constitutional impasse was due to the fact that, when the Quebec Liberal party by force of circumstances became strong defenders of provincial autonomy against federal intrusions, they moved sharply towards the traditional position of Quebec nationalists. It had therefore become necessary for Johnson to take vigorous steps to re-establish the Union Nationale as the leading exponent of the nationalist persuasion in Quebec politics, and outstanding champion of the province's special interests within Confederation.

Lesage's Liberal party was not the only cause for concern on the part of Daniel Johnson in his determination to reassert the position of the Union Nationale as Quebec's major nationalist party. He also had to face the challenge of a number of small but growing nationalist groups on the fringes of his party which had taken the logical step, in their view, of moving along the road from provincial autonomy to complete independence for Quebec. The most important of these separatist parties were the left-wing Rassemblement pour l'Indépendance Nationale (R.I.N.), and the right-wing Regroupement National, whose name was later changed to Ralliement National (R.N.).[56]

Johnson's new manifesto on the constitutional controversy took the form of a book called, *Egalité ou Indépendance*,[57] whose publication was carefully timed to appear with considerable fanfare on the eve of the party convention of March, 1965 (the proceedings of the convention are fully discussed later in this chapter). The first part of the book is mostly historical, dealing with the French Canadian's struggle for survival, the conflicts between Canada's two founding peoples, and the failure of past attempts to resolve the country's constitutional problems. It is only in the latter part of this rather slim book that Johnson puts forward his basic ideas for a new constitutional regime.

Johnson's starting point is that Canada consists of two nations, one English, and one French. Following Larousse's dictionary, he defines a nation as: "Communauté humaine, le plus souvent installée sur un même territoire, et qui, du fait d'une certaine unité historique, linguistique, religieuse ou même économique, est animée d'un vouloir-vivre commun."[58] The French-Canadian nation, it is emphasized, does not consider Quebec as just another province but as its homeland; it

[56]The origin and policies of these two parties are dealt with more fully in chap. XI, pp. 243–8.
[57]Montreal, 1965.
[58]*Ibid.*, p. 22.

is looked upon as a true nation state. While each of Canada's national communities has the basic right to self-determination, Johnson argues that the French-Canadian nation needs much greater powers than it received under the constitution of 1867: "Ce que nous voulons en fait, c'est le droit de décider nous-mêmes ou d'avoir part égale aux décisions dans tous les domaines qui concernent notre vie nationale."[59]

The solution to the problem of the continuing constitutional conflict as seen by the Union Nationale leader is to discard the B.N.A. Act in its entirety and draw up a completely new constitution. This constitution would be based on an alliance of two nations, each having all the sovereignty necessary to achieve fully its cultural, social, and economic goals, and both working together as equal partners in the management of their common interests.[60] It would be drawn up by a constituent assembly made up of delegates from the two Canadian nations, with some representation from other ethnic groups. Among other things it would clearly state the fundamental principle of the equality of both languages and cultures throughout Canada. Johnson was not too concerned whether the new constitutional arrangement was called—federation, associate states, confederation, or some other term; the essential thing was that it must give the French-Canadian nation "tous les pouvoirs qui lui sont nécessaires pour assumer son propre destin."[61]

As the title of his book implies Johnson was not only making a constitutional proposal but was also making a threat—the threat of Quebec breaking away from Canada if its essential demands were not met. The separatist solution was not to be rejected a priori: "Si la sécession devenait pour les Canadiens français le seul moyen de rester eux-mêmes, de rester français, alors ce ne serait pas seulement leur droit, ce serait même leur devoir d'être séparatistes."[62] The alternative of independence is put forward rather reluctantly and as a last resort, and before having recourse to it Johnson would like to do everything possible to resolve the problem of English-French relations in a less extreme way. At the same time he points out that there are some serious minded separatists who contend that if independence could be achieved first it would then be easier to establish a basis of co-operation between English and French Canada on a basis of equality.[63]

The proposals put forward in Johnson's book received enthusiastic support in the ranks of his party and general approval in other nationalist circles throughout the province. There was some criticism, however,

[59]*Ibid.*, p. 120.
[60]The proposals for a new constitution are to be found in *ibid.*, chaps. IX and X.
[61]*Ibid.*, p. 123.
[62]*Ibid.*, p. 110.
[63]*Ibid.*, pp. 108–9.

that the Union Nationale leader was ambiguous in places, particularly in his use of the term "égalité." One critic asked whether Johnson was talking about equality for individuals of French origin throughout the country, equality for French Canadians as a national community spread across Canada, or equality for a political society called Quebec.[64] Another criticism was that his proposals were too general and did not provide enough details.[65]

The vagueness and ambiguities in some of Johnson's use of terms may not have been accidental. He was aware that within the Union Nationale there were nationalists who were federalists and also a smaller group of nationalists who were separatists.[66] A position which was too clear-cut one way or the other could have split the party. From statements made by Johnson in later years it seems that what he had in mind was that Quebec, acting as the spokesman for the French-Canadian nation, would negotiate a new constitution with the federal government, acting as the spokesman for English Canada; the new constitution would give Quebec such a dramatic increase in legislative powers that it would be in fact, if not in name, practically a sovereign state.[67]

In spite of any shortcomings of Johnson's book from the point of view of clarity, it was nevertheless an important new departure in the constitutional debate and achieved Johnson's goal of clearly re-establishing the Union Nationale as the major spokesman of Quebec nationalism. While Johnson was calling for vastly increased legislative powers for Quebec in a completely new constitution, the Liberals up to then had been mostly concerned with repossessing those legislative powers under the B.N.A. Act which had been invaded by the federal government. While it is true that in its later years the Lesage administration began to call for special status for Quebec, it never went as far as Johnson in presenting independence as a possible option, thus giving that solution a certain respectability it never had before.

Around the same time as the publication of *Egalité ou Indépendance* Johnson scored another point against the Liberals over a proposal put forward by the federal government for a new amending procedure for the Canadian constitution which was known as the "Fulton-Favreau

[64]Richard Arès, S.J., "Egalité ou indépendance: quelle égalité? pour qui et par qui?" *Relations*, no. 321 (nov. 1967).

[65]Editorial, *Le Devoir*, 23 mars 1965.

[66]Johnson specifically mentioned that there were separatists in his party; see *Egalité ou Indépendance*, p. 106.

[67]See *infra*, pp. 233–4. One Union Nationale member who later went over to the Parti Québécois contended that Johnson knew that the people of Quebec were not yet ready for independence, and he therefore attempted to bring them along slowly and progressively towards their "libération." See Proulx, *Le Panier de crabes*, pp. 198–9.

formula." Briefly stated, this formula would have given the Parliament of Canada the power to amend the constitution, with certain important subjects excepted, provided that such amendment was agreed to by the legislatures of two-thirds of the provinces representing at least 50 per cent of the population of Canada. The exceptions concerned such areas as the use of the French and English languages, legislative powers of the provinces under the existing constitution, and a number of other matters. In the case of these exceptions any amendment had to be agreed to by all the provinces, or in some cases only by the provinces affected.[68]

Prime Minister Lesage at first gave Quebec's endorsement to the Fulton-Favreau formula because it meant repatriation of the Canadian constitution. However, from the very beginning the federal proposals were under attack from a good section of the French-language press and from the official opposition. The Union Nationale leader contended that they would eliminate the possibility of any special status for Quebec, and any modification of the existing constitution would only be in the direction of increased federal powers. He vowed to fight the proposals to the bitter end. The agitation of the Union Nationale against the formula, together with resistance from other groups in the province, forced Lesage to reconsider and shortly afterwards he withdrew Quebec's endorsement of the federal proposals.[69] While Lesage had lost face, Johnson's self-appointed role as the champion of Quebec's constitutional interests had been reinforced.

The second major step in Johnson's drive to rejuvenate the Union Nationale and give it a new image was taken in December, 1964, when he called a party caucus in a resort area north of Montreal to make plans for a party convention to be held in March, 1965, to discuss reforms in policies and party structures. The convention would be made up of three delegates from each electoral district, at least one of whom would be a woman and one a young person. Preparatory regional assemblies were to be held in Montreal and Quebec City in January and February. A beginning was made at the caucus in healing the breach between Johnson and Bertrand when the Union Nationale leader stressed that one of the major purposes of the convention would be to give the party a fully democratic structure all the way from the poll level up.[70]

The Union Nationale convention of 1965 was held in Montreal on March 19, 20, and 21, under the slogan of "Québec d'abord." The con-

[68]For text of Fulton-Favreau Formula see Paul Fox, *Politics: Canada* (3rd ed., Toronto, 1970), pp. 465–9.
[69]The controversy over the Fulton-Favreau proposals is described in Jones, *Community in Crisis*, pp. 119–21.
[70]*Le Devoir*, 12 déc. 1964.

vention, or "assises" as Johnson preferred to call it, was attended by around 1,200 official delegates, most of whom had paid their own expenses, even though they came from remote corners of the province. In addition, there were a thousand or more party supporters who attended all or part of the sessions. The delegates, a good many of whom were young people, participated enthusiastically in one or the other of the various committees which had been set up on such matters as the constitution, labour, education, and so on.[71]

In addition to official delegates and other party members the Union Nationale was also successful in obtaining the participation in the convention of an impressive number of non-party specialists representing various interests groups throughout the province: chambers of commerce, trade unions and co-operatives, teachers' associations, patriotic and student organizations, school commissions, and classical colleges. There were a good number of university professors, journalists, educators, and other intellectuals. For the most part these specialists acted as discussion leaders or resource people on the different panels. Points of view on economic and social matters ranged from far right to left of centre, and on constitutional options from revised federalism to separatism.

After their deliberations each of the committees put forward a number of resolutions for consideration in plenary session. These resolutions fell into two broad categories: reformulation of party policy, and reform of party structures. In regard to party policy it was to be expected that there would be a good deal of discussion on constitutional questions and specifically on the proposals put forward in *Egalité ou Indépendance*. The conference gave enthusiastic support to Johnson's ideas and at the same time strongly endorsed the party's stand on the Fulton-Favreau formula. There were also two highly controversial resolutions put forward in the constitutional committee which were side-tracked or amended before reaching plenary session. One of them, a proposal to make Quebec an officially unilingual state, was deferred for further study, but only after a heated debate. Another one from the separatist faction at the convention called for the complete independence of Quebec. This was amended to read that "the French-Canadian nation has the right to self determination," and that a referendum of all voters would be held to determine the means of applying this principle.[72]

Aside from constitutional matters, the convention passed a large

[71]The proceedings of the convention and the resolutions passed, as described here, are based on reports in *Le Devoir*, 19, 20, 22 mars 1965; *Montreal Star, March* 22, 1965; also Vien and Lapointe, *L'Union Nationale*, pp. 99–102.

[72]*Le Devoir*, 22 mars 1965.

number of other policy resolutions, only a few of which can be mentioned here: the establishment of a ministry of economic planning and a ministry of immigration; a policy of free education at all levels; the establishment of a complete health insurance scheme; enactment of an "anti-scab law" (a law banning strike-breakers); a law to promote agricultural unionism; creation of a provincial industrial fund; a proposal that property taxes be reserved exclusively for municipalities whose autonomy must be safeguarded; opposition to forced mergers of cities and towns; and a proposal for a Bill of Rights.

In regard to the second main task of the convention, the democratization of party structures, the key problem was that although there were fairly democratic local associations at the level of the electoral district, there was no way in which these associations could directly make their influence felt in the decision-making process at the provincial level. At that level it was the party leader, and to some extent the parliamentary caucus, who decided on policies and other party matters. In order to rectify this situation the convention took the important step of setting up a National Council made up of the party leader, the parliamentary caucus, and three delegates from each local association. The Council was to meet at least once a year, call a policy convention every two years, and had the power to call a leadership convention whenever it was needed. Ordinarily such a convention would only be called when a leader died or retired, but it could also be called if the National Council considered the performance of the existing leader unsatisfactory. The interesting thing about the latter proposal was that it was suggested by Johnson himself.[73]

There is little doubt that the convention's reforms in the area of party structures were an important step towards democratization. They were sufficient to satisfy Jean-Jacques Bertrand's consistent policy in this matter, and he explicitly made a statement to this effect at the end of the convention. At the same time he formally announced his full support for Johnson's leadership, thus ending the schism in the party which had existed since 1961.[74]

The Union Nationale convention of 1965 was in many ways an unusual as well as a successful party gathering. The organization and proceedings of the convention left the impression of an open gathering of people from all walks of life and with all points of view, who were being asked to come forward with policies which would guide the party in formulating its programme and rebuilding its structure. In contrast to the practices of the party in the past, the press was not only permitted but welcomed to attend all sessions including the meetings of the commit-

[73]*Montreal Star*, March 22, 1965.
[74]*Ibid.*

tees. In a leading editorial one Montreal newspaper referred to the convention as the most open and popular of any ever held in the province by a political party.[75] Although the resolutions passed were not binding on the party leadership, it seemed obvious that with the wide publicity they had received they were bound to have an impact on the future orientation of party policy.

The Union Nationale came out of the convention of 1965 revitalized, more democratic in its internal structure, and with a new set of policies and a new public image. There was increased enthusiasm and sense of purpose in the ranks of the militants and the party was strongly united behind the uncontested leadership of Daniel Johnson. Johnson was now ready to move to the next stage in his drive to bring the Union Nationale back to power: getting the party organization into a state of readiness for the forthcoming election which was expected to take place the following year.

HOW THE ELECTION OF 1966 WAS WON

When Jean Lesage announced on April 18, 1966, that the legislature would be dissolved and an election held on June 5th of that year, it was apparent that it would mainly be a struggle between the Liberals and the Union Nationale in spite of the participation for the first time of two new parties. The new parties, both of them separatist, were the left-wing Rassemblement pour l'Indépendance Nationale (R.I.N.), and the right-wing Ralliement National (R.N.). The two major parties contested all of the 108 constituencies, while the R.I.N. entered candidates in 73 seats and the R.N. in 90.

The leading role in the Liberal campaign was left to Lesage, although a few other cabinet ministers like Lévesque, Kierans, and Gérin-Lajoie also did some general campaigning. When announcing the election Lesage had stated that the government was seeking a mandate from the voters to strengthen its hand in negotiations with Ottawa for a larger share of the tax dollar.[76] In spite of this initial statement the Liberals did not fight the election as much on the issue of federal-provincial relations as on the party's record of accomplishments and the legislation it proposed to introduce if returned to power.[77]

The Liberal programme, under the slogan of "Québec en marche,"

[75]*Le Devoir*, 24 mars 1965; see also Gérard Bergeron, *Du Duplessisme au Johnsonisme, 1956–1966* (Montreal, 1967), pp. 376–9.

[76]*Le Devoir*, 19 avril 1966.

[77]The Liberal party had full-page advertisements in the daily press listing its accomplishments since coming to power and its plans for the future, see *Le Devoir*, 11, 24, 31 mai 1966; in the English press the heading was, "Six Years of Achievement, Six Years of Unparalleled Progress," *Montreal Star*, June 4, 1966.

called for the federal government to turn over to the province a greater share of corporation and personal income taxes and succession duties, and demanded that Ottawa transfer to the province full control over family allowances, old age security pensions, and other programmes considered to be constitutionally under provincial jurisdiction. These were essentially the same kind of demands that the Quebec Liberals had been making on the federal government for the previous six years. One new proposal was that Quebec should have greater input to federal immigration policies.

The other major proposals of the Liberals could be considered policies essential for the continuation of the Quiet Revolution, although in a somewhat more restrained fashion: introduction of a system of universal health insurance, subsidized housing, a raise in the minimum wage, guaranteed anual income, the creation of a new French-language university in Montreal, establishment of a new department of economic development, abolition of the Legislative Council, a Bill of Rights, and steps to be taken to ensure the priority of French as the language of work and of communication.[78]

From the very beginning of the election campaign the Liberal party assumed that it would be easily returned to power as it had been in 1962. It had an impressive record of accomplishments behind it and Lesage's "politique de grandeur" had given the province a new sense of purpose. It is true of course, that the party was faced with some problems: the reforms of the Quiet Revolution had been costly, resulting in a heavy burden of public debt and increased taxation; there were rumblings of discontent from certain parts of the province over the forced reorganization of school commissions and the plans for amalgamation of small municipalities; the rural areas were unhappy about the building of autoroutes rather than rural roads and the neglect of the agricultural sector generally; the Minister of Labour was under attack from the trade unions for not intervening in some of the strikes which were in progress.

While the Liberals were aware of these weaknesses in their position they did not consider them sufficiently important to endanger seriously their victory at the polls. The Union Nationale, as the Liberal party's main opponent, was not believed to be strong enough to constitute a threat, and its leader, "Danny Boy," was not taken too seriously. It was precisely here that the Liberals made their biggest mistake as subsequent events were to demonstrate.

[78]The official Liberal programme, *Québec en marche: Le Programme politique du parti Libéral du Québec*, is reprinted in Jean-Louis Roy, *Les Programmes électoraux du Québec: Un Siècle de programmes politiques québécois* (Montreal, 1971), II, 425–49; see also summary of programme, *Le Devoir*, 23 avril 1966.

The Union Nationale election campaign of 1966 was to firmly establish Daniel Johnson as a master of political strategy. The campaign, which had been planned well in advance of the election, had two main characteristics: one was the formulation of a well thought-out programme which gave the party the "new look" which Johnson had been trying to achieve since the 1965 convention; the other one was a strategy of concentrating the party's energies on a restricted number of constituencies and winning the election seat by seat, rather than trying to pile up the largest possible number of votes in every electoral district.

The Union Nationale programme appeared in early May with the slogan of "Québec d'abord." In line with Johnson's goal of presenting the Union Nationale as the most authentic spokesman of Quebec nationalism, the programme put great emphasis on constitutional matters. The proposals were essentially the same as those found in *Egalite ou Indépendence*: Quebec's drive for self-determination was to be achieved by the election of a constituent assembly made up of representatives of Canada's "two nations" who would meet on a basis of equality and draw up a new constitution. More immediate goals were for the federal government to turn over to Quebec 100 per cent of the taxation fields of corporation and personal income tax and succession duties, and to withdraw completely from all social security programmes.

The other main planks in the party platform were: the establishment of a ministry of economic planning, a ministry of immigration, a ministry of youth and recreation, and a Quebec radio and television network; the appointment of a provincial ombudsman, abolition of the Legislative Council, and enactment of a Quebec Bill of Rights; French was to be given the status of the province's national language; a new University of Quebec was to be set up; confessional schools would be maintained, but with the full recognition of the rights of those who wanted non-confessional education for their children; the autonomy of municipalities would be safeguarded and they would be given more adequate sources of revenue; there would be an increase in family allowances, a reduction in income taxes at the lower levels, subsidized housing, and crop insurance for the farmers; a health insurance scheme was to be introduced, although it was not stated whether or not it would be universal.[79]

There were several interesting aspects to the new Union Nationale programme. One was the significant contrast in certain areas with the

[79]The official Union Nationale programme, *Objectifs 1966 de l'Union Nationale, un programme d'action pour une jeune nation; Québec d'abord*, is reprinted in Roy, *Les Programmes électoraux du Québec*, II, 405–25; see also summary of programme, *Le Devoir*, 2 mai 1966; for an analysis and comparison of the programmes of the two major parties see Vincent Lemieux, ed., *Quatre élections provinciales au Québec, 1956–1966* (Quebec, 1969), pp. 22–5, 49–66.

party's programme of 1961.[80] No longer was "l'agriculture familiale" referred to as one of the principal bases of the province's economy; while confessional schools were still emphasized, the rights of parents who wanted non-sectarian schools were also recognized; in references to Quebec's culture it was "our French language and culture," rather than "our French and Catholic culture." Another feature of the programme was that in many areas it was the same or close to that of the Liberals, although there were still important differences in matters of health, welfare, and the constitution. All of these changes did not mean that the Union Nationale had taken a sharp turn to the left and become a radical party, but it certainly had moved from the far right towards the centre.

The second characteristic of Johnson's strategy, fighting the election at the local level in a limited number of seats, was clearly spelled out by the Union Nationale leader: "Chez nous, c'est simple, on veut gagner les comtés un par un. Lorsque nous aurons 55, nous aurons alors renversé le gouvernement."[81] Candidates were advised to concentrate solely on winning their own seats and not to be too concerned about how the party was doing in the province as a whole. Said Johnson, "Que chacun de vous se fasse élire, et je serai premier ministre le 5 juin."[82] The number of seats on which the party focused its main efforts numbered about sixty. These seats had been selected on the basis of a careful study made of seats won and lost in the 1962 election which had indicated where the party had its best chances. For obvious reasons the party did not publicize the constituencies on which it was directing its heavy artillery, but it was apparent that not too many of them, perhaps about ten, were in the Montreal area. In particular, little time or money was wasted on the predominantly English seats in western Montreal, the graveyard of nationalist candidates since the thirties.

If Johnson's strategy of winning the election seat by seat was to be successful, two key requirements had to be fulfilled: the type of candidate selected must have strong local appeal; and the party had to put the emphasis on local issues and local grievances. In regard to the first requirement the party concentrated its efforts on selecting candidates whose activities had made them well known in the electoral district: members of school commissions, chambers of commerce, co-operatives and credit unions, farm organizations, and in general people who were

[80]See *supra*, pp. 203–5.

[81]Lemieux, *Quatre élections provinciales au Québec*, p. 23; for Johnson's electoral strategy see Proulx, *Le Panier de crabes*, pp. 7–8; Claude Ryan, "Quebec Changes Governments," *Foreign Affairs*, XLV, 1 (Oct. 1966), pp. 148–61.

[82]Vien and Lapointe, *L'Union Nationale*, p. 108.

influential "local notables."[83] The party was particularly successful in recruiting local government officials: fourteen of the party's candidates were mayors and ten were municipal councillors.[84] There were also ten of the party's candidates who were listed as professors.[85] Although these candidates were mostly younger men from small colleges in the vicinity rather than from the large city universities, this was still a bit unusual for a party which had never been particularly successful in attracting intellectuals.

One type of candidate very much sought after by the Union Nationale was the individual who was not only influential in his own electoral district, but could also influence voters in surrounding districts. In rural Nicolet, for instance, the candidate, a former federal Conservative, had been active in agricultural organizations and could be expected to swing a good portion of the farm vote in adjacent constituencies. In working-class Maisonneuve in Montreal's east end, the candidate, a trade union leader, had the support of the President of the Montreal Labour Council (Q.F.L.).[86] This would help the Union Nationale candidates in other working-class districts along the Montreal waterfront. One other characteristic of the Union Nationale candidates was that 80 per cent of them had never run in a provincial election before; many were in their thirties, and the average age was just above forty.[87] Not only had the party's programme and style been given a new look, but its personnel as well.

The way in which the Union Nationale's election campaign was focused on the special grievances and interests of different regions can be seen in the type of appeal made by the party in various parts of the province: in the electoral districts of Beauce in the Eastern Townships and Rivière du Loup on the lower St. Lawrence the emphasis was on the threat to confessional schools, the long bus rides for children going to the new regional schools, and the high school taxes;[88] in the district of Yamaska, a farming area, the promise was made of establishing a "Chamber of Agriculture," which would enable the farmers to participate in the formulation and administration of laws relating to agriculture;[89] in Lévis, across the river from Quebec City, an improvement

[83]See Thomas Sloan, "NU Recruits Quality for North Shore Campaign," *Montreal Star*, May 19, 1966.

[84]Lemieux, *Quatre élections provinciales au Québec*, p. 23.

[85]*Le Devoir*, 14 mai 1966.

[86]*La Presse*, 6 juin 1966; *Montreal Star*, June 7, 1966.

[87]See Ryan, "Quebec Changes Governments," *Foreign Affairs*, p. 150.

[88]*Montreal Star*, May 16, 1966; *Le Devoir*, 27 mai 1966; "Le Quebec à l'heure du 5 juin," *Le Devoir*, 20 mai 1966.

[89]"La Campagne électorale," *Le Devoir*, 6 mai 1966.

was promised in the Québec-Lévis ferry service, and the new regional schools were denounced as "gigantisme scholaire."[90]

The focus on local issues was particuluarly evident in some of the speeches made by Johnson in his tour of the province: in the industrial town of Magog in the Eastern Townships where the textile workers were on strike the Union Nationale leader promised that if elected to power he would introduce a labour code more favourable to the workers, and reminded the strikers that at one time he had been a lawyer for a trade union;[91] at Shawinigan in the Laurentian region he stressed the depressed economy of the area and its high level of unemployment, and criticized the Liberals for taxing people of modest means in order to redistribute it to people who did not need it (a reference to the universality of family allowance and other social services);[92] moving on to Mont Laurier in the same region he promised an expansion of the local hospital, a new sports centre, and lower school taxes;[93] in the Abitibi region, the heartland of the social credit movement, Johnson invited Créditistes, as well as separatists, to join forces with the Union Nationale.[94]

The attention which the Union Nationale devoted to local and regional issues did not mean that those matters of province-wide concern were neglected. Johnson gave a good number of speeches to service clubs and business and professional associations, as well as regular radio broadcasts in which all aspects of the party programme were covered. In the Montreal area he carried out several "opérations tornades," or whirlwind tours of a number of electoral districts in the same evening, ending up with a large mass meeting just before election day. On every occasion the party's stand on the constitutional question was emphasized. Two days before the election an advertisement appeared in the newspapers entitled, "Jean Lesage a trahi le Québec,"[95] referring to the Liberal leader's original acceptance of the Fulton-Favreau formula. Presumably this was meant to be a last minute reminder as the voters made their way to the polls.

The outcome of the election of 1966 turned out to be one of the greatest surprises in Quebec's political history. The Union Nationale was returned to power with a slim majority of 56 seats to the Liberals 51. The results left the Liberals stunned and the daily press and political

[90]*Montreal Star*, May 16, 1966; *Le Devoir*, 16 mai 1966; "La Campagne électorale," *Le Devoir*, 18 mai 1966.
[91]*Le Devoir*, 1 juin 1966.
[92]*Le Devoir*, 19 mai 1966.
[93]*Le Devoir*, 23 mai 1966.
[94]*Le Devoir*, 23 mai 1966; *Montreal Star*, May 24, 1966.
[95]*Le Devoir*, 3 juin 1966.

forecasters considerably embarrassed by the unexpected turn of events. The Union Nationale victory seemed all the more paradoxical when one examined the popular vote won by the various parties. While the Union Nationale emerged triumphant it had actually lost a little ground, down from 42.1 per cent in 1962 to 40.9 per cent in 1966. The Liberals on the other hand, with a popular vote of 47.2 per cent were ahead of the Union Nationale, although they too had lost some ground compared to the 56.4 per cent they won in 1962. Neither of the two separatist parties won any seats, but the Rassemblement pour l'Indépendance Nationale (R.I.N.) obtained 5.6 per cent of the popular vote and the Ralliement National (R.N.) 3.2.[96] It was the consensus among political analysts that the reason for both of the major parties losing ground was the participation in the election of these two minor parties. The R.I.N., which was strongest in the Montreal area, took votes away from the Liberals, while the R.N. cut into Union Nationale strength in the small towns and rural areas.[97]

While the Union Nationale was once more back in power, the discrepancy between popular vote and seats won prompted some to ask whether the party had really won the election. One political commentator referred to the election as "la prise du pouvoir par erreur."[98] However, in a single-member constituency system the kind of distortion one finds here between seats won and percentage of popular vote polled is not unusual where there are several parties in the contest. It happened before in Quebec elections, was to happen again, and has happened in other provinces.[99] The distortion is, of course, intensified where there is maldistribution of seats between rural and urban populations as in the present case.

One widely held assumption on the part of the press and political commentators on the morrow of the election was that the Union Nationale victory was above all due to its support in the rural areas and small towns. However, before too readily accepting this assumption one should remember that during the Duplessis administration there

[96]The source of election statistic for the two major parties is *Annuaire du Québec*, 1974, p. 120; for the minor parties, *Le Devoir*, 6 juin 1966.

[97]See analysis in Editorial, *Le Devoir*, 10 juin 1966; also Robert Boily, "Montréal, une forteresse libérale," *Socialisme 66*, no. 9 (oct.–déc. 1966), pp. 158–9.

[98]Bergeron, *Du Duplessisme à Trudeau et Bourassa*, p. 498.

[99]The Union Nationale won the election of 1944 with 52.8 per cent of the seats, but only 35.8 per cent of the popular vote, *Annuaire du Québec*, 1974, p. 120; the Parti Québécois was to win the election of 1976 with 63.6 per cent of the seats, but only 41.37 per cent of the vote; André Bernard, *Québec: élections, 1976* (Montreal, 1976), p. 21; in 1972 the New Democratic party won the election in British Columbia with 69 per cent of the seats and 39 per cent of the vote, *Canadian News Facts*, VI (1972), pp. 869–70.

had always been a tendency among political observers in Quebec and the rest of Canada to look upon the Union Nationale as essentially a rural-based party and consistently underestimate its strength in urban areas.[100] The question of whether or not this was the case in the 1966 election can only be answered by making a careful analysis of the type of electoral district where the Union Nationale was successful. Such an analysis would also serve the useful purpose of indicating the sources of strength and weakness of the party in the last election before it began its steady decline as described in the next chapter.

Table IV shows the regional distribution of Union Nationale support as well as the rural-urban breakdown of the seats won by the party. The first thing to be observed is that the strength of the party lay outside of the Greater Montreal area (Montreal and Jesus Islands); there it won only six of the 27 seats. In practically every other part of the province the party was strong. Approximately 60 per cent of the party's seats were in three regions: the Eastern Townships, the Lower St. Lawrence, and the Laurentian region on the north shore of the St. Lawrence between Montreal and Quebec City. In contrast to the Union Nationale, the greatest Liberal strength was in Montreal and the electoral districts immediately surrounding it: the party captured twenty seats in Greater Montreal and eight others within a 25–35 mile radius.[101] This represents almost 60 per cent of the seats won by the Liberals. It is not surprising that at the time Montreal was referred to as "une forteresse libérale."

In regard to the rural-urban breakdown of Union Nationale support, Table IV shows that 22 of the party's 56 seats were predominantly rural and 11 were mixed rural-urban. The latter category consisted mostly of industrial towns surrounded by farming or forest areas. These two categories combined make up around 60 per cent of the seats won by the Union Nationale and indicate clearly its dependence on the voters in rural areas and small cities and towns.

In spite of the Union Nationale's strong rural orientation, Table IV shows that 23 of the party's seats, roughly 40 per cent of the total, were predominantly urban, indicating some success with important segments of the urban population. However, as some of these urban seats had sizable rural minorities, a closer look at the urban pattern of voting is called for. Here we must refer to Table V showing the popular vote in

[100]See *supra*, pp. 98–9.

[101]For Liberal seats won in Greater Montreal see, "Carte politique de Montreal," *La Presse*, 6 juin 1966; the seat won by an independent Liberal in Robert Baldwin is included in our figures; the eight other seats referred to were: Beauharnois, Chambly, Chateauguay, Deux Montagnes, Napierville-Laprairie, Taillon, Verchères and Vaudreuil-Soulanges.

Greater Montreal and Greater Quebec, and in cities throughout the province with populations of 20,000 or over.

As we can see from Table V the two main parties were almost equal in strength in the seventeen cities around the province outside of the Montreal and Quebec regions, the Liberals having a majority or plurality in nine and the Union Nationale in eight. Nor were the Union Nationale victories all in the smaller towns. The party captured three out of the four regional capitals: Three Rivers in the St. Maurice region; Sherbroke in the Eastern Townships; and Chicoutimi in the Lac St. Jean area. The Liberals retained their traditional stronghold of Hull in western Quebec. In Greater Quebec the Liberals had a slight plurality in spite of the fact that their opponents won four out of the six seats in this area.[102] The Liberal plurality was almost completely due to Jean Lesage piling up a huge majority in the fashionable Louis Hébert constituency.

When we turn to the Greater Montreal area our analysis becomes more complex for we have to take into consideration the English-French factor. Greater Montreal is about one-third English-speaking if we include those ethnic groups which have adopted English as their language of daily usage; moreover approximately 80 per cent of the non-French population of the province live in Montreal or in the satellite cities and towns surrounding it.[103] For this reason the vote in Greater Montreal has been broken down into predominantly English and predominantly French electoral districts.

In Montreal as a whole the Union Nationale captured only 30.07 per cent of the votes compared to 55.74 per cent for the Liberals.[104] From Table V, however, it is apparent that the Liberals relied rather heavily on the English voters for their large plurality over the Union Nationale. The English districts gave the Liberals 75.34 per cent compared to the 47.71 per cent which the party received in the French districts. If Montreal was "une forteresse libérale" it is clear that one of the reasons was that it was also "une forteresse anglaise." The Union Nationale on the other hand had insignificant support in the English areas of only 12.80 per cent. However, it won a sizable vote of 37.15 per cent in the French districts, although this was still considerably less than the Liberals.

[102]The Liberals won only Jean Talon and Louis Hébert.

[103]Jacques Henripin, "Quebec and the Demographic Dilemma of French-Canadian Society," in Thomson, ed., Quebec Society and Politics, p. 157.

[104]The total vote in Greater Montreal was 724,917; the Union Nationale had 217,979 votes and the Liberals 404,100; calculations made from official figures in Quebec, Président général des élections, Rapport sur les élections générales de 1966 (Quebec, 1967).

There is one other point worth mentioning: the six seats the Union Nationale won in Montreal were strongly French working-class in the south-eastern part of the city. In Quebec City the party also captured the two strongly working-class districts of St. Sauveur and Limoilou.

In summing up the results of our analysis, we can say that although the hard core of the Union Nationale's support was undoubtedly the

TABLE IV

ELECTORAL DISTRICTS WON BY THE UNION NATIONALE PARTY, RURAL AND URBAN (R & U), BY GEOGRAPHIC REGIONS, IN THE QUEBEC ELECTION OF 1966[a]

Greater Montreal[b]		Montreal Plain[c]		Greater Quebec[d]	
St. Henri	U	L'Assomption	U	St. Sauveur	U
St. Jacques	U	Terrebonne	U	Limoilou	U
Ste. Marie	U	St. Jean	U	Chauveau	U
Maisonneuve	U	Iberville	R-U	Lévis	U
Bourget	U	Richelieu	U	———	
Lafontaine	U	St. Hyacinthe	U	TOTAL	4 U
———		Rouville	R-U		
TOTAL	6 U	———			
		TOTAL	5 U		
			2 R-U		

SOURCES: For seats won by the Union Nationale, Quebec, Président général des élections, *Rapport sur les élections générales de 1966* (Quebec, 1967). The main source for the division of electoral districts into those which are predominantly rural or urban is *Census of Canada*, 1971 (Ottawa), I, Part I, Table 11; in most cases the comparative figures for the 1966 census are also shown, and it is the latter which have been used wherever available, although there is usually no significant difference between them. Where the boundaries of census districts do not coincide with those of electoral districts, which is often the case, the breakdown of rural and urban polling stations in each electoral district as found in the official election report has been referred to. A number of maps showing regional distribution of seats won by the two major parties are to be found in *La Presse*, 6 juin 1966.

[a]The category R-U refers to those electoral districts where the rural and urban populations are almost equal, that is, where the breakdown either way is roughly between 45 and 55 percent.

[b]Montreal and Jesus Islands.

[c]The term used by geographers to describe the lowlands surrounding Montreal.

[d]The city of Quebec and the satellite cities and towns surrounding it, including those directly opposite the City on the south shore of the St. Lawrence.

[e]The north shore of the St. Lawrence between Montreal and Quebec City.

[f]The region southeast of Montreal bordering on the state of Vermont and part of the state of Maine; a few seats on the fringes of the Eastern Townships have been included in this group.

[g]The south shore of the St. Lawrence River between Quebec City and Gaspé; the electoral district of Montmorency has been included in this group, although it is actually on the north shore just east of Quebec City.

[h]The far northern section of the province between the Abitibi and Saguenay regions.

[i]On the border of Ontario.

TABLE IV—Concluded

North Shore–Laurentian[e]		Eastern Townships[f]		Lower St. Lawrence[g]	
Labelle	R	Yamaska	R	Bellechasse	R
Montcalm	R	Bagot	R	Montmagny	R-U
Joliette	R-U	Missisquoi	R-U	L'Islet	R
Berthier	R	Shefford	U	Kamouraska	R
Maskinongé	R	Nicolet	R	Temiscouta	R
Three Rivers	U	Arthabaska	R-U	Rivière-du-Loup	R-U
St. Maurice	U	Sherbrooke	U	Montmorency	R
Champlain	R-U	Lotbinière	R	Gaspé Nord	R
Laviolette	U	Mégantic	U	———	
Portneuf	R	Wolfe	R	TOTAL	6 R
———		Compton	R		2 R-U
TOTAL	5 R	Dorchester	R		
	3 U	Beauce	R		
	2 R-U	Frontenac	R		
		———			
		TOTAL	9 R		
			3 U		
			2 R-U		

Northern Quebec[h]		Western Quebec[i]	
Rouyn-Noranda	U	Papineau	R-U
Roberval	R	Pontiac	R
Lac St. Jean	R-U	———	
Dubuc	R-U	TOTAL	1 R
Chicoutimi	U		1 R-U
———			
TOTAL	1 R		
	2 U		
	2 R-U		

rural areas and the smaller cities and towns, the party also had a considerable amount of support in French-speaking urban areas, particularly outside the Montreal area. Indeed, it could hardly have won the
election without such support. In those urban districts where it managed
to do well it depended to a large extent on working-class voters. In
comparing the Union Nationale under Johnson with that of Duplessis
it is apparent that the sources of party support were much the same,
but the extent of that support was much less than Duplessis received in
his last election of 1956.[105]

In spite of the controversy surrounding the Union Nationale's return
to power with a smaller popular vote than the Liberals, from Johnson's
point of view the election results could be considered satisfactory for
several reasons. One was that he had brought the party a long way from

[105]See Table I, *supra*, p. 99.

TABLE V

PERCENTAGE OF POPULAR VOTE POLLED BY VARIOUS PARTIES IN CITIES OF
20,000 AND OVER, AND IN GREATER MONTREAL AND GREATER QUEBEC,
IN QUEBEC ELECTION OF 1966[a]

Cities	Population (1966)	Liberal	U.N.	R.I.N.	R.N.
Alma	22,195	40.17	51.97		7.80
Cap-de-la-Madeleine	29,433	38.80	55.55		5.64
Chicoutimi	32,526	41.71	47.78		10.08
Drummondville	29,216	51.93	45.43		2.63
Granby	34,349	41.76	48.79	4.78	4.66
Hull	60,176	54.11	35.84	10.04	.14
Jonquière	29,663	45.51	32.14	2.91	18.80
Longueuil	25,593	54.89	27.53	17.28	1.16
Rimouski	20,330	56.46	41.32	2.23	
St. Hyacinthe	23,781	48.27	44.21	7.51	
St. Jean	27,784	33.20	49.13	4.60	.90
St. Jérôme	26,511	37.40	52.96	8.29	1.33
Shawinigan	30,777	43.14	42.75	14.10	
Sherbrooke	75,690	43.23	50.33	3.86	2.55
Thetford Mines	21,614	46.27	45.14		8.57
Three Rivers	57,540	45.63	48.96	5.39	
Valleyfield	29,111	39.76	32.15	3.89	.31
Greater Montreal	2,436,817				
French districts[b]		47.71	37.15	10.66	1.46
English distrcts[c]		75.34[d]	12.80	6.26	.57
Greater Quebec[e]	413,397	48.42	44.75	4.94	1.87

SOURCES: For population of cities, 20,000 and over, *Annuaire du Québec*, 1974, p. 229, Table VI, and for Greater Montreal and Greater Quebec, *ibid*, p. 234, Table X; popular vote percentages for each party have been calculated from official figures in Quebec, Président général des élections, *Rapport sur les élections générales de 1966* (Quebec, 1967); the breakdown of electoral districts in Greater Montreal into those which are predominantly English or French is based on statistics in Robert Boily, "Montréal, une forteresse libérale," *Socialisme 66*, no. 9 (oct.–déc. 1966), p. 144; two of the electoral districts not covered in Boily's statistics, Laval and Fabre, together make up the City of Laval which in 1971 was 80.75 per cent French, *Annuaire du Québec*, 1974, pp. 242, Table XX.

[a]In some cities total percentages fall considerably short of 100 per cent due to votes for independent or splinter party candidates not included in table.

[b]Includes electoral districts of Ahuntsic, Bourassa, Bourget, Dorion, Fabre, Gouin, Jacques Cartier, Jeanne Mance, Lafontaine, Laurier, Laval, Maisonneuve, Mercier, Olier, Ste. Anne, Ste. Marie, St. Henri, St. Jacques, Verdun.

[c]Includes electoral districts of D'Arcy McGee, Marguerite Bourgeoys, Notre-Dame-de-Grâce, Outremont, Robert Baldwin, St. Laurent, St. Louis, Westmount.

[d]Figures include Independent Liberal in Robert Baldwin.

[e]Includes electoral districts of Chauveau, Jean Talon, Louis Hébert, Lévis, Limoilou, St. Sauveur.

its state of disintegration after the defeat of 1960. The party's popular vote which had fallen by 5.4 per cent between 1956 and 1960, and a further 4.5 per cent between 1960 and 1962,[106] had only declined a little over 1 per cent in the present election. The erosion in its support had been stemmed and the gap between the Union Nationale and the Liberals had narrowed. Another factor was that the emphasis on winning seats rather than popular votes meant that a good many electoral districts were largely ignored by the party. If the Union Nationale had conducted the election in the usual fashion of blanketing the province with propaganda, it would very likely have won a larger percentage of the popular vote but lost the election. Finally, the party could point out that like any Quebec nationalist party it started out with a bloc of some 18–20 per cent of the electorate, the English voters, almost solidly against it. This voting bloc makes it extremely difficult, although not impossible, for any nationalist party to win a large majority vote.

THE UNION NATIONALE CONTINUES THE QUIET REVOLUTION

After recovering from the shock and surprise of the unexpected Union Nationale victory, the most widespread reaction in the press and in political circles was a strong fear that the modernizing policies of the Lesage administration would be reversed and that the patronage system and other questionable practices of the Duplessis era would return. These fears turned out to be groundless. There was no return to "la grande noirceur," as some people called the Duplessis era. Under both the Johnson administration from 1966 to 1968 and the Bertrand administration which followed it until 1970 the Quiet Revolution continued. Although some changes were made at the higher levels of the public service, there were no sweeping dismissals, and the technocrats appointed by the Lesage administration retained their posts. Hydro Québec was not denationalized, nor were the other government corporations dismantled; the Department of Education was not reorganized nor the educational revolution reversed; the declining influence of the clergy in education, health, and welfare continued and no attempt was made to restore the role of the Church in these areas; government employees retained their right to organize and the right to strike; although there was tension at times between the trade unions and the government—as indeed there had been under the Lesage government—there was no massive crackdown in the Duplessis style.

[106]From 52 per cent in 1956 to 46.6 per cent in 1960 and down to 42.1 per cent in the 1962 election; *Annuaire du Québec*, 1974, p. 120.

From the beginning of his administration Johnson used every opportunity to make it clear that the Union Nationale would continue in the spirit of reform and renovation of its 1965 convention. At a press conference shortly after his victory Johnson stated that there would be no general purge of government personnel, although there might be a few individual cases of dismissal at the senior level.[107] At the same time he also clarified the Union Nationale position on the two key areas of educational reform and economic policy. The Union Nationale leader stated, "Dans le domaine de l'éducation, il faut que ça continue, il faut même que la cadence soit accélérée."[108] He also made the rather unrealistic prediction that this could be accomplished without an increase in expenditures. In regard to economic policies, Johnson stated that although the party was committed to the principle of private enterprise this did not mean that it would favour the large English-dominated business enterprises to the detriment of the interests of French Canadians.

In forming his cabinet Johnson made an obvious effort to appoint ministers who would express the new spirit of renewal and reform within the party. While some of them had served under Duplessis, others represented the newcomers to politics whom Johnson had recruited. Among the veterans were: Jean-Jacques Bertrand, Vice-Prime Minister, who was made Minister of Education, and of Justice; Paul Dozois, the party's financial critic, Minister of Finance; and Maurice Bellemare, one-time trade union leader, Minister of Labour. Among the newcomers who showed some promise the most notable were: Jean-Noël Tremblay, a former professor at Laval University, Minister of Cultural Affairs; Clément Vincent, an agricultural expert, Minister of Agriculture; and thirty-year-old Marcel Masse, the man who had drawn up the party programme, Minister of State for Education. The following year Bertrand turned over the Education portfolio to a new appointee, Jean-Guy Cardinal, former Dean of the Faculty of Law at the University of Montreal.

Although Johnson's cabinet no doubt had some very competent people, and a number with considerable potential, as a team it still could not match up to the dynamism, intellectual ability, and long-term vision of Quebec's future, which characterized Lesage's "Equipe du tonnerre" of the early sixties. Johnson had a much more limited choice when it came to selecting capable and imaginative ministers; the Union Na-

[107]See *Gazette*, June 7, 1966. Johnson's commitment that there would be no return to the old patronage system was reiterated by his two close associates, Jean-Jacques Bertrand and Paul Dozois. *Le Devoir*, 10 juin 1966.
[108]*Le Devoir*, 7 juin 1966.

tionale was just not that kind of party. Its members in the legislature may have been good representatives of their constituencies, but this did not necessarily make them good administrators.

It has sometimes been observed that while the Union Nationale during its period in power between 1966 and 1970 continued the Quiet Revolution, the pace of reform was considerably slower and there were few new or innovative programmes.[109] This is largely true, but it should not be attributed altogether to the caution or conservatism of the Johnson and Bertrand administrations. With a heavy burden of public debt and high level of taxation there were severe financial restraints on undertaking further expensive programmes. If the Liberals had been returned to power they would have been faced by the same problem. Union Nationale policies, therefore, were to a considerable extent the completion of projects drawn up or started under the Lesage administration. In spite of this, a close look at the Union Nationale record during its period in office shows that the party's contribution to the modernization process of the sixties was by no means negligible.[110]

In the field of education the Union Nationale carried through with considerable vigour the recommendations of the Parent Commission and the earlier reforms started by the Liberals. A network of Colleges of General and Professional Education, or CEGEPs, was established in various parts of the province, and by 1970 there were 34 of them in operation. The system of government bursaries for students and annual grants for universities was not only continued but expanded. Another important and badly needed step was taken with the establishment of a new multi-campus state university, the University of Quebec. Although centred in Montreal, it had regional branches in Quebec City, Three Rivers, Chicoutimi, and Rimouski. Affiliated with it was a new National School of Public Administration, located in Quebec City.

In spite of the Union Nationale's strong commitment to the private enterprise system it was just as ready as the Liberals to intervene actively in the economy, particularly in the field of natural resources, where it could be argued that such intervention was necessary in the public interest. The integrated steel complex, SIDBEC, which had been planned by the Lesage government, only came into full operation in 1968 under the Johnson administration; Hydro-Québec continued to expand with a major development at Churchill Falls; a new govern-

---

[109]See Dale Postgate and Kenneth McRoberts, *Quebec: Social Change and Political Crisis* (Toronto, 1976), pp. 166–7.

[110]On the subject see André Larocque, "Political Institutions and Quebec Society," in Thomson, ed., *Quebec Society and Politics*, p. 79; also Vien and Lapointe, *L'Union Nationale*, pp. 113–15.

ment corporation known as Société Québécoise d'Initiatives Pétrolières (SOQUIP), was created in 1969 for the purpose of the discovery and development of natural gas and oil; a somewhat similar public corporation was established for the conservation as well as the exploitation of the province's forest resources called Société de Récupération et d'Exploitation Forestières (REXFOR).

The readiness of the Union Nationale to give the state an active rather than a passive role was indicated by the large number of new departments and other administrative agencies created: a Department of Inter-governmental Affairs; a Department of the Public Service; a Department of Immigration; a Department of Financial Institutions, Companies, and Co-operatives; and a Department of Communications. Other new governmental bodies established were an Office of Planning and Development, and a Quebec radio and TV system called Radio-Québec.

Another important contribution the Union Nationale made to the modernization of Quebec's political institutions was the abolition of the anachronism of the Legislative Council, the only upper house left in any province. The co-operation of the Council in its own demise was made easier by the retirement of its members on fairly generous pensions. The name of the lower house itself was changed from Legislative Assembly to National Assembly. One other important innovation of the Union Nationale was the establishment of the Office of Public Protector, or Ombudsman.

Not all the policies pursued by the Union Nationale were a continuation of those of the Lesage administration. Some of them were a reflection of the different nature of the party's clientele: the people in the small towns and villages, the farmers, the small business and professional men, and the lower income groups in the urban areas. The Liberal plan to regroup the hundreds of small towns and villages into larger municipal units moved at a much slower pace; the same applied to the reorganization of the smaller school commissions into larger regional units; crop insurance for farmers was introduced and more attention was paid to the building of local roads; with an eye on lower income groups in general, the basic income tax exemption was raised and a provincial system of family allowances was set up. One important project of the Liberals which the Union Nationale failed to carry out was a universal health insurance scheme. The party still had a strong tendency to consider that health and welfare services should not be universal, but provided only to those in need among lower income groups.

In spite of the differences mentioned above, the fact that the Union Nationale continued the more important of the modernizing policies of the Liberals indicated that from 1966 onward the two parties were becoming more similar.[111] There was, however, one notable exception. After losing the election of 1966 the Liberal party began to move away from such goals as special status and its brief flirtation with nationalism. For the Union Nationale, on the other hand, and we are dealing here specifically with the Johnson administration from 1966 to 1968, it was the constitutional and other related issues which were the main concern. Johnson had accepted the Quiet Revolution essentially for pragmatic reasons: he was aware that most of the Liberal reforms were not only popular but also long overdue, and that there was little point in going against the trend. More important, his all-absorbing interest as a politician and a nationalist lay elsewhere.

From the time of his appointment as head of the Quebec government in 1966 until his sudden death in 1968 Johnson threw all his energies into a drive to achieve two goals: vastly increased powers for Quebec under a completely new constitution along the lines outlined in his *Egalité ou Indépendance*; the establishment of some form of international status for Quebec, particularly among the French-speaking community of nations. At federal-provincial conferences, meetings with the governments of other provinces, addresses to national organizations or service clubs, Johnson waged a tireless campaign to achieve these two goals.

In the course of his campaign the Union Nationale leader clarified some things which were not too clear in his book. First of all it became apparent that he was primarily interested in obtaining increased powers for Quebec, "the homeland of the French-Canadian nation;" his interest in the rights of French-Canadians in other provinces was peripheral. Secondly, he spelled out more exactly than had ever been done before precisely what Quebec was looking for in a new constitution. At an interprovincial conference called in 1967 by Premier Robarts of Ontario on the topic, "The Confederation of Tomorrow," Johnson presented Quebec's demands: "As the mainstay of a nation, it wants free rein to make its own decisions affecting the growth of its citizens as human beings (*i.e.*, education, social security and health in all respects), their economic development (*i.e.*, the forging of any economic and financial tool deemed necessary), their cultural fulfillment (which takes in not only arts and literature, but the French language as well), and the presence abroad of the Quebec community (*i.e.*, relations with certain countries and international organizations)."[112]

---

[111]These similarities are analyzed in Vincent Lemieux, "Heaven is Blue and Hell is Red," in Martin Robin, ed., *Canadian Provincial Politics: The Party Systems of the Ten Provinces* (Scarborough, Ont. 1972), pp. 269–70.

[112]Reprinted in Daniel Johnson, "What Does Quebec Want?—1967," in J. Peter Meekison, ed. *Canadian Federalism: Myth or Reality* (2nd. edition, Toronto, 1971) p. 430.

Johnson was ready to admit that the negotiation of a new constitution shifting such extensive powers from the federal to a provincial legislature would take time to implement. He therefore proposed that while awaiting a new constitution the Quebec government immediately take over from the central government all existing federal programmes involving public expenditures in education, old-age security, family allowances, health, regional development, municipal aid, research, culture, as well as any other social or cultural service within provincial jurisdiction under the existing constitution.[113] This transfer of power would of course have to be accompanied by an increase in the taxing power of Quebec.

A close look at Johnson's sweeping constitutional proposals, whether for the short or long term, quickly indicates that, if agreed to, they would not only drastically weaken the powers of the central authority but would leave Canada quite a different kind of federal state (if it could be called a state at all; it would have a closer resemblance to a loose confederation of sovereign states). Johnson's "égalité" was looking more and more like his "indépendance."

Although the governments of the other Canadian provinces were for the most part opposed to Johnson's constitutional proposals, the most determined opposition came from the federal government in the person of Pierre Elliot Trudeau, Minister of Justice in the Pearson cabinet, who became Prime Minister in 1968. Trudeau's position in the constitutional debate was to play such an important role in the conflict between Quebec and Ottawa over the next ten years that it is essential to outline briefly the reasoning behind his stance.

Trudeau's opposition to widespread constitutional changes which would seriously weaken the central authority was based on two strongly held convictions. As a French Canadian and a Quebecer he rejected separatism, special status, or other nationalist positions because he considered that the best guarantee for the maintenance of French language and culture in North America was the continued partnership of French and English Canada in a strong federal system—a federal system modified wherever necessary to make Canada a truly bilingual and bicultural state where members of both language groups in every part of the country would have equal access to educational, cultural, legal, and other such facilities in their own language.[114]

The second reason for Trudeau's opposition to any weakening of the central government arose from his strong belief that the federal authority had a responsibility to see that every Canadian citizen, irrespective of

---

[113]*Ibid.*
[114]See Pierre Elliott Trudeau, *Federalism and the French Canadians* (Toronto, 1968), Part I, pp. 3–62.

the province in which he lived, received a basic minimum in the way of health, welfare, educational, and similar services. Trudeau's views, which were the same as other members of the cabinet, were expressed in a White Paper presented by the government to the Constitutional Conference of 1968. The White Paper stated that, "the Government of Canada must have the power to redistribute income between persons and between provinces." This involved making payments to individuals for the purpose of supporting income levels, such as old age security pensions and family allowances, and payments to provinces to equalize the level of provincial services provided. It followed that the federal authority must also have the powers of taxation which would enable it to tax those best able to contribute to these equalization measures.[115]

The diametrically opposed constitutional positions of Trudeau and Johnson made it inevitable that there would be serious clashes between the two leaders.[116] This conflict was accentuated by Johnson's determination to carry through, although with much more vigour, the initiatives taken by the Lesage government to establish a Quebec presence on the international scene. An indication of the Union Nationale's intent in this respect was the establishment of a Department of Inter-governmental Affairs shortly after the party came to power. Like Lesage, the Union Nationale leader argued that Quebec had a constitutional right to make argeements with other countries in those matters which were under provincial jurisdiction in the B.N.A. Act, and the right to participate directly in international agencies of a non-political nature, such as the International Labour Organization and UNESCO. From Johnson's point of view the achievement of international status for Quebec was all part of the drive for self-determination: recognition abroad would strengthen the argument for special status within Canada. The attitude of the Ottawa government to the international aspirations of Quebec remained the same: all agreements made by a province with another country must be finalized through the federal authority.

While the Union Nationale government was interested in expanding its international contacts wherever possible, for obvious historical and cultural reasons close relations with France were of particular importance; as Johnson put it, "cet oxygène indispensable à notre vie collective."[117] In May, 1967, Daniel Johnson made a five-day visit to France where President de Gaulle received him with all the honours of a head of a sovereign state. The purpose of the visit was to discuss ar-

[115]Canada (L. B. Pearson), *Federalism for the Future* (Ottawa, 1968), p. 38.
[116]For one of the more spectacular confrontations see *Constitutional Conference, Proceedings of the First Meeting, Feb. 5–7, 1968* (Ottawa, 1968), pp. 225–55.
[117]Proulx, *Le Panier de crabes*, p. 77.

rangements for educational, cultural, scientific, and economic co-operation between the two governments

General de Gaulle's return visit to Canada two months later, officially to participate in Canada's centennial celebrations, was to result in a major diplomatic clash between the Canadian and French governments. The French president arrived in Quebec City first and was given a warm welcome by the Johnson government. He then went on to Montreal where he delivered a speech to a large crowd in front of the City Hall. De Gaulle ended his address before a wildly cheering audience with the historic cry, "Vive le Québec, Vive le Québec Libre." Although there was considerable controversy over the question of whether de Gaulle intentionally used one of the slogans of the Quebec separatists to support their cause, the federal government looked upon the speech as an intolerable intrusion into Canada's domestic affairs.[118] Prime Minister Pearson delivered a public rebuke to the French president with the result that the latter cancelled his plans to go on to Ottawa and instead returned immediately to Paris. In defence of de Gaulle, Daniel Johnson contended that he was merely stating in his own way that the people of Quebec, like peoples everywhere, were free to determine their own destiny and had the incontestable right to decide on their own political status.[119]

There was one other major conflict between Quebec and Ottawa during the Johnson administration. In 1968 the government of Gabon invited Quebec, but not Canada, to send a delegation to a conference of ministers of education of French-speaking countries. The federal government was so incensed at this action that it suspended diplomatic relations with that African country. Prime Minister Pearson also wrote several letters to Johnson concerning the matter, but received little satisfaction.[120] When the Bertrand administration succeeded that of Johnson a few months later tension eased between the central government and Quebec, for Bertrand attempted to achieve the province's international goals by making working arrangements with Ottawa rather than by a policy of confrontation.

Daniel Johnson died suddenly in September, 1968, of a heart attack while visiting a Hydro-Québec power project in Northern Quebec. This was the third time within a ten-year period that a Union Nationale leader had died suddenly while heading the government. During his

[118]For the varied interpretations of the de Gaulle affair in the English and French press see, *Canadian Annual Review*, 1967, pp. 49–54; see also, Gilles Lalande, "Quebec and International Affairs," in Thomson, *Quebec Society and Politics*, p. 245.
[119]*Le Devoir*, 29 juillet 1967.
[120]Lalande, "Quebec and International Affairs," in Thomson, *Quebec Society and Politics*, p. 246.

seven-year term of office as leader Johnson had served the Union Nationale well. He had taken a party on the point of disintegration, reorganized and rejuvenated it, given it a modern programme, and brought it back to power. He had faced and overcome the challenge of Lesage's Quiet Revolution, and the Union Nationale had made its own contribution to many aspects of that important development in Quebec's political history.

His main contribution to the nationalist cause lies in his persistent demands for increased powers for Quebec, "the homeland of the French-Canadian nation," in a new constitution; and his hard fight to obtain for Quebec an international status. As leader of a major Quebec party he made the question of independence a respectable option which should not be rejected *a priori*, even though he himself seemed undecided on the question.

In evaluating the Johnson administration it should always be remembered that whatever its accomplishments, they were largely the work of Johnson himself. Unlike Lesage, he never had the same number of brilliant and energetic collaborators surrounding him whom he could call upon to assist him in achieving his goals. A political commentator who in general tended to be critical of Johnson stated "Au total, on est bien forcé d'admettre qu'il ne fait pas si mal, qu'il surprend même assez agréablement parfois—compte tenu, bien entendu, de la situation qu'il a trouvée et des effectifs dont il dispose."[121]

[121]Bergeron, *Du Duplessisme à Trudeau et Bourassa*, p. 499.

CHAPTER XI

The Decline and Eclipse of
Conservative Nationalism

THE SUDDEN DEATH of Daniel Johnson in 1968 and the appointment of Jean-Jacques Bertrand as his successor was a turning point in the history of the Union Nationale. From that time onward the strength of the party steadily declined and in the election of 1970 it was badly defeated, although it still remained the official opposition in the legislature. After that election its decline accelerated and in the following election of 1973 it did not win a single seat in the legislature. The disappearance of the Union Nationale as one of Quebec's major parties also meant the end of that particular brand of conservative nationalism of which it had so long been an outstanding exponent.

The fact that the decline of the party coincided with the changeover from the Johnson to the Bertrand administration does not mean that the waning of party fortunes can be attributed solely to this development. It is true that certain policies pursued by Bertrand were a contributing factor, but the situation was much more complex. The most important reason was that in the late nineteen-sixties the Union Nationale found itself faced by an entirely new challenge with which it was not as successful in coping as it had been with the Quiet Revolution: the growth of a new nationalist movement which had started at the beginning of the Lesage administration and ultimately resulted in the formation of a new political party, the Parti Québécois, which quickly emerged as a major rival to the Union Nationale as the spokesman for Quebec nationalism. In seeking to understand the reasons for the decline of the Union Nationale, therefore, our starting point must be an examina-

tion of the origins of the new nationalism, its main characteristics, and
how it gave birth to the Parti Québécois.

THE NEW NATIONALISM AND THE PARTI QUÉBÉCOIS

The new wave of nationalism which swept Quebec in the late fifties
and early sixties penetrated the universities, the teachers' associations,
at least part of the trade union movement, the professional associations,
the co-operatives, and a section of the French middle classes. It even
had some impact on the old political parties, the Liberals and the Union
Nationale. It expressed itself in the formation of countless patriotic
associations, leagues, fronts, and political parties, and the appearance
of new weekly or monthly nationalist publications.[1] Many of these new
organizations and publications were short-lived and disappeared within
a year or two due to lack of supporters or financial problems. There were
others, however which became more solidly implanted: the Parti Québécois was one of them.

The new nationalism of the sixties has usually been referred to as
"the separatist movement." This term is not so much incorrect as in-
complete as a description of the new nationalism. Certainly the proposal
that Quebec separate from Canada was one of its most outstanding
characteristics. However, it had two other features which should not
be overlooked: it was left-wing or radical on economic and social matters; and it was concerned with an issue which up to now had not been
a major concern of Quebec nationalists, the threat to the predominance
of the French language within Quebec. These three characteristics must
be looked at more closely if we are to grasp all aspects of the new
nationalism.

The separatist idea, that is, the proposal that Quebec separate from
Canada and become a completely independent and sovereign state, had
been suggested by isolated individuals and groups in Quebec in the past,
but it had never had a significant following or major impact on politics.[2]
The question of why the separatist movement arrived on the political
scene in Quebec with such force in the nineteen-sixties is a complicated
one and it is not proposed here to explore all aspects of it, but merely
to point out a few key factors in this new development.

[1]On the new nationalism see James W. Hagy, "Quebec Separatists: The First
Twelve Years," *Queen's Quarterly*, LXXVI, 2 (Summer, 1969), pp. 229–38; Juris
Dreifelds, "Nationalism and Socialism in French Canada," in Paul W. Fox, ed.
Politics: Canada (4th ed., Toronto, 1977), pp. 162–75; Léon Dion, *Quebec: The
Unfinished Revolution* (Montreal, 1796), pp. 141–62.

[2]See *supra*, chap. III, p. 44.

There is fairly general agreement among students of Quebec politics that the decolonization movement which took place in Asia and Africa following the Second World War had a dramatic impact on the thinking of a good number of Quebec nationalists.[3] For them the province's situation was similar to that of a former African colony like Algeria. Quebec had been conquered two centuries earlier by a colonial power, Great Britain, and that country's successor, the English-dominated Canadian federal government, continued to hold Quebec in colonial subjection; the right to self-determination of "the Quebec nation" involved throwing off the colonial yoke and making Quebec a separate sovereign state. The alleged similarity between an underdeveloped African colony and highly industrialized Quebec, a province which had provided "the colonial power" with three prime ministers and two governors general, is to say the least exaggerated.[4] However, the important point for our purposes is that this was the way in which many Quebec nationalists saw the situation and as such was a strong factor in their separatist motivation.

There is another less controversial and simpler explanation of why separatism became one of the characteristics of the new nationalism. The idea of an independent Quebec state can be looked upon as the end product of a natural process of evolution in the nationalist movement since its beginnings in the nineteen-thirties. There is a straight line from Duplessis' defence of provincial rights, to Lesage's more positive affirmation of those rights, to Johnson's demands for increased power in a new constitution, to the next logical step, that the people of the province assume complete control over their destiny by setting up an independent Quebec state. It seems apparent that, although all separatist groups like to use the vocabulary of decolonization now and then, the reason for most of them turning towards separatism was the failure, in their eyes, of the efforts of Lesage and Johnson to achieve Quebec's cultural and economic goals within the Canadian framework.

The second aspect of the new nationalism, its radical or left-wing position on economic and social matters, was in sharp contrast with the conservative nationalism of the Union Nationale. Radical nationalism was by no means an entirely new development on the Quebec political scene. This particular brand of nationalism had appeared before as an opposing force to the Union Nationale: there was the Action Libérale Nationale of Paul Gouin in the thirties, the Bloc Populaire in the forties,

[3]The influence of the decolonization movement on Quebec separatism is described in Dion, *Quebec: The Unfinished Revolution*, p. 144.

[4]The prime ministers were: Sir Wilfrid Laurier, 1896–1911; Louis St-Laurent, 1948–57; Pierre E. Trudeau, 1968– . The governors general were: Georges P. Vanier, 1959–67; Jules Léger, 1973–79.

and the social nationalists of the fifties. The radical nationalism of the sixties was in many respects the successor of these earlier movements, although it was in general much more left-wing. The earlier radicals had based their reforms on papal encyclicals with some modifications applicable to the Quebec situation. The new radicals drew their inspiration from a number of other sources, such as Marxism, Marxism-Leninism, or Swedish type social democracy. Some of them were parliamentary and democratic, while others were revolutionary, anti-parliamentary, or semi-anarchist. The most famous of the revolutionary movements was the Front de Libération du Québec (F.L.Q.), which was responsible for the 1970 kidnapping of James Cross, the British trade commissioner in Montreal, and the kidnapping and assassination of Pierre Laporte, a minister in the Bourassa Liberal cabinet.[5] Although the revolutionary and terrorist organizations such as the F.L.Q. made the headlines, the mainstream of the new nationalism, the political formations with the widest popular support, were social democratic and committed to the parliamentary process in achieving their aims.

The new concern in nationalist circles about the continued predominance of the French language in Quebec began during the Lesage administration. Evidence began to accumulate that French was slowly losing ground, and there was a possibility that in time English would become the dominant language, if not in Quebec as a whole, at least in the Montreal area.[6] However, over 40 per cent of the population of the province lived in Montreal and the surrounding area and this percentage was steadily increasing.

One of the factors behind the fears of the nationalists about the future of the French language was Quebec's rapidly falling birth rate. The high French-Canadian birth rate which had for several centuries maintained the French fact in North America began to drop rather sharply from the nineteen-fifties onward. Quebec, which at one time was the province with the highest birth rate in Canada, by the late sixties had one of the lowest.[7] One of the explanations for this development was the movement of population from a rural to an industrial and urbanized society where, among other things, the large family constituted such a heavy financial burden on the parents. There was another reason, how-

[5]For a factual day-by-day description of the 1970 crisis see John Saywell, *Quebec 70: A Documentary Narrative* (Toronto, 1971).

[6]See Jacques Henripin, "Quebec and the Demographic Dilemma of French-Canadian Society," in Dale C. Thomson, ed., *Quebec Society and Politics: Views from the Inside* (Toronto, 1973), pp. 157, 161–2.

[7]The birth rate dropped from 28.8 per 1000 population in 1958 to 16.0 per thousand in 1969. The latter figure contrasts with Ontario's 17.7 the same year. *Annuaire du Québec*, 1974, p. 299.

ever, which perhaps requires a fuller explanation: the decline in the influence of the Church and its code of morality.

Quebec in the era of the Quiet Revolution was no longer the society described earlier in this book made up of a people whose "whole pattern of thinking, . . . system of values and way of life had been moulded by the doctrines and social philosophy of Roman Catholicism."[8] After the Second World War, and particularly in the sixties, large segments of French Quebecers, although still nominally Catholics, began to drift away from the Church. There was not only a dramatic fall in Church attendance, but also a rejection of the teaching of the Church on such matters as the virtue of large families and opposition to divorce, birth control, and abortion.[9] With the decline of the influence of what might be called "the Catholic ethic," those practices which would result in the restriction of births became more widely accepted.[10] Perhaps the best illustration of the declining influence of the Church was to be found in the changing terminology of nationalist leaders: no longer did they refer to the survival of "our French and Catholic culture"; now it was "our French language and culture."[11]

A second cause for concern about the future of the French language in Quebec, aside from the falling birth rate, arose from the fact that the vast majority of immigrants coming to the province, most of whom settled in the Montreal area, assimilated into the English rather than the French section of the population.[12] For these immigrants it was a matter of mobility: occupational mobility, because English was the language of work, particularly at the higher levels in the offices and factories of the large English-dominated business corporations; geographical mobility, because they were living on a continent which was overwhelmingly English-speaking.

[8]*Supra*, p. 9.

[9]On the decline of Catholicism in Quebec see, Fernand Dumont, "Le Silence de l'Eglise du Québec," *Relations*, no. 344 (déc. 1969), pp. 348–50; Nikke Finke, "Government has Taken Over from the Church in Quebec," *Gazette*, Dec. 8, 1977; see also the extensive study initiated by the Quebec bishops on this problem, Commission d'étude sur les laïcs et l'Eglise, *L'Eglise du Québec: un héritage, un projet* (Montreal, 1971).

[10]The changing attitudes of Quebec women towards birth control and abortion are described in Jacques Henripin and Evelyne Lapierre-Adamcyk, *La Fin de la revanche des berceaux: qu'en pensent les Québécoises* (Montreal, 1974), pp. 103–17.

[11]This was true even of a conservative party like the Union Nationale; see *supra*, p. 220.

[12]Henripin, "Quebec and the Demographic Dilemma of French-Canadian Society," in Thomson, ed. *Quebec Society and Politics*, p. 159; various aspects of the language question are discussed in Richard Jones, *Community in Crisis: French-Canadian Nationalism in Perspective* (Toronto, 1972), pp. 31–6.

There was another aspect to the language question which added fuel to the controversy: the growing resentment among the population that in a predominantly French-Canadian province the language of work in the big business enterprises was English. This meant that French-speaking employees were at a disadvantage in regard to promotion if their command of English was not good enough. The problem became more acute when the educational reforms of the Quiet Revolution began to turn out young people equipped with the skills for an industrial society in which their mother tongue was a handicap. This particular problem, together with the others mentioned above, made it clear to Quebec leaders, and not merely the nationalists, that steps had to be taken by the government not only to maintain but to expand the role of the French language in Quebec. The so called "language question" was to quickly become as controversial as the constitutional question.

The three characteristics of the new nationalism which we have been discussing—the goal of an independent Quebec, radical economic and social policies, and concern for the survival of the French language—found their most effective expression with the formation of René Lévesque's Parti Québécois in 1968. This new party was the result of a coalition of three different separatist movements: the Rassemblement pour l'Indépendance Nationale (R.I.N.), the Ralliement National (R.N.), and Lévesque's own Mouvement Souveraineté-Association (M.S.A.).

The R.I.N., founded in 1960 by a small group of intellectuals headed by Marcel Chaput and André d'Allemagne, was the first separatist movement of any importance on the Quebec political scene. Chaput, a former federal civil servant, was elected leader of the R.I.N. in 1961, and in the same year published a book, *Pourquoi je suis séparatiste*, which caused quite a sensation at the time. Shortly after, Chaput left the R.I.N. over an internal dispute, and formed his own separatist movement. In 1964, Pierre Bourgault, a much more dynamic leader, became head of the R.I.N. and forged it into a well-organized political party in preparation for the elections expected in 1966. The programme of the R.I.N. rested mainly on the twin policies of complete independence for Quebec and complete unilingualism throughout the new state. The party also had a programme of economic and social reform based on the principles of European social democracy which put it in the mainstream of the radical nationalism of the sixties.[13]

The Ralliement National (R.N.), originally called Regroupement

[13]The origins, history and political philosophy of the R.I.N. are described in François-Pierre Gingras, "Le Rassemblement pour l'Indépendance Nationale ou l'indépendantisme: du mouvement social au parti politique," in Réjean Pelletier, ed., *Partis politiques au Québec* (Montreal, 1976), pp. 219–46.

National, was a splinter group led by René Jutras, which had broken away from the R.I.N. in 1964 because it considered Bourgault was moving the party too far to the left. Jutras joined forces with a small group of social creditors led by Laurent Legault who had left the federally oriented Ralliement des Créditistes in order to get involved in provincial politics. It was at this point that the name of the party was changed to Ralliement National, with Jutras and Legault as joint leaders. Although as strongly separatist as the R.I.N., the R.N. was much more conservative in economic and social matters.[14]

As we saw in the last chapter, both the R.I.N. and the R.N. entered candidates in the election of 1966 and won 5.6 and 3.2 per cent respectively of the popular vote; however, neither party won any seats. Although Bourgault considered his party had done well in its first venture into politics and claimed a "moral victory,"[15] the fact remained that the combined separatist vote was only around 9 per cent and the future of the two minor parties was uncertain. Moreover, the R.I.N. was weakened by a split between Bourgault and a far left group in the party with Marxist tendencies led by Madame Andrée Ferretti. It was just about this time that the third separatist movement, the Mouvement Souveraineté-Association, appeared on the political scene.

The M.S.A. had the advantage that its leader, René Lévesque, was a much better known and more experienced political figure than the separatist movement had come up with until then. As Minister of Natural Resources in the Liberal government of the early sixties, Lévesque was probably the member of Lesage's cabinet with the largest popular following. A politician with considerable charm, his greatest asset was his remarkable ability to communicate with people in an open and frank style. He was master of the techniques of television broadcasting, a skill which he had acquired while a political commentator for Radio-Canada. While he could not be classed as an outstanding intellectual, he was nevertheless a man of ideas and imagination. His style of oratory was improvised and spontaneous rather than a closely reasoned exposition and his thoughts seemed to come "off the top of his head," as it were. Lévesque's main weaknesses as a politician were that he found it difficult to compromise and had a certain impatience about getting things done that sometimes resulted in over-simplified solutions to complex problems.[16]

[14]For a brief history of the R.N., see Michael B. Stein, *The Dynamics of Right-Wing Protest: A Political Analysis of Social Credit in Quebec* (Toronto, 1973), pp. 99–103.

[15]*La Presse*, 6 juin 1966.

[16]Lévesque's political style and ideas are analysed in: Peter Desbarats, *The State of Quebec* (Toronto, 1966), pp. 94–100; Věra Murray, *Le Parti Québécois: de la*

Even when a member of the Lesage government Lévesque was strongly nationalist with leanings toward a moderate form of socialism in which private enterprise would still have an important role to play. As long as the Liberal cabinet was willing to go along with his ideas, such as the nationalization of the power companies, he was content to remain within the party. In the latter years of the Lesage administration, however, he became increasingly dissatisfied with some of the party's policies, and he was particularly disillusioned about its inability to win from the federal government the legislative and fiscal powers which he considered essential for Quebec's economic and cultural development. The seemingly endless negotiations and bargaining between the province and the central government were a continual source of irritation for him, and the term, "federalism does not work" became one of his favourite expressions.[17]

At the 1967 convention of the Quebec Liberal Federation Lévesque attempted to persuade the party to move towards the goal of an independent state of Quebec which would negotiate an economic association with Canada. When he failed to win the support of the convention for his proposal he left the party and formed the M.S.A. Some members of the executive of the Liberal Federation joined him, as well as a few constituency associations, but he failed to win over the vast majority of the Liberal members of the legislature or most of the rank and file of the party.

After leaving the Liberals, Lévesque entered into discussions with the R.N. and the R.I.N. with the goal of bringing about the union of all separatist groups. An agreement with the R.N., now under the leadership of Gilles Grégoire, a former Créditiste M.P., was arrived at quite easily and the two movements agreed to form a new party whose primary goal would be the independence of Quebec.[18] Negotiations with the R.I.N. were more difficult and presented a number of problems from

---

fondation à la prise du pouvoir (Montreal, 1976), chap. VIII; see also René Lévesque, *Option Québec* (Montreal, 1968). Two biographies of Lévesque which have appeared in recent years are: Jean Provencher, *René Lévesque: Portrait d'un Québécois* (Montreal, 1974); and Peter Desbarats, *René: A Canadian in Search of a Country* (Toronto, 1976).

[17]Lévesque has often appeared to be critical not only of Canadian federalism, but of the federal form of government as such. On occasion he has expressed the view that such a system is only suitable for a "melting pot" type of society like the U.S.A. See *Le Devoir*, 24 avril 1970.

[18]The term "independence," rather than "separatism," has always been insisted upon by Lévesque because of what he considers to be the negative connotations of the latter word. However, as Quebec must separate from Canada in order to become independent, the use of the term "separatism" is not inappropriate. It was the term used by Marcel Chaput, one of the founders of the movement. See *supra*, p. 243.

the point of view of Lévesque. Bourgault insisted upon absolute separation without any association with Canada and a unilingual Quebec in which the rights of the English minority would be eliminated, two points on which Lévesque strongly disagreed. Another cause for concern was the tendency of members of the R.I.N., including Bourgault, to get involved in street demonstrations which sometimes resulted in violent clashes with the police. This was not the public image Lévesque wanted for his new party, and he therefore broke off negotiations with Bourgault.

In October, 1968, representatives of the M.S.A. and R.N. came together in a founding convention which resulted in the birth of the Parti Québécois. The convention drew up a constitution and programme and elected René Lévesque as its first leader. About two weeks later Bourgault, realizing that his party had little chance of competing with the P.Q., persuaded his colleagues to dissolve the R.I.N. and join Lévesque's party as individual members. All the separatist forces in the province were now fused into one party.[19]

Before describing the main principles and goals of the Parti Québécois as outlined in its programme there are two points which must be made. The first one is that during its ten-year history from 1968 to 1978 there have been a number of fairly significant changes in some of the party's original policies, particularly from 1972 onward. It is not proposed here to trace the evolution of these policies over this decade, but to direct our attention solely to the basic principles and programme of the party between 1968 and 1970, that is, from the founding convention to the election of the latter year.[20]

The second point is that the key to an understanding of the Parti Québécois is to realize that it is at the same time three different things: it is a nationalist party committed to the maintenance of Quebec's French language and culture; it is a social democratic party like those in the Scandinavian countries or like the New Democratic Party (N.D.P.) in the western provinces; it is a separatist party whose main goal is to have Quebec secede from Canada. From the viewpoint of the leaders and militants of the P.Q. these three characteristics are interdependent: if the first two goals are to be reached it is essential that the third one be achieved. This assumption of interdependence is debatable and there

[19]The various steps leading up to the formation of the Parti Québécois are described in: Murray, Le Parti Québécois, pp. 11–22; Desbarats, René, chap. XX; Michel Roy, "René Lévesque's Very Special Kind of Federalism," Saturday Night, Jan. 1969, pp. 30–2.

[20]The evolution of Parti Québécois policies between 1968 and 1976 have been carefully analysed in Murray, Le Parti Québécois, Part I. The programme described here for the period 1968–70 is largely based on this study; see also report of the party's 1969 convention, Gazette, Oct. 20, 1969.

have been political movements in the province which have thought otherwise: most nationalist parties and organizations in the forties and fifties did not consider Quebec's separation necessary for cultural survival;[21] there have been left-wing parties in Quebec which never believed that the province had to separate in order to establish a socialist or social democratic society;[22] some separatist movements have been conservative rather than leftist.[23] The question of interdependence aside, one advantage the three-sided character of the Parti Québécois gave the party was that it could always emphasize one of its goals while largely ignoring the others if the political situation at any given time made such a strategy electorally rewarding.

As a nationalist party the main objective of the Parti Québécois was the survival and strengthening of the culture of "the Quebec nation." Culture was defined essentially in terms of language with no reference to the former role of Catholicism as an important ingredient of French-Canadian culture.[24] French would be the only official language in a sovereign Quebec, and was to become the language of communication, not only of the government, but also of school commissions, municipalities, and parapublic institutions like hospitals and welfare agencies; the publicly owned broadcasting system would function entirely in that language. French would be the language of work and communication in all industrial and commercial businesses and the people of Quebec would be guaranteed the right to be served in French in stores, restaurants, and other establishments.

An important part of the Parti Québécois's francization programme was that all immigrants would be compelled to send their children to French schools. However, the government would continue to finance the existing public school system and universities of the English-speaking minority, the amount of money allocated being proportional to the size of that language group in the total population. This particular commitment, although insisted upon by René Lévesque, was not popular with the more radical members of the party.

The social democratic aspects of the P.Q. programme put a strong emphasis on the role of the state in directing and planning the economy. A key agency in this planned economy would be an "Office du Plan"

[21]This was true not only of the Union Nationale but also of the radical nationalist parties and the patriotic societies.

[22]One of the best examples was the Quebec wing of the New Democratic Party. See *Manifeste 1970 du Nouveau Parti Démocratique du Québec* (mimeographed), p. 2.

[23]The Ralliement National, for instance; also Raymond Barbeau's Alliance Laurentienne. See Dreifelds, "Nationalism and Socialism in French Canada," p. 167.

[24]See Murray, *Le Parti Québécois*, p. 112 n19.

which would initiate, co-ordinate, and organize various sectors of the economic system in accordance with broad directives laid down by the government. Although private enterprise would continue to play the major role, the government reserved the right to intervene and nationalize certain areas such as the forest product industries. Public corporations which were already established like SIDBEC and SOQUEM would be strengthened and expanded, and the state in certain cases would acquire part of the shares of foreign-owned companies thus increasing the number of "mixed enterprises." Foreign capital would be welcomed but Quebecers must play an increasing role in the middle and upper management of these firms, and their activities must conform to the state's over-all economic plan. A Bank of Quebec would be established to perform the fiscal and financial functions hitherto carried out by the Bank of Canada.

Some of the more important social reforms planned were: a government housing policy which would include rigorous rent controls and the progressive nationalization of urban land; a complete, universal, and obligatory system of health insurance with doctors paid on a salary basis; a substantial increase in the minimum wage, equal pay for equal work for women, and government allowances to married women working in the home; all workers would be required to join a trade union, and all employers would be compelled to negotiate collective agreements with these unions; taxation reforms, including a capital gains tax.

The third and most controversial aspect of the Parti Québécois, its proposal for Quebec to secede from Canada and form an independent state, would take place through negotiations with the federal government, or if the latter refused to co-operate, Quebec would unilaterally declare its independence. In the new Republic of Quebec the existing cabinet-parliamentary system would be retained, but with a President as chief of state. After independence was achieved some form of economic association would be negotiated with Canada. At the time this was seen not only as desirable, but also as inevitable because of the reciprocal advantage to both countries. The details of this proposed association have never been clearly spelled out by the Parti Québécois. At times it has been referred to as a customs union, or a common market, or possibly a monetary union; it might also include agreements covering air, water, and rail transportation.

Before leaving the subject of the aims and goals of the Parti Québécois there is one question which must be raised: are there any similarities between René Lévesque's sovereignty-association and Daniel Johnson's proposal for a new constitution drawn up by Canada's two founding nations meeting on a basis of equality? If we can assume that Quebec would receive all the powers in a new constitution that Johnson was demanding in the late sixties,[25] it seems apparent that the province would in effect establish a new association with the rest of Canada in which it would be almost as powerful and independent as Lévesque's sovereign state. A key difference is that while Johnson's new constitution would be negotiated while Quebec was still part of Canada, Lévesque would have nothing to do with discussions with Ottawa concerning association until Quebec was independent. In spite of this, it appears that the position of the two political leaders on the constitutional question was closer than the Parti Québécois would probably admit.[26]

In the first two years following the founding convention of 1968 the Parti Québécois quickly gained in membership. Its adherents came not only from the R.I.N., and to a lesser extent from the older parties, but particularly from the intellectual elite, young people in the CEGEPs and universities, and members of the provincial public service. On the eve of the 1970 election it was obvious that René Lévesque's party would present a serious challenge to the major parties. Our particular interest here, however, is the impact that this new political force expressing the ideology of the new nationalism would have on the fortunes of the Union Nationale. Before attempting to answer this question it is first necessary to turn back and have a look at some of the problems facing the Union Nationale in the period immediately following the death of Daniel Johnson.

PARTY DISSENSIONS UNDER THE BERTRAND ADMINISTRATION

The appointment of Jean-Jacques Bertrand as Prime Minister in 1968 to succeed Daniel Johnson was a logical choice to make. As we saw earlier he had narrowly missed being elected leader at the convention of 1961, he had been Johnson's right-hand man since the 1965 convention, and at the time of Johnson's death he was Vice-Prime Minister. His appointment as head of the government had the unanimous approval of the cabinet and was later overwhelmingly endorsed by the Assembly caucus. The new Prime Minister continued with the same cabinet and retained Johnson's senior personal advisers.

Bertrand was quite a different type of leader from Johnson. He did

[25]*Supra*, pp. 233–4.

[26]Jérôme Proulx, a member of the Union Nationale under Johnson who later joined the Parti Québécois, claimed that the only real difference between the two leaders on this question was in the choice of terms. See his *Le Panier de crabes: Un Temoignage vécu sur l'Union Nationale sous Daniel Johnson* (Montreal, 1971), pp. 200–1. Essentially the same viewpoint has been expressed by Jean-Jacques Bertrand's son, Jean-François, who also joined the P.Q. See interview, *Gazette*, Oct. 4, 1977.

not have the latter's aggressiveness or skill in political manoeuvring. With a rather old-fashioned style of oratory he was not as adept as Johnson in the sharp thrust at the opponent's most vulnerable point. Bertrand, however, was universally liked and although he had many opponents in the Assembly, he had no enemies. Possessed of considerable charm, he was widely respected for his honesty and integrity, and no matter how heated the political battle, he invariably retained his sense of dignity. Some of his critics said that he had difficulty making up his mind, and he was often referred to as the province's Hamlet. Part of this may have been due to his tendency to study all sides of a question before making a decision and to his continued search for compromises.[27]

There were also differences between Johnson and Bertrand on the ideological level, even though this might only be a matter of emphasis. If Johnson was a nationalist and a conservative, Bertrand was a conservative and a nationalist. It was possible to conceive of Johnson turning to separatism as a last resort; it was very difficult to envisage Bertrand taking such a step, for he always looked upon himself as a Canadian as well as a Quebecer. In regard to the question of democratic processes within the party, Bertrand was a true believer from the start, while Johnson had to be converted to that point of view.

From the beginning of his administration Bertrand was faced with serious internal divisions within the party on constitutional and other questions. These divisions had existed under the Johnson administration, but the former leader with his adeptness in political manoeuvring managed to keep these divisions from surfacing. The most important split within the party was between the moderate nationalists led by Bertrand and a group which we will refer to as the "ultra-nationalists," whose unofficial leader was Jean-Guy Cardinal, Minister of Education. Bertrand had the support of most of the cabinet and the vast majority of the caucus. In contrast, there were only two other members of the cabinet of the same persuasion as Cardinal: Jean-Noël Tremblay, Minister of Cultural Affairs, and Marcel Masse, Minister for the Public Service. About a dozen members of the Assembly could also be considered ultra-nationalists.

Bertrand and his followers were federalists who believed that Quebec's goal of increased legislative and taxation powers could be achieved within the framework of the Canadian constitutional system by pursuing a policy of patient negotiations with Ottawa. Cardinal, who considered

[27]A short biography of Bertrand is to be found in Gérard Bergeron, *Du Duplessisme à Trudeau et Bourassa, 1956–1971* (Montreal, 1971), pp. 501–7. See also Hal Winter and Brian Stewart, "Two Men in Conflict: Battle for Control of a Party," *Gazette*, June 21, 1969.

himself as the heir of the Johnson tradition, believed in an aggressive nationalism involving a policy of continual confrontation with the federal government. He and most of his followers were probably not separatists at that point, but they felt a strong gravitational pull in that direction.

There was one other group in the Assembly which should be mentioned, and which one might call "the rural conservatives." It consisted of a certain number of members from the rural areas and small towns who were not particularly concerned with constitutional issues and similar matters. Their main interest was in such things as assistance to agriculture and anything the government might be able to do for their *comtés* in the way of local roads and other public services. This type of member, who had always existed in the Union Nationale, could be expected to support Bertrand in any party crisis.

The split in the party between the moderates and the ultra-nationalists only became fully evident when a leadership convention was announced for June, 1969. The constitution of 1965 had stipulated that on the death or resignation of a leader a convention made up of delegates from each electoral district must meet to select a successor. Bertrand, with his large support in the cabinet and in the caucus, could easily have ignored the constitution and avoided such a convention. He insisted, however, that a convention must be held in accordance with the democratic principles for which he had always fought. He also wanted to have his position strengthened by having his leadership clearly endorsed by the full membership of the party. The constitution stipulated that the convention was to be made up of twenty-one delegates chosen by the party members in each electoral district, adding up to a total of something over 2200. One-third of the delegates must be young people between 18 and 30, one-third women, and the other third men over thirty.[28]

Bertrand had assumed that the confirmation of his leadership would be a mere formality, particularly as forty-one of the party's fifty-five deputies announced their support for his candidacy. The situation was to change dramatically when Jean-Guy Cardinal decided to enter the contest and make the leadership campaign an all-out struggle between the ultra-nationalists and the moderates. Cardinal had the open support of only two members of the cabinet, Jean-Noël Tremblay, and Jean-Marie Morin, and a handful of members of the Assembly, the most important of whom was Jérôme Proulx, chairman of the Education Committee in the Assembly. However, he was also supported by André

[28]For a brief description of the Union Nationale convention of 1969 see Richard B. Holden, *Election 1970: Le Point tournant* (Montreal, 1970), pp. 19–24; and Proulx, *Le Panier de crabes*, chap. VI.

Lagarde, the party treasurer, by a number of the former advisers of Daniel Johnson, and by Pierre Marc Johnson, the son of the former leader. There was also reason to believe that he had considerable support from the party's rank and file.[29]

The convention itself was preceded by about a month of campaigning as each of the candidates sought to capture the support of the delegates who would make the final decision. It was a leadership campaign which tore the party apart, perhaps even more so than the convention of 1961.[30] The bitterness of the feelings and antagonism on both sides was due to something more than differences over constitutional questions. Ministers and deputies who sided with one or the other of the contenders knew that their political futures were at stake, for the winner would become not only leader but also Prime Minister with all that that implied. If Cardinal won, for instance, it was not likely that he would carry on with the same cabinet. Bertrand would not be inclined to reward with cabinet posts or other appointments those members and organizers who were attacking his policies.

In spite of the diverse points of view of the two contenders on the constitutional question, this particular issue did not play a predominant role in the campaign for the leadership, Cardinal, however, made a point to identify himself with the policies of Johnson and was usually accompanied on his tours by Pierre Marc Johnson. The presence of the latter was helpful in winning the support of the younger members of the party. Cardinal also never hesitated to make an appeal for the backing of separatists as well as federalists in his fight for the leadership.[31]

There were three other themes which Cardinal continually emphasized in his tour of the province. One was the necessity for the government to exercise more control over the civil servants whom, he contended, had become too powerful. The second theme had an authoritarian tinge: it was a criticism of the way in which the parliamentary system put restraints on the activities of the government and the large amounts of time spent in debate. The other main topic in his speeches was the urgent need to stimulate the economy and provide more employment for the graduates of the CEGEPs and universities.[32]

Under the slogan "Pour un nouveau Québec" Bertrand called for the maintenance of the democratic structure of the party introduced at the

[29]Aside from Bertrand and Cardinal, there was a third candidate in the race, André Léveillé, who ended up with about two dozen votes. Marcel Masse was chairman of the convention and therefore neutral.

[30]See Proulx, Le Panier de crabes, pp. 137–9, and Hal Winter, "N.U. Bitterness Rips Delegates at Convention," Gazette, June 20, 1969.

[31]Proulx, Le Panier de crabes, p. 131.

[32]For Cardinal's programme see, La Presse, 21 juin 1969; Gazette, June 21, 1969.

convention of 1965, the continuance of the fight to win back from Ottawa the powers which rightfully belonged to the province under the constitution, and the necessity of accelerating the economic development of Quebec for the benefit of all its people. He also proposed that a referendum be called on the question of introducing the presidential system of government in Quebec.[33] Unlike his opponent, Bertrand did not appeal for the support of the separatists, but instead suggested that they leave the party and join the Parti Québécois.[34]

The Union Nationale convention of June 19–21, 1969, was probably the most spectacular political extravaganza the province had ever seen. It was estimated that the total amount spent by the two candidates was around a million and a half dollars, which in present currency would be close to three million. Thousands of supporters were brought in at the candidates' expense by buses and trains from all parts of the province. There were marches and demonstrations, brass bands, placards and streamers everywhere, and hats and buttons supplied by the candidates. There were majorettes, dancing girls, hostesses, and impromptu chorus lines in the lobby of the stately Chateau Frontenac. There were singers and other entertainers, and liquor was plentiful and free in the hotel rooms of the candidates' organizers. Robert Charlebois, the well-known Quebec singer, brought in to sing the praises of Cardinal, ended up by comparing the convention to a Nazi Congress and praising the Parti Québécois. Although the delegates to the convention were supposed to participate in various committees to discuss different aspects of party policy most of these committees had to be cancelled because few people showed up.[35]

The voting for the leadership took place on the last day of the convention after the candidates had given their final speeches. Although the Bertrand organization knew that Cardinal had been gaining ground among the younger delegates, it still expected to win by a large majority. When the final results were in Bertrand had received 1325 votes to Cardinal's 938. This was a solid majority, but not the overwhelming victory Bertrand had hoped for, particularly as he had the almost unanimous support of the approximately 250 English delegates.[36]

The bitterness of the struggle between the Cardinal and Bertrand forces in the Union Nationale convention of 1969 seriously damaged the party. In spite of the usual formal declarations of party solidarity when

[33]The text of Bertrand's address to the Convention is to be found in *Le Devoir*, 23 juin 1969.

[34]Proulx, *Le Panier de crabes*, p. 130.

[35]For a description of the American-style "hoopla" of the convention see *La Presse*, 21 juin 1969; *Le Devoir*, 23 juin 1969; *Montreal Star*, June 21, 1969.

[36]The attitude of the English delegates is described in Holden, *Election 1970*, pp. 22–3.

the convention was over, the divisions within the party still ran very deep. Although Cardinal decided to remain in the cabinet, and Bertrand made no move to oust him, many of Cardinal's younger grass roots supporters announced that they were going over to the Parti Québécois.[37] In addition, the political extravaganza which had characterized the convention had created a poor image in the eyes of the public and sharply raised the question of how seriously the Union Nationale should be taken as a responsible party. Montreal's *La Presse*, the province's main French-language daily, in an editorial entitled, "Le cirque et le pain," harshly criticized the convention as "une foire gigantesque en forme de carnaval populaire."[38]

The split in the party between the Cardinal and Bertrand factions was not the only problem facing the Union Nationale in the late sixties. Unfortunately for Bertrand the controversial language question which, as we have seen, had been building up for a good number of years became an explosive issue under his administration. The particular event which brought matters to a head had actually taken place just before Bertrand came into office in 1968: it was commonly known as "the St. Léonard Affair."[39]

The town of St. Léonard, a suburb of Montreal, was made up of a mixed population of French and English origin, and also had a very large group of recently arrived Italian immigrants. A nationalist organization called Mouvement pour l'Intégration Scholaire (M.I.S.), whose objective was to make French the language which all non-English immigrants must adopt, won control of the St. Léonard Catholic School Commission which then decreed that the Italian immigrants must send their children to French schools. The Italians staged protests and demonstrations for, like most immigrant groups, they wanted their children to attend the English schools. Their protests were of no avail for Cardinal, as Minister of Education, refused to intervene and establish a policy for all school commissions to follow. The issue did not die there, for the M.I.S. continued its campaign to have other school commissions follow the example of St. Léonard, while the province's English-language press loudly protested that the traditional educational rights of the English minority were endangered.

When Bertrand succeeded Johnson as Prime Minister in October, 1968, he decided that the government must act to end the agitation and

---

[37]*Le Devoir*, 23 juin 1969; *Gazette*, June 23, 1969.

[38]21 juin 1969.

[39]There is a brief description of the St. Léonard Affair in Jones, *Community in Crisis*, Introduction xiv–xv; see also *Canadian Annual Review*, 1968, pp. 86–9 and pp. 137–9.

settle the question of the right of entry into the English or French sections of the public school system. He therefore introduced a bill in the Assembly, known as Bill 85, which would give parents the right to choose the language in which their children were to be educated. While satisfactory to the English minority the bill resulted in protests and demonstrations from the M.I.S. and other nationalist groups who contended that it would threaten the predominance of the French language in Quebec, particularly in the Montreal area where most immigrants settled.[40] The problem for Bertrand was that the opposition to the bill was also to be found within his own party. In the cabinet Jean-Noël Tremblay was the most vociferous opponent, but he was known to have the support of Cardinal and Masse, and about a dozen members of the party in the Assembly. With the Union Nationale's small majority in that house of perhaps three or four, Bertrand could not afford to take a chance on a split in the party. As a result Bill 85 was shelved.

The decision not to proceed with Bill 85 did not end Bertrand's determination to settle the language question. Several months after his leadership had been endorsed by the party convention of 1969 he came back to this controversial issue. Bertrand realized that there was a problem surrounding the predominance of the French language in Quebec, and the government had appointed a commission of inquiry headed by Jean-Denis Gendron of Laval University to investigate thoroughly all aspects of the matter. He believed, however, that the extreme nationalists had exaggerated the problem, and that for the most part it could be solved by persuasion rather than by restrictive legislation. He also believed that this could be done while still maintaining the linguistic rights of the English minority.

Because of the emotions aroused on both sides of the language debate, Bertrand, in his characteristic fashion, sought to work out a compromise. The result was a bill introduced in the Assembly late in 1969 known as Bill 63, entitled "An Act to Promote the French Language in Quebec." The main features of the bill with amendments added later were: English students must aquire a working knowledge of French in order to graduate; all parents had the right to send their children to either English or French schools; immigrants would be encouraged to enrol their children in French schools; the government would look into the question of what steps should be taken to promote French as the language of work in offices and factories.[41]

The new language legislation was as vehemently opposed by the

[40]For a description of the Bill 85 controversy from the point of view of an ultra-nationalist see, Proulx, *Le Panier de crabes*, chap. V.

[41]A short summary of the Bill is to be found in *Montreal Star*, Feb. 2, 1970.

nationalist groups throughout the province as the previous one. They contended, with some justification, that in its most important aspect, freedom of choice in schooling, it was essentially the same as Bill 85. It was strongly attacked by the Mouvement pour l'Intégration Scholaire, by the province's main patriotic society, the Société Saint-Jean Baptiste, by the province's teachers' associations, and by certain sections of the trade union movement. There were protests organized by the faculty and students in the French universities and CEGEPs, and a hastily formed umbrella group of all organizations opposed to the bill, the Front du Québec Français, organized a mass demonstration in front of the National Assembly.[42]

Opposition to Bill 63 was also to be found within the ranks of the Union Nationale, although the cabinet itself managed to retain a semblance of unity. Jean-Noël Tremblay in a sudden turn-about strongly supported Bertrand; Cardinal and Masse were not happy about some aspects of the bill but nevertheless backed it. About a half-dozen members of the Assembly caucus were opposed but only two, Jérôme Proulx and Antonio Flamand, actually voted against the bill, the others abstaining.[43] The two dissidents subsequently left the party to join the Parti Québécois. Bertrand did not have to worry about defections in the party this time for he knew that the Liberals would support the bill. One reason was that it was in accordance with that party's own language policy; a second reason was that the Liberals were in the process of planning a leadership convention and the defeat of the Bertrand government followed by a sudden election was not in their interests. As a result Bill 63 was passed by a large majority of sixty-seven to five.[44]

The Bertrand government's enactment of Bill 63, coupled with the fact that it only passed with the assistance of the Liberals, sharply called into question the nationalist credentials of the Union Nationale in the eyes of many of its supporters. Moreover, Bertrand in his increasingly strong attacks on the separatists seemed to be moving towards a stronger federalist position.[45] It was legitimate to ask how did the Union Nationale, or at least the majority of the party who supported Bertrand, differ from the Liberals? Could the Union Nationale still be called a nationalist party? There was no question about Cardinal and

---

[42]In regard to the controversy over Bill 63 and the protests it aroused see, Holden, *Election 1970*, chap. V; Proulx, *Le Panier de crabes*, chap. VII; *Montreal Star*, Oct. 31, 1969.

[43]*Montreal Star*, Nov. 13, 1969.

[44]*Montreal Star*, Nov. 21, 1969.

[45]At one point in the debate over Bill 63 he referred to the province as: "a Quebec which still belongs, and as far as I am concerned will always belong to Canada." See *ibid.* It is difficult to imagine Daniel Johnson making such a strong statement.

his grass roots following on that score, but his faction only represented a minority of the party. The essence of the problem was that the Union Nationale was beginning to suffer from a crisis of identity, and was not quite sure in what direction it was moving. This problem was to become more obvious when a general election was called several months later.

THE ELECTORAL DEFEAT OF 1970

When Jean-Jacques Bertrand announced on March 12, 1970, that an election would be held on April 29 of that year it soon became apparent that it would be a multi-party contest. There were some who saw in this development, perhaps prematurely, the end of Quebec's two-party system. Three parties, the Union Nationale, the Liberals, and the Parti Québécois, had candidates in all 108 electoral districts. A fourth party, the Ralliement des Créditistes, had candidates in 99 districts. The New Democratic Party and some splinter groups also entered a few candidates here and there, but they were never in the running and the election was essentially a four-party fight.[46]

The Union Nationale went into the election in a weakened condition and the party was on the defensive almost from the beginning of the campaign. Although an attempt was made to present a united front for the purpose of the election, the cleavage between ultra-nationalists and moderates was still there, and the party sometimes spoke with different voices. On top of its internal problems the Union Nationale found that it had to fight on several fronts, each of which constituted a different kind of challenge. The nature of these challenges can be seen from a brief survey of the main policies which the other three parties presented to the electorate during the campaign. Our starting point will be "the traditional enemy," the Liberal party.

The Quebec Liberal party of 1970 had changed in some important respects since the mid-sixties. After the defeat of 1966 it began moving away from its flirtation with nationalism and such policies as special status, and became more federalist in its orientation. This shift was accentuated when René Lévesque and his followers in the party left

[46]The following are a few of the studies made of the 1970 election: Richard B. Holden, *Election 1970: Le Point tournant* (Montreal, 1970); Vincent Lemieux, Marcel Gilbert, and André Blais, *Une Election de réalignment: L'Election générale du 29 avril 1970 au Québec* (Montreal, 1970); James W. Hagy, "Le Parti Québécois in the 1970 Election," *Queen's Quarterly*, LXXVII, 2 (Summer, 1970), pp. 266–73; Maurice Pinard, "The Ongoing Political Realignments in Quebec," in Dale C. Thomson, ed. *Quebec Society and Politics: Views from the Inside* (Toronto, 1973), pp. 119–38; Daniel Latouche, "The Independence Option: Ideological and Empirical Elements," in *ibid*, pp. 179–96.

to form the Mouvement Souveraineté-Association in 1967. This new orientation did not mean that the party was no longer interested in such matters as the maintenance of provincial rights and increased powers of taxation. It was a matter of a change of emphasis from nationalistic themes to economic issues as having the highest priority for the people of Quebec. The Liberals contended that the goal of cultural survival could only be achieved by the establishment of a strong Quebec economy; this in turn was dependent on Quebec's continued association in the Canadian federation. Jean Lesage expressed Liberal thinking on the subject very clearly in a speech made several years before: "Si le Québec n'est pas économiquement fort, il n'aura pas les moyens de se séparer des autres provinces. S'il est économiquement fort, il n'aura pas besoin de se séparer."[47] It was more than a coincidence that when Lesage retired from the leadership of the party in 1970 the party convention of that year chose as his successor a young economist, Robert Bourassa.[48]

In line with the new Liberal approach, when Robert Bourassa embarked on the election of 1970 he decided to base his strategy on shifting the political debate to economic matters without, however, losing sight of constitutional issues. Under the slogan of "Québec au travail," the Liberal party focused on the need for economic development to solve the problem of unemployment, the key problem facing Quebec. Bourassa toured the province and in speech after speech sought the support of the voters on the pledge that a Liberal administration would create 100,000 new jobs in the province.[49]

Economic development was to be furthered by tax incentives, subsidies and technical assistance to business, encouragement of foreign investment, government incentives for increased productivity in industry, an emphasis on regional development, and manpower training and retraining programmes. While stressing the necessity for the creation of new jobs, the Liberal party also made a point of promising that if elected it would make French the language of work throughout the province.

[47]Le Devoir, 10 oct. 1962.
[48]The Liberal leadership convention of 1970 is described in Holden, Election 1970, chap. III. The Quebec Liberal party has always appeared to be more comfortable when dealing with economic matters than when it has tried to take on a nationalistic image in competition with such parties as the Union Nationale and Parti Québécois.
[49]See Gazette, April 4, 1970; Montreal Star, April 20, 1970; Le Devoir, 13, 20 avril 1970; La Presse, 4, 25 avril 1970; also party advertisement, Le Devoir, 27 avril 1970. Proposals to promote economic development were outlined in a party pamphlet, Quebec: On to Work: The Program and the Team for 1970 (Montreal, 1970), and a booklet, Bourassa Quebec! (Montreal, 1970).

The economic development which the Liberals were proposing to be achieved within the framework of a revised federalism, a fec alism adapted to the changing conditions of Quebec's economic a social life, or, as Bourassa liked to call it, "une fédéralisme rentable" (in rough translation, "profitable" or "productive federalism"). This revised federalism would involve an increase in Quebec's fiscal resources and legislative powers. The Liberal argument against the Parti Québécois' proposal for independence was that it involved serious economic, fiscal, and monetary risks, and that most of that party's social and cultural goals could be achieved within the Canadian framework.[50] In spite of his pro-federalism Bourassa was careful to keep his distance from Prime Minister Trudeau and the federal Liberals. When the Quebec wing of the Canadian Liberal party distributed literature during the election stressing the benefits of federalism, Bourassa openly denounced it for intervention in a provincial election.[51]

The Union Nationale's second opponent, the Parti Québécois, could be considered a left-wing contender for the role of spokesman for Quebec nationalism. Although, as pointed out earlier, the P.Q. was at the same time a nationalist party, a social democratic party, and a separatist party, in the present election most of the emphasis was on the independence issue.[52] Some attention was devoted to the party's cultural, economic, and social goals, but the general implication was that these goals could be easily achieved once Quebec had become "emancipated." Nor was much attention paid to the proposed association with Canada after independence was won, although when the P.Q. was formed in 1968 a good deal of emphasis had been put on "souveraineté-association."

The main argument the Parti Québécois presented to the voters was that independence was the logical goal of a mature society determined to assume control of its own destiny. The Canadian federal system was often referred to by Lévesque as a "strait-jacket" or "cage" which restrained the natural cultural development of the people of Quebec. It was also denounced as a system in which Quebecers paid out more than they received back, involved a costly duplication of services, and resulted in the federal government siphoning off through taxes large

[50]For the economic benefits of federalism and the risks of independence according to Bourassa, see La Presse, 8 avril 1970; Le Soleil (Québec), 23 avril 1970; L'Action (Québec), 17 avril 1970; Gazette, April 17, 20, 1970.

[51]La Presse, 27 avril 1970; Le Devoir, 22 avril 1970.

[52]See speeches by René Lévesque, Gazette, April 6, 13, 1970; La Presse, 6, 28 avril 1970; also speech by Jacques Parizeau, financial critic of the party, Le Devoir, 23 mars 1970. The party programme was published in a booklet, La Solution (Montreal, 1970).

sums of money which should have been retained in Quebec.[53] This point was driven home in an advertisement which appeared in the French language newspapers showing the equation, "Souveraineté = Prospérité: 100% de nos impôts."[54] It was contended that an independent Quebec with all taxes and financial resources in its hands, and in full control of all the levers of the economy, would be able to solve the problems of unemployment, lagging industrial development, and regional stagnation.

Because of its emphasis on the goal of independence and rejection of federalism the focus of Parti Québécois attacks was the Quebec Liberal party and "les patrons libéraux à Ottawa." Behind the Liberals the P.Q. saw the controlling hand of English-Canadian financiers in Montreal and Toronto. In answer to Bourassa's contention that independence involved serious economic risks Lévesque accused the Liberals of pursuing "une campagne de peur."[55]

The third opponent facing the Union Nationale, the Ralliement Créditiste, was an unexpected late arrival to the electoral contest. Up until now the Créditistes, under the leadership of Réal Caouette, had limited their activities to the federal field where they had been relatively successful. However, at a party convention in January, 1970, they decided to form a provincial party and enter candidates in the forthcoming election. The leader chosen was thirty-five-year-old Camil Samson, a former president of the youth section of the party.

Although the Ralliement presented candidates in almost all electoral districts they were only serious contenders in those areas where the party had done well in the federal election of 1968 when they won fifteen seats: the Abitibi and Quebec City regions, the Eastern Townships, and to a lesser extent the Lac St. Jean region.[56] The Ralliement from its origins had always been a regional party with strength limited to certain areas of the province. Its supporters were mainly in the rural areas and small industrial towns and consisted of farmers, merchants, lower-level white collar workers, and industrial workers.[57]

Like the Liberal party, Camil Samson and his Créditistes put the emphasis on the revitalization of the economy as Quebec's main prob-

[53]*Montreal Star*, March 16, 1970; *Le Devoir*, 9, 24 avril 1970.

[54]*Le Devoir*, 22 avril 1970; *La Presse*, 25 avril 1970; see also the party's economic study, *La Souveraineté et l'économie* (Montreal, 1970).

[55]See statements by Lévesque, *La Presse*, 11, 25 avril 1970; and by Parizeau, *Le Devoir*, 23 mars 1970; *La Presse*, 17 avril 1970.

[56]See electoral map showing regional distribution of seats, 1968 election, *Montreal Star*, June 26, 1968.

[57]In regard to the socio-economic basis of support of the Ralliement Créditiste see, Maurice Pinard, *The Rise of a Third Party: A Study in Crisis Politics* (enlarged ed., Montreal, 1975), pp. 92–4; Stein, *The Dynamics of Right-Wing Protest*, pp. 4–6.

lem, but the similarity ended there. For the Ralliement the sole solution to the province's economic and social problems was monetary and fiscal reform. Its main proposal was the creation of a Quebec branch of the Bank of Canada which would make interest-free loans to provincial and municipal governments and school commissions. This would make it possible to reduce income and sales taxes and at the same time increase social welfare benefits. The party also stressed the necessity of maintaining the confessional school system and denounced the "socialisme d'état" of all the other parties. Although the Ralliement Créditiste was pro-federalist it insisted on maintenance of provincial autonomy and demanded that French be made the language of work. However, in general little attention was paid to constitutional and other nationalistic issues; the party's social credit philosophy led it to assume that once the proper monetary and fiscal system was instituted all other problems could be easily solved.[58]

Now that we have seen the various policies presented to the electorate by the other three parties we are in a better position to understand the nature of the problem with which the Union Nationale was faced. The Liberal party's stress on economic development and its concept of "fédéralisme rentable" would appeal to those moderate nationalists strongly opposed to separatism who were also concerned with the economic situation. It has already been pointed out that the Parti Québécois' proposal for independence had a strong attraction for the ultra-nationalist and semi-separatist wing of Bertrand's party.[59] At the same time the social democratic aspects of the P.Q. provided an opportunity for the Union Nationale's lower-income and working-class supporters to support a party which was not only nationalist but also reformist.

The threat to the Union Nationale from the Ralliement Créditiste was perhaps the most obvious of all. The latter party had considerable strength in some of those areas like the Quebec City region, the Eastern Townships, and Lac St. Jean which had been Union Nationale strongholds in 1966. Moreover, the socio-economic groups which supported the Ralliement tended to be similar to those of the Union Nationale, people in farming areas and lower middle class and industrial workers in the smaller industrial towns.[60]

In concluding this survey of the policies of the Union Nationale's opponents there is one observation which might be made. Without too

[58]For the programme and policies of the Ralliement Créditiste see speeches by Camil Samson and Réal Caouette, La Presse, 6, 27 avril 1970; Montreal Star, April 6, 16, 1970; L'Action, 2 avril 1970.
[59]Supra, chap. XI, pp. 250–1.
[60]Supra, chap. X, p. 224.

much exaggeration, it can be said that each one of these opponents presented a single solution to Quebec's problems: for the Liberals, it was economic development; for the Parti Québécois, independence; for the Ralliement, a new monetary and fiscal system. What was the Union Nationale's solution to be?

Prime Minister Bertrand's would probably have preferred to fight the election on the Union Nationale record in office and proposals for more legislation of a similar nature.[61] However, because of the prominent role which the issue of independence versus federalism played in the election he was forced to take a position on the constitutional question. He, therefore, asked for a mandate from the voters to put pressure on Ottawa for the formulation of a new constitution which would satisfy Quebec's special legislative and financial needs. Furthermore, Bertrand gave the federal government four years in which to meet these demands. If a new constitution was not forthcoming by 1974 the party would call a referendum on the question of independence.[62]

On the surface Bertrand's referendum proposal would appear to be a capitulation to the ultra-nationalists, but actually it was a compromise between the two wings of the party. First of all, the referendum would not take place for four years and from the point of view of the federalists quite a few things could happen by that time; and secondly Bertrand did not stipulate which side the Union Nationale would support in such a referendum, or whether it would take any stand at all.

The uneasy nature of the truce between the two factions in the party was indicated by an incident during the course of the campaign. In a speech in a suburb of Quebec City, Marcel Masse, a close associate of Cardinal, was reported to have stressed the similarities in goals between the Union Nationale and the Parti Québécois and that they differed only in the timing of the achievement of independence; he was also reported as saying that in the event of a minority government the Union Nationale might form a coalition with the Parti Québécois.[63] The speech caused such alarm in the federalist wing of the party that Bertrand quickly jumped in and strongly rejected any possibility of such a coalition, stating, "Je ne suis pas séparatiste, je crois au Québec dans le Canada et je le dis avec force."[64] Masse claimed that he was misquoted, and

---

[61]The format of the party's official programme, *Québec plus que jamais: Objectifs '70* (Laval, Que., 1970), was to list party accomplishments between 1966 and 1970 in such areas as agriculture, education, labour, etc., and then outline plans for future legislation in each of these areas. A proposal for negotiating a new constitution was mentioned, but nothing about the referendum discussed below.

[62]See Bertrand's speech at Cowansville April 5, reported in *Gazette*, April 6, 1970; *La Presse*, 6 avril 1970.

[63]*Le Soleil*, 23 avril 1970; *Gazette*, April 23, 1970.

[64]*Le Devoir*, 24 avril 1970; for other reports on the Masse affair see, *Le Devoir*, 22 avril 1970; *La Presse*, 23 avril 1970.

denied proposing a coalition with the P.Q. This seemed to be true, at least in part, but the damage had been done: the incident left the impression that the Union Nationale was a party which did not know in what direction it was going.

Aside from constitutional matters, there were a number of other proposals in the Union Nationale programme which should be mentioned: the establishment of a presidential system of government, the opening of an office of consumer protection and a legal aid service, a guaranteed minimum annual wage, the introduction of a comprehensive system of health insurance and certain measures to help the farmer, such as crop and livestock insurance. In regard to taxation, always a favourite theme with the Union Nationale, income taxes were to be reduced on lower incomes, school taxes progressively decreased, and succession duties abolished. The main proposal in regard to stimulation of the economy was the establishment of an Industrial Development Corporation which would promote the establishment of key industries and encourage the mergers of small business firms; the party also planned to adopt a more scientific approach to the province's manpower requirements and job training programmes.[65]

The Union Nationale's election campaign had not progressed very far before it became apparent that the party was in trouble. Most of its meetings were poorly attended compared to the other parties, audiences were often apathetic or hostile, and there was a good deal of heckling.[66] In the face of this adverse reaction from the electorate Bertrand and his colleagues fell back on one of the tactics characteristic of the Duplessis regime: the promise of large public expenditures in each electoral district in an attempt to win over the voters. In all parts of the province the party pledged that if it were returned to power it would build new local roads and highways, bridges, hospitals, and old people's homes; municipalities were to be given provincial grants to build swimming pools and sports and recreation centres; one county was promised a tourist park, and Montrealers were told that the city would receive seven and a half million dollars for the construction of its subway system.[67]

The Union Nationale's attempt to seduce the voters by the promise of large public expenditures was not particularly successful. When the results of the first public opinion poll were announced about ten days

[65]See *Québec plus que jamais: Objectifs '70*; also party advertisement, *L'Action*, 17 avril 1970; *Montreal Star*, April 6, 1970.

[66]At one meeting Bertrand was loudly booed, *L'Action*, 17 avril 1970; for reports of other meetings of the Union Nationale leader see *La Presse*, 8 avril 1970; *Gazette*, April 13, 1970; *Montreal Star*, April 14, 1970.

[67]Examples of the party's promises are to be found in Pierre-L. O'Neill, "Les Elections du 29 avril," *Le Devoir*, 13 avril 1970; *Montreal Star*, April 13, 21, 1970; *La Presse*, 8, 11 avril 1970; *Gazette*, April 11, 1970.

before the election the Union Nationale was running third behind the Liberals and the Parti Québécois; subsequent polls showed the same trend.[68] With this clear evidence of the steady deterioration in the party's position Bertrand discarded his usual low-key style of campaigning and began to strike out more aggressively at his political opponents, particularly the Liberals. In his attacks he made little distinction between the federal and provincial wings of that party, contending that Bourassa was merely "une marionette" manipulated by the Ottawa Liberals. In addition to the usual charge that the federal government was monopolizing the most lucrative sources of tax revenue, Bertrand argued that its anti-inflation policies were responsible for Quebec's high level of unemployment. Like the Parti Québécois he linked the Liberals with powerful financial interests in Montreal and Toronto. He also accused the English-language press in Montreal, as well as the leading French newspaper, La Presse, of being involved in a conspiracy against his party and manipulation of the public opinion polls.[69]

Although the Liberals were the Union Nationale's main focus of attack particularly in the latter part of the campaign, the other parties were not ignored. The Parti Québécois was often referred to by Bertrand as a group of adventurers and on one occasion he stated that a P.Q. victory would eventually lead to a left-wing dictatorship because of Lévesque's inability to control "l'aile anarchiste ou avant-gardiste" of his party.[70] On the few occasions Bertrand mentioned the Créditistes he quickly dismissed them as "démagogues." In his final appeal to the electorate the Union Nationale leader asked the voters to support his party because of its middle position between the two extremes: the Liberal party, which was federalist at all costs, and the Parti Québécois, which was separatist at all costs. According to Bertrand, the Union Nationale offered "le meilleur dossier constitutionnel."[71]

In view of the difficulties encountered by the Union Nationale throughout the election campaign and the trend shown in the public opinion polls there was little surprise on election night when the results

[68]The results of the first poll by Centre de Recherche sur l'Opinion Publique (C.R.O.P.) in La Presse, 18 avril 1970, were: Liberal, 25.6 per cent; Parti Québécois, 24.9 per cent; Union Nationale, 13.4 per cent; Ralliement Créditiste, 11.7 per cent; other 2.1 per cent; undecided, 22.2 per cent. The figures for the second poll by C.R.O.P. in La Presse, 25 avril 1970, were: Liberal, 24 per cent; Parti Québécois, 19 per cent; Union Nationale, 10 per cent; Ralliement Créditiste, 10 per cent; others, 2 per cent; undecided, 35 per cent. For comparisons with polls taken by other newspapers see La Presse, 28 avril 1970.

[69]Le Devoir, 27, 28 avril 1970; La Presse, 27, 28 avril 1970.

[70]Le Devoir, 22 avril 1970.

[71]Le Devoir, 28 avril 1970.

of the voting indicated that the Bertrand government had been defeated. The aspect of the election which was really surprising was the extent of that defeat. The Liberal party won the election with 72 seats and 45.4 per cent of the popular vote, while the Union Nationale won only 17 seats and had a popular vote of 19.6 per cent. The party had dropped 39 seats and its popular vote was slightly less than half of what it had received in 1966. The Parti Québécois had won only 7 seats, all but one in the east end of Montreal, but it won 23.06 per cent of the popular vote. The Ralliement Créditiste won 12 seats and had a popular vote of 11.19 per cent.[72]

Although the Union Nationale emerged from the election as the official opposition because of the number of seats won, the Parti Québécois had a higher share of the popular vote. Moreover, while Bertrand's party was losing ground, the Parti Québécois did remarkably well for the first election it had contested since its formation two years previously. The Ralliement Créditiste had also done fairly well in its first venture into provincial politics, although its strength was basically limited to those areas where the federal wing of the party was strong.

The serious nature of the Union Nationale decline can be seen more clearly if we compare the seats it won in various regions in the present election, as shown in Table VI, with those it captured in the electoral victory of 1966.[73] The first thing to be noted is that the party's representation was wiped out completely in the Montreal and Quebec City areas; in the Montreal Plain only one seat remained out of the seven it had won in 1966, and in Northern Quebec only two were retained out of the five won earlier. The other fourteen seats retained were scattered about equally in the other three regions of North Shore-Laurentian, Eastern Townships, and Lower St. Lawrence.

In regard to the rural-urban breakdown of seats won by the Union Nationale it will be observed that fourteen of the party's seventeen seats were in rural or rural-urban electoral districts. Not only had the party lost whatever urban base it had in Montreal and Quebec City, but it had also lost the regional capitals of Three Rivers and Sherbrooke, retaining only Chicoutimi in the Lac St. Jean region. The Union Nationale had finally become the almost exclusively rural-based party which many political commentators had always believed it to be.

In the process of losing its urban seats the Union Nationale also lost its working-class support. In Montreal the Parti Québécois captured the working-class districts of St. Jacques, Ste. Marie, Maisonneuve, Bourget, and Lafontaine, all of which had been won by the Union Nationale in

[72]Election statistics are from *Annuaire du Québec*, 1974, p. 120.
[73]See Table IV, *supra*, chap. X, pp. 226–7.

TABLE VI

ELECTORAL DISTRICTS WON BY THE UNION NATIONALE PARTY, RURAL AND URBAN
(R & U) BY GEOGRAPHIC REGIONS, IN THE QUEBEC ELECTION OF 1970[a]

North Shore–Laurentian[b]		Eastern Townships[c]		Lower St. Lawrence[d]	
Labelle	R	Bagot	R	Bellechasse	R
Montcalm	R	Missisquoi	R-U	Montmagny	R-U
Berthier	R	Shefford	U	Temiscouata	R
Maskinongé	R	Nicolet	R	Gaspé Nord	R-U
St. Maurice	U	Wolfe	R		
				TOTAL	2 R
TOTAL	4 R	TOTAL	3 R		2 R-U
	1 U		1 U		
			1 R-U		

Northern Quebec[e]		Montreal Plain[f]	
Dubuc	R-U	Iberville	R-U
Chicoutimi	U		
		TOTAL	1 R-U
TOTAL	1 U		
	1 R-U		

SOURCES: For seats won by the Union Nationale, Président général des élections, *Rapport sur les élections générales de 1970* (Quebec, 1971). The main source for the division of electoral districts into those which are predominantly rural or urban is *Census of Canada*, 1971 (Ottawa), I, Part I, Table 11. Where the boundaries of census districts do not coincide with those of electoral districts, which is often the case, the breakdown of rural and urban polling stations in each electoral district as found in the official election report has been referred to. A number of maps showing regional distribution of seats won by various parties are to be found in *Montreal Star*, April 30, 1970, and *La Presse*, 30 avril 1970.

[a]The category R-U refers to those electoral districts where the rural and urban populations are almost equal, that is, where the breakdown either way is roughly between 45 and 55 per cent.

[b]The north shore of the St. Lawrence between Montreal and Quebec City.

[c]The region southeast of Montreal bordering on the state of Vermont and part of the state of Maine.

[d]The south shore of the St. Lawrence River between Quebec City and Gaspé.

[e]The far northern section of the province between the Abitibi and Saguenay regions.

[f]The term used by geographers to describe the lowlands surroundings Montreal.

1966. In Quebec City the party's working-class stronghold of St. Sauveur was lost to the Ralliement Créditiste, while the Liberals took Limoilou.

At the same time as the Union Nationale was losing its working class clientele in the cities, the Ralliement was making inroads into its rural and small-town supporters in the Eastern Townships and the Quebec region: nine out of the twelve seats won by the Ralliement had been

Union Nationale seats in 1966.[74] The rest of the seats lost by the party went to the Liberals, many of them electoral districts where the P.Q. or Ralliement siphoned off enough support from Bertrand's party to enable the Liberals to emerge with a plurality.

The election of 1970 was the beginning of a realignment taking place in the Quebec party system. The main aspect of this realignment was the strong challenge the Parti Québécois was presenting to the Union Nationale as the spokesman for Quebec nationalism and major opponent of the solidly entrenched Quebec Liberal party. The defeat of a major party in a single election does not necessarily mean its early demise, but unfortunately for the Union Nationale the election of 1970 was the continuation of a decline which had started with the death of Daniel Johnson and was to accelerate in the next few years. As for the Ralliement Créditiste, its future role in provincial politics was not clear at this point, but it did seem likely that it would turn out to be a regional rather than a province-wide party.

THE DISINTEGRATION OF THE UNION NATIONALE

The Union Nationale emerged from the electoral defeat of 1970 as a party searching for a political doctrine to justify its existence. The crux of the problem was the polarization which was beginning to take place among the electorate towards either the Liberal party or the Parti Québécois. As we have seen, even before the 1970 defeat Bertrand had tried without success to find a middle position between the two parties. The difficulty for the Union Nationale was that if it attempted to maintain its image as a nationalist party it was clearly overshadowed by the more radical nationalism of the Parti Québécois. If, on the other hand, it adopted a strong anti-separatist stance and defended federalism it was moving into an area already effectively occupied by Bourassa's Liberal party.

If the Union Nationale could not find a middle position between the Liberal party and the Parti Québécois on constitutional and similar issues there was one other possibility open to it: it could focus on the other role it had traditionally played in Quebec politics as the outstanding defender of conservative economic and social values. In other words, it could become an essentially provincial conservative party basing its

[74]The electoral districts of Beauce, Dorchester, Frontenac, Lévis, Lotbinière, Mégantic, Portneuf, Rouyn-Noranda, and St. Sauveur. The other three seats won by the Ralliement were Abitibi East, Abitibi West, and Richmond. Seats won by various parties are listed in *Annuaire du Québec*, 1972, pp. 93–4.

support on the rural areas and small commercial and industrial towns. Such a step would have been a logical one to take, for the seats the party had won in the 1970 election indicated that whatever strength it retained was among that section of its supporters referred to earlier as "rural conservatives," that is, voters who were more interested in the solution of local problems than in constitutional and language questions.[75]

If the Union Nationale were to follow the orientation suggested here it would have to give up all pretensions of being a major spokesman for Quebec nationalism and accept the role of a minor party with support probably limited to a few regions outside of Montreal and other large urban areas. These were limitations which most of the key figures in the party, still hoping that it could return to the dynamic role it had played under Duplessis and Johnson, were not yet ready to accept. Moreover, as a party of rural conservatives the Union Nationale could expect to face the strong competition of the Ralliement Créditiste which had already cut into its rural and rural-urban support.

Faced by the dilemma described here, the Union Nationale, like all parties whose members are accustomed to looking for direction from above, began to consider the possibility of finding a new leader who would somehow provide a solution to the party's problems. The delicate task of replacing Bertrand as leader was facilitated by the fact that for some time he had been thinking of resigning for health and family reasons. Moreover, his relations with some of his former cabinet ministers were strained because in a press interview shortly after the election he had singled out Cardinal, Masse, and another minister, Mario Beaulieu, as being partly responsible for the party's defeat due to their ambiguous position on constitutional questions.[76] In the fall of 1970 Bertrand announced his intention to retire and shortly after the National Council of the party called a leadership convention for June of the following year.

The Union Nationale's leadership convention of June 18–19, 1971, was a subdued affair compared to previous ones. There were no great ideological conflicts to split the party such as the struggle between the old guard and the reformers in 1961, or between the ultra-nationalists

[75]Out of the seventeen seats won by the Union Nationale in the 1970 election all but three, Missisquoi, Montcalm, and Shefford, had populations which were over 95 per cent French-speaking; only Missisquoi was less than 90 per cent French. Calculations based on statistics, *Annuaire du Québec*, 1974, pp. 244–5. In these electoral districts the threat to the survival of the French language would probably appear rather remote.

[76]*Gazette*, Aug. 6, 1970. Bertrand later retreated somewhat when he accepted full personal responsibility for the party's defeat; *Gazette*, Aug. 8, 1970.

and the moderates in 1969. Nor was there much evidence of the "hoopla" which characterized the previous convention.[77] All of this could be an indication of the increased solidarity and seriousness of the party membership, but it could also be due to apathy and lack of vitality. The reality was that the attention of the delegates was focused on one thing: an overriding concern to find a leader who could provide the party with a set of policies and strategy which would keep it afloat.

Although there were five candidates in the contest only three of them were serious ones, all of them former members of the Bertrand cabinet: Gabriel Loubier, Marcel Masse, and Mario Beaulieu.[78] Loubier had been Minister of Tourism, Fish and Game, in the Johnson cabinet and retained the same post under Bertrand. Masse had started out as Minister of State for Education under Johnson, later Minister of State for the Public Service and then Minister of Inter-governmental Affairs under Bertrand. Beaulieu had been Minister of Finance and of Immigration under Bertrand and had been in charge of party organization in the 1970 election.

Marcel Masse, the candidate with the most carefully thought-out programme, attacked the party establishment and called for structural reforms which would bring about greater participation of the rank-and-file membership in the decision-making process; he also contended that urban problems had been neglected by the party and that it should devote more attention to such matters as town planning and the elimination of slums; his solution to unemployment was that the government put greater emphasis on the development of the manufacturing sector of the economy which in turn would stimulate the service industries. Although retreating from his former semi-separatist position he called for greatly increased powers for Quebec in a new constitution which would take into consideration Quebec's special situation as a province with a different language and culture.[79]

Loubier's programme indicated his strong conservative tendencies. In his speeches he emphasized the importance of maintaining the private enterprise system and the defence of the social order against "les têtes chaudes qui veulent tenir le Québec sur un volcan"[80] (a reference to the radical groups involved in street demonstrations); although a strong federalist and anti-separatist, he favoured greater

[77]See La Presse, 19 juin 1971; Gazette, June 21, 1971.

[78]The other two candidates were André Léveillé, who had been an unsuccessful candidate at the 1969 convention, and Pierre Sévigny, a former member of the Conservative cabinet of John Diefenbaker.

[79]For a description of Masse's policies see La Presse, 12, 19 juin 1971; Gazette, April 29, June 15, 1971.

[80]La Presse, 19 juin 1971.

powers for Quebec in a new constitution which would be negotiated between Canada's two founding nations; he also proposed a presidential system of government for the province and the stimulation of private investment to reduce unemployment.[81] Beaulieu's appeal to the delegates was based almost exclusively on one particular theme, the formation of a North American common market of Quebec, Canada, and the United States. This was an original idea, but the exact relationship between Quebec and the federal government under such a scheme was not clearly spelled out, although Beaulieu, like the other candidates, favoured increased powers for the province.[82]

On the basis of background and qualifications Masse appeared to have the best chance of winning the leadership. At thirty-five he was the youngest of the three, had the most varied administrative experience, and was the best orator; he was an intellectual in a party which did not have too many in that category. Unfortunately, however, for the Union Nationale's "brilliant young man," as Johnson used to call him, it was Loubier who had the support of the party establishment: practically all of the members in the Assembly and most of the key organizers were behind him.[83] Even Masse's former ultra-nationalist colleague, Jean-Guy Cardinal, went over to the Loubier camp. Masse ended up with the backing of only a few members of the legislature, although he could expect to receive the support of whatever strong nationalists remained in the party. As for Beaulieu, there was no clear indication of support from any specific group, but as party organizer in the previous election he had made many contacts. He had the disadvantage, however, of being a poor speaker, and he was the only one of the three candidates who did not have a seat in the Assembly.

When the time came for the delegates to make their decision it took three ballots to select a leader based on a system where the winner had to emerge with an over-all majority. After the first ballot it was clear that the contest was between Masse and Loubier. Beaulieu retired after the second ballot without indicating to his supporters whom they were to support. On the final ballot Loubier emerged as victor in an extremely close vote of 607 to 584.[84] Although Loubier was the new leader, it was obvious that his opponent had a strong following to be reckoned with.

Gabriel Loubier was an amiable, friendly politician, with an air of informality and a good sense of humor, although it could sometimes

---

[81]*La Presse*, 12 juin 1971; *Gazette*, June 16, 1971.
[82]*La Presse*, 12 juin 1971; *Gazette*, June 12, 1971.
[83]See François Trepanier, "Une troisième victoire pour la vieille garde," *La Presse*, 21 juin 1971.
[84]*Le Devoir*, 21 juin 1971.

get the better of him. As a party leader, however, he was not particularly successful. He had neither the imagination or political skill of a Johnson, nor the democratic idealism and quiet dignity of a Bertrand. His record in office was characterized by a number of serious mistakes and unsuccessful attempts to revive the party which ended up in the disaster of the 1973 election. All the blame for the party's problems after 1971 cannot, of course, be attributed to Loubier's leadership, but his policies did little to stem the process of disintegration.

Loubier's first mistake was that he did not make a strong enough effort to integrate Masse into the party team. With Masse having the support of half the membership it would have been logical, indeed essential, to form a Loubier-Masse partnership, even if it meant making substantial concessions to the ideas of the defeated candidate. An even more serious mistake was Loubier's decision, several months after he became leader, to change the name of the Union Nationale to Unité-Québec in the hope of winning wider support. This move, it should be noted, was made with the concurrence of the party executive, key organizers, and a majority of the parliamentary group. However, the rank-and-file membership was never fully consulted.[85]

The underlying factor behind Loubier's decision to change the name of the party was his tendency to look back continually at the policies and strategies of the Union Nationale which had been successful in the past in order to find solutions for the present. He hoped that the new name would enable the party to form a great anti-Liberal coalition of all the opposition parties like the one formed in 1935 between Duplessis' Conservative party and Paul Gouin's Action Libérale Nationale. Unfortunately for Loubier, however, his call for a regrouping of "les forces vives et valables de l'opposition" behind the Unité-Québec was unsuccessful: the Parti Québécois ignored it, while Camil Samson, leader of the Ralliement Créditiste, vehemently rejected the idea.[86]

The change in name of Loubier's party not only failed to widen its supporters but actually weakened it by causing dissensions within its ranks. Marcel Masse resigned from the party denouncing Loubier for changing the name of the Union Nationale without full consultation of its membership. A good number of his supporters among the rank and file followed him, thus reducing further the nationalist and urban-oriented wing of the party.[87] More than ever it was a party of rural conservatives, although Loubier still attempted to maintain its image as a major spokesman for Quebec nationalism.

[85]*Gazette*, Oct. 26, 1971; *Montreal Star*, Oct. 26, 1971.
[86]*Le Devoir*, 26 oct. 1971.
[87]*Gazette*, Nov. 2, 1971; *Montreal Star*, Nov. 2, 1971, March 4, 1972.

The Unité-Québec was no more successful than the old Union Nationale in finding a clearly defined position between the Liberals' "fédéralisme rentable" and the Parti Québécois' "indépendance." Its main
proposal in this area was reform of the constitution which would turn
Canada into a federation of co-operating states in which Quebec would
have an equal voice to the rest of Canada.[88] This was a reformulation of
Johnson's two nations proposal but without the threat of "indépendance." The Unité-Québec revived a number of other former Union
Nationale ideas like Bertrand's presidential system, but none of
Loubier's efforts succeeded in providing the party with a coherent and
imaginative programme or in winning new supporters. In January,
1973, after sounding out the feeling of the membership, the Unité-
Québec's fifteen-month experiment was terminated and the party went
back to its original name, the Union Nationale.

After the party changed back to its former name Loubier pursued a
somewhat more realistic political approach. One of his more astute
moves was to redouble his efforts for some kind of working arrangement
or alliance with the Ralliement Créditiste.[89] The two parties were similar in several important respects: they were both federalist, emphasized
the same economic and social values, were defenders of private enterprise, and opposed the centralized control by the governmental bureaucracy over such matters as education, municipal affairs, and health
services. Furthermore both parties now found their support among the
same socio-economic groups.[90] There was, of course, the problem of
the Créditistes' monetary theories, but Loubier was a flexible politician
who could probably arrange some compromise in this area. Such an
alliance would be an important step towards the formation of a party
of rural conservatives.

The timing of Loubier's overtures to the Créditistes seemed favourable. At the leadership convention of that party in February, 1973, Yvon
Dupuis, a former Liberal with a pragmatic approach to politics, won
out over several more doctrinaire social creditors. The new leader appeared to be more interested in policies which would put his party into
power than in implementing its monetary theories, and there were
indications that he might be interested in some form of working arrangement with the Union Nationale. Unfortunately for Loubier, however,
Dupuis had to move cautiously because his commitment to Social

[88]*Le Devoir*, 29 mai 1972; *Montreal Star*, May 29, 1972.
[89]See *La Presse*, 3, 6 fév. 1973; *Gazette*, Feb. 7, 1973.
[90]The similarities between the two parties are described in Maurice Pinard, "La
Scission au sein du Ralliement Créditiste et ses conséquences électorales," in Pelletier, ed., *Parti politiques au Québec*, pp. 188–90.

Credit doctrine was suspect among important sections of the party, and he finally had to back away from any negotiations.[91]

In spite of the Union Nationale's setbacks and declining support Loubier never gave up on a dream he had of repeating "le miracle de Johnson," referring to the former leader's success in bringing the party back to power in 1966. As that victory had been preceded by a rejuvenation of the Union Nationale at a policy convention, or "assises générales," held a year earlier, Loubier would attempt to do the same. He therefore called for a general convention to be held in the spring of 1973 to plan a new course for the party and prepare it for the next election which was expected to take place the following year.

The policy convention of May 18–20, 1973, followed as closely as possible the pattern of the previous one in 1965. Attended by around 1200 delegates, the party had also invited a number of non-party specialists to act as resource people in various fields. A comprehensive working document had been drawn up to serve as a basis for discussion in the different committees on such matters as the constitution, the economy, language and culture, and other topics. Resolutions from the committees were to be passed on to the plenary session.

In spite of the obvious effort and careful planning which went into the convention of 1973, it failed to give the party the reformed, rejuvenated, and impressive new look which Johnson had achieved in 1965. Nor did it arouse the same popular interest, and the showmanship of the former leader was badly missing. The policies which emerged from the deliberations were largely a revival of time-worn Union Nationale proposals, like the presidential system of government, or policies borrowed from the programmes of other parties, particularly the Ralliement Créditiste.[92]

Like the Créditistes the convention put a great emphasis on the maintenance of the principle of private enterprise including the "co-existence" of a private as well as a public sector in the fields of medical care and hospitalization. In his defence of the rights of the individual Loubier often referred to "le respect de la personne humaine," a favourite theme with the Social Crediters. Other policies similar to the Ralliement programme were the establishment of a guaranteed annual

[91]For Dupuis' political ideas see Michael B. Stein, "Le Crédit social dans la province du Québec: sommaire et développements," *Canadian Journal of Political Science*, VI, no. 4 (Dec. 1973), pp. 573–4.

[92]A summary of the more important policy resolutions of the Convention is to be found in, *Le Devoir*, 21 mai 1973; *Montreal Star*, May 21, 1973; *Gazette*, May 19, 21, 1973; for a complete report of proceedings see, Union Nationale, Assises générales, St. Léonard, 18, 19, 20 mai 1973, *Un Programme pour l'avenir du Québec* (Montreal, 1973).

income and the participation of the provinces in the administration of the Bank of Canada.

As one might anticipate the convention endorsed Loubier's proposal for a new constitution agreed upon by the "contracting states" of Canada. In a more radical departure, it also repudiated Bill 63 passed by the Bertrand administration and proposed that French become the official language of Quebec and the language of work, and that immigrants be required to send their children to French schools. This was a move in a nationalist direction, but these proposals had been part of the Parti Québécois programme for several years. Moreover, even the Liberal party now favoured French as the language of work and was moving towards adoption of some of the other language policies. The main thing missing in Loubier's attempt to project a nationalist image was that, in contrast to Johnson in 1965, he failed to come up with a ringing manifesto like "Egalité ou Indépendance" to capture the popular imagination and arouse controversy. As a result, the convention left the impression of a party more interested in attracting the Créditiste vote than in playing a new and dynamic nationalist role.

When Prime Minister Bourassa rather unexpectedly called an election for October 29, 1973, instead of waiting until the following year, the Union Nationale started out with some serious disadvantages. A public opinion poll a few months previous had shown that it ranked fourth among the province's parties, with only 3.8 per cent of the popular vote, although 31 per cent were still undecided.[93] A second factor was that in 1972 the Bourassa government had eliminated the more serious distortions of the electoral map by increasing substantially the number of urban seats and reducing the rural ones, a serious blow for a rural-oriented party like the Union Nationale. There was also a continuing desertion of former Union Nationale organizers, candidates, and other key personnel to the other parties, particularly the Parti Québécois.[94] Two important recruits for that party were Pierre Marc Johnson and Jean-François Bertrand, sons of the former Union Nationale leaders; Jean-Guy Cardinal was about to make a move in the same direction. In the face of all these discouraging developments there was, however, one favourable factor: Loubier had a fairly substantial campaign chest from the sale of the Union Nationale's two Renaissance Clubs in Montreal and Quebec City, and the sale of the party-owned daily, *Montréal-Matin*.

[93]The results of a poll taken by C.R.O.P. in June 1973 were: Liberal party, 34.7 per cent; Parti Québécois, 17.7 per cent; Ralliement Créditiste, 12.6 per cent; Union Nationale, 3.8 per cent; Undecided, 31.2 per cent. *Le Devoir*, 15 juin 1973.
[94]Claude Beauchamp et Claude Saint-Laurent, "Des heures difficiles," *La Presse*, 5 oct. 1973.

The same four parties contested the election of 1973 as in 1970: Liberals, Parti Québécois, Parti Créditiste (formerly Ralliement Créditiste), and Union Nationale. However, while the earlier election had been a lively four-party struggle in most electoral districts, the 1973 election was dominated by the clash between Bourassa's Liberals and Lévesque's Parti Québécois over the economic consequences of independence, with the two other parties playing a much more minor role. The main feature of the Parti Québécois campaign was its presentation of "le budget de l'An I," a projection of receipts and expenditures in Quebec's first year as an independent state; the purpose was to show how the province would be better off economically if it were separated from Canada. The Liberals countered by presenting their own financial statistics showing the economic advantages of federalism and calling for "cultural sovereignty" in a revised constitution.[95] The "battle of the budget" was not a particularly effective strategy for the Parti Québécois: the results of the conflicting statistics were inconclusive, the debate was too technical for the average voter, and attention was diverted from adequate scrutiny and criticism of the record of the Liberal administration. Aside from the two main parties, the Parti Créditiste under its new leader, Yvon Dupuis, attracted the most attention because of its determined effort to get a foothold in Montreal and other urban areas. The policies proposed by Dupuis were sometimes vague and inconsistent, but it was clear that he was a strong advocate of private enterprise and a harsh critic of trade union leaders and other "radicals."[96]

The Union Nationale, fully aware of its low standing in the polls, put up a strong fight to the end of the campaign in an effort to reverse the trend. Loubier's main hope was to win over some of the undecided voters with a programme which was essentially the same as the proposals put forward at the policy convention of the previous May.[97] In his attacks on the other parties Loubier focused particularly on the Parti Québécois, contending that the Union Nationale was the party of "vrais nationalistes," and one which would "humaniser le système."[98]

On a number of occasions Loubier referred to his intention to follow Johnson's strategy in 1966 of fighting the election seat by seat. He was inconsistent, however, in following this plan, tending to give the same

[95]On the 1973 election, and particularly the struggle between the Liberals and the Parti Québécois see Murray, *Le Parti Québécois*, pp. 181–8, 200–4; and John Saywell, *The Rise of the Parti Québécois, 1967–1976* (Toronto, 1977), pp. 73–105.

[96]See *La Presse*, 13, 24 oct. 1973; *Montreal Star*, Oct. 16, 24, 1973; for the party's full programme see *Un Programme humain pour un Québec fort* (Montreal, 1973).

[97]See "Le Manifeste électoral de l'Union Nationale," *Le Devoir*, 9 oct. 1973; and in English, *For the Future of a Strong Quebec* (St. Eustache, Qué., 1973).

[98]*La Presse*, 29 oct. 1973; for attacks on the Parti Québécois see *La Presse*, 13, 20 oct. 1973; *Le Devoir*, 10 oct. 1973; *Montreal Star*, Oct. 12, 1973.

speech wherever he went instead of concentrating on local issues. The real problem, however, was his inability to find strong candidates, a key factor in Johnson's strategy. Although he had announced early in the campaign that the Union Nationale would be presenting a large number of "prestigious candidates," this not only failed to happen, but the party had difficulty in some districts to find anyone who would accept the nomination.[99] Another damaging blow to the Union Nationale morale was that throughout the campaign the other parties largely ignored it. At the end Loubier was spending a good deal of time insisting that the Union Nationale was not about to disappear from the political scene.

The election of 1973 had a number of unexpected results. The Liberal party won with a crushing majority of 102 out of the 110 seats, but with 54.7 per cent of the popular vote; the Parti Québécois was next with only six seats in spite of the fact that it won 30.2 per cent of the vote and was now the official opposition; the Parti Créditiste won only two seats, but its popular vote of 9.9 per cent was only about 1 per cent less than in 1970 when it won twelve seats; the Union Nationale was last, without a single member elected and only 4.9 per cent of the vote.[100]

The distorted results which the single-member constituency system can produce when there is a multi-party contest have been pointed out before and need no further comment here. The one aspect which does call for comment is the disaster which befell the Union Nationale: the party went down from 56 seats and 41 per cent of the vote in 1966 to no members elected and only 4.9 per cent of the vote in 1973, just seven years later. We have here a political development which probably has no parallel in Canadian politics: a party which had been one of the main parties in a two-party system and which had been in existence for almost four decades completely disappeared from the legislature within a seven-year period, to be replaced as the official opposition by another party which did not even exist seven years before. This new party, the Parti Québécois, might have had only a handful of seats in the Assembly, but the size of its popular vote indicated quite clearly that it had become the successor to the Union Nationale as the spokesman for Quebec nationalism; radical nationalism had finally triumphed over conservative nationalism (the question of whether the Union Nationale was re-born in the election of 1976 is dealt with in a brief postscript below).

In retrospect it can be said that some of the reasons for the decline and demise of the Union Nationale were due to fairly obvious errors in policy and strategy, while others were related to profound changes

[99]Loubier's strategy and its weaknesses are described in *Le Devoir*, 15 oct. 1973; *Montreal Star*, Oct. 9, 20, 1973; *Gazette*, Oct. 10, 20, 1973; *La Presse*, 22 oct. 1973.
[100]Election statistics from *Annuaire du Québec*, 1974, p. 120.

taking place in the structure of Quebec society to which the Union Nationale was unable to adjust. One of the more obvious mistakes of the party was its failure to recognize the increasing importance of the language question for Quebec's French-speaking majority in the nineteen-sixties, particularly in regard to the language of work. Another weakness was the Union Nationale's long period of indecision over the question of whether it would remain federalist or move in the direction of separatism. This issue seriously split the party until it was finally resolved by the strong federalist and anti-separatist position of Loubier. By this time the Union Nationale was hardly more nationalist than the Liberal or Créditiste parties.

A more basic problem underlying the Union Nationale's decline was that it had become in some respects an anachronism, a party which was representative of a type of society which was rapidly disappearing. Even though the Union Nationale had always had a certain amount of urban support, its approach to politics was strongly rural-oriented, with policies, priorities, and a system of values which were in sharp contrast to the advanced industrialized, urbanized, and secularized society which Quebec had become by the early sixties. Although for a short period between 1966 and 1968 the party appeared to be on the road to modernization and recovery, it soon became apparent that Johnson's efforts had only slowed down the party's decline, not reversed it. The appearance of a more modern and dynamic nationalist party which reflected more accurately the aspirations and goals of the Quebec nationalist movement of the sixties and seventies was the finishing touch for the Union Nationale.

There is one final observation which must be made. The reference above to the Parti Québécois as the successor to the Union Nationale suggests a similarity between the two parties which René Lévesque and his colleagues might be reluctant to accept, for they have always been inclined to look upon the Union Nationale as "a reactionary party." However if we leave aside for the moment the vast gap between the economic and social philosophies of the two parties, and consider them purely in terms of *their nationalist ideology* there is undoubtedly a direct line from Duplessis, to Johnson, to Lévesque. Although he was no admirer of Duplessis, René Lévesque could hardly disagree with the following statement made by Le Chef in 1945: "Il y a un autre point important. C'est le droit d'être maître chez soi . . . L'Autonomie, c'est le droit . . . de faire des lois pour nous et par nous, de faire régler les questions qui regardent Québec par Québec, plutôt que de les faire régler par Ottawa."[101]

[101]*Le Devoir*, 19 nov. 1945.

Postscript

ALTHOUGH I NEVER INTENDED to continue this history of Quebec nationalism beyond the replacement in 1973 of the Union Nationale by the Parti Québécois as the official opposition in the legislature, some brief comment must be made concerning the apparent resurrection of the Union Nationale in the election of 1976. In that election the party, now under a new leader, Rodrigue Biron, won eleven seats and around 18 per cent of the popular vote. With two or three exceptions, the seats won were rural or rural-urban electoral districts in the Eastern Townships or adjacent to that area. Making allowances for the changes in the electoral map in 1972, a rough survey of seats won seems to indicate that Biron regained for the Union Nationale most of the ground lost to the Créditistes in 1970 (the Ralliement's popular vote fell from approximately 10 per cent in 1973 to 5 per cent in 1976). Another aspect of the Union Nationale's support was the large gain made among English voters in western Montreal, and its victory in one seat in that region, the electoral district of Pointe Claire.

It is my contention that, although there is a certain continuity between Biron's Union Nationale and the one which disappeared from the legislature in 1973, in several important respects Biron's party is a different one from the traditional Union Nationale of Duplessis and Johnson, or even from that of Bertrand. This conviction has been arrived at for three different reasons: the leading figures in the party for the most part are not the same; although its economic and social policies are conservative like those of the old Union Nationale, the party is not significantly more nationalist than the Liberals or the Ralliement Créditiste; its clientele, or sources of support, with the exception of some rural voters, are considerably different from those of the traditional Union Nationale.

In regard to the leading figures in the party, it should be noted first of all that Rodrigue Biron, the head of a family-owned business firm, only joined the Union Nationale two months before he was chosen leader, and his candidacy was opposed by whatever was left of the old party establishment. Only around a dozen of the candidates in the 1976 election had been Union Nationale members of the legislature at one time or the other. With the exception of Maurice Bellemare, an old-time politician from the Duplessis era, and one or two others, these former members had been back-benchers. Conspicuously absent were the key figures of the party in the early seventies: Jean-Jacques Bertrand had died in 1973, while the others, Cardinal, Masse, Loubier, Beaulieu, Tremblay, had either retired from active politics or joined another party. Biron had personally to choose a majority of the candidates in the election because local party associations were moribund or had withered away. He recruited them largely from the ranks of the federal Conservative party, from the Ralliement Créditiste, and from his business acquaintances throughout the province.

The reason why the nationalist credentials of Biron's Union Nationale must be questioned is because of its stand on certain issues in the 1976 election. Although the party presented the usual arguments in defence of provincial rights made by all Quebec parties, it was clearly and unquestionably a strong federalist party. Its position on the language question was even more surprising for it was more liberal than that of the Liberal party. Biron called for the abolition of Bill 22 passed by the Bourassa government which put certain restrictions on the freedom of recently arrived non-English speaking immigrants to send their children to English schools. Instead he proposed that these immigrants be given freedom of choice between the English and French school systems. He also proposed that while French would become the "national language" of Quebec, both French and English would become "official languages." Whatever one thinks of these constitutional and language policies, one thing was certain: this was not the voice of Quebec nationalism.

The type of regional and socio-economic support which Biron's party received from the electorate in the 1976 election raises further questions about its similarity to the old Union Nationale. While the party managed to obtain a considerable amount of rural support as in the past, it failed to make inroads into the working-class districts of Montreal and Quebec City and in the regional capitals of Chicoutimi, Three Rivers, and Sherbrooke, areas which had been Union Nationale strongholds from the party's early days to the election of 1970. Even more unusual was the spectacular gains made by Biron's party in Montreal's predominantly English-speaking west end, and its victory in the electoral district of Pointe Claire which was 80 per cent English. How could an authentic

Quebec nationalist party conceivably win a seat in a region which has been consistently referred to here as, "the graveyard of nationalist candidates?" The answer is that, although the viewpoint and goals of the English voter had not changed, those of the Union Nationale had.

If the party led by Biron bears only a slight resemblance to the traditional Union Nationale party, what is its place in the Quebec political spectrum and what is its future role likely to be in the political life of the province? Political prediction is always a hazardous business, but it seems probable that the new Union Nationale will end up as a party of rural conservatives, a regional party whose main support lies outside large urban areas like Montreal and Quebec City. As we saw earlier, this trend was developing in the old Union Nationale in the final days of Loubier's leadership. Two developments since 1976 seem to strengthen this possibility. The English voters in western Montreal after their brief flirtation with Biron's party are now returning to their original allegiance, the Liberal party under its new leader Claude Ryan. Secondly, the Ralliement Créditiste, the main rival to the Union Nationale in the rural areas and small towns, appears to be disintegrating. It might very well be that the new Union Nationale will become the successor to the Créditistes as the party of rural conservatives, just as the Parti Québécois has become the successor to the old Union Nationale of Duplessis and Johnson as the spokesman for Quebec nationalism.

CHAPTER XII

Conclusion

WHEN A POLITICAL SCIENTIST undertakes a study of a political party such as Union Nationale he usually has two purposes in mind. The first and most obvious one is to provide some useful information on the pattern of politics in a particular area over a certain period of time. A second purpose, however, is to throw some additional light on those complex theoretical and methodological problems involved in any attempt to develop a scientific approach to the study of politics. The nature of the contribution which the political scientist can make in this respect will inevitably be related to the historical and cultural background of the society whose political processes are being studied.

This analysis of Quebec politics has provided at least part of the answer to three questions which cannot help but be of particular interest to the political scientist: what type of political behaviour can one expect to find in a society constituting an ethnic minority whose main preoccupation is the maintenance of its cultural identity and the defence of its group interests? How is the reaction of the voter to the economic and social problems of an industrial society affected by strong adherence to the doctrines and social philosophy of Roman Catholicism? How does a lack of democratic convictions and of an adequate understanding of parliamentary government affect the proper functioning of that type of political system and change the nature of the party struggle?

In regard to the first question, this study has shown that in a society where an ethnic minority has reason to believe that its interests as a distinct cultural group are threatened, the struggle to defend and protect those interests tends to become the dominant issue in politics and encourages the growth of strong nationalistic sentiments. As a result, purely economic issues, which ordinarily play an important role in any capitalist society, are likely to be pushed into the background. The average voter in this ethnic group may be more interested in the problem of maintaining his right to speak and use his language in everyday life than in the enactment of social legislation. His ability to retain the particular set of values found in his educational system may be more important to him than the struggle for higher wage scales. He may be more concerned about the possibility of the dominant group forcing upon him some policy in the realm of foreign affairs to which he is opposed, such as participation in a war, than with the question of introducing reforms in the capitalist system.

In pointing out this readiness on the part of an ethnic minority to place cultural survival ahead of economic interests, it is not meant to imply that such interests are of no concern whatsoever to the group, or that the cultural issue is always the dominant one. We are merely saying that when a question of priorities arises in certain periods of crisis "ethnic consciousness" will turn out to be stronger than "class consciousness."

This preoccupation of a minority group with the maintenance of its cultural values has some interesting implications for the party struggle. It means that the political party which is the staunchest defender of those values is in an excellent position to capture the support of a majority of the voters, including the working class, even though it may be a party of economic conservatism closely allied with business interests and even strongly anti-labour. It means that it is possible for a party which is the bitter enemy of the trade union movement to capture the support of a large proportion or even a majority of the trade union vote.

The important role that such non-economic factors as ethnic (or religious) interest can play in the motivation of the voter has not, in the opinion of the writer, always received adequate attention in the analysis of political parties. Many political analysts, even those who are not of Marxist persuasion, have tended to assume that the economic philosophy of a political party is *in every case* that party's most important characteristic. One cannot deny, of course, the extremely important role that the clash of economic interests plays in politics. However, undue emphasis on this factor may in certain cases obscure other aspects of a party which must be taken into consideration if we are to understand all the reasons for that party's strength. For instance, a description of the Union Nationale as a right-wing or ultraconservative party is correct as far as it goes, but it misses completely the most important characteristic of the party *from the point of view of those who support it,* many of whom may not be economic conservatives at all. Although one may disagree with such a point of view, the fact that it is there must be recognized and given adequate weight in the analysis of that party.[1]

In making a plea that much more consideration be given to the non-economic aspects of politics it is contended that only in that way can we explain satisfactorily why parties of private enterprise, such as the British Conservative party and the Christian Democratic Union in the German Federal Republic, have been successful in obtaining substantial support from manual and white collar workers, and other groups in the lower income brackets.[2] Such an approach might also lead us to question the fairly common assumption that the growth of communism in certain underdeveloped and former colonial areas is solely due to the economic benefits promised by that movement. Is there not a strong possibility that the appeal of the communists to nationalistic and anti-Western sentiments is at least of equal importance in many situations? How important a factor has the anti-religious bias of Marxism been in attracting the support of middle and upper class intellectuals who are in revolt against religious beliefs and practices in these areas?[3] Although the writer does not have the answer to questions such as these, he does believe that they suggest problems of politics which are well worth investigating.

A second conclusion which can be drawn from our study of Quebec politics is that where economic unrest develops in a capitalist society which is at the same time strongly Roman Catholic, proposals for

[1]In a short study made some years ago of Canadian federal politics between 1935 and 1949 the writer arrived at somewhat similar conclusions concerning the importance of non-economic factors in voting behaviour. See Herbert F. Quinn, "The Role of the Liberal Party in Recent Canadian Politics," *Political Science Quarterly,* LXVIII, (Sept., 1953), 396–418.

[2]It is estimated that in the British election of 1951 the Conservative party received the support of 28 per cent of the manual workers, 48 per cent of the lower paid white collar workers, and 41 per cent of an "intermediate" group consisting of sales clerks, policemen, postmen, waitresses, and so on. See John Bonham, *The Middle Class Vote* (London, 1954), pp. 129 and 173. In regard to Western Germany, a public opinion poll taken in 1952 showed that 32 per cent of the voters with monthly incomes of less than 250 DM (roughly $57.00) were supporters of the Christian Democratic Union. See Michael P. Fogarty, *Christian Democracy in Western Europe,* 1820–1953 (Notre Dame, Ind., 1957), p. 369. In the German election of 1957 the C.D.U. received strong support in several areas containing a high percentage of industrial workers. See Uwe Kitzinger, *German Electoral Politics* (Oxford, 1960), pp. 280-4.

[3]The important role that intellectuals have played in the growth of Communism in Asiatic countries is described in Morris Watnick, "The Appeal of Communism to the Peoples of Underdeveloped Areas," in Richard Bendix and Seymour M. Lipset, eds., *Class, Status and Power* (Glencoe, Ill., 1953), pp. 651–62.

reform are likely to be inspired by the principles of social Catholicism rather than those of socialism.[4] The Catholic social movement originated in France, Germany, and a number of other European countries around the middle of the last century.[5] It was led by a few prominent laymen and certain members of the clergy who were interested in social reform and opposed to the conservative semi-feudal tradition within European Catholicism. This movement received little support from Pope Pius IX, but it was strongly endorsed by his successor Pope Leo XIII. The social Catholics attempted to find a middle way between economic liberalism and Marxian socialism. While they were in agreement with a good deal of the Marxist critique of liberal capitalism, they were strongly opposed to the solution which Marx put forward with its emphasis on state control and ownership of the means of production. The Catholic reformers proposed the redistribution of private property rather than its elimination through government ownership.

If we make allowance for certain conditions peculiar to Quebec, we can say that this study has given us a fairly good idea of the aims and goals of the Catholic social movement during the periods from 1920 to 1945 and from the end of the Second World War to the late 1950's. In the first period Catholic reformers proposed to bring about a redistribution of wealth in a number of different ways: the establishment of a scale of wages which would enable the worker to acquire property; the organization and expansion of co-operatives; family assistance and other forms of social legislation; the encouragement of small- and medium-size industry rather than the large-scale enterprise; government assistance to the small farmer to enable him to stay on the land. In contrast to the laissez-faire attitude of the economic liberals, and the rigid state controls of the socialists, the programme of social Catholicism called for the establishment of professional associations, or corporations, similar to the guilds of the Middle Ages, which would regulate and co-ordinate a wide range of economic activities. Although the emphasis was on the private ownership of property, it was recognized that certain forms of enterprise, such as some public utilities, might have to be taken over by the government in the public interest.

[4]It must be emphasized here that the term "strongly Roman Catholic" describes a people who fully accept the directives and social philosophy of the Church. It does not apply to those areas, such as certain sections of France and Italy, where the people are only nominal Catholics. For a more extensive consideration of this distinction, see *supra*, p. 9n.

[5]Probably the best study of the Catholic social movement to appear in English is Fogarty, *Christian Democracy in Western Europe, 1820–1953*.

In the period following the Second World War a new orientation in Catholic social thought took place, but the proposals mentioned above were by no means completely discarded. This new orientation expressed itself in a growing lack of interest on the part of many Catholic reformers in the establishment of a corporative system. At the same time the state was given a somewhat more active role in the regulation of the economy and in the provision of social services. The fact that most sectors of the economy would continue to be characterized by large- rather than small-scale business enterprise was now fully recognized. The most important new development in the postwar years was the emphasis placed on the participation of the workers in the management, ownership, and profits of these large industrial enterprises. It would appear that these new trends in Catholic social thinking have been endorsed by Pope John XXIII in his encyclical, *Mater et Magistra*, which appeared in 1961.[6]

Social Catholicism, in providing an alternative to liberal capitalism, has in the past made it difficult for socialist and communist parties to make much headway among industrial workers in strongly Catholic areas such as Quebec, the Rhineland, Alsace-Lorraine, and certain industrial sections of Belgium, even during periods when there has been a great deal of economic unrest and dissatisfaction with the capitalist system. It should also be noted that the development of this left-wing movement within Catholicism in modern times has coincided with a shift to the right on the part of social democratic parties in western Europe. These parties have gradually discarded their Marxist ideology with its anti-religious overtones and its sweeping proposals for the nationalization of private enterprise.[7] As a result of these changes, the possibility of co-operation at the political level between the socialist and the social Catholic has greatly increased. This can be illustrated by the friendly relationship which existed between the French Socialist party and the Mouvement Républicain Populaire during the Fourth Republic, and by the coalition government in Austria composed of the Social Democratic party and the People's party, which has been in power since the end of World War II. There is, however, one other aspect of social Catholicism which should always be borne in mind. In spite of the influence and strength of this movement within Catholicism, it must not be assumed that

---

[6] (New York, 1961). See in particular, pp. 16–29.

[7] At the meetings of the Socialist International in 1951 and 1953 resolutions were passed which indicated a desire on the part of members of that organization to free themselves from the accusation that they had any anti-religious bias. See Fogarty, *Christian Democracy in Western Europe, 1820–1953*, p. 383–4.

it has the support of all members of that faith in any given country. There are many right-wing Catholics who are staunch defenders of industrial capitalism in its existing form and are therefore highly critical of the reformers. These conservative Catholics provide a good deal of support for such right-wing political formations as the Independents in France.

A third aspect of this study has interest for the political scientist. It has demonstrated that in a society where democratic institutions are not accompanied by democratic convictions, and where the electorate lacks a real understanding of the principles of parliamentary government, a political party, once it is in office, has effective means of perpetuating its power irrespective of what economic and social policies it decides to adopt. It can use its control over the administration and the legislature to build up its electoral support by pursuing certain tactics which would not be tolerated in a society with a strong commitment to democratic ideals. These tactics fall into three main categories: (a) the administration can threaten to restrict essential governmental services and expenditures in any community which refuses to support the party; (b) it can build up a huge campaign chest by compelling business enterprises dependent on the government for orders, contracts, and other favours, to contribute regularly to the party fund; (c) it can fashion the electoral machinery along lines which will be most disadvantageous to the opposition parties. The only time such a régime is likely to be seriously threatened is when the voters make up their minds that they will no longer stand for such questionable practices.

The various means which a party has at its disposal to perpetuate its power once it is firmly entrenched in office has a direct bearing on the important question of the control which business and financial interests can exercise over government policy in a capitalist society. According to a theory held by many socialists, political parties in any country with a private enterprise economy are always the captives of the business community because they are dependent on the latter to provide funds for election campaigns. If one of these parties manages to win an election it can remain in power only as long as its policies are in conformity with the interests of the business world.

It is not proposed here to discuss whether the many and varied forms of business enterprise are ever completely united on any given policy, or whether money is the only factor in the ability of a political party to win an election, although both of these are interesting questions. It can be conceded, however, that this theory of capitalist domination does have some relevance for a party which is out of office,

or even for a party in power in certain kinds of societies.[8] The point
to be made here is that in a society with the type of politics found in
Quebec the relationship between a political party and the business
community is completely reversed once that party is in office. It is not
a case of the party remaining in power because it has the support of
the business interests. Because it is in power it can demand the support of the business interests whether they like it or not. It is in a
position to levy tribute because the business world is dependent on
the government for favourable legislation, tax concessions, licences,
and the other privileges essential for the profitable operation of many
enterprises. The most reliable source of financial support is the
manufacturers, contractors, and merchants who wish to do business
with the government. The independence of the party in power is
strengthened still further by the fact that its control over the treasury
enables it to use government funds for electoral purposes. It can buy
the support of large sections of the press by subsidies and by exerting
various forms of pressure. Its control over the electoral machinery
enables it to determine the conditions under which opposition parties
supported by big business will be permitted to operate.

Although a party in power operating under the conditions described
need not be dominated by the business interests, it does not necessarily follow that such a party will adopt a hostile attitude towards
these interests. Whether or not this happens will depend upon the
economic ideas which find favour with the party, and which may, of
course, be subject to change over a period of time. Our basic argument here is that even a radical party opposed by the economic *élite*
will have, under the special conditions noted, adequate means of
financing its operations once it is in power, and will even be able to
wring contributions from firms opposed to its policies. In V.O. Key's
study of Louisiana politics under Huey Long, whose régime incidentally bore some striking resemblances to that of Duplessis in
Quebec, the author points out the peculiar power that accrues to
those in office:

If a political leader cannot annex the support of a segment of the
economic upper crust, once in office he can manufacture a new economic
elite attached to the regime. Public purchases provide one means. In
Louisiana state control of petroleum production permitted favoritism worth
millions. Louisiana's gambling habits make gambling concessions profitable.
. . . By these and other methods the Long organization created its own

---

[8]In regard to this reference to "certain kinds of societies," see the first few lines
of the last paragraph of the present chapter.

vested interests, which were tied to it by golden bonds and could help pay the cost of politics.[9]

In another part of the same study this statement is made:

. . . the contractor-donor is more concerned with whether a candidate will win than with his ideology. The consequence is that 'radical' gubernatorial candidates frowned on by the vast majority of businessmen sometimes attract substantial financial support.[10]

It is rather paradoxical that in a more authentically democratic society than Quebec under Duplessis, or Louisiana under Huey Long, a party which came into power with the support of big business would find it more difficult to free itself from its control because in such a society the voters would not stand for such questionable practices as the spending of government money for partisan purposes and the raising of campaign funds by making deals with government contractors and suppliers. In other words, whenever a political party cannot finance itself out of public funds, it is more dependent on and influenced by private interests. The most equitable solution to this problem would be for the state to defray part of the campaign costs of *all* parties contesting an election. (France has had such a system since the days of the Third Republic.) At the same time the over-all costs of elections should be reduced by placing a limitation on the amount of money which can be spent by any candidate or party. Any action along these lines would eliminate the basis of a good deal of the criticism heard from time to time concerning the way in which democratic government functions in the Western world.

[9]V. O. Key, Jr., *Southern Politics* (New York, 1949), p. 163.
[10]*Ibid.*, p. 473.

Appendices, Bibliography, and Index

Appendix A

TABLE VII

Seats Won by Various Parties in Quebec Provincial Elections, 1867–1976

Election	Liberal[a]	Conservative[b]	Union Nat.	Action Libérale Nat.	Bloc Populaire	Parti Nat.	Parti Québécois	Ralliement Créd.	Other	Total Seats
1867	14	50								64[e]
1871	20	45								65
1875	25	40								65
1878	32	32							1	65
1881	12	53								65
1886		30				35[d]				65
1890		26				46[d]			1	73
1892	18	52							3	73
1897	57	17								74
1900	67	7								74
1904	66	8								74
1908	57	15							2	74
1912	63	16							2	81
1916	75	6								81
1919	74	5							2	81
1923	64	21								85
1927	75	9							1	85
1931	79	11								90
1935	48	16		26						90
1936	14		76							90
1939	69	1	14						2	86
1944	37		48		4				2	91
1948	8		82						2	92
1952	23		68						1	92
1956	20		72						1	93
1960	51		43						1	95
1962	63		31						1	95
1966	51		56						1	108
1970	72		17				7	12		108
1973	102		0				6	2		110
1976	27		11				70	1	1	110

Sources: Inasmuch as the party affiliation of some of the members of the Legislative Assembly between 1867 and 1900 was rather uncertain, two sources have been checked for this period, Quebec, Department of Trade and Commerce, "Members of the Legislative Assembly, by Electoral District, Since 1867," *Statistical Year Book*, 1953, pp. 35–53, and Robert Rumilly, *Histoire de la Province de Québec* (Montreal, n.d.), Vols. I–X; for the elections from 1904 to 1960, see *Canadian Parliamentary Guide*, 1905–1961; from 1962 to 1973, *Annuaire du Quebec*, 1975–76, p. 154; for election of 1976, André Bernard, *Quebec: élections 1976* (Montreal, 1976), p. 21.

[a]Includes independent Liberals.

[b]Includes independent Conservatives.

[e]There were actually sixty-five seats, but no election was held in the electoral district of Kamouraska until 1869.

[d]This figure includes member who referred to themselves as Liberal nationalists, Conservative nationalists, or merely nationalists, but who supported the government of Honoré Mercier, the leader of the Parti National.

TABLE VIII
Administrations in the Province
of Quebec, 1867–1976

Prime minister	Party	Length of administration
Pierre J.-O. Chauveau	Conservative	July 1867–Feb. 1873
Gedéon Ouimet	Conservative	Feb. 1873–Sept. 1874
C.-B. de Boucherville	Conservative	Sept. 1874–March 1878
Henri-C. Joly	Liberal	March 1878–Oct. 1879
J.-Adolphe Chapleau	Conservative	Oct. 1879–Aug. 1882
J.-Alfred Mousseau	Conservative	Aug. 1882–Jan. 1884
John Jones Ross	Conservative	Jan. 1884–Jan. 1887
L.-Olivier Taillon	Conservative	Jan. 1887–Jan. 1887
Honoré Mercier	Parti National	Jan. 1887–Dec. 1891
C.-B. de Boucherville	Conservative	Dec. 1891–Dec. 1892
L.-Olivier Taillon	Conservative	Dec. 1892–May 1896
Edmund J. Flynn	Conservative	May 1896–May 1897
F. Gabriel Marchand	Liberal	May 1897–Oct. 1900
S. Napoléon Parent	Liberal	Oct. 1900–March 1905
Sir Lomer Gouin	Liberal	March 1905–July 1920
L.-Alexandre Taschereau	Liberal	July 1920–June 1936
Adélard Godbout	Liberal	June 1936–Aug. 1936
Maurice Duplessis	Union Nationale	Aug. 1936–Nov. 1939
Adélard Godbout	Liberal	Nov. 1939–Aug. 1944
Maurice Duplessis	Union Nationale	Aug. 1944–Sept. 1959
Jean-Paul Sauvé	Union Nationale	Sept. 1959–Jan. 1960
Antonio Barrette	Union Nationale	Jan. 1960–July 1960
Jean Lesage	Liberal	July 1960–June 1966
Daniel Johnson	Union Nationale	June 1966–Oct. 1968
Jean-Jacques Bertrand	Union Nationale	Oct. 1968–May 1970
Robert Bourassa	Liberal	May 1970–Nov. 1976
René Lévesque	Parti Québécois	Nov. 1976–

Source: *Annuaire du Québec,* 1975–76, p. 150.

TABLE IX
Number of Industrial Wage Earners, and Membership
of Trade Unions in the Province of Quebec,
for the Census Years, 1931, 1941, 1951

Census	Industrial wage earners[a]	Trade union membership	Trade union membership as a percentage of industrial wage earners
1931	550,032	58,620	10.66
1941	616,998	121,280	19.65
1951	808,372	259,950	32.15

Source: The source of the figures for industrial wage earners is: Canada, Dominion Bureau of Statistics, *Census of 1931,* Vol. V, Table 31 (Wage earners, 10 years of age and over, male and female); *Census of 1941,* Vol. VI, Table 6 (Wage earners, 14 years of age and over, male and female); *Census of 1951,* Vol. V, Table 6 (Wage earners, 14 years of age and over, male and female). The source for trade union membership is Quebec, Department of Trade and Commerce, *Statistical Year Book*, 1947, p. 560, and 1953, p. 584.

*This includes wage earners in the following categories as shown in the census: Mining and Quarrying, Manufacturing and Mechanical, Electric Light and Power, Construction, Transportation and Communication, Trade and Commerce, Service (excluding professional), Labourers Unspecified. These types of employment are roughly equivalent to what we usually refer to as "working class."

TABLE X

Total Trade Union Membership in Quebec and Membership of the Confédération des Travailleurs Catholiques du Canada, for the Years 1932 to 1951 Inclusive

Year	Total trade union membership	C.T.C.C. membership	C.T.C.C. membership as a percentage of total membership
1932	42,680	25,000	58.58
1933	41,309	26,894	65.10
1934	53,798	30,346	56.41
1935	51,240	38,000	74.16
1936	74,572	45,000	60.34
1937	108,566	50,000	46.05
1938	114,856	47,000	40.92
1939	104,876	49,401	47.10
1940	114,707	46,341	40.40
1941	121,280	46,032	37.96
1942	151,605	46,447	30.64
1943	188,714	53,384	28.29
1944	175,993	65,249	37.07
1945	171,203	61,723	36.05
1946	208,546	62,960	30.19
1947	210,260	70,176	33.38
1948	229,621	82,218	35.81
1949	236,399	83,272	35.23
1950	239,800	83,112	34.66
1951	259,950	88,081	33.88

Sources: For trade union membership in Quebec, Quebec Department of Trade and Commerce, *Statistical Year Book*, 1953, p. 584; for C.T.C.C. membership, Canada, Department of Labour, *Labour Organization in Canada*, 1952, p. 19. All figures shown are based on membership reported by the trade unions themselves, and are subject to a slight margin of error, as some locals fail to report their membership.

*All C.T.C.C. unions are to be found in Quebec, with the exception of one local in Ontario, and one local in Nova Scotia.

Appendix B

PROGRAMME DE L'ACTION LIBERALE NATIONALE, 1934*

La crise actuelle est due en grande partie à la mauvaise distribution dans le domaine économique, à l'avidité de la haute finance et aux abus de toutes sortes qui se sont glissés dans l'application du régime démocratique. Il est inutile d'espérer que l'équilibre se rétablira de lui-même et sans l'aide d'une formule d'action bien définie. La nécessité d'une évolution politique accompagnée d'une évolution économique est évidente. Aux Etats-Unis, le parti démocrate, régénéré, tend actuellement vers cette double transformation. Au Canada et dans la province de Québec, nous en sommes encore aux théories. Nos gouvernants n'ont pas encore pris attitude sur les réformes d'ordre politique, économique et social préconisées par nos esprits les plus avertis.

Le conflit de juridiction entre les pouvoirs municipal, provincial et fédéral (raison qui devient facilement un simple prétexte), la confiance aveugle que certains de nos dirigeants placent encore en des formules dont la crise a démontré le danger, l'influence néfaste de la caisse électorale, l'absence de collaboration entre nos hommes politiques et nos économistes, l'inorganisation de l'opinion publique retardent indéfiniment l'exécution des mesures les plus importantes et nous privent du plan d'ensemble qui seul nous permettra de remédier intelligemment à la situation.

Nous croyons qu'une évolution politique est nécessaire dans notre pays et dans notre province afin d'assurer la mise en œuvre des doctrines élaborées par nos économistes.

L'Action libérale nationale est née de la nécessité de cette évolution. L'Action libérale nationale est née de la nécessité d'une action politique vivante et constructive qui, tout en sachant reconnaître la valeur de certaines œuvres antérieures et le mérite de leurs auteurs, se préoccupe avant tout du présent et de l'avenir. L'Action libérale nationale est née de la nécessité d'adapter la politique provinciale aux besoins urgents d'aujourd'hui, but qui actuellement ne saurait être atteint que par la "relibéralisation" du parti libéral provincial.

L'Action libérale nationale offre donc le plan d'ensemble suivant qui, même s'il n'est pas parfait, tend vers cette double évolution politique et économique, seul moyen d'assurer une meilleure répartition des richesses, et partant, d'enrayer le chômage et de mettre fin à la crise.

I

RÉFORMES AGRAIRES

Nous croyons fermement, comme beaucoup d'autres, que l'œuvre de restauration économique se ramène principalement à une œuvre de restauration rurale, basée sur l'agriculture familiale et la coopération. C'est pourquoi nous plaçons à la base même de notre plan d'action, les réformes agraires.

*Reprinted from Le Devoir, July 28, 1934.

Ces réformes se ramènent à huit articles principaux qui doivent être réalisés simultanément. Ce sont :

1º—Préparation et exécution d'un vaste plan de colonisation;

2º—Redressement de notre agriculture par la conquête des marchés locaux et étrangers ainsi que par l'électrification des campagnes et, à ces fins, augmentation des subsides;

3º—Organisation de l'industrie complémentaire, petite et moyenne;

4º—Organisation professionnelle des agriculteurs;

5º—Etablissement d'un crédit agricole provincial, afin de remédier aux lacunes du crédit agricole actuel;

6º—Protection de l'ouvrier et du journalier rural et du bûcheron en particulier;

7º—Rachat des tenures seigneuriales par la province;

8º—Collaboration avec le Conseil de l'Instruction publique pour assurer la ruralisation de l'école de rang;

9º—Organisation de l'enseignement agronomique supérieur et réforme de l'enseignement agricole à tous les degrés;

10º—Inventaire de la Coopérative fédérée et, au besoin, paiement de sa dette par le gouvernement, et remise de cette institution aux cultivateurs organisés.

La restauration rurale, dont nous donnons ci-dessus les grandes lignes, comporte une étude préalable approfondie suivie de l'élaboration d'un plan d'ensemble et de la coordination des différents ministères et services intéressés : Terres et Forêts, Agriculture, Colonisation, Voirie, Trésorerie et Secrétariat provincial. Cette étude, ce plan d'ensemble, cette coordination, il suffit d'étudier la question, même superficiellement, pour s'en convaincre, ne peuvent être menés à bonne fin par un seul homme. Il faut le concours désintéressé de toutes les compétences. C'est pourquoi nous préconisons la création d'une Commission d'Agriculture et de Colonisation composée de spécialistes indépendants et de fonctionnaires.

II

Réformes ouvrières

1º—Loi sur le contrat de travail et codification en un seul volume de toutes nos lois ouvrières; (Code du Travail).

2º—Application du rapport de la Commission des Assurances sociales :

a) dans les mesures qu'il préconise pour la protection de l'enfance et l'extension de l'hygiène industrielle; (cf. 2º rapport, pp. 12 à 32 et 4º rapport, 2ème partie, pp. 113 à 125);

b) par la création d'une assurance maladie invalidité propre à répartir sur le plus grand nombre les charges d'hospitalisation, de façon à libérer le budget provincial; (cf. 7º rapport, pp. 275 à 321);

c) par l'institution d'allocations aux mères nécessiteuses et de pensions de vieillesse avec la collaboration du fédéral; (cf. 5º rapport, pp. 140 à 163 et 2º rapport, pp. 32 à 44);

3º—Revision de la Loi des Accidents du Travail;

4º—Réglementation de la vente à tempérament;

5º—Disparition des taudis par l'encouragement à la construction des logements ouvriers;

6°—Extension de la réglementation des heures de travail;

7°—Rémunération équitable pour le travail de l'ouvrier, à l'effet de lui faciliter l'accès à la propriété;

8°—Revision et extension de la Loi du salaire minimum;

9°—Primat du salaire sur les dividendes;

10°—Application rigoureuse de la Loi de l'Observance du dimanche.

III

RÉFORMES INDUSTRIELLES ET COMMERCIALES

1°—Création d'un ministère du commerce, aux fins suivantes;

a) recherche de nouveaux débouchés à l'étranger pour nos produits agricoles et industriels;

b) nomination de nouveaux agents commerciaux dans plusieurs pays étrangers pour stimuler le commerce de la province en ces pays;

c) création d'un laboratoire de recherches afin de trouver de nouveaux emplois pour nos ressources naturelles;

d) création d'un office de renseignements pour nos commerçants et nos industriels;

e) coopération avec les industriels pour améliorer l'industrie;

f) inventaire de nos ressources naturelles pour tâcher d'intéresser les propriétaires de capitaux à créer de nouvelles industries;

g) coopération avec les industriels pour essayer d'obtenir plus d'emplois pour les chômeurs;

h) coopération avec les industriels pour faire valoir leurs droits auprès du Gouvernement fédéral relativement à l'abaissement et au relèvement des tarifs;

2°—Changements dans l'administration de la Commission des Liqueurs de Québec :

a) abolition des achats par intermédiaires;

b) diminution du nombre des commissaires.

IV

RÉFORMES ÉCONOMIQUES

1°—Briser, par tous les moyens possibles, l'emprise qu'ont sur la province et les municipalités les grandes institutions financières, le trust de l'électricité et celui de l'industrie du papier;

2°—Afin d'obtenir la baisse des taux de l'électricité : aménagement par la province, au fur et à mesure des besoins, des pouvoirs d'eau non encore concédés ainsi que de ceux concédés mais non encore exploités; de plus, enquête immédiate, par une commission indépendante spécialement nommée dans ce but et possédant tous les pouvoirs nécessaires, afin de déterminer s'il est dans l'intérêt de la province d'acquérir graduellement, à un coût permettant de baisser substantiellement les taux actuels tout en amortissant le prix d'achat, les compagnies produisant ou distribuant l'électricité dans la province;

3°—Combattre les cartels du charbon, de la gazoline et du pain, en leur faisant une concurrence d'Etat si nécessaire;

4º—Combattre le trust du lait en réunissant dans une association fermée tous les producteurs de lait de la province de Québec;

5º—Enquête complète sur la structure et les méthodes financières des compagnies d'utilité publique et assainissement de leur capitalisation;

6º—Aggravation et application sévère de la Loi des Combines;

7º—Politique d'électrification rurale progressive selon un plan déterminé inspiré du système ontarien (ceci faisant partie, d'ailleurs, du plan de restauration rurale).

V

RÉFORMES FINANCIÈRES

1º—Revision de la Loi des Compagnies à fonds social, afin de prévenir l'exploitation du petit épargnant et d'assurer la protection de l'actionnaire et du porteur de débentures;

2º—Uniformisation de ladite loi dans tout le Canada;

3º—Création par la Province d'un organisme spécial pour assurer l'application compétente et rigoureuse de ladite loi.

VI

RÉFORMES POLITIQUES ET ADMINISTRATIVES

1º—Economie et honnêteté dans l'administration de la chose publique;

2º—Interdiction aux ministres d'être actionnaires ou intéressés d'une manière quelconque dans une compagnie obtenant des contrats du gouvernement;

3º—Interdiction aux ministres d'être directeurs d'une banque, d'une compagnie de fiducie, d'une compagnie d'utilité publique, d'une compagnie d'assurance ou d'une compagnie de chemin de fer;

4º—Transformation du Conseil législatif en un Conseil économique;

5º—Remise des fonctions et des pouvoirs du Lieutenant-gouverneur entre les mains du Juge en chef de la Cour d'Appel;

6º—Coordination des ministères fédéraux et provinciaux, afin de prévenir les doubles emplois, ladite coordination devant s'exercer plus particulièrement dans le cas des pêcheries maritimes, afin d'assurer l'élaboration et l'application d'un système efficace et de faire bénéficier nos pêcheurs des subsides fédéraux.

VII

RÉFORMES ÉLECTORALES

1º—Bulletin avec talon, comme autrefois;

2º—Vote obligatoire; (mesure sujette à plébiscite);

3º—Election partielle dans les trois mois qui suivent la date de la vacance;

4º—Cartes d'identité dans les villes de plus de 10,000 âmes;

5º—Diminution des dépenses d'élection;

6º—Réglementation des souscriptions aux fonds électoraux faites par les compagnies à responsabilité limitées;

7º—Limitation des souscriptions électorales individuelles;

8º—Supposition de personnes punissable par un an de prison au moins, et même sanction contre tous ceux qui ont employé, payé ou aidé toute personne se rendant coupable de cette infraction.

VIII

RÉFORMES FISCALES

1º—Loi temporaire donnant le droit de rachat à celui qui est dépossédé de ses propriétés par vente du shérif sur prêts hypothécaires, ledit droit de rachat devant s'exercer dans les deux ans de la vente sur remboursement du capital, des intérêts et des frais, le taux d'intérêt après la vente devant être le même que celui mentionné dans l'hypothèque;

2º—Rajustement du taux d'intérêt sur prêts hypothécaires;

3º—Diminution de l'intérêt chargé par les banques et ce, afin d'aider l'industrie et le commerce;

4º—Conversion de la dette provinciale au meilleur taux possible;

5º—Rajustement des subsides fédéraux afin de faire plus large la part des provinces;

6º—Redistribution des impôts, tant fédéraux que provinciaux et municipaux, afin que les sociétés commerciales et certaines classes d'individus qui souvent jouissent d'exemptions ou d'évaluations injustes, contribuent aux charges publiques de façon équitable.

IX

RÉFORMES JUDICIAIRES

1º—Réorganisation complète de la police provinciale sous la direction d'un seul chef dont les pouvoirs s'étendraient à toute la province et à l'application de toutes les lois;

2º—Réorganisation des tribunaux relevant du gouvernement provincial, de façon à assurer la distribution équitable du travail et afin de diminuer les dépenses;

3º—Revision des tarifs des frais judiciaires, de façon à assurer à tous les justifiables un recours moins coûteux.

———

Ainsi qu'on pourra le constater, certains articles de ce plan d'ensemble appellent des précisions. Nous fournirons au cours de nos premières assemblées les détails et les explications qui s'imposent.

Par ailleurs, ainsi qu'il a été dit plus haut, nous n'avons pas la prétention de croire que la formule que nous soumettons à l'opinion publique soit, dans son ensemble, définitive et parfaite. Elle est suffisamment élaborée, cependant, pour nous permettre de rechercher les adhésions et la collaboration dont nous avons besoin pour parfaire notre œuvre et la mener à bonne fin.

Les suggestions que l'on voudra bien nous faire seront accueillies avec plaisir et recevront toute notre attention. Il ne saurait évidemment y avoir de compromis sur les principes qui sont à la base même de notre mouvement, mais nous n'hésiterons pas à apporter à notre plan d'ensemble les modifications dont la nécessité nous sera démontrée par une saine critique. C'est pourquoi nous invitons tous ceux qui croient sincèrement à la nécessité d'une évolution politique et économique à communiquer avec nous à nos bureaux, à l'adresse suivante :

L'*Action libérale nationale*,
438, rue Saint-François-Xavier,
Montréal, P.Q.

Les personnes suivantes sont les officiers de l'*Action libérale nationale*:

MM. Paul GOUIN,
président général,
Fred MONK,
président,
Jean MARTINEAU,
vice-président,
Calixte CORMIER,
trésorier,
Roger OUIMET et
Robert DUFRESNE,
secrétaires-conjoints.

LE TEXTE DE L'ADRESSE PAR PAUL GOUIN A SAINT GEORGES DE BEAUCE, LE 12 AOUT 1934*

J'ai souvent regretté de ne pas posséder le don d'improvisation, ou tout au moins cette facilité de parole qui permet à tant de nos compatriotes de communiquer spontanément à leur auditoire, en phrases bien balancées et logiquement enchaînées, les sujets auxquels ils ont mûrement réfléchi. Et aujourd'hui plus que jamais je ne puis m'empêcher de déplorer la pauvreté de mes moyens oratoires. En effet, pour répondre comme il convient aux orateurs qui m'ont précédé, pour rendre à M. Lacroix et à vous-mêmes, mesdames et messieurs, l'hommage qui vous revient, pour exposer dignement un programme comme celui de l'Action libérale nationale, il me faudrait posséder l'éloquence vivantre et fougueuse des tribuns qui ont illustré notre histoire politique. Et mon trouble et mes regrets sont d'autant plus intenses que je sais qu'en entendant tout à l'heure pour la première fois le son de ma voix, vous avez évoqué du fond de votre mémoire deux autres voix, deux grandes voix qui, tour à tour, faisant appel au cœur ou à la raison, défendirent si souvent devant vous les intérêts de notre nationalité.

C'est vous dire, mesdames et messieurs, que ce n'est pas à la légère que j'ai accepté l'honneur de diriger les destinées de l'Action libérale nationale et d'exposer son programme au peuple de cette province.

GRANDEURS ET MISÈRES DE LA VIE POLITIQUE

J'aurais préféré, je ne vous le cache pas, un rôle plus modeste, une vie plus paisible. Mieux que tout autre peut-être, je connais les grandeurs et les misères de la vie publique. Je sais les joies et les tristesses qu'elle réserve

*Reprinted from *Le Devoir*, Aug. 13, 1934. This speech gives further clarification and explanation of the programme of L'Action Libérale Nationale.

à l'homme politique; je sais aussi les joies et les tristesses qu'elle réserve à sa famille. J'ai connu la souffrance et la torture morale de l'homme politique, qui, après avoir goûté aux plus grands triomphes, constate soudain, au soir de la vie, l'oubli, l'ingratitude et la lâcheté de certains hommes qu'il appelait ses amis. J'ai connu aussi la souffrance, la torture morale de l'enfant et de l'adolescent qui, malgré lui, doit sacrifier sur l'autel de la patrie les douces joies de la vie de famille.

Et ce spectacle si souvent douloureux, et cette jalousie instinctive d'enfant avaient fait naître en moi l'aversion, ou plotôt, ce qui est plus juste encore, la haine de la politique. Inspiré par ce sentiment, j'ai longtemps pensé que le bonheur pour moi se résumerait à bien peu de choses : une maison de pierre des champs, au bord du grand fleuve, sous l'arbre qui verdoie; une bibliothèque garnie de vieux bouquins et d'estampes anciennes, où je pourrais à loisir écrire l'histoire de notre province; une ronde d'enfants joyeux et espiègles autour de leur maman.

Et il faut être bien naïf ou bien méchant, mesdames et messieurs, pour écrire ou laisser entendre que, par seule ambition personnelle, je consentirais à vivre moi-même, jusqu'à un certain point, les heures qu'a vécues mon père à la fin de sa carrière; que par seule ambition personnelle, je consentirais à faire vivre à ma femme et à mon fils unique les jours que j'ai vécus dans mon adolescence; que par seule ambition personnelle, je consentirais à abandonner la vie heureuse, paisible et facile qui était la mienne. Grâce à la Providence, le nom que je porte n'a pas besoin d'autre fleuron et mon blason n'a pas besoin d'être redoré.

Le devoir de chaque citoyen

Si je suis aujourd'hui devant vous, mesdames et messieurs, si je m'adresse aujourd'hui au peuple de cette province, c'est parce que j'ai compris la leçon de patriotisme qui se dégageait de la vie de mes pères et la leçon d'abnégation que m'a enseignée la crise; c'est aussi parce que j'ai compris que la seule chose qui compte dans la vie d'un homme, la seule chose, qui puisse compenser pour toutes les misères, tous les sacrifices, tous les déboires et toutes les tristesses, c'est de pouvoir se dire, à la fin de sa vie, que l'on a fait son devoir, sans peur et sans reproche, jusqu'au bout. C'est là le vrai bonheur. Et le devoir de chaque Canadien français, aujourd'hui, mesdames et messieurs, le vôtre comme le mien, c'est de s'élever au-dessus de l'intérêt personnel, de l'intérêt de famille, de classe et même de parti pour s'occuper d'un seul intérêt : l'intérêt national.

Comme l'écrivait M. Edouard Montpetit, ce noble artisan de notre renouveau national : "A chaque génération, son rôle et sa peine." Le devoir de la génération qui a subi la conquête était de réparer la défaite et de se développer en nombre, quoi qu'il advint. Nos ancêtres n'ont pas failli à la tâche. Ce fut le miracle de notre survivance; les soixante mille Canadiens français de 1760 sont devenus des millions. Puis il nous a fallu acquérir des droits et les défendre. La génération des patriotes de 1837 les a conquis sous la mitraille et même jusque sur l'échafaud. Enfin, vient le moment de créer dans tous les domaines des compétences tout en perpétuant la double victoire de nos aïeux. C'était le rôle de nos aînés immédiats, prêtres et laïcs, qui eux aussi, ont compris leur de qui, eux aussi, ont compris leur de [sic] les d'où est sortie une véritable élite.

LE DEVOIR DE L'HEURE PRÉSENTE

Maintenant, mesdames et messieurs, le temps est venu d'utiliser le capital humain, les droits et les chefs de file que nous devons à nos pères; le temps est venu d'assurer la conquête nationale et économique de notre peuple. C'est le devoir de notre génération.

Certes, la tâche qui nous attend est lourde. Mais, grâce à Dieu, elle arrive à une heure particulièrement propice.

En effet, le branle-bas d'idées provoqué par la crise mondiale a permis un échange de vues entre toutes les classes de notre société. Les préjugés se sont dissipés; les cloisons quasi étanches qui existaient entre nos différents milieux se sont abattues; les portes des tours d'ivoire où s'étaient enfermés nos intellectuels se sont ouvertes sous la pression de l'opinion publique. Fermiers et ouvriers, professionnels et hommes d'affaires, théoriciens et praticiens, jeunes et vieux, prêtres et laïcs, ont enfin compris qu'ils avaient des intérêts communs à défendre et que la prospérité des uns dépendait du bien-être des autres.

Et les conséquences extérieures de la crise ont aussi contribué à faciliter grandement notre tâche. Le monde entier traverse actuellement une ère de mises au point et de rajustements économiques, sociaux et politiques. Il faut en profiter non seulement pour modifier notre structure économique, mais aussi pour assurer notre avenir national.

LA RESTAURATION NATIONALE

Dans certains milieux, s'inspirant mal à-propos de la doctrine du retour à la terre préconisée par Lucien Romier et par nos économistes les plus avertis, on semble croire que l'œuvre de restauration économique, que l'œuvre de survivance nationale, se résument chez nous à une question de colonisation et d'électricité. C'est là une profonde erreur qu'il faut dissiper à tout prix. Il ne faut pas nous engager dans cette voie, excellente en elle-même, sans avoir pris les précautions élémentaires. Les conséquences néfastes de la politique d'industrialisation à outrance, qui a été le crédo de cette province avant la crise, constituent une dure leçon dont il faut nous souvenir. Il ne faut pas verser dans les excès contraires; il faut garder un juste milieu.

Il est impossible, en effet, de séparer le problème de la colonisation et de l'électrification des campagnes des autres réformes agraires qui s'imposent. Comme je le disais le 30 juin dernier, au congrès général de l'A.C.J.C. à Nicolet, et comme le rappelle le manifeste de l'Action libérale nationale publié le 28 juillet dernier, l'œuvre de restauration rurale, qui est la clé de voûte du relèvement économique et qui doit être basée sur l'agriculture familiale et la coopération, se ramène à dix articles principaux qui doivent être réalisés simultanément si nous voulons que la colonisation ne soit pas seulement un palliatif mais bien un remède définitif.

RÉFORMES AGRAIRES

Ces articles sont les suivants :

1º Préparation et exécution d'un vaste plan de colonisation;

2º Redressement de notre agriculture par la conquête des marchés locaux et étrangers ainsi que par l'électrification des campagnes et, à ces fins, augmentation des subsides;

3º Organisation de l'industrie complémentaire, petite et moyenne;

4º Organisation professionelle des agriculteurs;

5º Etablissement d'un crédit agricole provincial, afin de remédier aux lacunes du crédit agricole actuel;

6º Protection de l'ouvrier et du journalier rural et du bûcheron en particulier;

7º Rachat des tenures seigneuriales par la province;

8º Collaboration avec le Conseil de l'Instruction publique pour assurer la ruralisation de l'école de rang;

9º Organisation de l'enseignement agronomique supérieur et réforme de l'enseignement agricole à tous les degrés;

10º Inventaire de la Coopérative fédérée et, au besoin, paiement de sa dette par le gouvernement, et remise de cette institution aux cultivateurs organisés.

Il est évident, en effet, mesdames et messieurs, pour ne donner que quelques exemples, qu'il faut assurer au colon devenu agriculteur, le moyen de vendre ses denrées; qu'il faut fournir à l'agriculteur déjà établi, le moyen d'écouler ses produits et aussi de se libérer des charges et des hypothèques qui l'étouffent; qu'il faut aussi pour prévenir la répétition toujours possible de la désertion des campagnes, apprendre aux fils de cultivateurs à connaître et à aimer la terre. Cela ne pourra s'effectuer que par le redressement de l'agriculture existante et l'organisation de la petite et de la moyenne industries, mesures qui procureront à l'agriculteur des marchés; cela ne pourra s'effectuer que par la création d'un crédit agricole et par la ruralisation de l'école de rang.

Et j'irai plus loin. Je dirai que si nous voulons mettre fin à la crise, c'est-à-dire enrayer le chômage et assurer une meilleure répartition des richesses, je dirai que ces réformes agraires doivent être accompagnées d'une série d'autres réformes non moins importantes, comme par exemple, les réformes ouvrières, les réformes économiques, financières, politiques et administratives.

Il est certain, en effet, comme nous l'avons vu plus haut, que la ruralisation bien ordonnée doit prévoir, un peu partout à travers la province, le maintien et même la création d'un certain nombre de centres industriels. Il convient donc, entre autres choses, d'assurer à l'ouvrier qui habitera ces centres, un salaire qui lui permettra d'acheter à prix convenable les produits de l'agriculteur. Le sort, le bien-être, l'aisance de l'agriculteur et de l'ouvrier, producteur et consommateur, sont intimement liés.

RÉFORMES OUVRIÈRES

Voici, d'après le manifeste de l'Action libérale nationale, les réformes ouvrières qui s'imposent :

1º Loi sur le contrat de travail et codification en un seul volume de toutes nos lois ouvrières;

2º Application du rapport de la Commission des Assurances sociales;

a) Dans les mesures qu'il préconise pour la protection de l'enfance et l'extension de l'hygiène industrielle;

b) Par la création d'une assurance-maladie-invalidité propre à répartir sur le plus grand nombre les charges d'hospitalisation, de façon à libérer le budget provincial;

c) Par l'institution d'allocations aux mères nécessiteuses et de pensions de vieillesse avec la collaboration du fédéral;

3° Revision de la loi des accidents du travail;

4° Réglementation de la vente à tempérament;

5° Disparition des taudis par l'encouragement à la construction des logements ouvriers;

6° Extension de la réglementation des heures de travail;

7° Rémunération équitable pour le travail de l'ouvrier, à l'effet de lui faciliter l'accès à la propriété;

8° Revision et extension de la loi du salaire minimum;

9° Primat du salaire sur les dividendes;

10° Application rigoureuse de la Loi de l'Observance du dimanche.

Et je conseille à ceux qui pourraient douter de l'opportunité de ces réformes, entre autres l'opportunité d'assurer une rémunération équitable pour le travail de l'ouvrier et le primat des salaires sur dividendes, je conseille, dis-je, à ceux-là, de demander à l'honorable M. R.-B. Bennett de leur transmettre une copie du fameux rapport Stevens. Ils constateront, je n'en doute pas, les injustices flagrantes, éhontées et révoltantes commises à l'égard de nos ouvriers. Ils comprendront, j'en suis sûr, la gravité de la situation et l'urgence d'y remédier sans tarder.

Mais, mesdames et messieurs, les réformes agraires et les réformes ouvrières que nous réclamons ne sauraient guérir tous les maux dont nous souffrons. Comme je le disais, il y a un instant, il faut y joindre, pour ne mentionner que celles qui nous intéressent particulièrement, les réformes économiques, les réformes financières, les réformes politiques et administratives.

En effet, il faut d'abord assurer le développement de l'agriculture et de la saine industrie. Pour cela, il faut briser l'emprise des trusts qui, parce que nous les avons laissés grandir sans les contrôler, étouffent littéralement notre vie économique. Nous croyons que les réformes économiques que nous avons placées dans notre programme, qui vous sera distribué tout à l'heure et que vous pourrez étudier, nous croyons, dis-je, que les réformes économiques que nous avons préparées atteindront sûrement et efficacement ce but. Je n'ai pas à m'étendre davantage sur ce sujet. Je sais que, grâce à la belle campagne poursuivie par l'honorable M. Bouchard et le Docteur Philippe Hamel, la question vous est suffisamment familière.

Il faut ensuite, mesdames et messieurs, empêcher que l'épargne de la classe agricole et de la classe ouvrière, qui normalement devrait leur assurer la prospérité, ne soit accaparée par la finance véreuse. Ici interviennent les réformes financières qui se lisent comme suit :

RÉFORMES FINANCIÈRES

1° Revision de la loi des compagnies, à fond social, afin de prévenir l'exploitation du petit épargnant et d'assurer la protection de l'actionnaire et du porteur de débentures;

2° Uniformisation de ladite loi dans tout le Canada;

3° Création par la province d'un organisme spécial pour assurer l'application compétente et rigoureuse de ladite loi.

Je sais, mesdames et messieurs, qu'il n'est pas nécessaire d'insister sur ce point. Vous connaissez tous ces voleurs de grand chemin qui, en échange de la vision dorée de châteaux en Espagne ou même de châteaux canadiens, vous arrachent vos économies. Pour empêcher ces escroqueries, qui sapent à la base même les possibilités de notre indépendance économique, nous croyons qu'il est nécessaire et possible d'organiser un système de police aussi efficace, par exemple, que celui de la Commission des liqueurs de la province de Québec.

Donc, mesdames et messieurs, réformes agraires, réformes ouvrières, réformes économiques et réformes financières, voilà quelques-unes des mesures auxquelles il faut avoir recours sans tarder pour assurer notre renaissance économique et notre survivance nationale. Mais, mesdames et messieurs, il est inutile d'espérer, et j'insiste sur ce point, que nous obtiendrons ces réformes essentielles si elles ne sont pas accompagnées de réformes politiques et administratives.

Réformes politiques

La crise que nous traversons, il ne faut pas l'oublier, est due en grande partie aux abus et aux erreurs de toutes sortes qui se sont glissés dans l'application du régime démocratique. Le principal de ces abus est l'avidité de la haute finance, qui, par l'entremise de la caisse électorale, depuis la fin de la grande guerre, surtout, a dirigé à son gré, à sa guise et suivant ses intérêts, les destinées des peuples; la principale de ces erreurs a été l'absence de collaboration entre les hommes politiques, les sociologues, les économistes et les techniciens.

Pour mettre fin à ces abus, pour réparer ces erreurs, il ne faut pas avoir peur d'avoir recours à une formule d'action bien définie. L'histoire nous fournit sur ce point un exemple qui est en même temps une mise en garde : les réactions violentes qui ont mis fin aux excès de la monarchie absolue et dont la Révolution française est restée le prototype. Et la situation actuelle nous offre des enseignements non moins significatifs; les régimes politiques nouveaux adoptés par certains pays comme l'Autriche et l'Italie. Sans verser dans le communisme ou le socialisme, sans verser dans le fascisme, il importe donc de libérer nos hommes politiques de la dictature économique et de permettre à nos économistes, nos techniciens et nos spécialistes de collaborer plus étroitement à la direction des affaires publiques.

Fonds électoraux

Nous parviendrons à ce double but en contrôlant d'abord les souscriptions faites aux fonds électoraux par les compagnies à responsabilité limitée, en réglementant ensuite la participation des ministres aux conseils d'administration des grandes compagnies et, enfin, en transformant notre Conseil législatif en un Conseil économique.

Point n'est besoin, j'imagine, mesdames et messieurs, d'argumenter en faveur des deux premières réformes que je viens d'énoncer. Chaque citoyen intègre de cette province, électeur, député, conseiller législatif et ministre, sait jusqu'à quel degré d'asservissement abject nous a réduits la dictature économique, par le truchement de la caisse électorale, et jusqu'à quel point cet asservissement a été contraire à l'intérêt général du peuple de cette province, en dénaturant l'expression de l'opinion publique et ses justes réclamations. On me traitera sans doute d'idéaliste en me disant, suivant la formule consacrée, que les élections ne se font pas avec des prières. Je répondrai simplement en disant que si tous les intéressés, électeurs et gouvernants, ne se hâtent pas d'apporter un peu d'idéal, de désintéressement, de patriotisme, d'esprit chrétien et social dans l'application électorale de notre régime démocratique, celui-ci ira infailliblement à la ruine.

LE CONSEIL LÉGISLATIF

Passons maintenant, mesdames et messieurs, à la question primordiale : la transformation du conseil législatif en un conseil économique. C'est là la base logique de toute renaissance économique, la base nécessaire à notre survivance nationale, et la seule réponse honnête et définitive aux problèmes auxquels nous avons à faire face actuellement.

Le manifeste de l'Action libérale nationale est la preuve éclatante de cette affirmation. Notre programme, et je tiens à le proclamer hautement afin de leur rendre l'hommage et le mérite qui leur a été si souvent refusé dans le passé, notre programme, dis-je, tout comme la politique récemment inaugurée par le gouvernement provincial, tout comme les idées préconisées par le chef de l'opposition, est inspiré largement des réformes d'ordre politique, économique et social, élaborées par nos économistes, nos sociologues et leurs disciples.

L'ECOLE SOCIALE POPULAIRE

Nous avons pris comme base d'étude et de discussion, pour préparer notre manifeste, le programme de Restauration sociale publié sous les auspices de l'Ecole sociale populaire. Les contacts que nous avions établis préalablement avec les différentes classes de notre société nous ont permis de constater que ce document reflétait de façon assez juste non seulement l'opinion de nos esprits les plus avertis mais aussi les sentiments, les aspirations et les besoins populaires.

Nous avons donc jugé à propos, en définitive, de suivre les grandes lignes du programme de Restauration sociale. Nous y avons fait cependant plusieurs changements. Il fallait tenir compte de certains commentaires judicieux provoqués par la publication de ce premier plan d'ensemble et de la marche des idées. Il fallait surtout transposer ces doctrines dans le domaine de l'action politique et pratique, en y incorporant nos idées personnelles.

CEUX QUI ONT ÉTÉ LES PRÉCURSEURS

Donc, mesdames et messieurs, on peut affirmer que les principaux artisans de l'orientation nouvelle donnée à la politique de la province, par les hommes politiques de tout calibre, ceux qui sont sincères comme ceux qui ne le sont pas, on peut affirmer, dis-je, que les principaux artisans de cette orientation nouvelle sont MM. Edouard Montpetit, Esdras Minville, Olivar Asselin, les RR. PP. Papin Archambault, Chagnon et Lévesque, l'abbé Lionel

Groulx. MM. Albert Rioux, Eugène L'Heureux, Henry Laureys, Paul Riou, Thomas Poulin, Omer Héroux, Georges Pelletier et tant d'autres dont il me serait trop long d'énumérer les noms.

Et devant ce fait indéniable, je dis qu'il est de la plus élémentaire justice de faire participer ces hommes, intègres et renseignés, à la direction des affaires publiques. D'ailleurs, ce n'est pas uniquement une question de justice, c'est aussi une question d'élémentaire sagesse politique.

En effet, je tiens à vous en prévenir loyalement, pour mettre au point notre programme, pour scruter, approfondir chacun des points qu'il soulève, il faudra nécessairement rechercher et obtenir le concours de spécialistes et de techniciens. Et comme je le disais tout à l'heure, j'affirme que c'est là la seule réponse honnête et définitive aux problèmes actuels.

Réformes administratives

L'une des graves erreurs de notre régime démocratique a été d'abord de croire que la science d'administrer les choses de l'Etat était une science infuse, et ensuite, de croire que les représentants du peuple pourraient en même temps et à la fois, s'occuper de leurs intérêts personnels, des intérêts de l'Etat et des intérêts de leurs électeurs. Il ne faut pas oublier, en effet, et ce n'est pas faire ressortir avec justice l'ingratitude de son rôle, que l'homme politique actuel, ministre ou député, si bien doué ou si bien disposé soit-il, a peu de temps à consacrer à la lecture et à l'étude. Comme je le disais tantôt, l'administration de son département, la gestion de ses affaires personnelles, les intérêts immédiats de ses électeurs, occupent tout son temps. Et c'est là, dans ce désarroi d'idées, ce conflit d'intérêts, cette absence de temps pour l'étude, la réflexion et la méditation, qu'il faut chercher, je crois, la véritable raison pour laquelle des questions aussi importantes, par exemple, que celle du crédit agricole, n'ont pas encore reçu de solution.

Il faut un crédit agricole

Evidemment, je pourrais, comme beaucoup d'autres sans doutes, vous donner sur la question quelques aperçus généraux.

Je pourrais vous dire, entre autres, que l'expérience durant ces dernières années du crédit agricole fédéral ne paraît pas avoir donné des résultats satisfaisants au cultivateur de cette province; que je doute fortement que la nouvelle loi passée par le gouvernement Bennett à la dernière session fédérale, loi qui accorde aux cultivateurs le droit de faire des concordats, améliore grandement la situation actuelle; que je crois que ce problème est un des plus sérieux de l'heure présente, non seulement pour la classe agricole mais pour toute notre province, puisque notre système économique sera paralysé tant que nos cultivateurs ne pourront pas sortir de leur embarras financier; que pendant cette crise, le gouvernement fédéral a aidé nos grandes institutions bancaires en faisant ce que l'on appelle le réescompte, opération qui consiste à escompter à nouveau le papier ou valeurs de crédit que les banques avaient escomptés; que ce réescompte a été fait pour aider ces institutions à traverser la crise; que le même gouvernement a été jusqu'à garantir près de soixante millions pour une institution privée telle que le C. P. R.: qu'il a fait plus; qu'il a passé un ordre en conseil, le 31 décembre 1931, pour permettre de surévaluer les actions communes que les compagnies d'assurance sur la vie avaient en portefeuille et ce pour sauver ces institutions : que ce n'est que deux ans et demi après cette date que ce même gouvernement pense à la classe qui produit la plus grande partie de notre richesse nationale et ce, comme je l'ai dit plus haut, par une loi qui semble défectueuse et injuste à sa face même.

Crédit rural provincial

Je pourrais également ajouter que, devant l'expérience du passé, je crois que le seul moyen de remédier aux malaises de la classe agricole du Québec dans le domaine financier, c'est de créer un crédit rural provincial modelé en quelque sorte sur ceux déjà existants en Belgique, aux Indes, en Egypte et au Danemark qui, ainsi que vous le savez, sans doute, est un de nos grands compétiteurs sur le marché anglais; que ce même système a été établi récemment en Malaisie où il semble donner d'excellents résultats; que je crois que nos cultivateurs ont besoin de trois sortes de crédit : 1o Celui à courte échéance pour faire face à des circonstances imprévues comme le manque des récoltes, la maladie ou la mortalité; 2o Prêt à quelques mois pour achat d'animaux ou d'instruments aratoires; 3o Prêts à long terme pour achat de fermes ou pour améliorations à ces dernières; que je crois également que ces prêts devraient être faits à un meilleur taux d'intérêt que ceux consentis au commerçant et à l'industriel car le profit du cultivateur est moindre que celui des deux premiers et que je crois que le système actuel de nos banques à chartes est nuisible à "nos habitants" parce qu'il sert à drainer l'argent de nos campagnes dans les villes.

Et enfin, en terminant, je pourrais vous dire que je crois que le crédit rural devrait avant tout et en premier lieu servir à relever notre agriculture avant d'être envoyé à la ville pour aider l'industriel et le commerce et souvent, malheureusement, pour alimenter la finance malsaine.

Mais, il ne s'agit là, mesdames et messieurs, je le répète, que d'aperçus généraux qui ne sauraient, je le sais, vous donner entière satisfaction. Vous aimeriez sans doute à avoir quelque chose de plus précis. Je vous avoue franchement que je ne saurais le faire en ce moment et je soumets humblement que bien peu de personnes dans la province sont actuellement en état de fournir, sur ce point, une formule pratique et définitive. Pour régler, au moyen des Caisses populaires ou autrement, une question de cette envergure, où intervient entre autres, ne l'oublions pas, le conflit d'administration entre le pouvoir fédéral et le pouvoir provincial, il faut nécessairement la référer, ainsi que nous le disions, à une commission d'agriculture et de colonisation, composée de spécialistes indépendants et de fonctionnaires.

Prenons maintenant, si vous le voulez bien, mesdames et messieurs, pour illustrer par un dernier exemple la nécessité de cette commission, à laquelle devront être soumises toutes les réformes agraires, la question du redressement de notre agriculture par la conquête des marchés étrangers.

Les marchés étrangers

Beaucoup d'entre vous se souviennent sans doute de l'influence bienfaisante qu'avait eue sur l'industrie du beurre et du fromage le système de transports frigorifiques inauguré par le régime Laurier à son arrivé au pouvoir en 1896.

Nous croyons que la nomination par la province d'agents commerciaux, compétents, dans les vieux pays comme l'Allemagne, l'Autriche et les Etats de l'Europe centrale, amènerait une demande considérable pour vos produits. L'Allemagne, entre autres, dont la population de soixante-dix millions d'habitants est obligée, paraît-il, pour se nourrir, d'avoir recours à des produits artificiels, fournirait croyons-nous un marché illimité. Là encore intervient la nécessité d'avoir recours au conseil et à la collaboration des compétences et des techniciens.

C'est pour cela et aussi pour les raisons que je viens d'énumérer, que comme conclusion à nos réformes agraires nous avons écrit ce qui suit : "La restauration rurale, dont nous donnons ci-dessus les grandes lignes, comporte une étude préalable approfondie suivie de l'élaboration d'un plan d'ensemble et de la coordination des différents ministères et services intéressés : terres et forêts, agriculture, colonisation, voirie, trésorerie et secrétariat provincial. Cette étude, ce plan d'ensemble, cette coordination, il suffit d'étudier la question, même superficiellement, pour s'en convaincre, ne peuvent être menés à bonne fin par un seul homme. Il faut le concours désintéressé de toutes les compétences. C'est pourquoi nous préconisons la création d'une Commission d'agriculture et de colonisation composée de spécialistes indépendants et de fonctionnaires."

Et cette argumentation basée, je crois, mesdames et messieurs, sur le bon sens même, je pourrais l'étendre aux autres catégories de réformes que nous réclamons et qui, pour la plupart, devront être soumises à des comités d'études.

COMITÉ DE LÉGISLATION

Je vous rappellerai brièvement pour illustrer ce point par quelques exemples frappants, qu'au chapitre des réformes économiques, nous préconisons ou plutôt, nous préconisions, le 28 juillet dernier, la création d'une commission indépendante spécialement nommée dans ce but pour enquêter sur la question de l'électricité et que dernièrement, M. P.-E. Gagnon, avocat de Rimouski, faisait une suggestion très opportune et qui serait le meilleur moyen d'assurer des réformes financières, justes et équitables : la formation d'un comité permanent de législation composé de juges, des professeurs d'Universités et d'avocats éminents, pour collaborer avec le gouvernement dans l'élaboration des lois.

Examinons maintenant, mesdames et messieurs, si vous le voulez bien, comment nous pourrions introduire ces différents comités d'études dans notre système parlementaire, comment nous pourrions les coordonner, comment nous pourrions, sans aucune dépense additionnelle, assurer leur fonctionnement.

L'organisme qui nous permettra de grouper nos esprits les plus avertis, l'organisme conducteur qui nous permettra d'étudier simultanément tous nos problèmes et de remédier vraiment à la crise, c'est, je le répète, le conseil économique.

LE CONSEIL ÉCONOMIQUE

L'idée n'est pas nouvelle. MM. Montpetit, Minville, Eugène L'Heureux, Asselin et plusieurs autres ont, à maintes reprises, démontré la nécessité d'un organisme semblable pour notre province. J'ai, moi-même, eu l'occasion d'en causer assez souvent.

Cependant, jusqu'à date, on s'est surtout occupé de lancer l'idée, c'est-à-dire d'en démontrer les avantages et, comme je le disais tout à l'heure, la nécessité, sans entrer beaucoup dans les détails de l'organisation même du conseil, sans analyser d'autre part ce qui a été fait, dans ce sens, dans les autres pays.

J'essaierai donc, aujourd'hui, en quelques minutes, de faire une courte revue des différents conseils économiques qui ont surgi un peu partout dans le monde, quitte ensuite à chercher comment nous pourrions adapter cette nouvelle formule à la vie économique et politique de notre province.

Le temps, évidemment, ne me permettra pas d'entrer dans tous les détails techniques de l'organisation des différents conseils économiques. Pour cela, il me faudrait, à l'instar de quelques parlementaires très connus, vous faire subir un discours de quelque trois heures, chose que je n'aurai pas la cruauté de faire.

Disons donc que depuis la grande guerre et surtout depuis la crise où l'on a senti davantage, surtout chez le peuple, la nécessité d'une réforme, disons, dis-je, que cette idée de conseil économique pour diriger la vie économique des pays a fait lentement mais sûrement son chemin. C'est ce que nous voyons dans un très intéressant rapport préparé sous les auspices de la Société des Nations.

Nous voyons dans cet ouvrage que plus de vingt-cinq pays, y compris la Grande-Bretagne, la Belgique, la France, l'Allemagne, l'Italie, l'Autriche, la Grèce et les Etats-Unis, ont adopté, sous une forme ou une autre, cette nouvelle formule.

Deux groupes de conseils économiques

Il y a deux groupes principaux de conseils économiques. Le premier comprend ceux de l'Allemagne, de la France et de l'Italie. Créés sur la base d'une large représentation des organismes économiques, il s'ensuit qu'ils ont une influence considérable sur la politique économique des nations. Ils prennent part à la rédaction des projets de lois concernant les questions économiques. Cependant, en France et en Allemagne, les conseils sont purement consultatifs, tandis qu'en Italie le conseil économique peut, en certains cas, prendre des décisions qui sont sujettes cependant, au droit de veto de Mussolini, ce qui n'est pas peu dire.

La seconde catégorie, la plus nombreuse, comprend une variété de groupes, composés d'experts, de spécialistes ou de représentants de diverses professions que le gouvernement consulte au besoin.

Le nombre des différents conseils varie beaucoup. Celui de l'Allemagne comptait trois cent vingt-six experts du moins, avant l'avènement de l'expert unique : M. Hitler ! L'Italie a cent soixante-deux conseillers, la France quarante-sept pour en venir à l'Irlande qui n'en possède que six. Remarquons en passant que l'Ecosse n'a pas de conseil économique, sans doute, pour des raisons d'économie . . . politique !

Les membres sont choisis de cinq façons différentes : 1o Ils sont élus par le peuple; 2o nommés par les différents groupements économiques; 3o Choisis par le gouvernement; 4o Nommés par le gouvernement sur la recommandation de groupes professionnels tels que syndicats ouvriers, etc; 5° Membres ex officio de ce conseil par suite des postes qu'ils occupent dans l'administration gouvernementale.

Presque toujours les agriculteurs et les ouvriers sont représentés dans les conseils, tandis que les professions le sont rarement, probablement afin d'en exclure les avocats ! De même, les artistes, les professeurs et les autres êtres excentriques sont ordinairement soigneusement tenus à l'écart.

Tous les conseils ont un secrétariat permanent et rétribué par l'Etat, qui est la base de l'organisme.

Comme vous pouvez le constater, mesdames et messieurs, le conseil économique est une chose très simple sur le papier. C'est aussi une formule très à la mode. Voyons maintenant, en quelques mots, comment nous pourrions l'adapter à nos besoins et l'introduire dans notre organisme politique.

Ce qu'il nous faudrait

Voici les grandes lignes d'un conseil économique qui, je crois, nous conviendraient entièrement. Il s'agirait en dehors de toute influence politique, de grouper, ainsi que je l'ai dit tout à l'heure, nos compétences en un organisme qui, se basant sur le programme de l'Action libérale nationale, tracerait d'abord, une ligne de conduite générale conforme à nos besoins et à nos aptitudes et aiderait ensuite à en diriger l'exécution.

L'organisation de ce conseil, dont le président serait nommé par le gouvernement, comporterait un comité-directeur, autant de sous-comités qu'il y a dans la province de branches importantes de l'activité économique et un secrétariat général. Chacune des branches de l'activité économique serait représentée par un spécialiste dans le comité-directeur. Ainsi, il y aurait un économiste, un ingénieur agricole, un commerçant, un juriste, un sociologue, un banquier, etc. Désignés par les associations professionnelles, les syndicats ouvriers, les Chambres de commerce, les universités, etc., des candidats à la charge de membres du comité-directeur seraient proposés à l'Etat qui choisirait parmi eux le nombre nécessaire. Les membres des sous-comités seraient choisis de la même façon, avec cette différence que le comité-directeur aurait voix au chapitre pour désigner les candidats. Les membres du comité-directeur et des sous-comités ne recevraient pas de rémunération fixe mais auraient droit à un jeton de présence.

Le conseil économique procéderait par enquêtes, par l'intermédiaire de ses sous-comités. Une assemblée plénière, réunissant le comité-directeur et les sous-comités, déciderait des mesures à suggérer au gouvernement. En même temps que le rapport serait transmis aux ministres, il serait publié dans les journaux afin d'éclairer, d'orienter et d'alerter l'opinion publique.

Un conseil législatif de 12 membres

La façon d'introduire ce nouveau rouage dans notre machine administrative n'est pas très compliquée. Il suffisait, comme je l'écrivais dans le *Canada*, en 1932, et comme nous le disons dans notre manifeste, de transformer notre conseil législatif dont le rôle, il faut bien l'avouer, ne répond plus aux besoins du moment. En somme, notre conseil législatif, remanié et réduit à douze membres tout au plus, serait le comité-directeur de notre conseil économique.

Jetons de présence

Donc, mesdames et messieurs, parce qu'elle comporte la réduction du nombre de nos conseillers et parce que le travail de ceux-ci ne serait plus rétribué que par jetons de présence, cette transformation du conseil législatif en un conseil économique comporte deux grands avantages qu'il convient de faire ressortir: économie et collaboration de nos compétences dans l'administration de la chose publique.

Compression des ministères

Mais ce n'est pas tout. Grâce aux services que rendra ce conseil économique, il sera possible de réduire le nombre des ministères en combinant ceux qui logiquement devraient ne faire qu'un. Ainsi, nous pourrions, je crois, réunir en un seul ministère, la colonisation et l'agriculture. Nous pourrions joindre les travaux publics à la voirie, le travail au commerce, et ainsi de suite, sans compter que nous pourrions faire disparaître les ministres sans portefeuille qui, si je suis bien informé, ont tout de même un portefeuille puisqu'ils reçoivent deux mille dollars par année.

Le lieutenant-gouverneur

Ajoutons à ces économies substantielles celle qui résultera de la remise entre les mains du juge en chef de la Cour d'appel des pouvoirs du lieutenant-gouverneur, celle surtout qui résultera de la diminution des membres de la Commission des liqueurs et des intermédiaires qui alimentent le commerce de celle-ci. De ce dernier chef, je crois que nous pourrions économiser au moins un million de dollars par année.

Appel à la coopération

Voilà, mesdames et messieurs, les grandes lignes de notre programme. Comme nous l'écrivions lors de sa publication, nous n'avons pas la prétention de croire qu'il soit dans son ensemble, définitif et parfait. Il est suffisamment élaboré cependant pour nous permettre de rechercher les adhésions et la collaboration dont nous avons besoin pour parfaire notre œuvre et la mener à bonne fin. Et c'est votre collaboration et votre adhésion que je suis venu chercher aujourd'hui, mesdames et messieurs. Je sais que vous ne me la refuserez pas. Je sais que se rallieront à nous, tous ceux—et vous êtes de ce nombre—qui ont assez de clairvoyance pour comprendre qu'il est temps que nous ayons un programme de reconstruction nationale, qui, tout en sachant respecter les droits des autres branches de notre activité économique, soit nettement et intelligemment à base agricole.

Nous ne sommes ni révolutionnaires ni démagogues

Comme vous avez pu le constater, nous ne sommes ni des révolutionnaires, ni des démagogues, et nous savons mieux que tout autre peut-être respecter le passé dans ce qu'il a de bon, d'utile et de noble. Nous croyons simplement et fermement que les idées et les formules, qui étaient pratiques il y a cinq, dix, quinze ou vingt ans, doivent être remplacées par d'autres idées et d'autres formules conformes aux besoins de l'heure présente, et que nous pouvons faire cela sans renier en aucune façon l'œuvre de nos pères.

THE UNION NATIONALE

Nous croyons à la nécessité d'une action politique vivante et constructive qui, tout en sachant reconnaître la valeur de certaines œuvres antérieures et le mérite de leurs auteurs, se préoccupe avant tout du présent et de l'avenir. Nous croyons à la nécessité d'adapter la politique provinciale aux besoins urgents d'aujourd'hui.

LES PARTIS POLITIQUES

Sera-t-il nécessaire pour cela, et je réponds ici à la question que se pose en ce moment l'opinion publique, sera-t-il nécessaire pour cela d'établir une nouvelle division de nos partis politiques ? Je ne le crois pas.

La doctrine libérale, de par sa nature même, est la doctrine de la liberté de pensée et de parole, des idées nouvelles, des innovations, des réformes et des évolutions. Nous avons besoin actuellement, comme je le disais tout à l'heure, d'une évolution politique. C'est pourquoi j'estime que c'est le parti libéral, je ne dis pas un parti libéral, mais le parti libéral, "relibéralisé", si je puis dire, sur bien des points, qui normalement devrait opérer les réformes que nous réclamons.

Mais la couleur politique n'est qu'un point secondaire. Ce qui importe pour le moment c'est de nous rallier tous, généreusement et résolument, autour du programme de l'Action libérale nationale, pour enrayer le chômage, pour assurer une meilleure répartition des richesses, et pour ramener dans le cœur de chacun la part de joie, de bonheur et de paix à laquelle il a droit.

Pour cela, il faut le concours de toutes les bonnes volontés. Notre fleuve, dont la force herculéenne est formée des forces réunies des ruisseaux, des rivières et des torrents, est un magnifique symbole d'union dont nous devons nous inspirer davantage, si nous voulons, comme le fleuve atteint l'océan, atteindre notre destinée nationale.

Appendix C

EDUCATION AND CULTURE

It is the duty of the Government of this Province to evaluate what we possess . . . so that it may be developed in such a manner that Quebec may draw a lasting benefit and grow in the path of its traditions, its spirit and its culture. JEAN LESAGE

CULTURAL LIFE

ARTICLE 1 — Creation of a Department of Cultural Affairs, having under its jurisdiction the following:
  a) A Provincial Arts Council;
  b) An Historic Monuments Commission;
  c) A Provincial Office of Town Planning;
  d) A Provincial Linguistic Office;
  e) An Office for Cultural Relationships with French-speaking groups outside the Province.

Commentary—The history of Quebec Province starts with the early French settlers and, even today, its chief characteristic is the possession of two distinct cultures, existing side by side in harmony. This is a unique asset and must be developed and fostered for the benefit of the whole Province.

EDUCATION

ARTICLE 2—Free Schooling at all levels including University.

ARTICLE 3—Free text books for all schools under the jurisdiction of the Department of Education.

Commentary—The Province of Quebec has the lowest rate of school attendance in Canada. Fifty per cent of the pupils leave school at the age of fifteen. A recent study shows that 76% of the young unemployed did not go beyond eighth grade and thus face the prospect of being periodically unemployed, throughout their lives. In our universities the children of our farmers and our workers represent only the smallest percentage of the total student population. At the last session of the Legislature the Government did nothing to assist these students, or their parents who must carry the full burden of educating their children. Free schooling must be implemented immediately. Basically, every young person with ability should have the right to free education, at all levels. This can be accomplished through the adoption of the following program:

ARTICLE 4—Education must be compulsory to age 16.

ARTICLE 5—The Province must assume all school debts not already assumed.

ARTICLE 6—The establishment of a Provincial Universities Commission.

Commentary—The establishment of such a commission was requested by the University of Montreal and Laval University in the briefs they submitted to the Tremblay Commission. The role of the Commission would be to advise the Provincial government on matters of education and to provide liaison between the Universities and the Provincial Government.

ARTICLE 7—The Commission will be specifically instructed to recommend a plan for the financial assistance of students.

Commentary—Free schooling can only become a reality in the Province when an educational system has been instituted which recognizes the needs of the teaching profession as well as those of the students.

ARTICLE 8—Our technical schools must adopt a modern teaching curriculum, based upon the most up-to-date methods and techniques. The curriculum must be revised in accordance with latest scientific developments in industry.

Commentary—A recent study has shown that graduates of our technical schools are poorly trained and have not been taught the latest techniques. A survey of 265 graduates of nine technical schools or trade schools showed that only 33% were working at their trade, 40% were employed in other work and 27% were unemployed.

ARTICLE 9—The establishment of a Royal Commission on Education.

Commentary—The need for a Royal Commission on Education has been stressed by practically every organization concerned with the problem.

ECONOMIC DEVELOPMENT

The general improvement in living standards which should result from an expanding economy, will continue to pass us by, so long as we fail to exercise adequate control and sound management. JEAN LESAGE

AN ECONOMIC COUNCIL

ARTICLE 10—The establishment of an Economic Planning and Development Council.

Commentary—The membership of the Council would consist of representatives of Labor and Industry, engineers, sociologists, economists, and others. Its primary task would be the overall planning of our economic and industrial development. Acting as an advisory body to the government it would carry out continuing studies and direct the long range planning upon which government policy would be based. Scientific developments no longer permit government by improvisation.

A DEPARTMENT OF NATURAL RESOURCES

ARTICLE 11—The establishment of a Department of Natural Resources whose responsibilities would be:
  a) To develop industries for the conversion of our natural resources in the Province.
  b) To encourage the establishment of heavy industry in the Province with financial assistance from the government if necessary.

c) To encourage our people to invest their capital in the development of our natural resources.

d) To require that industries exploiting our natural resources employ personnel of the province in technical and administrative positions at all levels.

e) Establish an Institute of Mines.

f) Assure the ownership and development by Quebec Hydro of all undeveloped hydro-electric power wherever it is economically feasible to do so.

g) To standardize the rates for electricity and to reduce such rates when they are deemed to be too high.

h) After investigation by a Royal Commission into the sale of the gas facilities by Quebec Hydro, the distribution of natural gas will be returned to Quebec Hydro insofar as this will be to the benefit of the Province.

Commentary—The Province of Quebec possesses some of the richest natural resources in the world. If their exploitation is well planned they will assure the people of the Province a high and stable standard of living. These resources belong to the Province and should primarily benefit the people of Quebec.

In order to distribute job opportunities more equitably throughout the Province, the Liberal government will adopt a policy to encourage the decentralization of industry and to stimulate the establishment of new industries in distressed areas, or in areas not presently industrialized. As part of this program the Liberal Party proposes that the rates of electric power be standardized.

Royalties now being paid by companies exploiting our natural resources must be revised so that the return to the Province will bear an equitable relationship to the profits which these companies earn from their operations.

We will eliminate "company towns" with their inherent opportunities to exploit the labor force and the resulting disregard of fundamental freedoms.

UNEMPLOYMENT

ARTICLE 12—The Provincial government must assume its responsibilities in respect to unemployment.

Commentary—Unemployment in the Province of Quebec, in the month of March 1960, amounted to 42% of all the unemployed in Canada—actually 236,000. For the past number of years the Province of Quebec has always had the largest number of unemployed. This, surely is a situation which is unacceptable to a province with the greatest natural resources in the nation.

Unemployment is a problem that affects the whole family. Measures must be taken to strike at the roots of this problem which continues to undermine the security of thousands of our families.

Unemployment, whether it is local, regional or general can only be eradicated by a plan for the long term development of our economic resources. Stable employment in each locality and region can only be realized through an overall plan. A Council of Economic Planning and Development would assure the citizens of the province of a planned program for the industrial development and the exploitation of our natural resources.

Technological development presents us with another problem. Government, working with Labor and Industry, must remedy the effects of replacing men with machines. Displaced workers must be retrained for other jobs in new trades. A program must be evolved to provide free training centers and to provide, during the period of retraining, financial assistance over and above unemployment insurance.

The Council for Economic Planning and Development will also deal with the question of seasonal unemployment. It must determine the causes of such unemployment in each area and industry. It will recommend a program to alleviate this condition.

The government of the Province must collaborate with the government of other provinces and with the Federal government to devise programs to ease the effect of periodic unemployment through the stimulation of economic activity. The Council of Economic Planning and Development must propose to the government programs of Public Works to absorb the unemployed during periods of recession.

AGRICULTURE

ARTICLE 13—Agriculture must be made profitable through an imaginative program energetically implemented through:

    a) The Department of Agriculture giving high priority to its agronomy service and by research in soil utilization and conservation.

    b) The modernization of farming techniques so that the family farm will become a profitable venture.

    c) The establishment of an effective marketing, grading, and storage system.

    d) The Agricultural Marketing Law to be modified as regards the majority required for approval of a plan, the composition of lists of eligible producers, the definition of "buyer", the system of arbitration, and recognition of farm groups.

    e) Government assistance for the construction and maintenance of modern storage facilities, chemical fertilizer plants and marketing facilities for farm produce.

    f) A plan to permit the sons of farmers to purchase farms on loans advanced by the Province to 90% of the real value. Upon the repayment of two-thirds of the loan, the final third would be cancelled and considered as an establishment grant.

    g) Long and short-term loans to be made available through the Farm Credit Bureau to help improve the productivity of farms.

    h) Mechanization of farms.

    i) The payment of a premium on butter and cheese, if the present Federal subsidies are cancelled.

    j) The payment of a premium on pork so long as the present system of compensation payments remains in force.

    k) A more generous subsidy on the purchase of chemical fertilizers.

    l) The reorganization of the Dairy Commission in order to protect dairy farmers against exploitation and abuses and to assure them a fair price for their milk.

    m) Assistance to dairy farmers during the winter months.

n) The establishment of artificial insemination centers.

o) The adoption of herd loss and crop damage insurance.

p) The establishment of special wood lots to supplement the income of farmers.

q) Financial aid to industries consuming agricultural products as raw material; to mills producing potato flour; to the producers of cider; and to rendering plants and soapworks, etc.

r) Revision of the law to provide all rural municipalities with financial assistance for water-systems, sewer-systems and sewage disposal plants.

s) Maintenance by the government of all winter roads.

Commentary—For the first time since the great Liberal governments of the past the Province of Quebec will have a realistic agricultural program.

"The farm organizations of the Province have said time and again that the government of the Union Nationale has never had an Agriculture program. The present Minister of Agriculture, the officials of his department, and indeed the entire government, have advanced no plan nor new idea in the field of agriculture for the past quarter of a century. As long as the Union Nationale is in power it will have only one thought, and one policy, political patronage. In the meantime our agricultural community will continue to suffer, their livelihood decline and our farms deteriorate. The farmers realize that it is in their interest to change governments". (Extract from a speech by Jean Lesage given at St. Hyacinthe on the 5th of July 1959).

COLONIZATION

ARTICLE 14—In colonization matters, improvement of existing parishes must precede the forming of new parishes.

Commentary—There exists a large number of colonization parishes that have lost many of their settlers, leaving the cleared land unexploited. Instead of spending enormous sums of money to form new parishes, it is logical to start establishing settlers in existing parishes which already have municipal, school, and other services.

ARTICLE 15—Close cooperation between the Department of Colonization; colonization missionaries and the Colonization Society.

ARTICLE 16—For the development of settlers' land, it is imperative to revise the rates and the acreage limits.

Commentary—To adapt himself to his new mode of life the settler needs help. All colonization territories must be organized to permit settlers to establish themselves as farmers so that they may benefit from the additional revenues and advantages granted to other farmers in the Province. Therefore, it is urgent that premiums be raised and also that an additional premium be granted for every acre of land cultivated and maintained. In amending the Law of Colonization to permit the improvement of parishes, we must grant premiums to the new occupants of the cultivated lots which were abandoned. Land drainage must be intensified so that the maximum cultivation may be obtained.

Without access to the forest the settler cannot prosper. Therefore, as previously mentioned, it is important that wood lots accessible to the settlers be established in accordance with good reforestation practice.

Finally, the settler should benefit like the farmer, from all credits allotted by the Government.

PULP WOOD

ARTICLE 17—The setting of a minimum fixed price for pulp wood marketed by farmers and settlers as proposed by the U.C.C.

Commentary—The loss suffered by the farmers during the past few years, owing to the low price paid them for their pulp wood, is estimated at several million dollars. The proposed legislation, similar to that currently in effect in the Province of Ontario, would assure the farmer a fair price for his pulp wood.

INDUSTRY AND COMMERCE

ARTICLE 18—The Department of Industry and Commerce must have broader powers to provide industrial development on a regional basis according to an overall plan. The establishment of commercial representatives in Europe and elsewhere must be provided for.

MASTER PLAN FOR HIGHWAYS

ARTICLE 19—Communications are the key to economic development. A master highway plan is essential to a practical road construction program, taking into account the need for roads to resources, highways for tourists and regional requirements. A master highway plan would be coordinated by the Economic Planning and Development Council.

FISHERIES

ARTICLE 20—Improvement of the condition of fishermen:
  a) By instituting a research program, an aggressive publicity campaign to encourage the consumption of fish at home, and to stimulate the export of fish.
  b) By taking firm measures against the pollution of lakes and rivers.

Commentary—The fishing industry is one of our natural resources. The economic difficulties of our fishermen are traceable to the serious decline, during the past few years, of the value of our fish crop. This decline has occurred at a time when the export of fish from other provinces has increased.

TOURISM

ARTICLE 21—The government must give highest priority to a program to stimulate the tourist industry, the fourth largest industry in Canada.

Commentary—At present the government spends a negligible amount on the promotion of the Tourist Trade.

The French way of life offers an attractive and unique appeal to Tourists. A publicity campaign should feature this so that more Tourists will travel in the Province.

Parks and camping sites should be set up for the benefit of tourists. The government should enact legislation to permit the guarantee of long term loans for the improvement and development of tourist accommodation.

SOCIAL WELFARE

To be a Liberal is to support social justice. GEORGES E. LAPALME

THE FAMILY

ARTICLE 22—The Department of Youth will become the Department of the Family and Youth.

Commentary—The present basis of social security legislation is the individual rather than the family unit. In our society we have always insisted that the government and the individual respect the dignity and supremacy of the family. We will apply this principle to all social legislation which we may propose.

SOCIAL SECURITY

ARTICLE 23—At the next session of the Legislature, legislation will be passed to provide a supplementary family allowance of $10 a month payable to parents of children 16 to 18 years of age who are attending school.

ARTICLE 24—At the next session of the Legislature, legislation will be enacted to provide a supplementary pension of $10 a month to the following, according to their means:

   a) Persons 70 years or over who are receiving the Old Age Pension.
   b) Those between 65 and 70 years of age who are eligible according to present regulations.
   c) Those receiving pensions as invalids.
   d) Those receiving the Blind pension.

ARTICLE 25—Widows and spinsters aged 60 or over will be eligible to receive a pension equivalent to that payable to persons 65 to 70 years of age.

PUBLIC HEALTH

ARTICLE 26—The prompt initiation of a program of Preventive Medicine and Public Hygiene. The grave problem of water pollution will be given the highest priority in this program.

HOSPITAL INSURANCE

ARTICLE 27—The immediate adoption of a hospital insurance plan in consultation with the Medical profession, hospital associations, etc.

ARTICLE 28—The hospital insurance plan would assure the citizens of the province the same benefits as provided by the national hospital insurance plan, taking into account our constitutional rights, the particular needs of our people and of the institutions which serve them.

Commentary—The Liberal Party has advocated the adoption of a hospital insurance plan for the past 17 years.

We will establish diagnostic centers and hospitals for incurables.

LABOR LEGISLATION

ARTICLE 29—The publication of a Labour Code.

ARTICLE 30—The establishment of Labour Courts.

ARTICLE 31—Revision of the Workmen's Compensation Act.

ARTICLE 32—Revision of the Minimum Wage Commission Act.

ARTICLE 33—Publication of the decisions of the Labour Relations Board.

ARTICLE 34—Abolition of bills 19 and 20.

ARTICLE 35—The establishment of a Pension Fund.

Commentary—The Superior Labour Council should immediately prepare a completely revised Labour Code, and also create Labour Courts.

Management and Labour should be represented on the Minimum Wage Commission. The Commission will investigate the whole question of the administration of wage regulations, paying particular attention to the areas covered by parity ordinances. The object of the investigation would be the establishment of equitable minimum wages throughout the province, especially in the forest industry. Wages fixed by the parity ordinances should be reviewed regularly by the Commission and adjusted after consultation with representatives of industry and labour.

Legislation will be passed making employer dominated unions illegal.

Industry and Labour will be represented on the Workmen's Compensation Commission.

The decisions of the Commission can affect the whole future of an injured worker. The worker should have the right of appeal and also the right of access, for himself or his representative, to his medical file.

A contributory Pension Fund should be established. It would not replace existing pension plans. It would, first, assure those not presently covered by such a plan, a pension upon retirement. It would also assure the continuation of an employee's participation in a pension plan if he changed jobs.

HOUSING

ARTICLE 36—The establishment of Family Housing Loans.

Commentary—One of our great social problems is the lack of modern housing facilities especially those suitable for family living.

Generous financial assistance from the Provincial government is necessary for large families in the low-income group. We propose to assist these people in securing adequate living accommodation.

First, we propose to assist financially the housing cooperatives which have accomplished so much in providing modern housing. Second we will collaborate with any Municipality which wishes to take advantage of the Federal government grants for urban redevelopment to construct low rental housing units.

STATUS OF THE MARRIED WOMAN

ARTICLE 37—A married woman should have the same legal status as her husband in respect to her movable and immovable property, as well as the right to institute legal proceedings concerning such rights.

ARTICLE 38—A married woman, under the laws of community property, should enjoy the same legal status as her husband, in respect to her personal property.

CONSTITUTIONAL RIGHTS

The Canadian Confederation can progress only if there is mutual respect for the spirit which inspired its foundation. PAUL GÉRIN-LAJOIE

FEDERAL-PROVINCIAL RELATIONS

ARTICLE 39—The establishment of a Department of Federal-Provincial Relations.

ARTICLE 40—Quebec to call an Interprovincial Conference.

ARTICLE 41—Presentation by Quebec of a memorandum, based upon the recommendations of the Tremblay Commission, offering definite proposals for the solution of fiscal problems. The memorandum would be presented to the Interprovincial Conference.

ARTICLE 42—Quebec would propose to the Interprovincial Conference the establishment of a permanent Interprovincial Council.

ARTICLE 43—Quebec will propose the establishment of a permanent Federal-Provincial Secretariat.

ARTICLE 44—Quebec will propose to her sister provinces that the necessary legislation be passed to permit Canada to amend her own constitution.

ARTICLE 45—Quebec will propose the creation of a special court to deal with constitutional questions.

Commentary—The problems which face the Provinces in Canada urgently require that an Interprovincial meeting should take place before the scheduled Federal Provincial Conference next July and certainly before 1962 at which time the present agreements with the Federal government expire. Quebec's views must be forcefully presented. If they are to be accepted Quebec's representatives must take the initiative in submitting practical proposals at these conferences.

For many years the Quebec Liberal Party has suggested that the Tremblay Commission report form the basis for discussion. This report recommends that the present financial agreements with the provinces be abolished and replaced by a fiscal policy which would return to the provinces their constitutional rights.

The establishment of an Economic Planning and Development Council, of a Department for Cultural Affairs and a Department of Federal-Provincial Affairs will permit our province to take positive and realistic action.

The Administration

In politics as in finance, there are no mysteries, there may be mysterious events but I repeat, there are no mysteries. René Hamel

A ROYAL COMMISSION

Article 46—A Royal Commission will be established at once to investigate the conduct of public affairs by the governments of the Union Nationale Party.

Commentary—The need for such an enquiry has been made abundantly clear by the revelation of scandals, such as the Begin scandal, the Pouliot scandal, the natural gas scandal, and endless others.

REFORMS

Article 47—Reform of the Civil Service.

Commentary—Democratic government requires a loyal and competent civil service. The government administration needs able men and women who wish to make a career in government service knowing that employment and promotion may be secured without political patronage. The Liberal government will establish an independent Civil Service Commission.

Article 48—Electoral Reform.

Commentary—The democratic form of government requires a fair and equitable election procedure. All political parties must be treated as equals, electoral officers should be subject to the jurisdiction of the courts for their actions, election expenses should be limited, the freedom to vote and the secret ballot should replace dishonesty and fraud in elections. Redistribution of electoral ridings should be carried out in order to give fair and proper representation to all our people. The state should assume all essential election expenses of candidates.

Article 49—Debates of the Legislative Assembly will be published.

Commentary—The public, in a democracy, has every right to know what its representatives say in debate and what position they take in the business before the legislature.

PUBLIC MONIES

Article 50—The institution of rigid control of the spending of public monies, to end nepotism, patronage and waste.

Article 51—The awarding of government contracts only after competitive bidding.

Article 52—The abolition of the system of discretionary grants.

Commentary—The control of public monies, by the elected representatives of the people is a fundamental requirement of democracy. This control must be exercised by all the members of the Legislature.

MUNICIPALITIES

Article 53—Redistribution of taxation revenues between the provincial and municipal governments.

Commentary—The revenues of the municipalities are insufficient for their growing needs. A system of equalization payments will be set up to meet these needs.

TAXATION

ARTICLE 54—A complete study into all aspects of provincial taxation.

Commentary—Such a study is urgent and required for the following reasons:
   a) The levels of Provincial inheritance tax are too high, threatening deduction of family capital and posing a serious threat to the survival of many family businesses. (Ottawa should be called upon to abandon this field of taxation).
   b) The collection and administration of the sales tax is difficult for the province, a great inconvenience for our merchants and annoying to our consumers. (The sales tax should be abolished immediately on fuel oil, patent medicines and other articles which are basic necessities of life).
   c) Personal income tax is so poorly graduated that married people are taxed more than single persons.
   d) Many so-called nuisance taxes should be abolished.

Bibliography

THIS BIBLIOGRAPHY DOES NOT CLAIM to be exhaustive. Although it includes most of the sources referred to in the footnotes, I have eliminated those references which deal only indirectly with the main theme of the book or touch on some minor point. I have also added a number of books and articles which are not referred to in the text, but which contain valuable information for those who want to go more deeply into one of the topics covered in a particular chapter. Some of these publications appeared after the major part of this book had been completed and provide additional background for it. Further bibliographical material is to be found in Philippe Garigue, *A Bibliographical Introducton to the Study of French Canada* (Montreal: Department of Sociology and Anthropology, McGill University, 1956), and in Jean-Charles Bonenfant, "Inventaire des sources," *Recherches sociographiques*, II (3–4), July–Dec., 1961, pp. 483–566.

The general plan of the bibliography is to group the listings in accordance with the various chapters into which the book is divided, with a further subdivision into books, articles, and pamphlets. A few reference works contain useful information on the subject-matter of several chapters and these are listed at the beginning of the bibliography.

Inevitably a good deal of the data on a subject of this nature can only be found in the daily newspapers. This is particularly true of the more recent developments discussed in the latter part of the book. Among French language newspapers, *Le Devoir* of Montreal has always provided the best coverage of political events. *La Presse* of the same city, and *L'Action* (formerly *L'Action Catholique*) of Quebec City, should also be referred to. Among English language newspapers, the *Star* and the *Gazette*, of Montreal, are useful. The Union Nationale publishes a weekly newspaper, *Le Temps* (Quebec City). The Liberal party also has a weekly paper, *La Reforme* (Montreal).

YEAR BOOKS AND ELECTION STATISTICS

Canadian Annual Review. Toronto: Canadian Review Co. Ltd., 1920–38.
Canadian Parliamentary Guide. Ottawa: P. G. Normandin, 1905–61.

CLICHE, PAUL. "Les élections provinciales dans le Québec, de 1927 à 1956," *Recherches sociographiques*, II (3–4) (July–December, 1961), 343–65.

DEAN, E. P. "How Canada Has Voted: 1867 to 1945," *Canadian Historical Review*, XXX (Sept., 1949), 227–48.

HAMELIN, JEAN, et al. "Les élections provinciales dans le Québec," *Cahiers de géographie de Québec*, IV, 7 (oct. 1959–mars 1960), 5–207.

Quebec, Department of Trade and Commerce. *Statistical Year Book*. Quebec: Queen's Printer, 1920–61.

———— Legislative Assembly. *Report on the General Election*, 1923, 1927, 1931, 1935, 1936, 1939, 1944, 1948, 1952, 1956, 1960. Quebec: Queen's Printer.

GENERAL REFERENCES

BOVEY, WILFRID. *The French-Canadians Today*. Toronto: J. M. Dent & Sons (Canada) Ltd., 1938.

FALARDEAU, JEAN-CHARLES, éd. *Essais sur le Québec contemporain*. Québec: Les Presses de l'Université Laval, 1953.

LOWER, A. R. M. *Colony to Nation*. Second edition. Toronto: Longmans, Green & Co., 1949.

MINVILLE, ESDRAS, éd. *Notre Milieu*. Montréal. Editions Fides, 1946.

RUMILLY, ROBERT. *Histoire de la Province de Québec*. 33 vols. Montréal: Various publishers, 1940–62.

WADE, MASON. *The French-Canadians, 1760–1945*. Toronto: Macmillan Company of Canada, 1955.

CHAPTER I. THE HISTORICAL AND CULTURAL BACKGROUND OF QUEBEC POLITICS

Books

ARÈS, RICHARD. *Notre Question nationale*. 3 vols., Montréal: Editions de l'Action Nationale, 1945.

BRUNET, MICHEL. *La présence anglaise et les Canadiens*. Montréal: Librairie Beauchemin, 1958.

Congress on Canadian Affairs. *The Canadian Experiment, Success or Failure?* Québec: Les Presses de l'Université Laval, 1962.

FRÉGAULT, GUY. *Le Civilisation de la Nouvelle France, 1713–1744*. Montréal: Société des Editions Pascal, 1944.

French-Canadian Backgrounds: A Symposium. Toronto: The Ryerson Press, 1940.

MACKAY, R. A., and ROGERS, E. B. *Canada Looks Abroad*. Toronto: Oxford University Press, 1938.

MACRAE, C. F., ed. *French Canada Today*. Report of the Mount Allison 1961 Summer Institute. Sackville, N.B., 1962.

Quebec. *Report of the Royal Commission of Inquiry on Constitutional Problems*. 2 vols. Quebec: Queen's Printer, 1956.

WADE, MASON, ed. *Canadian Dualism*. Toronto: University of Toronto Press, 1960.

Articles

AYEARST, M. "The *Parti Rouge* and the Clergy," *Canadian Historical Review*, XV, 4 (Dec., 1934), 390–405.

BILODEAU, CHARLES. "Education in Quebec," *University of Toronto Quarterly*, XXVII, 3 (April, 1958), 398–412.

FALARDEAU, JEAN-CHARLES. "Rôle et importance de l'Eglise au Canada Français," *Esprit*, nos 193–4 (août–sept. 1952), 214–29.

—— "The Parish as an Institutional Type," *Canadian Journal of Economic and Political Science*, XV, 3 (Aug., 1949), 353–67.

FORTIER, D'IBERVILLE. "Les relations culturelles Franco-canadiennes," *Esprit*, nos 193–4 (août–sept. 1952), 247–58.

MAHEUX, ARTHUR. "French Canadians and Democracy," *University of Toronto Quarterly*, XXVII, 3 (April, 1958), 341–51.

PELLETIER, GÉRARD. "D'un prolétariat spirituel," *Esprit*, nos 193–94, (août–sept. 1952), 190–200.

SCOTT, F. R. "Canada et Canada Français," *Esprit*, nos 193–4, (août–sept. 1952), 178–89.

TRUDEAU, PIERRE-ELLIOTT. "Some Obstacles to Democracy in Quebec," *Canadian Journal of Economic and Political Science*, XXIV, 3 (Aug., 1958), 297–311.

CHAPTER II. THE PATTERN OF QUEBEC POLITICS, 1867–1920

Books

ARMSTRONG, ELIZABETH H. *The Crisis of Quebec, 1914–1918.* New York: Columbia University Press, 1937.

WILLISON, J. S. *Sir Wilfrid Laurier and the Liberal Party*, vol. I. Toronto: George N. Morang & Co., 1903.

Articles

AYEARST, M. "The *Parti Rouge* and the Clergy," *Canadian Historical Review*, XV, 4 (Dec., 1934), 390–405.

BONENFANT, JEAN-CHARLES, and FALARDEAU, JEAN-CHARLES. "Cultural and Political Implications of French-Canadian Nationalism," Canadian Historical Association, Report, 1946, 56–73.

LOCKHART, A. D. "The Contribution of Macdonald Conservatism to National Unity, 1854–78," Canadian Historical Association, Report, 1939, 124–32.

UNDERHILL, F. H. "The Development of National Parties in Canada," *Canadian Historical Review*, XVI, 4 (Dec., 1935), 368–75.

CHAPTER III. THE CHALLENGE OF INDUSTRIALISM AND THE
GROWTH OF NATIONALISM

Books

Canada. *Report of the Royal Commission on Dominion-Provincial Relations*, Book I, *Canada, 1867–1939*; and Appendix V, prepared by Esdras Minville. Ottawa: King's Printer, 1940.

DALES, J. H. *Hydroelectricity and Industrial Development: Quebec, 1898–1940.* Cambridge: Harvard University Press, 1957.

GARIGUE, PHILIPPE. *Etudes sur le Canada Français.* Montréal: Faculté des Sciences sociales, Université de Montréal, 1958.

HUGHES, EVERETT C. *French Canada in Transition*. Chicago: University of Chicago Press, 1943.

LÉTOURNEAU, FIRMIN. *L'U.C.C.* La Trappe, Qué.: Institut agricole d'Oka, 1949.

LOGAN, H. A. *Trade Unions in Canada*. Toronto: Macmillan Company of Canada, 1948.

OLIVER, MICHAEL K. "The Social and Political Ideas of French-Canadian Nationalists, 1920–1945. Unpublished doctoral dissertation, McGill University, 1956.

Articles

ALLARD, L. "Un demi-siècle de vie canadienne-Française," *L'Action Nationale*, XXXV, 2 (fév. 1950), 133–55.

BONENFANT, JEAN-CHARLES, and FALARDEAU, JEAN-CHARLES. "Cultural and Political Implications of French-Canadian Nationalism," Canadian Historical Association, Report, 1946, 56–73.

CHARPENTIER, ALFRED. "Historique de la C.T.C.C.," *Programme-souvenir, Congrès annuel, et vingt-cinquième anniversaire de la Confédération des Travailleurs Catholiques du Canada*, 1946, 13–36.

DUGRÉ, ALEXANDRE. "La Défense de notre capital humain: par la colonisation," *L'Action Française*, XVI, 3 (sept. 1926), 130–53.

GUINDON, HUBERT. "The Social Evolution of Quebec Reconsidered," *Canadian Journal of Economics and Political Science*, XXVI, 4 (Nov., 1960), 533–51.

LEMELIN, CHARLES. "Social Impact of Industrialization on Agriculture in the Province of Quebec," *Culture*, XIV, 1 (mars 1953), 34–46; XIV, 2 (juin 1953), 157–69.

PELLETIER, GEORGES. "Les Obstacles économiques à l'indépendance du Canada Français," *L'Action Française*, VIII, 2 (août 1922), 66–75.

PERRAULT, ANTONIO. "La Défense de notre capital humain: utilisation de notre capital humain," *L'Action Française*, XVI, 4 (oct. 1926).

CHAPTER IV. THE FORMATION AND RISE TO POWER
OF THE UNION NATIONALE

Books

ANGELL, HAROLD M. "Quebec Provincial Politics in the 1920's." Unpublished master's thesis, McGill University, 1960.

GOUIN, PAUL. *Servir, I, La Cause nationale*. Montréal: Editions du Zodiaque, 1938.

LAROQUE, HERTEL. *Camillien Houde: le p'tit gars de Ste-Marie*. Montréal: Editions de l'Homme, 1961.

OLIVER, MICHAEL K. "The Social and Political Ideas of French-Canadian Nationalists, 1920–1945." Unpublished doctoral dissertation, McGill University, 1956.

Articles

LAPORTE, PIERRE. "Il y a 25 ans, la convention de Sherbrooke," *Le Devoir*, 1–3 oct. 1958.

QUINN, HERBERT F. "The Bogey of Fascism in Quebec," *Dalhousie Review*, XVIII, 3 (Oct., 1938), 301–8.
ROTHNEY, GORDON O. "Nationalism in Quebec Politics since Laurier," Canadian Historical Association, Report, 1943, 43–9.

Pamphlets

ANGERS, FRANÇOIS-ALBERT, et al. *Vers un ordre nouveau par l'organisation corporative*. Montréal: L'Ecole Sociale Populaire, 1940.
CARON, M. MAXIMILIEN. *La Corporation professionnelle*. Montréal: L'Ecole Sociale Populaire, 1939.
DUTHOIT, M. EUGÈNE. *L'Organisation corporative*. Montréal: L'Ecole Sociale Populaire, 1935.
LEO XIII (Pope). *Rerum Novarum*. New York: The Paulist Press, n.d.
PIUS XI (Pope). *Quadragesimo Anno*. London: Catholic Truth Society, 1931.
Pour la restauration sociale au Canada. Montréal: L'Ecole Sociale Populaire, 1933.
RIOUX, A., et al. *Le Programme de restauration sociale*. Montréal: L'Ecole Sociale Populaire, 1933.
Union Nationale. *Le Catéchisme des électeurs*. Montréal: J. B. Thivierge & Fils, 1936.
———— *Maurice Duplessis: A Great Canadian*. Montreal, 1948.

CHAPTER V. THE ECONOMIC POLICIES OF THE UNION NATIONALE
IN TWO ADMINISTRATIONS

Books

DALES, J. H. *Hydroelectricity and Industrial Development: Quebec, 1898–1940*. Cambridge: Harvard University Press, 1957.
DESPRÉS, J. P. *Le Mouvement ouvrier canadien*. Montréal: Editions Fides, 1946.
LOGAN, H. A. *Trade Unions in Canada*. Toronto: Macmillan Company of Canada, 1948.
———— *State Intervention and Assistance in Collective Bargaining: The Canadian Experience, 1943–1954*. Toronto: University of Toronto Press, 1956.
MINVILLE, ESDRAS, éd. *L'Agriculture*. Montréal: Editions Fides, 1944.
PUTNAM, DONALD F., ed. *Canadian Regions*. Second ed., Toronto: J. M. Dent & Sons, 1954.
TRUDEAU, PIERRE-ELLIOTT, éd. *La Grève de l'amiante*. Montréal: Editions Cité Libre, 1956.

Articles

ROGERS, L. J. "Duplessis and Labour," *Canadian Forum*, Oct., 1947, pp. 151–2.
SIROIS, JACQUELINE. "Asbestos Strike," *Montreal Standard* (magazine section), May 28, 1949, pp. 2–8.

Pamphlets

BOLTÉ, P. E., et al. *Structural Reforms in the Enterprise*. Québec: Université Laval, 1949.

Commission sacerdotale d'études sociales. *La Participation des travailleurs à la vie de l'entreprise.* St. Hyacinthe, Qué.: Secrétariat national d'Action sociale, 1947.

Maritime Labour Institute. *Labour and Learning.* Halifax: Dalhousie University, 1949.

Union Nationale. *L'Administration de la Province de Québec: 1936-1939, 1944-1952.* Québec, 1952.

CHAPTER VI. THE UNION NATIONALE AND THE FEDERAL GOVERNMENT

Books

DAWSON, R. M. *The Conscription Crisis of 1944.* Toronto: University of Toronto Press, 1961.

LAMONTAGNE, MAURICE. *Le Fédéralisme canadien, évolution et problèmes.* Québec: Les Presses de l'Université Laval, 1954.

LAURENDEAU, ANDRÉ. *La Crise de la conscription.* Montréal: Editions du Jour, 1962.

PICKERSGILL, J. W. *The Mackenzie-King Record,* I, 1939-1944. Toronto: University of Toronto Press, 1960.

Quebec. *Report of the Royal Commission of Inquiry on Constitutional Problems,* vols. I and II. Quebec: Queen's Printer, 1956.

Articles

ANGERS, FRANÇOIS-ALBERT. "Pourquoi nous n'accepterons jamais la conscription pour service outre mer," *L'Action Nationale,* XIX, 2 (February–March, 1942), 86–105.

―――― "Un vote de race," *L'Action Nationale,* XIX, 4 (mai 1942), 299–312.

ANGUS, H. F. "Two Restrictions on Provincial Autonomy," *Canadian Journal of Economics and Political Science,* XXI (Nov., 1955), 445–6.

DUPLESSIS, MAURICE. "J'ai sacrifié le pouvoir à l'accomplissement de mon devoir," *L'Œil* (Montréal), 15 juin 1942, pp. 11–16.

FRASER, BLAIR. "Crisis in Quebec," *Maclean's Magazine,* Aug. 15, 1944, pp. 5–6, 43–6.

MORIN, PIERRE. "Causons d'autonomie," *Renaissance* (Quebec City), juillet 1948, pp. 19–37.

QUINN, HERBERT F. "Parties and Politics in Quebec," *Canadian Forum,* May, 1944, pp. 32–4.

―――― "Can the Liberals Hold Quebec?" *Canadian Forum,* Dec., 1944, pp. 201–2.

VIGNON, PIERRE. "Qui nous protègera du communisme," *Renaissance,* juillet 1948, pp. 38–52.

Pamphlets

DION, GÉRARD. *Le Communisme dans la Province de Québec.* Québec: Université Laval, 1949.

DORION, NOEL. *Le Communisme et le parti Libéral.* Québec: Organisation de l'Union nationale, 1948.

DUPLESSIS, MAURICE. *Mémoire du gouvernement de la Province de Québec présenté à la conférence fédérale-provinciale.* Québec: King's Printer, 1946.

Union nationale. *La Conscription hypocrite.* Québec, 1944.

—————— *Manuel des orateurs de l'Union nationale.* Québec, 1956.

CHAPTER VII. ADMINISTRATIVE AND ELECTORAL PRACTICES UNDER THE UNION NATIONALE

Books

HAMELIN, JEAN et MARCEL. *Les mœurs électorales dans le Québec de 1791 à nos jours.* Montréal: Editions du Jour, 1962.

LAPORTE, PIERRE. *Le Vrai Visage de Duplessis.* Montréal: Editions de l'Homme, 1960.

Articles

FRASER, BLAIR. "Shakedown," *Maclean's Magazine,* Nov. 15, 1945, pp. 5–6, 59–61.

KEATE, STUART. "Maurice the Magnificent," *Maclean's Magazine,* Sept. 1, 1948, pp. 7, 71–5.

LAPORTE, PIERRE. "La Machine électorale," *Cité libre,* II, 3 (déc. 1952), 42–6.

—————— "Les Elections ne se font pas avec des prières," *Le Devoir,* 1 oct.– 7 déc. 1956.

MARTIN, HAROLD H. "Quebec's Little Strong Man," *Saturday Evening Post,* Jan. 15, 1949, pp. 17–19, 102–4.

PARENTEAU, ROLAND. "Finances provinciales, 1953," *L'Actualité Economique* (juillet–sept. 1953), pp. 343–51.

RIOUX, MARCEL. "L'Élection, vue de l'Anse-à-la-Barbe," *Cité libre,* II, 3 (déc. 1952), 47–52.

SIROIS, JACQUELINE. "Beauce Battle Hotly Waged," *Standard* (Montreal), Nov. 17, 1945.

TRUDEAU, PIERRE-ELLIOTT. "Some Obstacles to Democracy in Quebec," *Canadian Journal of Economics and Political Science,* XXIV, 3 (Aug., 1958), 297–311.

Pamphlets

DION, GÉRARD, and O'NEILL, LOUIS. *Political Immorality in the Province of Quebec.* Montreal: Civic Action League, 1956.

CHAPTER VIII. THE GROWTH OF OPPOSITION TO THE UNION NATIONALE

Articles

COUSINEAU, JACQUES. "Une Modèle de règlement de grève," *Relations,* no 200 (août 1957), 208–9.

DION, GÉRARD. "L'Eglise et le conflit de l'amiante," in PIERRE-ELLIOTT TRUDEAU, éd., *La Grève de l'amiante.* Montréal: Editions' Cité libre, 1956.

DION, GÉRARD, and PELCHAT, JOSEPH. "Repenser le nationalisme," *L'Action Nationale,* XXXI, 6 (juin 1948), 403–12.

FRASER, BLAIR. "The Religious Crisis in Quebec Politics," *Maclean's Magazine,* Nov. 10, 1956, pp. 13–15, 90–1.

LÉGER, JEAN-MARC. "Aspects of French-Canadian Nationalism," *University of Toronto Quarterly,* XXVII, 3 (avril 1958), 310–29.

LEMELIN, ROGER. "The Silent Struggle at Laval," *Maclean's Magazine*, Aug. 1, 1952, pp. 11, 36–8.

"Mgr Charbonneau et l'opinion publique dans l'Eglise," *Cité libre*, jan.–fév. 1960, pp. 3–7.

QUINN, HERBERT F. "The Social Credit Movement in Quebec," *Canadian Forum*, March, 1947, pp. 275–6.

RAYMOND, MAXIME. "What Does the Bloc Populaire Stand For?" *Maclean's Magazine*, Jan. 1, 1944, pp. 8–10, 35.

ROBILLARD, J. P. "Pour un nationalisme social," *L'Action Nationale*, XXXI, (avril 1948), 284–96.

Pamphlets

Archevêques et Evêques de la Province de Québec. *Le Problème ouvrier en regard de la doctrine sociale de l'Eglise*. Québec: Service extérieur d'éducation sociale, Université Laval, 1950.

Bloc populaire. *Programme provincial du Bloc*. Montréal, 1943.

DION, GÉRARD, and O'NEILL, LOUIS. *Political Immorality in the Province of Quebec*. Montreal: Civic Action League, 1956.

Parti social démocratique. *Programme du partie social démocratique*. Montréal, 1956.

Union des électeurs. *Programme de l'Union des électeurs*. Montréal, 1946.

CHAPTER IX. THE ELECTION OF 1960

Books

DION, GÉRARD, et O'NEILL, LOUIS. *Le Chrétien et les élections*. Montréal: Editions de l'Homme, 1960.

LAPORTE, PIERRE. *Le Vrai Visage de Duplessis*. Montréal: Editions de l'Homme, 1960.

LESAGE, JEAN. *Lesage s'engage*. Montréal: Editions de l'Homme, 1959.

Articles

ALLEN, RALPH. "The Hidden Failure of Our Churches," *Maclean's Magazine*, Feb. 25, 1961, pp. 11–15, 44–50.

BERGERON, GÉRARD. "Political Parties in Quebec," *University of Toronto Quarterly*, XXVII (April, 1958), 352–68.

DION, LÉON. "De l'ancien au nouveau régime," *Cité libre*, juin–juillet 1961, pp. 3–15.

LAURENDEAU, ANDRÉ. "Le Parti libéral se lance dans l'aventure de la démocratisation," *Le Magazine Maclean*, May, 1961.

"Maurice Duplessis," *Relations*, oct. 1959, p. 253.

"Programme du parti libéral," *La Réforme* (Montréal), 6 juin 1956.

TRUDEAU, PIERRE-ELLIOTT. "L'élection du 22 juin 1960," *Cité libre*, août–sept. 1960, pp. 3–8.

Pamphlets

Parti libéral. *Le Guide de l'orateur libéral*. Montréal, 1948.

——— *Le Digeste de la justice sociale*. Montréal, 1952.

——— *Le Parti libéral provincial s'engage* . . . Montréal, 1952.

——— *1960 Political Manifesto of the Quebec Liberal Party*. Montreal, 1960.

CHAPTER X. THE REJUVENATION AND RECOVERY OF THE UNION NATIONALE

Books

BARRETTE, ANTONIO. *Mémoires*. Montreal: Librairie Beauchemin, 1966.

BERGERON, GÉRARD. *Du Duplessisme au Johnsonisme, 1956–1966*. Montreal: Editions Parti Pris, 1967.

———— *Du Duplessisme à Trudeau et Bourassa, 1956–1971*. Montreal: Editions Parti Pris, 1971.

Canada. *Constitutional Conference, Proceedings of the First Meeting, Feb. 5–7, 1968*. Ottawa: Queen's Printer, 1968.

———— L. B. Pearson. *Federalism for the Future*. Ottawa: Queen's Printer, 1968.

CARDINAL, MARIO, LEMIEUX, VINCENT, and SAUVAGEAU, FLORIAN. *Si l'Union Nationale m'était contée*. Montreal: Editions du Boréal Express, 1978.

DAWSON, R. MacGREGOR. *The Government of Canada*. Revised by NORMAN WARD. Fifth edition. Toronto: University of Toronto Press, 1970.

DESBARATS, PETER. *The State of Quebec*. Toronto, McClelland and Stewart, 1966.

FOX, PAUL W. *Politics: Canada*. Third Edition. Toronto: McGraw-Hill Co. of Canada, 1970.

GÉRIN-LAJOIE, PAUL. *Pourquoi le Bill 60?* Montreal: Editions du Jour, 1963.

JOHNSON, DANIEL. *Egalité ou indépendance*. Montreal: Editions Renaissance, 1965.

JONES, RICHARD. *Community in Crisis: French-Canadian Nationalism in Perspective*. Toronto: McClelland and Stewart, 1972.

LAPORTE, JEAN-LOUIS. *Daniel Johnson, cet inconnu*. Montreal: Librairie Beauchemin, 1968.

LEMIEUX, VINCENT, éd. *Quatre élections provinciales au Québec, 1956–1966*. Québec: Les Presses de l'Université Laval, 1969.

MORIN, CLAUDE. *Quebec versus Ottawa*. Toronto: University of Toronto Press, 1976.

POSTGATE, DALE, and McROBERTS, KENNETH. *Quebec: Social Change and Political Crisis*. Toronto: McClelland and Stewart, 1976.

PROULX, JÉRÔME. *Le Panier de crabes: Un Témoignage vécu sur l'Union Nationale sous Daniel Johnson*. Montreal: Editions Parti Pris, 1971.

Québec, Président général des élections. *Rapport sur les élections générales de 1966*. Québec: Imprimeur de la Reine, 1967.

Québec. *Mémoire à la Commission Royale d'Enquête sur les méthodes d'achat utilisées au Département de la Colonization et au Service des Achats du gouvernement*. Deuxième Partie. Québec: Imprimeur de la Reine, 1963.

ROY, JEAN-LOUIS. *Les Programmes électoraux du Québec: Un Siècle de programmes politiques québécois*, vol. II. Montreal: Les Editions Leméac, 1971.

SCOTT, FRANK, and OLIVER, MICHAEL, eds. *Quebec States her Case*. Toronto: Macmillan of Canada, 1964.

SLOAN, THOMAS. *Quebec: The Not-So-Quiet Revolution*. Toronto: Ryerson Press, 1965.

SMILEY, DONALD V. *Canada in Question: Federalism in the Seventies*. Second Edition. Toronto: McGraw-Hill Ryerson, 1976.

THOMSON, DALE C., ed. *Quebec Society and Politics: Views from the Inside.* Toronto: McClelland and Stewart, 1973.

TRUDEAU, PIERRE ELLIOTT. *Federalism and the French Canadians.* Toronto: Macmillan of Canada, 1968.

VIEN, CHRISTIAN, and LAPOINTE, DOMINIQUE. *L'Union Nationale: Son Histoire, ses chefs, sa doctrine.* Quebec: Les Editions du Mercredi, 1969.

Articles

ANGELL, HAROLD M. "The Evolution and Application of Quebec Election Expense Legislation, 1960–66," in Canada, *Report of the Committee on Election Expenses.* Ottawa: Queen's Printer, 1966.

ARÈS, RICHARD, S. J., "Egalité ou indépendance: quelle égalité? pour qui et par qui?" *Relations*, no. 321 (nov. 1967).

BOILY, ROBERT. "Montréal, une forteresse libérale," *Socialisme, 66*, no. 9 (oct.-déc. 1966), 138–60.

GELINAS, ANDRÉ. "The Quebec Public Service," in Dale C. Thomson, ed., *Quebec Society and Politics: Views from the Inside.* Toronto: McClelland and Stewart, 1973.

GINGRAS, PAUL-EMILE. "L'Ecole des technocrates," *Relations*, no. 344 (déc. 1969), 337–41.

GUAY, JACQUES. "Johnson par lui même," *Le Magazine Maclean*, oct. 1966, pp. 11–13, 26, 28, 30–2.

HENRIPIN, JACQUES. "Quebec and the Demographic Dilemma of French-Canadian Society," in Dale C. Thomson, ed., *Quebec Society and Politics: Views from the Inside.* Toronto: McClelland and Stewart, 1973.

JOHNSON, DANIEL. "What Does Quebec Want? — 1967," in J. Peter Meekison, ed., *Canadian Federalism: Myth or Reality.* Second Edition. Toronto: Methuen Publications, 1971.

LALANDE, GILLES. "Quebec and International Affairs," in Dale C. Thomson, ed., *Quebec Society and Politics: Views from the Inside.* Toronto: McClelland and Stewart, 1973.

LAROCQUE, ANDRÉ. "Political Institutions and Quebec Society," in Dale C. Thomson, ed., *Quebec Society and Politics: Views from the Inside.* Toronto: McClelland and Stewart, 1973.

LATOUCHE, DANIEL. "Le vrai nature de la Révolution tranquille," *Canadian Journal of Political Science*, VII, 3 (Sept. 1974), 525–36.

LEBLANC, JULES. "L'Education au Quebec," *Canadian Annual Review*, 1963, pp. 364–80.

——— "En Education ça ne va pas trop vite!" *Le Magazine Maclean*, sept. 1966, pp. 24, 32–3, 36.

LEMIEUX, VINCENT. "Heaven is Blue and Hell is Red," in Martin Robin, ed., *Canadian Provincial Politics: The Party Systems of the Ten Provinces.* Scarborough, Ont.: Prentice-Hall of Canada, 1972.

MORIN, JACQUES-IVAN. "The Treaty-Making Power of Quebec," in Frederick Vaughan, *et al, Contemporary Issues in Canadian Politics.* Scarborough, Ont.: Prentice-Hall of Canada, 1970.

RYAN, CLAUDE. "Quebec Changes Governments," *Foreign Affairs*, XLV, 1 (Oct. 1966) 148–61.

STEWART, JAMES. "First Step: Repeal Law on Fixed Ridings," in *Election*

Analysis Pinpoints Reform Need. (Reprinted from Montreal Star, May 30–June 5, 1970).

Pamphlets

Parti Libéral du Québec. *Québec en marche: Le Programme politique du parti Libéral du Québec.* Montreal, 1966.

―――― *Address by Jean Lesage to the Quebec Liberal Federation, Sept. 30, 1962.* Mimeographed. Montreal, 1962.

Union Nationale. *Action Plan for a Young Nation.* Quebec, 1962.

―――― *Objectifs 1966 de l'Union Nationale, un programme d'action pour une jeune nation; Québec d'abord.* Quebec, 1966.

CHAPTER XI. THE DECLINE AND ECLIPSE OF CONSERVATIVE NATIONALISM

Books*

BERNARD, ANDRÉ. *Québec: élections 1976.* Montreal: Editions Hurtubise HMH, 1976.

CHAPUT, MARCEL. *Pourquoi je suis séparatiste.* Montreal: Editions du Jour, 1961.

Commission d'étude sur les laïcs et l'Eglise. *L'Eglise du Québec: un héritage, un projet.* Montreal: Editions Fides, 1971.

DESBARATS, PETER. *René: A Canadian in Search of a Country.* Toronto: McClelland and Stewart, 1976.

DION, LÉON. *Quebec: The Unfinished Revolution.* Montreal: McGill-Queen's University Press, 1976.

HENRIPIN, JACQUES, and LAPIERRE-ADAMCYK, EVELYNE. *La Fin de la revanche des berceaux: qu'en pensent les Québécoises.* Montreal: Les Presses de l'Université de Montreal, 1974.

HOLDEN, RICHARD B. *Election 1970: Le Point tournant.* Montreal: Les Editions Ariès, 1970.

LATOUCHE, DANIEL, LORD, GUY, and VAILLANCOURT, JEAN-GUY. *Le Processus électoral au Québec: les élections provinciales de 1970 et 1973.* Montreal: Editions Hurtubise HMH, 1976.

LEMIEUX, VINCENT, GILBERT, MARCEL, and BLAIS, ANDRÉ. *Une Election de réalignement: l'Election générale du 29 avril 1970 au Québec.* Montreal: Editions du Jour, 1970.

LÉVESQUE, RENÉ. *Option Québec.* Montreal: Editions de l'Homme, 1968.

MURRAY, VĚRA. *Le Parti Québécois: de la fondation à la prise du pouvoir.* Montreal: Editions Hurtubise HMH, 1976.

Parti Libéral du Québec. *Bourassa/Quebec.* Montreal: Editions de l'Homme, 1970.

Parti Québécois. *La Solution: Le Programme du Parti Québécois.* Montreal: Editions du Jour, 1970.

―――― *La Souveraineté et l'économie.* Montreal: Editions du Jour, 1970.

---

*Some of the books listed under Chapter X are also useful as references for material covered in this chapter.

PELLETIER, RÉJEAN, éd. *Partis politiques au Québec*. Montreal: Editions Hurtubise HMH, 1976.

PINARD, MAURICE. *The Rise of a Third Party: A Study in Crisis Politics*. Enlarged Edition. Montreal: McGill-Queen's University Press, 1975.

PROVENCHER, JEAN. *René Lévesque: Portrait d'un Québécois*. Montreal: Editions de La Presse, 1974.

Quebec. Président général des élections. *Rapport sur les élections générales de 1970*. Québec: Imprimeur de la Reine, 1971.

SAYWELL, JOHN. *Quebec 70: A Documentary Narrative*. Toronto: University of Toronto Press, 1971.

————— *The Rise of the Parti Québécois, 1967–1976*. Toronto: University of Toronto Press, 1977.

STEIN, MICHAEL B. *The Dynamics of Right-Wing Protest: A Political Analysis of Social Credit in Quebec*. Toronto: University of Toronto Press, 1973.

Union Nationale. Assises générales, St. Léonard, 18, 19, 20 mai 1973. *Un Programme pour l'avenir du Québec*. Montreal: Editions du Mercredi, 1973.

Articles

DREIFELDS, JURIS. "Nationalism and Socialism in French Canada," in Paul W. Fox, ed., *Politics: Canada*. Fourth Edition. Toronto: McGraw-Hill Ryerson, 1977.

DUMONT, FERNAND. "Le Silence de l'Eglise du Québec," *Relations*, no. 344 (déc. 1969), 348–50.

GINGRAS, FRANÇOIS-PIERRE. "Le Rassemblement pour l'Indépendance Nationale ou l'indépendantisme: du mouvement social au parti politique," in Réjean Pelletier, éd., *Partis politiques au Québec*. Montreal, Editions Hurtubise HMH, 1976.

HAGY, JAMES W. "Quebec Separatists: The First Twelve Years," *Queen's Quarterly*, LXXVI, 2 (Summer, 1969), 229–38.

————— "Le Parti Québécois in the 1970 Election," *Queen's Quarterly*, LXXVII, 2 (Summer, 1970), 266–73.

HENRIPIN, JACQUES. "Quebec and the Demographic Dilemma of French-Canadian Society," in Dale C. Thomson, ed., *Quebec Society and Politics: Views from the Inside*. Toronto: McClelland and Stewart, 1973.

LATOUCHE, DANIEL. "The Independence Option: Ideological and Empirical Elements," in Dale C. Thomson, ed., *Quebec Society and Politics: Views from the Inside*. Toronto: McClelland and Stewart, 1973.

PINARD, MAURICE. "The Ongoing Political Realignments in Quebec," in Dale C. Thomson, ed. *Quebec Society and Politics: Views from the Inside*. Toronto: McClelland and Stewart, 1973.

————— "La Scission au sein du Ralliement Créditiste et ses conséquences électorales," in Réjean Pelletier, éd., *Partis Politiques au Québec*. Montreal: Editions Hurtubise HMH, 1976.

ROY, MICHEL. "René Lévesque's Very Special Kind of Federalism," *Saturday Night*, Jan. 1969, pp. 30–2.

STEIN, MICHAEL B. "Le Crédit social dans la province du Québec: sommaire et développement," *Canadian Journal of Political Science*, VI, no. 4 (Dec. 1973), 563–81.

Pamphlets

Nouveau Parti Démocratique du Québec. *Manifeste, 1970.* Mimeographed. Montreal, 1970.

Parti Créditiste du Quebec [formerly Ralliement Créditiste]. *Un Programme humain pour un Québec fort.* Montreal, 1973.

Parti Libéral du Québec. *Quebec, On to Work: The Program and the Team for 1970.* Montreal, 1970.

———— *Un Nouveau programme d'action.* Montreal, 1973.

Parti Québécois. *Un Gouvernement du Parti Québécois s'engage* ... Montreal, 1973.

Union Nationale. *Québec plus que jamais: Objectifs, 1970.* Laval, Que., 1970.

———— *For the Future of a Strong Quebec.* St. Eustache, Que., 1973.

Index